What Makes Health Public?

John Coggon argues that the important question for analysts in the fields of public health law and ethics is 'what makes health public?'. He offers a conceptual and analytic scrutiny of the salient issues raised by this question, outlines the concepts entailed in, or denoted by, the term 'public health', and argues why and how normative analyses in public health are inquiries in political theory. The arguments expose and explain the political claims inherent in key works in public health ethics. Coggon then develops and defends a particular understanding of political liberalism, describing its implications for critical study of public health policies and practices. Covering important works from legal, moral, and political theory, public health, public health law and ethics, and bioethics, this is a foundational text for scholars, practitioners, and policy bodies interested in freedoms, rights, and responsibilities relating to health.

JOHN COGGON is a research fellow in the School of Law, University of Manchester. His research focuses principally on legal, moral, and political issues relating to health and welfare. He was the winner of the 2006 Mark S. Ehrenreich Prize in Healthcare Ethics Research, awarded by the Pacific Center for Health Policy and Ethics at the University of Southern California, in conjunction with the International Association of Bioethics. From 2007–10 he held a British Academy postdoctoral fellowship.

Cambridge Bioethics and Law

This series of books was founded by Cambridge University Press with Alexander McCall Smith as its first editor in 2003. It focuses on the law's complex and troubled relationship with medicine across both the developed and the developing world. In the past twenty years, we have seen in many countries increasing resort to the courts by dissatisfied patients and a growing use of the courts to attempt to resolve intractable ethical dilemmas. At the same time, legislatures across the world have struggled to address the questions posed by both the successes and the failures of modern medicine, while international organisations such as the WHO and UNESCO now regularly address issues of medical law.

It follows that we would expect ethical and policy questions to be integral to the analysis of the legal issues discussed in this series. The series responds to the high profile of medical law in universities, in legal and medical practice, as well as in public and political affairs. We seek to reflect the evidence that many major health-related policy debates in the UK, Europe and the international community over the past two decades have involved a strong medical law dimension. With that in mind, we seek to address how legal analysis might have a trans-jurisdictional and international relevance. Organ retention, embryonic stem cell research, physician assisted suicide and the allocation of resources to fund health care are but a few examples among many. The emphasis of this series is thus on matters of public concern and/or practical significance. We look for books that could make a difference to the development of medical law and enhance the role of medico-legal debate in policy circles. That is not to say that we lack interest in the important theoretical dimensions of the subject, but we aim to ensure that theoretical debate is grounded in the realities of how the law does and should interact with medicine and health care.

Series Editors
Professor Margaret Brazier, *University of Manchester*
Professor Graeme Laurie, *University of Edinburgh*
Professor Richard Ashcroft, *Queen Mary, University of London*
Professor Eric M. Meslin, *Indiana University*

Books in the series

Marcus Radetzki, Marian Radetzki, Niklas Juth
Genes and Insurance: Ethical, Legal and Economic Issues

Ruth Macklin
Double Standards in Medical Research in Developing Countries

Donna Dickenson
Property in the Body: Feminist Perspectives

What Makes Health Public?

*A Critical Evaluation of Moral, Legal, and
Political Claims in Public Health*

John Coggon

CAMBRIDGE
UNIVERSITY PRESS

CAMBRIDGE UNIVERSITY PRESS
Cambridge, New York, Melbourne, Madrid, Cape Town,
Singapore, São Paulo, Delhi, Tokyo, Mexico City

Cambridge University Press
The Edinburgh Building, Cambridge CB2 8RU, UK

Published in the United States of America by Cambridge University Press,
New York

www.cambridge.org
Information on this title: www.cambridge.org/9781107016392

John Coggon 2012

First published 2012

Printed in the United Kingdom at the University Press, Cambridge

A catalogue record for this publication is available from the British Library

ISBN 978-1-107-01639-2 Hardback
ISBN 978-1-107-60241-0 Paperback

Dedicated to Hosam Bang: a gentleman, scholar, and great friend

Contents

Foreword

Lawrence O. Gostin
Linda D. and Timothy J. O'Neill Professor of
Global Health Law
Director, O'Neill Institute for National and Global Health
Law, Georgetown University

John Coggon, in this seminal book, asks a question of such simplicity, but also of such profound importance: What makes health public? The rigor with which he examines this critical question will make this book a classic in the field of public health ethics – an essential reference point for scholars, students, and policy-makers. Coggon's essential claim is that any normative analysis in the field of public health, or argument in favor of, or against, a particular public health measure, is based in political theory. This remains true whether the proponent favors a limited model of public health (with a narrow public sphere) or an expansive model. In both cases, Coggon treats these as political questions, exposing the political nature of public health claims.

What I wish to do in this foreword is to demonstrate why Coggon's question is so significant in contemporary academic and public discourse. In short, understanding the public/private dimensions of health is indispensible for ascertaining the appropriate scope of governmental public health in a liberal democracy. And that issue, as Coggon points out, is as socially and politically charged, as it is important to the population's wellbeing.

To begin with, scholars often refer to "health" with some imprecision. Health, of course, is a *status* of high value to humanity. Health has intrinsic, but also instrumental, value through its contribution to human functioning – happiness, creativity, and productivity. Health is also essential for the functioning of populations – engaging social interactions, participating in the political process, exercising rights of citizenship, and generating wealth.

But what produces health? There is no definitive answer to that question, but one might divide health-producing interventions as including three overlapping spheres: health care (individual clinical services), public health (population-based approaches), and broader socio-economic determinants (fair distribution of income, jobs, housing, and social support). There are public/private dimensions to each of these, and they are the subjects of pitched political battles.

The public/private dimensions of health care

Much of the discourse about health is devoted to health care – a complex system of primary, emergency, and hospital services designed primarily to diagnose and treat individuals who become ill or injured. Political disagreements about the public/private domains of health care are rife. If health care is a human right, as many argue, the State has a duty to ensure health goods and services that are available, accessible to everyone (including being affordable and geographically accessible), acceptable (including culturally), and of good quality.

The State's obligation to ensure the right to health under international law, however, has not tamped down the division between those who see health care as a core public obligation and others who see it as a market commodity. Most States broadly accept that health care is a public responsibility, which takes many different forms ranging from a national health service to a single or multiple payer system. The private sphere, however, can dominate in certain countries such as the United States. In the debates over President Obama's health care reform, political adversaries cast public financing and quality standards (even comparative cost effectiveness) as government-imposed "death panels." And even in primarily public systems, the tension between public and free market principles is palpable. Consider, for example, the Canadian Supreme Court, which struck down a prohibition on private medical insurance because it violated patients' "liberty, safety and security" under the Quebec charter.[1]

Another dimension of the public/private divide is whether individuals have primary responsibility for their own health. In the health care context, conservatives argue that individuals who fail to take good care of their health ought to pay more for their insurance or even be excluded from coverage for certain conditions. Increased premiums for smokers is common in private run systems, but conservative scholars argue that it should extend to persons who are obese, abuse alcoholic beverages or drugs, and even individuals with sexually transmitted infections such as HIV. Those who engage in high-risk activities, such as skydiving, would also have reduced coverage or pay higher premiums. Conversely, many private insurance companies are now offering premium discounts

---

[1] *Chaoulli* v. *Quebec (Attorney General)* [2005] 1 SCR 791, 2005 SCC 35.

for those who engage in healthy behavior, such as going to the gym or maintaining a favorable mass/body index.

Consequently, John Coggon's question, "what makes health public?" becomes exceedingly important in evaluating how health care is financed and provided, and whether and to what extent health goods and services should be governed by free enterprise principles.

The public/private dimensions of public health

One might assume that controversies about the public dimension of public health would be less intense than with health care. After all, health care professionals serve individuals, while public health agencies serve the population as a whole.

The word "public" in public health can be understood to have two overlapping meanings – one that explains the entity that takes primary responsibility for the public's health, and another that explains who has a legitimate expectation of receiving the benefits.[2] The government is the public entity that acts on behalf of the people and gains its legitimacy through a political process. And it is the population that has a legitimate expectation of benefiting from public health services. What best serves the population, of course, may not always be in the interests of all its members, making public health highly political. What constitutes "enough" health? What kinds of services are necessary? How will services be paid for and distributed? These remain political questions.

Almost everyone understands that the level and kinds of services that government offers are political. There are finite resources and public officials will take differing views about the relative value of health as opposed to other public goods, such as energy, defense, transportation, or even tax relief. But it is not only the allocation of public health resources that are within the political realm, but also the very role of government together with its relationship to the individual.

The dominant liberal perspective holds that the State can interfere with individual autonomy only to prevent harm to others. It is for this reason that conventional infectious disease services (e.g., screening, reporting, and quarantine) are relatively uncontroversial. But when the State intervenes in personal choices that are primarily self-regarding (e.g., what to eat, whether to smoke, or even whether to wear a helmet) the political divisions are at their height.

---

[2] Lawrence O. Gostin, *Public Health Law: Power, Duty, Restraint* (2nd edn) (Berkeley: University of California Press, 2008), available at www.ucpress.edu/books/pages/11023.php.

The political fault line is between a government that actively orders society for the good of the people (a "nanny state") on the one hand, and a government that leaves individuals to make their own personal and economic choices on the other. Arguments over the nanny state range from mandating motor cycle helmets and fluoridating drinking water, through to a tax on sweets, a ban on trans fatty acids, and zoning or taxation to incentivize shops that sell whole foods and disincentivize fast food establishments.

Paternalism remains at the heart of the political debates over the appropriate role of the State in creating the conditions in which people can be healthy. Public health paternalists rely on the fact that people face constraints (both internal and external) on the capacity to pursue their own interests, including cognitive and informational deficits, as well as limited willpower. They may objectively know what is in their best interests but find it difficult to behave accordingly. Finally, individuals face social and cultural constraints on their behavior. Human behavior is influenced by many external factors including parents and family, peers and community, media and advertising.

Perhaps it is not even accurate to think of public health paternalism as directed to the individual at all but instead towards overall societal welfare. Public health practices are "communal in nature, and concerned with the well-being of the community as a whole and not just the well-being of any particular person."[3] Public health aims its policies toward the community and it counts its results in improved health and longevity in the population. Even if conduct is primarily self-regarding, the aggregate effects of persons choosing not to wear seatbelts or helmets can be thousands of preventable injuries and deaths.

Again, Coggon's question, "what makes health public?" becomes exceedingly important in social and political life. Do we allow individuals to make their own choices, even if they will suffer adverse consequences and the population as a whole will bear considerable burdens? Or is this purely a matter of personal choice? So much about what the State does, and its relationship with its citizens, is intricately tied to how these questions are resolved in the political realm.

---

[3] Dan Beauchamp, "Community: The Neglected Tradition of Public Health", in D. Beauchamp and B. Steinbock (eds.), *New Ethics for the Public's Health* (New York: Oxford University Press, 1999), p. 57.

The public/private dimensions of socio-economic determinants of health

A strong and consistent finding of epidemiological research is that socio-economic status (SES) is correlated with morbidity, mortality, and functioning. SES is a complex phenomenon based on income, education, and occupation. Material disadvantage, diminished control over life's circumstances, and lack of social acceptance all contribute to poor health outcomes. Some researchers go further, concluding the overall level of economic inequality in a society correlates with (and adversely affects) population health. That is, societies with wide disparities between rich and poor tend to have worse health status than societies with smaller disparities, after controlling for *per capita* income. The World Health Organization's Commission on Social Determinants of Health concluded, "the social conditions in which people are born, live, and work are the single most important determinant of good health or ill health, of a long and productive life, or a short and miserable one."[4]

Assume that these data are as robust as the public health community believes them to be. Does it follow that the State is obliged to ensure more plentiful, and more equal, distribution of socio-economic goods? This may be the most politically contentious question of all because it goes to the heart of political life – whether government's first duty is to redistribute wealth across the population. The Social Determinants Commission, for example, recommends equity across the life span, beginning with child development and education, through to fair employment and housing, as well as social protection for everyone, including the elderly. Must the State tackle inequitable distribution of power and resources, with health equity becoming a marker of government performance?

On one level, it is only the State that can exercise the legitimate power to redistribute socio-economic goods through its power to tax and spend – for example, steeply progressive taxation and generous social welfare programs. On another level, each individual is positioned to provide these goods for themselves in a free enterprise system. Even the most free market advocates often make allowances for particularly vulnerable groups, such as children, the elderly, and persons with physical or mental disabilities – allowing a modicum of State support services.

[4] Commission on Social Determinants of Health, *Closing the Gap in a Generation: Health Equity Through Action on the Social Determinants of Health* (Geneva: World Health Organization, 2008).

But they would make no such allowance to able-bodied adults who, in their view, are capable of meeting their own needs. In relation to the fully capable, free market theorists posit that state services actually incentivize less productive activities.

Here, the familiar divide between State and individual responsibility is acute. There are certain conditions of life (e.g., food, housing, education, and work) that are well known for their positive influence on health. Yet, Coggon's question remains as pertinent as ever – what makes health (in this case mediated through socio-economic conditions) public?

The book's three broad projects

I have sought to briefly show why the public/private domains involving human health are critically important, and why they are so political. I hope this foreword makes the reader want to know more. John Coggon's penetrating analysis is essential for understanding the public sphere, and its deep political dimensions.

Coggon engages in three broad projects. First, he offers a thorough conceptual analysis, in particular of the different things people mean when they use the term "public health." Unpacking the variety of meanings of this much-used term will significantly improve scholarly and public discourse in the field. Secondly, Coggon provides an analytic framing for arguments in public health law and ethics, discussing what he means by politics (as compared with and sometimes opposed to morality), and then using this framing to explain some of the most influential arguments in public health ethics. Finally, he develops his own preferred understanding of political liberalism, and discusses its implications for arguments about public health ethics.

The field of public health ethics – still relatively young – owes a great debt to John Coggon. His book will be much discussed, and highly influential, as the field matures and integrates with broader social and political discourse.

Lawrence O. Gostin
Washington, D.C.
March, 2011

Acknowledgements

Over the course of this project, I have met and discussed ideas with more people than I can possibly thank here individually. I have learned so much, and am deeply grateful. The work between these covers is the result of many hours of (sometimes heated) debate, careful reading, and deep thought. In particular I need to express my profound gratitude to people who have read all or part of earlier drafts of the work. Madison Powers was incredibly generous in the time he took reading the first draft of Part I, and in taking time to discuss the wider aspects of the project during my trips to Georgetown in 2008 and 2010. Thanks also to Stephen John, Ania Pacholczyk, and Elen Stokes for feedback on other incarnations of this part of the book. On top of writing his very thoughtful foreword, Larry Gostin offered kind and careful comments on the first complete draft of the work, as well as finding time to meet and discuss the evolving ideas on both my Washington visits. I must state my thanks too to Barry Lyons, Suzanne Ost, and Adam Tucker, all of whom also read the whole piece and came back with encouraging and insightful comments.

I owe an enormous debt to Margot Brazier, John Harris, and Søren Holm, my mentors in Manchester, who have gone well beyond the call of duty in supporting my work, subjecting it to diligent critique, and helping me through the drafting and redrafting. The environment these three people have created in the Centre for Social Ethics and Policy, and the Institute for Science, Ethics, and Innovation, makes coming to work a pleasure.

Beyond these, there are countless people who have taken the time to discuss the ideas that I explore and arguments that I make. I can not name everyone, but must say thank you to Roger Brownsword, Angus Dawson, Matti Häyry, Richard Ingleby, Bruce Jennings, Tom Koch, Jean McHale, Jonathan Montgomery, Ollie Quick, Keith Syrett, and Tuija Takala. Each of these people has been a fantastic source of support, and provided much needed critical guidance on a whole range of ideas with which I have struggled. I must thank also organisers and audiences of various seminars and conferences at which I have been able to test some of the ideas found below, in particular at the Universities of Georgetown, Keele, Liverpool, Oxford, and University College London, the 2008 conference of the International Association of Bioethics in Croatia, the 2008 International Conference of the British Association for Canadian Studies' Legal Studies Group in London, and the 2010 meeting of the Society of Legal Scholars in Southampton. I must thank my wonderful colleagues at Manchester, especially for the superb feedback they gave to papers presented at the Institute for Science, Ethics, and Innovation's internal seminar series. Finally, I owe thanks to Cambridge University Press, and would like particularly to express my gratitude to Helen Francis, Finola O'Sullivan, Cheryl Prophett, Sarah Roberts, Elizabeth Spicer, and Richard Woodham.

I have researched and written this book during the course of a British Academy Postdoctoral Fellowship. The freedom and support afforded by this scheme have allowed the experience to be most enjoyable and rewarding. I have been able to visit some inspirational people and places, and enjoyed the processes of scholarship at their most stimulating and intellectually gratifying. As well as expressing my thanks for choosing to support my postdoctoral project, it is important to acknowledge the additional ways in which the Academy has taken care of me throughout my research. The value it gives to nurturing young scholars is something of which all within the academic community, and beyond, should be proud. I would also wish to state my thanks to the Wellcome Strategic Programme on the *Human Body: Its Scope, Limits, and Future*, which has supported me during the final stages of drafting this work.

Of course I could have done none of this without the love and support of friends and family. Although I can't thank everyone by name, from my side of the family I must say thank you for the great care and encouragement to Grandma, Granny, Mum and Dad, Ruth, Tim, James, Matthew, and (latterly) Daniel, Roz, Simon, and Lyra, Rattus, and Meredith. And my socio-in-laws have also been superb, and remarkably tolerant, so thank you to Maura and Killian, Jane and Niall, Chuck K. McGuinness (whose health is his wealth) and Lou, Rosemarie, Cathal, and Sarah, and last but by no means least Evelyn.

Too many friends to list have kept me going during this project. I daren't try to name them all, for fear of upsetting those I might forget, but I must mention by name Big Ade, Caroline and Alex, Fatima, Joe, Nash, Stokes (again), and Suzie. I also can't fail to mention the Thursday lunch club at the Kennedy Institute of Ethics: the warmth and welcome offered by the brilliant people in Georgetown has been truly fantastic.

Finally, and above all, I need to say in woefully inadequate words how thankful I am to Sheelagh, for all her patient support, care, and love. Cursed with a shared interest in the sorts of issues discussed in this book, she has suffered more discussions than anyone should have to do as I've tried to straighten out my thoughts on public health law and ethics. Thank you.

John Coggon
Manchester

What makes health public?
Introduction

This book is about public health, and the imperatives and responsibilities we might associate with the protection of health. These issues are of central importance in policy, practice, education, and research. They raise and would address a whole range of concerns, whose number and urgency are growing exponentially: for example, how governments should respond to alcohol and tobacco use, the obesity 'epidemics', and the need to care for members of an aging population; whether people should ensure that they eat 'healthy foods', exercise frequently, and contribute to 'herd immunity' by participating in vaccination programmes; why employers should safeguard the health of their staff, why industry should 'educate' consumers about the potential health effects of certain products, and why sports events should not promote or advertise 'unhealthy brands'. To come to useful conclusions from moral, legal, and political perspectives, the crucial task is to establish whether any of such matters are *shared concerns*, and if so, why, or if not, why not. In other words, anyone concerned about health, and about whether, when, how, and why it gives rise to meaningful responsibilities, needs to address the question *what makes health public?*

The significance of exploring this question should not be underestimated. Across the globe, public health is central to major debates in ethics, law, and politics. It has an increasing presence in the academic literature, in university teaching, and for policy, regulatory, and governmental bodies. Greater and greater attention is focused on the good of health, and the ethics relating to public health. Concern is not limited to (public) healthcare systems: the entire social and physical environments are the context of contemporary analysis of 'health law and ethics'. Governments and analysts are concerned with the social determinants of health, and the attendant links to practical health-related responsibilities. There has been much consideration of questions such as the regulation of tobacco, alcohol, and food; resource allocation, especially within healthcare; containment and control of contagious diseases; bioterrorism; and climate change. All of these, and many

1

other issues, are portrayed as public health problems, demanding public health solutions.

Yet there are important, and often too easily ignored, prior questions that require close analytic scrutiny before defensible conclusions can be reached on any individual, practical, health-related matter. What does 'health' meaningfully denote in policy arguments? It may, for example, be conceived as something that is a foundation, an aspiration, a means to other ends, a discrete facet of the human good, or a value-free scientific concept that just happens generally to correlate with a desirable state. And how can it, and things that affect it, be a 'public' matter? By treating something as public, we invite analysis from political philosophy, and necessarily any substantive response to a public health issue will imply more fundamental points about the nature, basis, and scope of political obligation. Recognition of this allows us to establish and assess what other public concerns legitimately conflict with apparent imperatives concerning health. As the literature on public health law and ethics grows, there is a need for critical, comprehensive analysis of this theoretical landscape, providing the means for analysts and policy-makers to understand and explain the import of their concerns. This book is a contribution to such an endeavour.

Structure of the book

Absent a detailed groundwork it is impossible to make sound examination of the salient issues raised in debates on practical health issues, and to move towards a useful understanding of how and why policy should be developed or resisted. *What Makes Health Public?* addresses the conceptual and the analytic framing, other theorists' moral, legal, and political responses, and my own conclusions on the best means of approaching the regulation of public health issues. The book is divided into three parts.

Part I

The first part of the work is directed to a foundational conceptual analysis. It begins with an exploration of the concepts 'health' and 'public'. Throughout the work, each of these concepts receives further attention, in particular where the analysis is directed specifically at their employment in key scholarship in public health law and ethics, and where they bear on issues such as the regulation of smoking tobacco. I argue in Chapter 1 that useful conceptions of health are necessarily value-laden, and that in the relevant literatures we need to be able to account for 'positive' as well as 'negative' accounts of health; i.e. it does not suffice simply to engage with arguments about the absence of disease. I also raise the contentious issue of deciding *who* is given the effective responsibility for deciding what health means: should it be a matter of subjective judgement for the individual, or an externally judged, apparently objective question? This groundwork provides the scope for more substantive conclusions on the use of health in political argument.

Similarly, in Chapter 2 I provide a foundational analysis of the term public, whose implications are then examined in close detail throughout the book. The chapter tests what is meant when people talk about *a* or *the* public, and what it means to describe an issue as being public. In regard to the former, I adopt and defend the use of a non-reified concept of the public, as advocated by Bruce Jennings. The chapter examines the conceptual difficulties associated with treating the public as something other than a collection of individuals, albeit a collection that may be bound by a shared purpose that has important normative implications. As for discussion of things being public, the chapter looks at the public/private distinction, and its relationship to things being 'the law's business'. Amongst the important conceptual considerations are defences of the idea that 'all law is public', that the State is necessarily (though not unproblematically) the final arbiter on whether a matter should be private, and the distinct matters protected by reference to public or private interests. Finally, I present the idea of public as it features specifically in debates on public health, and the perspectives it may be seen to add to these.

Following those two more general conceptual analyses, Chapter 3 is directed to understanding quite what 'public health' itself might mean. My aim in this chapter is ambitious: by looking both at how the term is defined and how it is used, I present what I take to be a comprehensive means of categorising the different 'faces' of public health. I suggest that there are seven such faces, and explain how and why I have met this conclusion. In some senses the categorisations seem rough or imperfect; for example, at times there may be uncertainty about whether something should be classified under one heading or another. Nevertheless, I suggest that it is important for analysts to be aware of, and able to account for, the distinct ways that public health features in the literature, from a highly directive, value-driven concept, to a scientific shorthand for health distribution or prevalence within or between populations. It is not ultimately my aim to present a strong defence of one understanding of public health over the others. Rather, I seek to demonstrate how variously the term is used and the implications of this, and to provide others with a 'tool' to assist their own analyses of matters that are advanced under the heading of, or in the name of, public health.

Chapters 4 and 5 explore these concepts in the contexts of practical regulation and academic study. First, Chapter 4 explains what it might mean to describe something as a 'public health policy'. It presents the practical and normative natures of policy and regulation, and the breadth of interventions that regulators may choose to employ in response to perceived public problems. Chapter 5, by contrast, explains what scholars and analysts are engaging in when they study 'public health law and ethics'. An important upshot of each of these chapters is a recognition that the fields described are potentially without boundary, or within the competence of any single government department: prior to analysis, it is hard to see what might not be of concern or relevance to someone interested in the public health implications of some law, policy, or practice. Issues as diverse as tax and town planning may all be seen to raise potential 'public health issues'. In Chapter 6, these and other conclusions from Part I are brought together, and I highlight their pertinence to analyses of matters that are said to be public health issues.

Part II

The second part of the book develops and defends the work's core thesis: that if we are to produce a coherent means for undertaking normative evaluations of public health policy (and non-policy) we need a complete political theory. Notably, this framing seems to run counter to two alternative approaches that are also dominant in the literature: first, that to establish normative conclusions we should look simply to the ethics 'of' public health; or second, that we should assess public health issues according to a theory of morality. Notwithstanding these distinct framings, I seek to demonstrate first that our concern should be political, and second that other analysts working in public health ethics should already be regarded as working within political theory. To make this case, Part II is split into two substantive chapters, followed by a short concluding chapter.

Chapter 7 addresses what I mean by describing something as a political issue, and distinguishes this from moral and legal framings. I recognise that this is just one way of advancing these different approaches: i.e. some would suggest that political philosophy is just a part of moral philosophy; others may suggest that what I describe as political philosophy is a branch of legal theory. Nevertheless, I present substantive reasons for the separations I propose. The approach distinguishes the following under the heading 'political': *universalist ideal type* theories that are based on claims of unitary liberal rationalism and the best means of protecting it in a community of 'substandard' agents; *pluralist ideal type* theories that are based on claims of equally legitimate, diverse, incommensurable accounts of the good and the best means of protecting these in a community; and *anti-ideal type* theories that are based on amoral considerations of facts about the world, people, and power relations. I argue that analysis has to be able to account for and respond to matters raised by each of these three approaches.

The argument then moves to an engagement with establishing the basis, nature, and scope of political normativity. It engages with the literature on philosophical anarchism, suggesting that analysts may find their answers to questions of legitimacy in relation to (public health) policy by exploring their reasons (should they exist) for shunning anarchy. The development of defensible political theory is what gives the crucial insights needed in assessments undertaken in public health law and ethics. Chapter 7 ends with a short discussion of two issues that are taken to be of particular pertinence in regard to public health: paternalism and the 'population perspective'. Regarding paternalism in a policy context, I emphasise the particular importance of 'collateral paternalism', suggesting that the strength of a policy can not be assessed by reference to individual cases that alone present a non-ideal application of principle. In regard to the population perspective, I note that whilst this may (rightly) be viewed as affording insights to scholars in law and ethics, we should not lose sight of the fact that policy-makers will naturally take such a perspective. Its adoption is thus less controversial than some analysts may wish to suggest.

Chapter 8 demonstrates the plausibility of my thesis, and exemplifies how pervasive it is by applying it to key works in the field. My argument maps politically the positions of some of the most noted and influential scholars in public health law and ethics. The chapter moves from an extreme of small State libertarianism, through different presentations of the 'middle ground', to an extreme of 'health theocracies'. At each stage several approaches are examined, with a view to ascertaining various points: in particular, I demonstrate why the theories should be categorised as political; what manner of reasoning underpins each of them; what they imply for health policy, and – where this is clear – what their authors take 'health' to mean. It is possible to distinguish ideal and non-ideal theories, and theories that are bound by side-constraints (e.g. people's 'natural rights' to be free from State interference) and theories that are grounded on consequentialist concerns (e.g. political systems that are defended for being conducive to the best achievable equality of human flourishing). A key point that the chapter emphasises is that once an analyst accepts the idea of the State, it is equally important to be able to defend both policy and failures to make policy. Some analyses suggest favour for a 'liberty bias', wherein it is necessary to justify any manner of regulation. However, once it is accepted that some regulation is better than no regulation, even the most 'liberty-friendly' theory presents a base concern for something other than non-regulation, and thus States' omissions as well as their acts must be equally open to critical scrutiny.

Chapter 9 concludes Part II, highlighting the principal points made, and relating them to the whole area of public health law and ethics. At this stage, the arguments have clearly presented and defended the position that public health law and ethics are political fields of inquiry, and that analysis of a public health problem can not be undertaken without a complete background political theory.

Part III

Parts I and II of the book offer substantive and methodological points that are of general application to normative work relating to public health. It is my argument that analysts ought to find persuasive the thesis developed in these parts of the book, regardless of their particular moral and political commitments. In Part III, my project is distinct; here I develop and defend a particular theory of political liberalism.

Chapter 10 constructs this theory. The work assumes a critical, self-reflective mode, considering each stage of the argument as it develops. The controversy and contestability in *any* political theory naturally beset my own position. Given this, I have presented the discussion in such a way that even a reader who is not persuaded by the argument itself might see the distinct stages of difficulty that must be overcome when producing a practically applicable, normatively robust, theory. In particular, it is necessary to overcome problems of establishing who is included in (and thus who is excluded from) the political community, establishing how to allow values to underpin policy measures in a system of moral pluralism, and accounting for claims against people's liberty in the name of political obligation. The theory I defend falls into the tradition of Millian liberalism, and works around a central 'harm and benefit principle'. To illustrate how it might function, the chapter ends with a practical, step-by-step presentation of the claims it gives rise to, using the example of a law that deems it obligatory to wear a seatbelt when travelling in a car. Chapter 11 then discusses this idea of political liberalism in relation to problems in public health law and ethics. I argue that a concept of health is best conceived as an aspect of welfare, and that this wider concept should be crucial to normative evaluations of proposed and actual health policy. I explore the complexity of endorsing ideas about welfare in a system of pluralism, and relate this also to the difficulty of accommodating both 'internalist' and 'externalist' accounts of health; i.e. establishing who should have the (legal) right to decide whether the effect of some policy is good or bad for health, and to what extent that matters. To explore how the theory provides access to the salient insights into policy, the chapter employs short examples from alcohol and tobacco regulation.

Chapter 12 gives a brief conclusion to the whole book. It stresses the important point that it is wrong-headed to presume that health and health-related issues will either always or never be public. Instead it reiterates the view that knowing that something relates to health does not, of itself, answer the question of whether it is a shared concern. Thus, analysts and policy-makers need to establish in any given case why health is or is not public, and work from there to a practical conclusion on what would form defensible regulation. They need a political theory, and in coming to this they will present an account that tells us what responsibilities exist in relation to health, whether these are enforceable, and if not, whether they are nevertheless the sound and appropriate basis for non-coercive policy.

Health and politics

Against a backdrop of moral pluralism, this book therefore offers a fundamental addition to the wide and sometimes disparate literature on public health. The analysis works within a liberal political paradigm for a practical and a principled reason, both of which are explored and defended. Practically speaking, the frameworks the book addresses *are* found in liberal political States, and thus demand consideration, at least to begin with, on these terms because they are relevant to them. At the level of principle, political liberalism represents a defensible means of grounding regulation and interference with individuals' freedom to act. Whilst many things beyond these ideas are considered along the way, the central thread of political liberalism is, I argue, what holds together – and should hold together – contemporary debates that claim to speak to public health law and public health ethics. It is true that the work can be seen in places to uphold a 'presumption of liberty', which seems to preoccupy so many engaged in debates on liberalism. But, through the analysis of anarchism and what would lead us to accepting the authority of a State, I argue that this presumption misplaces an emphasis that is core to political debates, and thence to establishing the legitimacy or otherwise of measures instigated or debarred in the name of health. Although liberty may be a natural default – no one should defend a government that makes policy randomly, negligently, or capriciously – non-regulation is not the presumption underpinning political liberalism, even where this is seen as the system needed to *maximise* or *optimise* the net amount of liberty that citizens can enjoy. The real presumption is that a sound conception of the public good can be established, and that *it* will be protected and promoted. We thus need an inquiry into this, and an articulation of its implications, if we are to understand when, how, and why health may be made public.

The following chapters give the groundwork to analyse the debates on responsibility and public health, and offer my own critique of them. I demonstrate that the arguments are about politics, that consciousness of this allows us better to understand them, and that that enables easier moves to practical, defensible outcomes. Given the strong focus on politics, a reader flicking through the book may think that 'public health' is only engaged in about half of it. Superficially this is true, but the crucial point is that *all* of the analysis is engaged *in* public health law and ethics, whether tacitly or explicitly. While some readers might not be convinced by the theory of liberalism that I defend in Part III, I hope that it will at least provoke useful further engagement in fields concerned with public health, and debates in moral, legal, and political philosophy, and that it sits well with other theories considered and presented in this book. The literature around these issues is expanding rapidly. Although there is a lot of disagreement, I have sought to draw out similarities as well as differences, and emphasise places where apparently contradictory approaches can be combined coherently. Part of my own presentation of an overall theory is aimed at advancing that project. Both in its separate parts, and taken as a whole, I hope that the book will be a useful, worthy, and valuable contribution to a fast-growing literature, and more importantly to a crucial subject of considerable personal and governmental concern.

Part I

Basic concepts in public health
Introduction to Part I

The conceptual framing and critical analysis undertaken throughout this book are directed to investigating normative claims made in relation to public health. My central argument is that the meaningful studies that would apply practical philosophy to this are in politics. They should be informed by works from disciplines including moral philosophy, law, economics, and sociology, but the interesting and important health-related responsibilities – of States, private companies, and individuals – are political. Ideological differences, concerns for competing goods, and distinct forms of partiality at the base of disputes in political theory are therefore the relevant sources of contention. And it is in answers to these disputes that questions on public health are meaningfully answered. Some might suggest that this book should have explored the question "What makes health private?"; they might argue that I beg the question and presume a 'liberal bias'. Others might contend that I beg the question by presuming that health could even be a public matter. In what follows I seek to vindicate my analysis against such accusations. In brief, I contend that it is wrong to take it that everything relating to health can just be either 'private' or 'public'. I also argue that most theorists agree with this, and that all policy-makers do. However, our reasons for doing so differ. Thus my analysis lends itself to various important tasks. The first of these is to provide a conceptual and analytic 'groundwork' to understand the nature and scope of arguments in public health ethics and law. This is the purpose of Part I of the book.

The first chapter provides an overview of the key disputes concerning concepts of health, presenting three dichotomies that present themselves: normative/naturalist; positive/negative; and internalist/externalist. I suggest that any useful concepts of health are normative, but that this need not denote political normativity. I then, in Chapter 2, consider the ideas of publics and things being public. Although it is not possible just to assess the terms health and public independently and then come to an understanding of the term 'public health', this conceptual exploration is fundamental, and leads to Chapter 3, where I describe seven distinct faces of public health. In Chapters 4 and 5 I reflect on the meanings of public health policy, and the areas of public health law and ethics. This conceptual work allows me to conclude that we do not find useful answers to public health problems *in* public health, and must instead engage in a wider analysis if the answers we come to develop can be related to defensible practical outcomes.

1   Health, normativity, and politics

1.1   Introduction

If we are concerned to know what practical imperatives health can give rise to, we need to know what it is. This chapter presents the *framing* of theoretical arguments on this issue. The conceptual points raised can then be applied to the distinct substantive conceptions of health that fall under consideration throughout the book. I should be clear that the debates on how best to understand health do not seem close to resolution, and I do not intend to try to find a final answer. The simple truth is that health means many things, and it is practically futile to approach a general analysis of public health as if this were not the case. Rather, analysts need to be prepared to recognise what issues might be raised when the term 'health' is presented in an argument or policy document. With a view to this end, I consider the three most pressing points of contention that arise, and see how they relate to political evaluation of health-related issues.

1.2   Health and three dichotomies

Two apparent quandaries beset normative analyses concerning health. First, people tend to take it as analytic that health is good, yet there is considerable resistance to its taking consistent priority, or being a fundamental value to govern our lives. This challenge is not quite as problematic as it seems. Many moral and political theories accommodate plural goods without incoherence or contradiction.[1] Equally, many theories accommodate the fact that people behave in ways that they

---

[1] To exemplify the great differences in approach that permit this, contrast Isaiah Berlin, *Four Essays on Liberty* (Oxford University Press, 1969); John Finnis, *Natural Law and Natural Rights* (Oxford University Press, 1980); Joseph Raz, *The Morality of Freedom* (Oxford University Press, 1988); Ronald Dworkin, *Life's Dominion: an Argument about Abortion and Euthanasia* (London: Harper Collins, 1993); John Gray, *Two Faces of Liberalism*, (Cambridge: Polity Press, 2000); Amartya Sen, *The Idea of Justice*, (London: Penguin, 2009).

would themselves consider irrational, foolish, or harmful.[2] For some a natural response to people's disregard for health is to seek a means of sharing responsibility for it (amongst other things), and through a political society not leave government of every health issue to the wisdom of each individual.[3] The second quandary that may prove problematic can be seen in one of two ways, and presents a more insidious difficulty: either no one quite knows what health is, making it a nebulous subject of analysis and policy; or too many people 'know' what it means, but they contradict each other in the certainty of their knowledge.[4] A root problem, then, is not just to relate concerns for health with those for other important goods; it is to ascertain that when someone mounts an argument about health we understand at least approximately what it is about. In the following three sections, I will highlight three dichotomies that feature prominently in debates over the meaning of health. It is essential to have an awareness of them, and where critiques are formed to take a position on them. Doing so helps analysts to overcome the problem of conceptual opacity when discussions claim to be about health. Before engaging with health as it features in policy or argument, it is necessary to recognise that it may be used as a 'normativist' or 'naturalist' concept; that it may be 'negative' or 'positive'; and that assessments of health may be made from 'internal' or 'external' perspectives. It is important also to emphasise that the first dichotomy represents a mutually exclusive pairing; the latter two can coherently be employed simultaneously.

1.2.1   *Normative* versus *natural*

One of the long-running debates in the philosophy of medicine explores the question of whether health – whatever it means – is a necessarily normative concept; in other words, whether it is of necessity value-laden.[5] Many analysts claim that it is. When they do so, their contention is that health refers to something that is (taken to be) by definition

---

[2] See e.g. discussions of 'second-order desires' in Gerald Dworkin, *The Theory and Practice of Autonomy* (Cambridge University Press, 1988); Harry G. Frankfurt, "Freedom of the will and the concept of the person", *Journal of Philosophy* (1971) 68:1, 5–20. Consider too Richard Thaler and Cass Sunstein, *Nudge: Improving Decisions About Health, Wealth, and Happiness* (London: Penguin Books, 2009), which seems to have become an instant classic in debates in public health ethics.

[3] See Chapter 8.

[4] See also Bjørn Hofmann, "The concept of disease – vague, complex, or just indefinable?", *Medicine, Health Care, and Philosophy* (2009).

[5] Mahesh Ananth, *In Defense of an Evolutionary Concept of Health* (Aldershot: Ashgate, 2008), ch. 1.

good, and therefore something imbued with values. These values may be 'metaphysical',[6] moral,[7] social,[8] or even political.[9] Whatever their source, as normative values they present *directive* claims; health is said to be good, and thus something that we ought to value and ought to act to protect. Health entails imperatives. Normative perspectives take a wide range of sources, from arguments concerning the 'natural human good'[10] or 'human flourishing',[11] through claims about its representing a desirable end-state given an understanding of welfare,[12] to claims that health denotes states that are not desirable in themselves but rather as a means to some further end.[13] For different reasons in each case, people may argue that health is intrinsically or instrumentally valuable. The important common point, though, is that the concept of health will only be as strong as the normative theory that houses it. Furthermore, even where people claim that health is normative, but seek to move beyond a 'biomedical model' towards a 'social model', necessary medical or scientific connotations will remain and should be acknowledged as doing so.[14] Indeed, the focus of health concerns will tend to be on things that are subject to scientific understanding: there are scientific experts in the matter of normative concepts of health. So if we take it that cancer is a disease, and it is to be labelled a disease for normative reasons, study of its causes or treatment can still be purely scientific. However, this does mean that wariness is sometimes voiced by people concerned that undue normativity is smuggled into conceptual, analytic, or practical claims about health, which may be presented as *scientifically indicated* when in fact a moral, social, or political judgement is being expressed.[15] To put it crudely, an epidemiologist can tell us the

---

[6] Petr Skrabanek, *The Death of Humane Medicine and the Rise of Coercive Healthism* (St Edmundsbury Press: Bury St Edmunds, 1994).

[7] Ivan Illich, *Limits to Medicine – Medical Nemesis: The Expropriation of Health* (London: Marion Boyars, 1995 [1976]).

[8] Juha Räikkä, "The social concept of disease", *Theoretical Medicine* (1996) 17:4, 353–361.

[9] Clare Bambra, Debbie Fox, and Alex Scott-Samuel, "Towards a politics of health", *Health Promotion International* (2005) 20:2, 187–193.

[10] E.g. Finnis, *Natural Law and Natural Rights*.

[11] E.g. Madison Powers and Ruth Faden, *Social Justice: The Moral Foundations of Public Health and Health Policy* (Oxford University Press, 2006); Jonathan Wolff and Avner de-Shalit, *Disadvantage* (Oxford and New York: Oxford University Press, 2007).

[12] E.g. Lennart Nordenfelt, "On the relevance and importance of the notion of disease", *Theoretical Medicine and Bioethics* (1993) 14:1, 15–26.

[13] E.g. David Seedhouse, *Health: The Foundations of Achievement – second edition*, (Chichester: John Wiley & Sons, 2005).

[14] Peter Sedgwick, "Illness: mental and otherwise", *The Hastings Center Studies* (1973) 1:3, 19–40.

[15] Most famously, see Illich, *Limits to Medicine*.

incidence of coronary disease, and the likely reduced incidence if statins were widely used. But his[16] expertise does not tell us that they should be used. However, the normativity within the concept of disease may be taken to suggest that this is precisely what his claim amounts to. And where this is the case, it becomes more controversial when discussions relate, for example, to 'lifestyle diseases', mental health, or matters of distant or improbable benefit for individuals.

In response to concerns about the validity of health as a normative concept – for example for fears that it is defined wrongly by someone with power, that it should itself denote a plurality of definitions – some seek to define health as a 'naturalist' concept, arguing that it carries no intrinsic normative baggage whatsoever.[17] In such cases, it is suggested that we are better to conceive it as analytic that health is a purely scientific term. Perhaps the most noted advocate of a non-normative understanding of health is Christopher Boorse, who advances and defends a position that defines health as 'species-typical functioning'. Writing in the mid-1970s, Boorse contends that:

> With few exceptions, clinicians and philosophers are agreed that health is an essentially evaluative notion. According to this consensus view, a value-free science of health is impossible. This thesis I believe to be entirely mistaken. I shall argue in this essay that it rests on a confusion between the theoretical and practical senses of 'health,' or in other words, between disease and illness.[18]

Against this predominance of contrary opinion, Boorse develops and defends a concept of health that opposes itself with disease. Health reflects an organism's (or its parts') functioning normally given their evolutionary purpose: "the normality is statistical and the functions biological".[19] Boorse summarises the position as follows:

1. The *reference class* is a natural class of organisms of uniform functional design; specifically an age group of a sex of a species.
2. A *normal function* of a part or process within members of the reference class is a statistically typical contribution by it to their individual survival and reproduction.

---

[16] In this book I use the pronouns 'he', 'his', and 'him' as shorthand for the more cumbersome 'he or she', etc. They can be read as 'she', 'her', and 'her' if that is preferred.

[17] See Christopher Boorse, "Health as a theoretical concept", *Philosophy of Science* (1977) 44:4, 542–573. See also Christopher Boorse, "On the distinction between disease and illness", *Philosophy and Public Affairs* (1975) 5:1, 49–68, and more recently Christopher Boorse, "A rebuttal on health", in James Humber and Robert Almeder (eds.), *What is Disease?* (Totowa, NJ: Humana Press, 1997).

[18] Boorse, "On the distinction between disease and illness", 49.

[19] Boorse, "Health as a theoretical concept", 542.

3. *Health* in a member of the reference class is *normal functional ability*: the readiness of each internal part to perform all its normal functions on typical occasions with at least typical efficiency.
4. A *disease* is a type of internal state which impairs health, i.e. reduces one or more functional abilities below typical efficiency.[20]

The main problem[21] with Boorse's scientific concept of health – as with non-normative concepts of health more generally – is found in the very distinction he draws in the first passage cited above: it is practically useless. Scientific neutrality, and no intrinsic connection to a necessary ill, come at the cost of our knowing little on the back of a state of disease. Investigations that lead to the conclusion that someone, or a part of someone, is unhealthy give at most a hint that perhaps something should be done about that.[22] Knowing that someone is in some way healthy or unhealthy on this understanding is as useful as knowing that he has green eyes, likes Mozart, or prefers watching international rugby fixtures to watching episodes of *Coronation Street*. This now commonly rehearsed observation is well highlighted by Germund Hesslow,[23] who argues that the value of knowing if someone is healthy in Boorse's sense is only *secondary*: if we take Boorse's definition of health – a definition to which Hesslow is most sympathetic[24] – we find nothing directive in it. Even in his works prior to Hesslow's critique, Boorse seems wise to this, and suggests that it strengthens the theory's robustness. "Health," he argues, "is functional normality, and as such is desirable exactly insofar as it promotes goals one can justify on independent grounds."[25] Through *illness*, rather than disease, does Boorse think we have a concept that tells us that something is wrong in a sense that should concern us. Health relates to normal biological function. Sometimes this will

---

[20] Boorse, "Health as a theoretical concept", 555.
[21] I mean here the main problem given this book's focus: i.e. if we choose not to engage in a critique of the tenability of Boorse's theory on its own terms. From amongst the literature that does this, see: Richard Hare, "Health", *Journal of Medical Ethics* (1986) 12, 174–181; Elselijn Kingma, "What is it to be healthy?", *Analysis* (2007) 67:2, 128–133; Ananth, *In Defense of an Evolutionary Concept of Health*.
[22] This may seem an unsympathetic reading of Boorse, bearing in mind his acknowledgement of the possible "view that health is a descriptively definable property which is usually valuable", like, for example, intelligence: Boorse, "On the distinction between disease and illness", 54 (see also 60–62). I stand by the claim made, however, as from a policy, or action-guiding perspective this general truth (if it is one) provides only a presumption and we are better to find our way to problems directly, rather than through a generally right secondary route.
[23] Germund Hesslow, "Do we need a concept of disease?", *Theoretical Medicine* (1993) 14:1, 1–14.
[24] Hesslow, "Do we need a concept of disease?", note 2.
[25] Boorse, "On the distinction between disease and illness", 61–62.

be good, sometimes neutral, and sometimes bad. It is because "health judgments" need not be "practical judgments" that Boorse sustains his position concerning its scientific objectivity.[26] Yet, as Hesslow points out, such a concept "does not coincide with any clinically important or morally relevant categories".[27] When conducting a moral or political critique, we are in no way helped by knowing whether a person is diseased or healthy in Boorse's sense. It is perhaps in part for this reason that Norman Daniels, a long-standing – and in some senses a celebrated – advocate of Boorse's concept, argues for "a modest form of normativism"[28] in understandings of disease (and, by implication, health).

For any, even minimally, practical purposes, a value-neutral concept of health is of little use. Some, such as Daniels, may suggest that a naturalist concept provides a useful baseline for analysis, but it is clear that more work is needed before recognition of a physiological atypicality indicates that something should be done, or before we accept that physiological typicality is to be embraced or aspired to. For those who hold that work in science for its own sake is a good in itself, Boorse's conception may be useful. But for those interested in legal, moral, political, practical, and social issues relating to something usefully termed "health", it is a redundant concept.[29] To claim otherwise is either disingenuous (and possibly done in the hope that the concept's scientific objectivity, or (moral) value neutrality,[30] will imply a wider objectivity or neutrality), or unduly narrow (privileging health problems over non-health problems, when there is no good reason to do so[31]). Given the prevalence of endorsements of naturalist concepts, species-typical models do need to be accounted for in analysis. However, I am wary of them for three reasons. First, of themselves they are useless to normative

---

[26] Boorse, "Health as a theoretical concept".

[27] Hesslow, "Do we need a concept of disease?", 3.

[28] Norman Daniels, *Just Health: Meeting Health Needs Fairly* (Cambridge University Press, 2008), p. 42.

[29] See also Daniel Callahan, "The WHO definition of health", *The Hastings Center Studies* (1973) 1:3, 77–87, especially 86.

[30] A developed account of Boorse's concept is advanced and defended in Ananth, *In Defence of an Evolutionary Concept of Health*, where it is argued at p. 4 "that although *epistemic norms* (e.g., predictive power, replicability, parsimony, etc.) are an integral part of a naturalistic account, *non-epistemic norms* (e.g., social, moral, desirability, etc.) are not".

[31] That is to say, as James Wilson puts it, missing "the question of whether health is of fundamental importance" prior to theorising on the basis that health is special: James Wilson, "Not so special after all? Daniels and the social determinants of health", *Journal of Medical Ethics* (2009) 35:1, 3–6, at 6. If species-typical functioning *simpliciter* is our definition of health, then surely health is not a fundamental good.

inquiries into public health. Second, they do not help at all if we take it that disease is non-normative but that illness is of normative concern; it just means we have chosen not to substantiate our concept of illness, and must now return to doing so. And third, noting, for example, a general correlation between species atypicality and bad conditions for people in society seems misleading. Whilst it is apparent that there is a correlation between atypical functioning and undesirable states, it is far from clear that we can infer that a majority of statistical aberrances are undesirable; in other words, even if it is generally true that undesirable states are also unusual, it does not follow that the reverse is true. It is fallacy to suppose that because undesirable often equates with atypical, atypical will often equate with undesirable. We should thus be careful in accepting the apparently benign pragmatism that seems to favour a naturalist model

1.2.2   Negative and positive

The second health dichotomy to consider relates to distinctions between positive and negative accounts of health. It is useful to begin with the World Health Organization's (WHO) definition:

Health is a state of complete physical, mental and social well-being and not merely the absence of disease or infirmity.[32]

This short formulation encapsulates a commitment to two relevant conceptions, which are generally labelled positive and negative definitions of health. In its negative form, health may assume a 'biomedical definition': the absence, for example, of disease or illness. As Daniel Callahan notes, to an extent this negative definition is problematic, apparently providing only "the tautological proposition that health is the absence of non-health".[33] Nevertheless, it carries currency in many circles, and thus is not to be disregarded without some consideration. Whatever we seek an absence of – be it disease, infirmity, pathology, disorder, illness, or something else – negative definitions rest on the proposition that, absent the malady, health by default obtains. To establish that, or the extent to which, someone is healthy demands that we show that he is not *not* healthy in some way. When contemplating this conception, it is important to recall the allusion above to the role of scientific expertise. To some it seems that biomedical definitions of health

---

[32] See the declaration in the WHO's constitution, available at http://apps.who.int/gb/bd/ PDF/bd47/EN/constitution-en.pdf.
[33] Callahan, "The WHO definition of health", 85.

have some sort of scientific neutrality or objectivity to them, which may be taken to imply a wider, normative neutrality: health is the absence of disease, disease is objectively demonstrable, so health is value-free. However, even if we limited our focus to physical health we would see that negative conceptions still either carry a normative concept of disease, or are useless. There is no point seeking to eradicate a harmless disease presented merely as a benign and risk free aberration. Expertise in disease may be held by those with special knowledge or training, but should not be taken to present the concept itself as value-neutral.

At a more pragmatic level, the negative conception does not account for all matters of concern to policy-makers and practitioners in professions associated with public health.[34] The negative conception, therefore, is of interest, but can not tell us all that we need to know to perform a complete analysis of 'public health issues'. The WHO's definition accounts also for concerns for a more positive state of being – and in so doing seems to ensure great breadth to the borders of its own 'jurisdiction' – by expressing concern not only for an *absence* of non-health in a 'biomedical' sense, but also for the *presence* of "complete physical, mental and social well-being". Stephen Holland warns that positive conceptions of health risk a problem of explanatory opacity: "we are in danger of defining one unclear concept, 'health', in terms of another equally opaque concept, 'well-being'".[35] This may be true, but it is no truer than a comparable problem with regard to negative conceptions. In each case, we are dealing with a normative concept, and in each case that requires some unpacking.[36] It seems that the principal problem is that health may become too broad-spanning a term if it is equated with well-being.[37]

Given the myriad constructions of disease and well-being that exist, we must be prepared for both negative and positive conceptions to come under analysis. It is useful to be aware of the conceptual distinction between the two, but to remember, as Holland notes, a commitment to one in no way precludes a commitment to the other. Governments and public health professionals may seek both negative and positive health ends; positive welfare or well-being may be an end, just as the eradication or means of remedying disease are.[38] However,

[34] See Department of Health, *The NHS Constitution for England* (London, 2010), available at www.dh.gov.uk/en/Publicationsandstatistics/Publications/Publications-PolicyAndGuidance/DH_113613; Nuffield Council on Bioethics, *Public Health–Ethical Issues* (London: Nuffield, 2007).

[35] Stephen Holland, *Public Health Ethics* (Cambridge: Polity, 2007), p. 92.

[36] Holland, *Public Health Ethics*, pp. 96–98.

[37] Powers and Faden, *Social Justice*, p. 17.

[38] Holland, *Public Health Ethics*, p. 106.

it is worth recognising an important point of frailty in the hinge of the positive/negative dichotomy. The biomedical definition is considered of principal use as relating to a matter of expertise, or professional competence. Under close investigation, however, the supporting concepts and normative drivers that give meaning to the negative definition are likely to be the same as those that give substance to the positive definition. The negative definition may only be a part of a wider model of well-being or welfare, and indeed the positive model may well only be part of a wider theory of the human good. In this sense, they should in some manner be able to commensurate or fit coherently together. As well as in internationally relevant documents, such as the WHO's constitution, politically significant national documents and policy tools also find a seemingly natural harmony and propriety in advancing both negative conceptions of health and positive conceptions of well-being.[39] This is not necessarily problematic, but where health may be related to ideas such as welfare or flourishing, a positive/negative divide may not prove as helpful or clear cut as it at first appears to be.

1.2.3 *Internal* versus *external*

The final conceptual issue concerning health to consider here relates to how we might choose to measure health. It is already evident that there is radical disagreement over the very meaning of health. Furthermore, some analysts feel strongly about its 'misappropriation' in order to advance power claims and exert control beneath the disguise of a benign and altruistic concern for what is good for people (be the power claims from expert cliques or governments).[40] When we move into practical discussions about health, then, not only is there the problem of establishing precisely what a theorist, practitioner, or policy-maker means by 'health'; there is also the issue of working out who for practical purposes gets to define it in a given circumstance. The importance of this is clear.[41] Amartya Sen usefully describes the divide in approaches

[39] See e.g. *The NHS Constitution for England* (NHS, 8 March 2010).
[40] Hints of this are found in Boorse "Health as a theoretical concept", 572. More forcefully, see Illich, *Limits to Medicine*; Ivan Illich, "Disabling professions", in Ivan Illich, Irving Kenneth Zola, John McKnight, Jonathan Caplan, and Harley Shaiken, *Disabling Professions* (New York and London: Marion Boyars, 1977); Thomas Szasz, *The Theology of Medicine – The Political-Philosophical Foundations of Medical Ethics* (Oxford University Press, 1979); Skrabanek, *The Death of Humane Medicine*; see further the discussion in Chapter 8, especially sections 8.2 and 8.4.
[41] Mark Sullivan, "The new subjective medicine: taking the patient's point of view on health care and health", *Social Sciences and Medicine* (2003) 56, 1595–1604.

by reference to 'internal' and 'external' evaluations of health.[42] At the first extreme on this understanding, we can say that health should be defined relative only to internal perspectives; it is for the subject himself to decide when and whether he or something in his environment is healthy or unhealthy. The practical implication is that we leave it to individuals to define health for themselves, only allowing health-based interferences in instances that *they* recognise as mandating these. This has perceived advantages for those concerned about some issues related to autonomy, liberty, and pluralism. It has disadvantages when we consider questions of people's ignorance and incomplete capacity for rational decision-making.[43]

At the opposite extreme, we find that health is to be defined by an external agent, whose authority stems, for example, from expert knowledge. In this sense, people are objects whose health is evaluated regardless of their own perception. This view has perceived advantages for those concerned that particular individuals or groups are entrenched in situations (social or otherwise) that render them unable to recognise objectively identifiable harms that they would do well to escape or avoid. It has disadvantages where access to information requires a subjective perspective (e.g. to measure pain or suffering), where health's practical evaluation recommends an individual assessment of relative merits and demerits of alternative options, or in the face of fears about 'moral imperialism' through 'medicalisation' or 'healthism'.

As with positive and negative conceptions of health, it is possible here to adopt an approach that accounts for both internal and external approaches. Sen is amongst those who advocate a combined approach, and this is something I explore further in Chapter 11. It is important here to stress the relevance of this third dichotomy, and keep in mind its potential bearing on understandings of health and the limits and strengths of distinct justifications for political claims about imperatives driven by health concerns.

1.3   Health and politics

In anticipation of the detailed arguments in the remainder of this book, I will make brief mention here of the relationship between arguments about health's normativity in (potential) contrast with political

---

[42] Amartya Sen, "Health achievement and equity: external and internal perspectives", in Sudhir Anand, Fabienne Peter, and Amartya Sen (eds.), *Public Health, Ethics, and Equity*, (Oxford University Press, 2004). Cf. *ibid*.

[43] These issues are considered thoroughly in Parts II and III.

normativity. I seek in this section just to begin to explain the import of the term 'political' in what will follow, and why the relevant normativity for understanding what makes health public is derived from a political theory, rather than a theory of health (unless the two are the same[44]).

As already suggested, normative claims are ones that purport to say what *should* be, or be done, given some background theory, framework, or condition that provides authoritative and directive reasons. Similarly, normative assessments are judgements or evaluations made given such a theory. In many works we find reference to distinctions between normative claims and descriptive or empirical claims. Often the difference is seen to be crucial; on one hand, some analysts seek to ensure that we not infer an 'ought' from an 'is', on the other some are concerned that our arguments actually bear on the world as it is. However, for several reasons, reference to 'the normative' can prove troublesome. One of these reasons is that there are various sources of normativity, meaning a normative claim may denote something that provides a favourable reason given one account, but that is indefensible on another.[45] Morality is clearly a source of normativity, and when people make normative critiques under this heading, they will be analysing something – e.g. a vaccination policy – in accordance with a moral theory. They might ask, for example, whether there is a 'natural moral right' not to be subjected to such a policy. 'The law' is another source of normativity, and analysts could likewise evaluate a measure such as a vaccination policy according to legal norms. Here they might assess, for example, whether it is constitutional, or conforms with human rights obligations. Clearly the 'right' answer found in each case may imply a different judgement of the favourability of the policy. Where there is disagreement, or the risk of moral and legal discord is even voiced, the moral theorist may simply hold the law to be 'normatively irrelevant', or an 'illegitimate' source of normativity. Similarly, for some the relevant or interesting normativity is that which governs us practically in a political society, with its 'voice' found through legal and other regulatory measures, and in this case 'the moral' is an irrelevant, or only partially or indirectly relevant normativity.

I have said that useful concepts of health are normative; they imply something good or desirable. However, as long as the concept remains

---

[44] See Chapter 8, section 8.4.
[45] In Parts II and III this idea is developed at some length, and is well articulated in Simmons' reference to distinct "favorable evaluations" that might be used to assess the legitimacy and desirability of a State: A. John Simmons, "Consent theory for libertarians", *Social Philosophy and Policy* (2005) 22:1, 330–356.

hollow, we do not know its *political* (or indeed moral, or other normative) implications. The values in health may, for example, be morally or
socially defined. Thus, while I make the strong claim that for our purposes health can not be used in a value-neutral way, I also do not take
it that its inherent directivity automatically provides conclusions on, or
necessarily even hints to, what practical, political (or other) obligations
there ought to be concerning or because of health.

As I will argue in the next chapter, a 'public realm' denotes shared
concerns, where there is a mandate for an external authority – the
State – to encourage or enforce certain norms. It also implies a particular form of community, which is rightly viewed according to political paradigms. Looking at issues through a political lens sharpens our
focus on what matters most in practice: where health is discussed as a
public issue, the questions are about what people will be allowed to do,
forced to do, encouraged to do, or forced to take responsibility for *by
the State*.[46] It allows assessment of the sorts of obligations we have, but
with vital reference to how these obligations may be mediated through
the State. Whilst arguments based in 'pure morality' may help individuals assess what *they* should do, arguments about politics consider
what should be made or encouraged to happen given a particular form
of association. There is a movement from abstracted or 'in principle'
evaluations to practically implemented measures that actually bear on
people's lives. It is within this context that questions about health are
most important. It is crucial to see how moral arguments inform political debates. But the variety both of views and of people within political
communities demands its own form of analysis. Arguments directed at
the State draw from distinct concerns to those directed at 'moral self-
governors'.[47]

Taken in isolation these short assertions open and leave unanswered
a great many difficult questions. They are the subject of this book, and
in what follows I will demonstrate clearly what I take 'the political' to
mean, how it differs from 'the moral', and why politics provides the
proper focus for our analysis.[48] The reason for presenting these ideas in
sketch form here is to set the scene for what is to come, and indicate the
direction the arguments will take.

---

[46] As indicated, the substantive discussion will be addressed below. In particular, the
analytic divide between morality and politics draws from Thomas McPherson,
Political Obligation (London: Routledge and Kegan Paul, 1967).
[47] *Ibid.*
[48] See Part II.

1.4   Conclusions on health

This chapter has presented the nature of disputes about the idea of
health itself. The meaning of this concept is contested at various levels,
suggesting possible problems when people unquestioningly debate it, or
seem to debate it when in fact they are conceiving quite different things.
The key point, then, is to note that we must be prepared to scrutinise
the way the term health is used, to ensure we understand what it means
in a given case and what sort of weight is being given to it. I have argued
that whilst some urge the adoption of value-free understandings, these
have no practical use and are to be treated with sceptical caution. In
the context of public health analyses, I have also suggested that it is
important to allow both for 'positive' and 'negative' understandings of
health, and to be aware of the practical problem of deciding whose concept of health is used in a given situation. Having explained the reasons
for considering health to be normative, I ended the chapter by noting
how the fact of this normativity will not automatically imply any *political* imperatives. Useful concepts of health are value-laden, but it does
not follow that these values automatically imply imperatives within the
public sphere.

2   The public, and things being public

2.1   Introduction

The 'public' in 'public health' evokes different messages in different audiences.[1] For normative analysts, reference to 'public' is a reminder that evaluation of health-related matters must take place in a political and social context; a reminder that there is no use in simply identifying issues as they would relate to two abstracted individuals in their own discrete universe, as may (unhelpfully) happen in medical ethics.[2] Given the importance of the term 'public' in debates in public health law and ethics, further conceptual clarity is needed. Although the 'public' in public health takes its adjectival form, our focus may fall on 'the public' too. An analyst may claim to be concerned by the health of *the* public or *a* public, as well as by the public aspects of people's health. In regard to the former, we may then want to consider what the public is: is it some entity that is more than the sum of its parts, or is it just the aggregate of people it comprises? In regard to the latter, we might note that there may be overlapping, even universal, health-related issues that are not fair game for policy measures, unwanted third party interference, or as the basis of claims seeking to establish health-based rights or duties. Furthermore, the 'public' in public health may be considered as an administrative qualifier, referring to the work of government, or even specific agencies within government.[3]

---

[1] Marcel Verweij and Angus Dawson, "The Meaning of 'Public' in 'Public Health'". in Angus Dawson and Marcel Verweij (eds.), *Ethics, Prevention, and Public Health* (Oxford University Press, 2007).

[2] Ronald Bayer and Amy Fairchild, "The Genesis of Public Health Ethics," *Bioethics* (2004) 18:6, 473–492; Madison Powers, "Bioethics as Politics: The Limits of Moral Expertise", *Kennedy Institute of Ethics Journal* (2005) 15:3, 305–322; Lawrence Gostin, *Public Health Law: Power, Duty, Restraint* (2nd edn) (Berkeley: University of California Press, 2008), pp. 38–41; Angus Dawson, "Political Philosophy and Public Health Ethics", *Public Health Ethics* (2009) 2:2, 121–122.

[3] Mark Rothstein, "Rethinking the Meaning of Public Health," *Journal of Law, Medicine and Ethics* (2002) 30, 144–149. See chapter 3, section 3.2.2.

The extent to which matters are public, in some senses, depends on the extent to which they are not purely of concern to the individual; put positively, the extent to which they are all citizens' 'business'. To be this does not mean simply that people have similar or overlapping concerns, for example that they are all equally susceptible to the risk of a form of cancer, but that each person's susceptibility is also everybody else's concern. Establishing robust answers to these questions is an endeavour in political philosophy. Part II of the book considers a range of frameworks for such analytic assessment, ranging from the apolitical, wherein there is no public, to the strongly communitarian, wherein a concept of public is of great importance. Here I am concerned to establish the important conceptual groundwork to allow such analysis. The current chapter therefore explores 'public' as a noun and as an adjective, and presents the concepts around which analysis will most usefully be framed. I begin by considering 'the public', and note its association with a collective of citizens; a shared community. The implications of this are necessarily political, and expose the proper nature of our critical assessment. I then consider the public/private distinction, assessing its validity and utility. Before concluding, I note two senses of 'public' as it features in matters relating to public health, discussed in an influential paper by Angus Dawson and Marcel Verweij.[4] As public health of necessity focuses our attention on the idea that 'public' is of significance, it is crucial to consider what it might mean.

2.2   The public

For present purposes, let us take for granted a political system.[5] This means that we can coherently presume that there might be something worthwhile in discussing things labelled public health issues, *whatever* that means, because we accept a notion of shared community. In so doing, we accept that there will be matters of shared concern, and that health, or health-affecting behaviour, might in some instances be a part of this shared concern. This does not mean that we need presume here any consensus about the nature or source of legitimacy of the best political system. Although the practical implications will vary with distinct ideologies, the principle discussed in this section is true for extreme libertarians right through to extreme collectivists and communitarians. In brief, to have a public is to have an organised community; some sort of

---

[4] Verweij and Dawson, "The Meaning of 'Public' in 'Public Health'".
[5] In Chapter 7, I explore in detail the value and benefit of considering anarchism in analysis of public health.

political system identifiable as housing a collection of people who even taken individually share an identity and concerns with others in their community. It is crucial to recognise the import of this idea of sharing. In the context of an argument concerning civic republicanism, but in a manner that can speak more widely in political philosophy, Bruce Jennings puts the idea as follows:

Shared purposes or problems are not the same as individual purposes or problems that happen to overlap for large numbers of people. Of course, they do affect persons as individuals and as members of smaller groups, but they also affect the constitution of a 'people,' a population of individuals as a structured social whole. An aggregation of individuals becomes a people, a public, a political community when it is capable of recognizing common purposes and problems in this way; and what allows it to have this kind of political understanding and imagination has largely to do with a dynamic interplay between what I shall call *action* and *structure* over time.[6]

It is worth stressing that to make a claim concerning the existence of a public does not require a concession to some ontological or metaphysical assumption about group identity or a group as being more than the sum of its members. A public should be seen as a construction, and one that may only be sustained if it is recognised and supported by a sufficient number of the people it relates to. It requires the collective exercise of what Jennings, influenced by Benedict Anderson's *Imagined Communities*,[7] labels the "political imagination".[8] It is useful to reflect on Anderson's work. We need not worry about its focus – nationalism – or concern ourselves here with the development of his thesis, which works through a global, historical analysis. It is the way that Anderson frames nations that is key to our current deliberations. He defines "the nation ... as an imagined political community – and imagined as both inherently limited and sovereign".[9] He goes on:

It is *imagined* because the members of even the smallest nation will never know most of their fellow-members, meet them, or even hear of them, yet in the minds of each lives the image of their communion.[10]

---

[6] Bruce Jennings, "Public Health and Civic Republicanism," in Dawson and Verweij (eds), *Ethics, Prevention, and Public Health*, p. 48. See also on this understanding of public: Raymond Geuss, *Public Goods, Private Goods* (Princeton and Oxford: Princeton University Press, 2003), ch. III, especially pp. 36–41.

[7] Benedict Anderson, *Imagined Communities – Reflections on the Origin and Spread of Nationalism – Revised edition* (London: Verso, 1991).

[8] Jennings, "Public Health and Civic Republicanism", p. 49.

[9] Anderson, *Imagined Communities*, p. 6.

[10] *Ibid.*

For our purposes, the "limited" aspect of nationhood is a distraction as we are not immediately interested in inter- or multinational concerns. Although we need to suppose *a* jurisdiction, its limits need not in principle be exclusive: whilst Anderson can not allow that a nation embraces all of mankind,[11] the question is academic for present purposes as 'the public' in theory could.[12] The shared belief in community is important as it binds together those who otherwise would not be considered as one; a sense, as Anderson puts it, of "fraternity".[13] Although a community may be described as solid, organic even,[14] its very existence is reliant on this shared imagination; a shared belief throughout a group of people that they are members of the same community; the same public. In fact, a public is no more solid or organic than the imaginings that create it, notwithstanding that these imaginings may be quite powerful. To quote Anderson one final time:

> An American will never meet, or even know the names of more than a handful of his 240,000-odd fellow-Americans. He has no idea what they are up to at any one time. But he has complete confidence in their steady, anonymous, simultaneous activity.[15]

The, or a, public has this shared political imagination. It does not require harmonious political perspectives in the sense, for example, of being Labour or Tory, or Democrat or Republican. It rests upon a sharing of the view that there is something that renders a people a collectivity; a shared grouping.[16]

It is worth stressing that this manner of thinking is not (as may be implied pejoratively) 'leftist' or 'socialist' imagery; not 'communitarian' in a narrowly ideological sense of the word.[17] It captures all political

---

[11] *Ibid.*, p. 7.
[12] We might note abstractions such as the "world community" referred to in works on global health: see e.g. Lawrence Gostin and Allyn Taylor, "Global Health Law: A Definition and Grand Challenges", *Public Health Ethics* (2008) 1:1, 53–63. See also the 'in principle' comments on the plausibility of there being a single global state in comparably theoretical discussions, such as David Copp, "The Idea of a Legitimate State," *Philosophy and Public Affairs* (1999) 28:1, 3–45, e.g. at 25. There is a crucial sense of "limited" that does concern us, entailed in the question of who is included in "mankind" in the first place. This issue is explored in detail in Parts II and III. See in particular section 10.2.1.2, in Chapter 10, below.
[13] Anderson, *Imagined Communities*, p. 7.
[14] *Ibid.*, p. 26.
[15] *Ibid.*
[16] See also Richard Jenkins, "Rethinking ethnicity: identity, categorization and power", *Ethnic and Racial Studies* (1994) 17:2, 157–223; Rogers Brubaker, "Ethnicity without groups", *European Journal of Sociology* (2002) 43:2, 163–189.
[17] E.g. as it may be used to contrast the works of John Rawls, whose political theory has a strong communitarian base, and Robert Nozick, who argues that political legitimacy can only obtain in a minimal State: see John Rawls, *A Theory of Justice – Revised edition*

perspectives. One of the greatest sleights of hand in debates on ethics and public health is that which takes (right wing) libertarianism's being at one end of the 'political spectrum' to suggest that the 'burden of further justification' falls only on analysts arguing in favour of a position beyond libertarianism. Political imagination is exercised by all who believe in a political community, even those at the extremes of right wing, 'small state' libertarianism. Protagonists who argue against fluoridation of the clean water that is available to the public, yet take for granted that the public should have access to potable water, or, to generalise the point, those who argue as a matter of basic principle against legal coercive measures yet take for granted the need for a legal system, overstate the nature of the need for a defence from more communitarian protagonists.[18] *All* who engage in a dialogue that requires a political community – a public – as its subject are making a claim that there exists, and should exist, shared interests and identity (even if they would claim not to conceive matters thus). The complicated leap is not the one from libertarianism to a less individualistic political philosophy, but the leap that takes us into politics at all; the claim that a public exists whatsoever. These controversial points are central to the arguments explored and developed in the current book, and receive close attention in Part II. But in short, and contrary to how the issue can be caricatured, no one *forces* libertarians to drink water, fluoridated or otherwise; rather, they enjoy the access to clean water as members of a political community that provides this. It is question-begging to sustain without argument an apparently unquestionable premise that assurance of clean water is a State duty, whilst holding that fluoridated water is of necessity a step too far.[19]

Accepting these claims about the conceptual pervasiveness of 'the public', we can still hold that the public need not be given a more 'real' status than is feasible. This is well drawn out in Jennings' analysis. He argues for the need to reject a concept of the public that wrongly

---

(Oxford University Press, 1999); Robert Nozick, *Anarchy, State, and Utopia*, (Oxford: Blackwell, 1974).

[18] This is not intended to demonstrate that water should be fluoridated; it is a claim that apparently principled objectors to fluoridation can too easily overlook the normative work done in establishing that there is a 'right' to clean water in the first place, which may prove more than the simplistic 'autonomy-based' objections to fluoridation allow: in this regard, autonomy-based moral objections (as opposed to ones based on scientific uncertainty) do not bite as straightforwardly as some commentators suggest: see Rod Griffiths, "Fluoride: a whiter than white reputation?" *British Medical Journal* (2007) 355, 723.

[19] On this point, compare Gerald Dworkin, "Paternalism: Some Second Thoughts", in Gerald Dworkin, *The Theory and Practice of Autonomy* (Cambridge University Press, 1988), p. 125.

occupies space in arguments relating to public health, and political, legal, and bioethical thought more widely:

This is a reified concept of the public; it conceives of the public as if it were a natural thing – an organic whole with its own interests, needs, and being – as opposed to a socially constructed, imaginary life-world. Reification – treating social reality as if it were material or natural reality – leads the theorist to predicate to the entity moral, legal, and other normative properties that are predicated to human persons. The public has rights, interests, obligations. It can be harmed or injured. While it is often legally necessary to reify government or corporate agencies in this fashion, at least they have identifiable structures of authority, accountability, and responsibility. Like human persons, they are tangible actors in the social and natural world; they do things that have consequences.[20]

Setting the public up as an entity that is in and of itself ontologically separable from the individual people it comprises is formally problematic. It pulls something from nowhere – essentially off the back of a metaphor – and then obscures any sound purpose of the metaphor. Conceptual notions such as the public good, public purpose, or public interest do not require the conceptualisation and reification of an *abstract* concept. In fact, the creation of such an entity is problematic and can lead to considerable (and illusory) analytic problems: the public's interests enter into conceptual normative disputes, for example 'between the individual and society'. Such a formulation pits people outside of and against something of which they are supposed to be a part.[21] This is a point of crucial importance to the sound analysis of public health. We should reject as analytically crippling and conceptually invalid the idea that we can draw an antagonistic dichotomy between 'the individual and society' (and various similar manners of framing this ostensibly attractive notion: e.g. 'the individual and the community' or 'the individual and the public'). As shorthand, such phraseology is at times useful,[22] but it is best avoided for various reasons. Most importantly, to contrapose individuals and their communities is in fact to *exclude* individuals, or separate them, from themselves. It is to say they are not citizens; they are not part of the whole against whose interests they are said to act. This is theoretically flawed, and normatively useless. It is only plausible that someone may be the subject of obligation if he is

---

[20] Jennings, "Public Health and Civic Republicanism", p. 54.

[21] See Nozick, *Anarchy, State, and Utopia*, pp. 32–33.

[22] Stephen Holland, for example, reduces concerns in public health ethics down to "dilemmas between the rights and needs of the individual and the rights and needs of the community": Stephen Holland, *Public Health Ethics* (Polity: Cambridge, 2007), p. ix.

part of the system. The public is a political community; the collection of people subject to law in a jurisdiction. To place an individual outside of the public is also to place him outside of the law, and thus we can not consider any manner of legitimate legal regulation of his behaviour. Furthermore, if we reify 'the public', we must at least accept that this now 'real' entity assumes a different form than people. Though it may be described as 'organic', it will fail to be served by the same goods, face the same risks, or thrive in the same manner as people do. The health or welfare of a public on this understanding will bear no relation to any conception of health or welfare that may – even can – apply to a person.[23]

The public's shared interests are shared by all. Where we see arguments, for example, stating that 'individual autonomy must yield to the public interest', this is not 'society' knocking the individual on the head. Rather, it is the member of a public seeing foreclosed an option that is in fact available, but which is not viably permissible within the community. This stands whether we believe that legitimate political limitations to people's autonomous actions are very few, or if we allow for a more liberty-limiting communitarian philosophy. Through the creation of a public comes the creation of (politically) legitimate and illegitimate interests. The individual may be served by illegitimate interests – as an extreme example, he may have interests in killing a family member for financial gain – but those interests are not sustainable within the public he inhabits. The individual here is not 'bowing to the public', or being denied some 'right'. As he is part of the public, he can not simultaneously occupy this position and serve himself in a way that is incompatible with his and others' legitimate rights, duties, and other interests that are established through community membership.

In brief conclusion, we do best to think of the public as a collection of people with a shared sense that makes them a political community. In some analyses in public health, populations will be studied that can not, in a meaningful legal or political sense, be described as 'publics' in this way. Wendy Parmet gives the examples of populations of smokers, or of women drivers of SUVs in Boston aged below 35, who might be the focus of epidemiological research rather than bound by some common sense of identity.[24] In this regard, we may coherently choose to talk about 'a public' without implying any normative associations between

---

[23] See Richard Mohr, "AIDS, gays, and State coercion", *Bioethics* (1987) 1:1, 35–50. See also Chapter 3 for distinctions between individuals' and populations' health.

[24] Wendy Parmet, *Populations, Public Health, and the Law* (Washington: Georgetown University Press, 2009), p. 18. See also Chapter 3, especially sections 3.2.6 and 3.2.7.

its members. It is important to recognise this use of the term. As argued in Chapter 3, it can be helpful when describing scientific public health issues, with its use constrained to apolitical questions concerning human health. However, the wider project of this book, addressing ideas about public health as a source of normative concern, speaks to more than a collection of scientific subjects. In these normative considerations, by referring to the public, we are referring to a political community that is subject to the normative constraints it imposes on itself (or has imposed upon it), whatever they may be, and however they are established. It is not just a number of people; it is a community. Normative examination of the public is an endeavour in political philosophy. It can not be limited to 'public health perspectives', even if it is informed by these.

2.3   The public/private distinction: public as "the law's business"

Although it is crucial to have considered 'the public', the term 'public' is more commonly used adjectivally, and tends, at least within 'the liberal tradition', to be contrasted with 'private'. Neither of these terms means the same thing in every context in which it is used, and to that extent their use may lead to incoherence or apparent rather than substantial agreement or consistency. As Raymond Geuss argues, considering the public/private distinction as unitary is simplistic, leaving crucial questions unanswered, and thus providing only superficially useful argument. This does not mean that the distinction must be rejected altogether, or that works that have not made inroads on the back of it are redundant; simply, it calls for deeper scrutiny in order to formulate sufficiently robust and meaningful analyses.[25] Methodologically, the order of our investigation should run, Geuss suggests, as follows:

[F]irst we must ask what this purported distinction is *for*, that is, *why* we want to make it at all. To answer this question will bring us back to some relatively concrete context of human action, probably human political action, and it is only in the context of connecting the issue of the public and private to that antecedent potential context of political action that the distinction will make any sense. It is thus a mistake to answer the question, "Why shouldn't we interfere with that?" with "*Because* it is private," and think that this is the obvious end of the discussion. In itself it merely and tautologically says that we should not interfere because it is the kind of thing we think we ought not to interfere with. By saying it is private, we just shift the locus of the argument to the

---

[25] Geuss, *Public Goods, Private Goods.*

question of *why* we think we ought not to interfere, and the reasons we give will be highly diverse[.][26]

Clearly this approach cuts both ways: just as it is unsatisfactorily question-begging to say "Regulations that prevent me from smoking are illegitimate because smoking is a private matter" so it is to say simply that "The regulations are legitimate because smoking is a public matter". It is crucial not to use the terms 'public' or 'private' as unsophisticated sanctifiers; as lazy words that do our normative work for us. They are conclusions rather than start points. And, as I have noted, each can represent different conclusions.

Notwithstanding the scope for alternative accounts – contradictory ones even[27] – it is necessary here to provide a view of the public/private distinction that can operate within liberal political frameworks (broadly conceived), to discover whether analysis of public health is a coherent enterprise in the first place, and if it is, to demarcate it from other (i.e. non-public[28]) health issues. As in the likely case alluded to in Geuss' analysis, we are directly concerned here with political action. I propose to draw from paradigms set up (not uniquely) in the English courts' treatment of Article 8 of the European Convention on Human Rights (ECHR), which gives a qualified guarantee of "respect for private and family life". The formulaic clumsiness of the courts' position, discussed in the coming paragraphs, reinforces Geuss' claims about distinct meanings of public and private, but it is tolerably comprehensible and raises the issues that are of relevance in analysis of the public/private distinction in regard to public health. As well as a public/private dichotomy, there emerge distinctions in the meanings of public and private taken individually, thereby allowing the description of 'public private acts' and other such combinations, reflecting two distinct senses in which things may be private or public. The first sense is

---

[26] *Ibid.*, p. 107 (emphases in original).

[27] For example, adding a third conception to private and public, to accommodate the "grey area" the polarity seems necessarily to create: Alan Wolfe, "Public and private in theory and practice: some implications of an uncertain boundary", in Jeff Weintraub and Krishan Kumar (eds.), *Public and Private in Thought and Practice: Perspectives on a Grand Dichotomy* (Chicago and London: The University of Chicago Press, 1997).

[28] Geuss notes that private is not the only "opposite" of public: Geuss, *Public Goods, Private Goods*, pp. 8–9. Principally, I remain focused on private as *the* alternative concern in the present analysis as private connotes an element of legitimate "non-publicness" in a way, for example, that secrecy does not. In other words, private and public are not value neutral terms in the current analysis. It is for this reason that they are taken as conclusions rather than start points, and I echo Geuss and encourage analysts to unpack the arguments underpinning their positions on what makes things public.

'decisional privacy', referring to the autonomy of an individual, and the good (within reason) of individuals making their own decisions, and living in accordance with their own values. On this count, the less fundamental a decision is to a person's identity or values the 'less private' it is in a privileged legal or political sense. The second sense refers to the physical or social nature of the matter under question; for example, by reference to an act's physical character, or the degree to which it is performed 'in public'. The more public an act is in this sense, the less worthy it becomes of legal protection as a matter of respect for privacy.

To illustrate the distinctions, it is useful to focus particularly on the High Court judgment in the 'Rampton smokers' case'.[29] The applicants, resident in a secure psychiatric hospital, argued that the court should quash regulations that prohibit the smoking of tobacco in psychiatric hospitals in England (Rampton's being a secure psychiatric hospital means that going outside for a cigarette is not possible, and thus in effect there is a complete ban on smoking).[30] The lawfulness of the smoking ban was challenged as being an infringement of the human right to respect for private and family life, and was argued to be discriminatory (under Article 14 ECHR) as it does not apply similarly in prisons, hospices, or care homes. The court considered how 'private' may be understood in the light of previous Article 8 jurisprudence. Of particular prominence in the judgment was analysis of a challenge to a legislative ban on hunting with dogs,[31] and Dianne Pretty's case, where arguments were made that privacy rights incorporated a right to assisted suicide (in her case, the infringement of Article 8 was found to be justified under Article 8(2), in order to protect the vulnerable).[32]

As described above, the High Court in the Rampton smokers' case discerned two meanings of 'private' relevant to assessment of Article

---

[29] *R (G and B)* v. *Nottinghamshire Healthcare NHS Trust; R (N)* v. *Secretary of State for Health* [2008] EWHC 1096 (Admin). Note there was an unsuccessful appeal against the High Court's decision: *R (N)* v. *Secretary of State for Health; R (E)* v. *Nottingham Healthcare NHS Trust* [2009] EWCA Civ 795. On the issue discussed here, compare paras 30–52 of the Court of Appeal's judgment. For wider discussion and analysis, see John Coggon, "Public health, responsibility and English law: are there such things as no smoke without ire or needless clean needles?" *Medical Law Review* (2009) 17:1, 127–139; John Coggon, "No right to smoke in high security psychiatric hospitals," *Journal of Bioethical Inquiry* (2009) 6:4, 405–408; Neil Allen, "A human right to smoke?" *New Law Journal* (2008) 158 (7326), 886–887.

[30] Specifically, the court was asked to quash reg. 10(3) of the Smoke-Free (Exemption and Vehicles) Regulations 2007, drafted in accordance with s. 3 of the Health Act 2006.

[31] *R (Countryside Alliance)* v. *Attorney General* [2007] UKHL 52.

[32] *Pretty* v. *UK* (2002) 35 EHRR 1. Strictly, Dianne Pretty was arguing that *she* had a right that *her husband* should have an immunity from prosecution were he to assist her suicide.

8 claims. The first relates to privacy in the sense of personal decision-making. Private decisions are essentially ones made by an individual on his own behalf, according to his own values. The more "integral to a person's identity or ability to function socially as a person", the more "morally [and therefore politically and legally] worthy of respect" a matter will be.[33] Thus, the more fundamental to a person something is, the more pressingly private it is. This sort of privacy may be related to concepts of individual autonomy or moral agency, such as the "positive liberty" described by Isaiah Berlin.[34]

The second sense of privacy relates to the degree of 'publicness' that obtains in the exercise of decision-making. Whilst the first sense is in some ways abstract (though no less important for that), this second sense is about the physical or social manifestation of (autonomously made) choices. Looking analogically to earlier jurisprudence, the court reasoned that fox hunting was a 'private public' act; it is a matter of private choice whether to hunt, but it is an activity that takes place very publicly rather than 'in private'. This could be contrasted with a 'private private' act, which would take place out of the public gaze. And in Dianne Pretty's case, although the decision was deeply personal and would have been given effect 'in private', its potential social effect, its implication for others, was estimated as too far reaching to allow her this manifestation of a right to privacy.

An activity that is private in the first sense enjoys an increasing likelihood of ECHR protection in proportion with the extent that it is private in the second sense (and *vice versa*). The personal importance of an activity weighs on its strength as a protected act, as does the degree to which it is undertaken *in* private. (In the event, it was decided *inter alia* that the patients' decision to smoke was not of sufficient importance to their identity, and *their* home (i.e. Rampton Hospital) was too public a place, so the ECHR did not afford them rights against the policy).

The Court's approach in this area draws out usefully the senses of private that are of concern to a political analysis relating to public health. It is worth noting that, particularly with reference to US jurisprudence, privacy conceptions are often split into three, not two. The three are 'zonal', 'relational', and 'decisional'. I consider the two conceptions I have raised in this section to be sufficient and suitable for our analysis, capturing satisfactorily all that is covered by the alternative triad (decisional corresponding with the first sense, and zonal and relational

---

[33] These terms are taken from the court's account of a submission by counsel for the applicants: [2008] EWHC 1096 (Admin), para. 74.

[34] Isaiah Berlin, "Two Concepts of Liberty", in Isaiah Berlin, *Four Essays on Liberty* (Oxford University Press, 1969).

corresponding with the second sense). Whether an analyst assumes the two, three, or possibly some other dissection, it is good to remember that there will likely remain some artificiality, or 'grey areas', that the chosen framing will not overcome. And despite the dominance in some quarters of the three conception model, within the US context some prefer the two conception option. In footnoted text, Kendall Thomas makes well the point:

> The distinctions are largely ideal-typical, and thus should be understood as mainly heuristic. It is not unusual to find elements of one model present in others. Indeed, in his dissent in *Hardwick*, Justice Blackmun characterizes the Supreme Court's approaches to the question of constitutional privacy as being "along two somewhat distinct, albeit complementary, lines." 478 U.S. at 203–4. On the one hand, the Court "has recognized a privacy interest with reference to certain *decisions* that are properly for the individual to make." On the other, "it has recognized a privacy interest with reference to certain *places* without regard for the particular activities in which the individuals who occupy them are engaged." Id. At 204 (citations omitted) (Blackmun J., dissenting).[35]

For the purposes of the current analysis, and the framing it requires and recommends, the dual conceptions can accommodate satisfactorily the important senses of 'private' and 'public' raised in analysis of public health issues.[36]

What may be labelled 'the liberal presumption' tells us that we have (in some cases overrideable) reasons to privilege people's decisions and freedom to act, in particular where the matter seems to go to the core of what they consider fundamental or of importance to their personal existence, and when they take place 'in private'. And each of these concerns permits of degrees: things can be more or less private in either sense. According to the liberal presumption, the 'more private' a decision is, the more reason there is, *prima facie* anyway, to respect an individual's choice and thus his freedom to act on it. And the 'more private' the place where he seeks to perform the activity, the more reason there is, *prima facie* anyway, to permit him freedom to act. In critical analysis of public health, this normative sense within private is crucial. But why draw out this liberal framing?[37] In short, it is because public health issues become of practical importance when political questions are raised, and the context of our analysis is within systems of political

---

[35] Kendall Thomas, "Beyond the privacy principle", *Columbia Law Review* (1992) 92, 1431–1516, at 1443, fn. 26. Emphasis in original.

[36] It is worth noting that some theorists may be concerned to discuss 'informational privacy' under its own heading, rather than see it protected by the concepts of privacy that I consider adequate.

[37] Dawson, "Political philosophy and public health ethics".

liberalism.[38] We face questions such as: when is health, a health-affecting behaviour, or a health-affecting policy, a matter of shared concern? And when does this mean that practical freedoms might be limited? As Robert Mnookin has noted:

[A]cross a broad political spectrum there is a consensus that the power of government should be bounded and that certain 'private' activities should be presumptively beyond the bounds of legitimate government regulation or coercion … The rub comes with the second question, however. What are the dimensions of the private realm?[39]

The very acceptance of this conceptualisation – of there being useful categories of private and public – raises the question of practical, principled, and analytic importance that Mnookin goes on to ask: "Does it make sense to think there is a shared commitment to the liberal ideal of a private realm, when political opponents each pour such different content into the concept?"[40] Drawing from Ronald Dworkin's interpretation of the two (then, anyway) dominant political perspectives in the US,[41] Mnookin acknowledges the depth of tensions between substantial political theories, even if superficially each can be said to prize the idea of public and private realms: one may consider privacy as something for the market, whilst another may see privacy not as a fiscal principle but a moral one. From the analytic perspective of a lawyer-economist, Mnookin suggests the public/private distinction is unimportant; a view that seems sensible enough given the rather shaky reasons that might be offered to support the contention that there is a straightforward difference between 'public law' and 'private law'.[42] He does, however, also suggest that from moral and political perspectives, a proclaimed rejection of the distinction may not be as complete as analysts might claim. Commentators may wrongly confuse rejection, for example, of economic liberalism with wholesale rejection of the public/private distinction.[43] This is important. In echo of Emile Durkheim's

---

[38] Cf Holland, *Public Health Ethics.*

[39] Robert Mnookin, "The public/private dichotomy: political disagreement and academic repudiation", *University of Pennsylvania Law Review* (1982) 130:6, 1429–1440, at 1430.

[40] *Ibid.*, at 1433.

[41] Ronald Dworkin, "Liberalism", in Stuart Hampshire (ed.), *Public and Private Morality* (Cambridge University Press, 1978).

[42] See also Morton Horwitz, "The history of the public/private distinction", *University of Pennsylvania Law Review* (1982) 130:6, 1423–1428; Duncan Kennedy, "The stages of decline of the public/private distinction", *University of Pennsylvania Law Review* (1982) 130:6, 1349–1357.

[43] Mnookin, "The public/private dichotomy: political disagreement and academic repudiation", at 1440.

noted phrase, *all law is public*.[44] Formal and informal legal mechanisms protect 'private law' matters, and give authority to individuals' claims of 'private law' rights against other individuals. Their exercise, or the threat of their exercise, can be seen as a process of individuals' exercising public authority rather than simply exerting power in another (i.e. a 'private') realm.[45] The very fact that disputes over the terms in a legally valid[46] private contract can be settled by the judiciary, or limited by Parliament, is demonstrative of the public nature described here. Equally, that a 'right to privacy' is guaranteed by law, and adjudicated upon in the courts, demonstrates how a private realm, inasmuch as it is legally protected – and susceptible to legal protection – is public. This public protection of privacy is not just desirable, it is essential, and calls for workable regulation.[47]

However, the metaphor of private and public realms can still do its work, for our concern here is not with private law *versus* public law; it is with public *versus* private as *political* conceptions. The law's reach may be seen to represent the outer boundaries of the public, and its directions demarcating the limits of legitimate action; the bounds beyond which there is no proper place for public adjudication, enforcement, or interference.[48] Where the law does not speak, or should not speak, we have our private sphere.[49] There is, or at least in principle could be, a

---

44 Emile Durkheim, *The Division of Labour in Society* (trans. George Simpson), (New York: Macmillan, 1933 [1893]), p. 123.

45 Frances Zemans, "Legal mobilization: the neglected role of the law in the political system", *The American Political Science Review* (1983) 77:3, 690–703.

46 This necessary qualification is not, but may seem, question-begging: the issue is dealt with in the next paragraph (as it was by Durkheim in the discussion cited just above).

47 Christine Sypnowich, "The civility of law: between public and private", in Maurizio Passerin d'Entrèves and Ursula Vogel (eds.), *Public and Private – Legal, Political and Philosophical Perspectives* (London and New York: Routledge, 2000), pp. 97–98.

48 See Samuel Freeman, "Why libertarianism is not a liberal view", *Philosophy and Public Affairs* (2001) 30:2, 105–151, especially at 111–114, and 120–123: bringing some putatively private agreements into the public sphere, and making them the subject of public adjudication and enforcement, of necessity means they are "no longer merely a matter 'between consenting adults'; it becomes a matter of civic law and a publicly recognized right" (at 112). To be clear, then, our concern here is not with *legal* distinctions between, for example, private and public harms, as, once these are legally recognised, they both fall within the public realm under the current analysis (which thus contrasts, for example, with the nature of analysis in jurisprudence exploring the concept of 'public' in the crime of 'public nuisance': see *R* v. *Rimmington* [2005] UKHL 63).

49 Hence the allusion in the title of this section to the "Wolfenden report", which famously stated that: "There must remain a realm of private morality which is, in brief and crude terms, not the law's business" Wolfenden Committee, *Report of the Committee on Homosexual Offences and Prostitution* (Cmnd. 247) (London: HMSO, 1957), para. 13.

clear boundary between the realms of public and private.[50] And it makes sense to conceive this both in terms of physical as well as more abstract claims to a boundary between the private and the public.[51] As each qualifies and completes the other – i.e. it is tautological just to define the public as that which is not private – we are presented well with a conceptual framing for use in practical normative analysis relating to public health issues, and need then to see how to fill it with substantial, well-argued content. But to reiterate, the important conceptual point raised here is one that Christine Sypnowich describes as "an essential idea: certain aspects of life are the prerogative of the individual and should be safe from political interference".[52] If we want to know what makes health public, and thus the legitimate bounds of health-affecting actions, we need to know how to develop accounts of 'private', both in its decisional and social aspects, and to evaluate the bearing of it within a wider political theory. How such a theory may be and should be delineated is a matter considered in Parts II and III. For now, what does this all tell us about the contrast between private and public? What role does 'public' come to play? Regardless of where one sits politically, there is good reason to afford people a 'private sphere' within which to make decisions. The size of this sphere, and the reasons for allowing it, will vary depending on ideology and the nature of the people in a community, but all political views allow some sphere of privacy. What stands as fair game for State interference is what, for present purposes, is public. As it is a flipside to private, again it is a normative notion, which means that reason needs to be given for labelling something public. However, there is also an important asymmetry that needs to be addressed.

People differ about what matters: What is their private concern? What is a public concern? What is fundamental to them? What is important to them? And how should others behave given their shared existence within a public? An 'anything goes' position, wherein our only criterion for assessing the importance of a decision is an individual's own appraisal of it, can not work.[53] Nevertheless, it is possible to allow a plurality of moralities to coexist within a political system[54] (just as it is possible to have a plurality of concepts of health). Pluralism does

---

[50] Cf Mark Elliott, "'Public' and 'private': defining the scope of the Human Rights Act", *Cambridge Law Journal* 66:3, 485–487.

[51] Sypnowich, "The civility of law: between public and private", p. 96.

[52] *Ibid.*, p. 97. See also Freeman, "Why libertarianism is not a liberal view," section I.

[53] This is clearly a strong claim about the necessity of law. I am taking the acceptability and good of political systems for granted in this chapter (without arguing for any specific political model).

[54] John Gray, *Two Faces of Liberalism* (Cambridge: Polity Press, 2000).

not require the permissibility of anything that anyone might consider appropriate; rather, it requires the acceptance and permissibility of a limited variety of conflicting takes on 'the good'. Susan Wolf summarises the position as follows:

> Pluralism in ethics ... is the view that there is an irreducible plurality of values or principles that are relevant to moral judgment. While the utilitarian says that all morally significant considerations can be reduced to quantities of pleasure and pain, and the Kantian says that all moral judgment can be reduced to a single principle having to do with respect for rationality and the bearers of rationality, the pluralist insists that morality is not at the fundamental level so simple. Moreover ... the pluralist believes that the plurality of morally significant values is not subject to a complete rational ordering.[55]

The public sphere that raises itself in the current analysis is not concerned with the 'rational ordering' of different accounts of the (moral) good that individuals may choose to follow. However, it does require two practical normative and epistemic roles for the State, which are possibly the source of the greatest controversy in debates concerning public health law and ethics, as well as being a source of great contention in wider philosophical debates concerning the legitimacy of the State. First, there is the need to legislate or adjudicate on the very boundaries of the public/private distinction. In other words, there is a need to deem that x is a matter within the private sphere or is a matter of public (or, synonymously here, shared) concern. Thus the very question of what is private is a public one, and requires some – likely controversial, or at least contestable – public means of ascertainment. Second, there is a need when making worthwhile policy (and it is hard to accept that a government could have legitimate reason not to seek to make worthwhile policy) to commit to some account, or accounts, of the good. And such an account may not be universally accepted, even if, in principle, it is universally acceptable. Thus, where the State claims governance of an issue – either by permitting its remaining in the private sphere, or by claiming public 'ownership' through positive advancement or prohibition in policy – we find substance to the meaning of public. The justifications for claiming that something ought to be public, whether it relates to foreclosing the exercise of choices, even if they are born of deeply held conviction, or limiting the places wherein choices can be exercised, will sit on one or both of two strata. This is parallel with the two senses of private in that realm: there will be a more ethereal (but not, of itself, unreal) claim about something along the lines of shared interests, identity, or good that transcends the legitimate

---

[55] Susan Wolf, "Two levels of pluralism", *Ethics* (1992) 102:4, 785–798, at 785.

scope of individual difference or indifference; and there will be a more practical claim about the physical or social 'publicness' of a place or activity.

Interesting scope for nuanced argumentation on these matters allows us to examine the nature of special or fundamental – i.e. 'more private' – reasons. In the context of arguments purporting to relate to public health, we might think of the provision of specific exemptions from general duties to wear protective clothing for those with 'religious reasons' for wanting this freedom: archetypally the freedom of Sikhs not to wear safety helmets on construction sites[56] or when riding a motorcycle.[57] As will be made clear in the following chapter, we can see from this that there is possibly an enormous breadth to the scope of 'public health issues'. Any health-related matter that might be contested, either as being private or as being public, will be open to public adjudication. And as so much activity can bear on health one way or another, it is very hard to imagine an area of State governance that can not therefore be said presumptively to raise public health issues.

In short, the idea of public has left us free, if not bound, to contemplate what may be meant by 'the public interest', and also to consider the very shape of ourselves as conceptually conceived. By not allowing ourselves to conceive of the public as some organic 'meta-entity', we are left, as Jennings argues, with a framing of people who *internalise* apparent tensions between the public and the private.[58] This internal dualism of people within a community is neither analytically nor ontologically problematic. An idea developed throughout this book is that we must see ourselves as political beings. Each of us is both public and private: a person is a custodian, but not the sole custodian, of his living being.[59] Both he and the State have obligations towards his welfare. If health is to be made public, it is to say that we are not just atomised, but sovereignty over our existence is to some extent shared. Where our health or health-affecting behaviour is public it is not only our individual concern.

It is too simplistic just to say that all of health could be private or public. For *analytic* purposes, 'public health' invites the dissection of these issues. 'Public health' may usefully denote the sum of health

---

[56] Employment Act 1989, s. 11.
[57] Road Traffic Act 1988, s. 16. See also Mark Hill and Russell Sandberg, "Is nothing sacred? Clashing symbols in a secular world", *Public Law* (2007), 488–506; Russell Sandberg and Norman Doe, "Religious exemptions in discrimination law", *Cambridge Law Journal* (2007) 66:2, 302–312.
[58] Jennings, "Public health and civic republicanism", p. 55.
[59] See further Parts II and III.

within a population, without regard to the aspects of *public* concern as contrasted with *private* concern. But when deciding what triggers obligation, we need to know what makes health public; what makes it of shared concern in any given situation. Public health *then* may denote the health-related matters that are everyone's business. It is necessary briefly now to consider alternative resonances that may be found in the term 'public' within the context of 'public health ethics'.

2.4   People, populations, and a healthy public

Marcel Verweij and Angus Dawson offer a critical exploration of the meaning of 'public' in 'public health'.[60] Whilst I would contend that for normative analysis of public health issues, the conceptual framing outlined in the previous sections is of principal use, it is important also to be aware of the distinct implications seen in the term 'public' as it arises in these more narrowly circumscribed debates. Inasmuch as it is taken in some contexts to denote specific or alternative senses, it is well that these be drawn out, both for conceptual awareness and for critical assistance.

Having considered a range of definitions of public health, Dawson and Verweij discern two salient and relatively common factors.[61] First is the idea that 'the public' is something that can be targeted in a special way. It suggests a 'population approach', both in action, and in understanding issues relating to health and the assessment of the health of populations. This is redolent, notably, of the distinction Geoffrey Rose famously draws between care for the health of populations and that of individuals.[62] Second is the idea that interventions can be 'public' in the sense that they entail coordinated, collective action, often orchestrated by the government or anyway some public body. Dawson and Verweij develop each of these senses of public in turn.

The public's health, they suggest, is only partly to be measured as the aggregate health of the population's members. This is not simply because, with an emphasis on population-targeted policies and on *prevention*, it is often impossible to identify the individuals who are direct beneficiaries of a measure, even as epidemiological analysis demonstrates that benefits accrue. The aggregate health alone does not account for *distribution* of health within a population. The authors argue that a

---

[60] Verweij and Dawson, "The meaning of 'public' in 'public health'".

[61] *Ibid.*, p. 21.

[62] Geoffrey Rose, "Sick individuals and sick populations". *International Journal of Epidemiology* (1985) 14, 32–38. This paper is discussed in further detail in the next chapter.

more equitable distribution of good health represents a better *public* health, even if the aggregate population health is the same as that in a population with marked differences in healthy and unhealthy individuals. It is possibly more controversial than Dawson and Verweij allow to suggest that a public is healthier because of greater equity in health. It seems hard for this not to entail wider claims about the normative value of equity in society, and then to fall into a claim about *better* versus *worse* societies, disguised as a more morally neutral claim about *healthier* versus *less healthy* societies.[63] And even if this wider claim need not be inferred, the sense of the term 'health' seems inevitably to be different to that which the authors apply to individuals and then imagine aggregated. 'Health' when applied to a healthy public in this second, more idealistic sense, may be more metaphorical than it is in the earlier, person-based sense. In his discussion of *res publica*, Geuss captures this in the following phrase:

> Since obviously one of the main factors of common concern to the *populus* is its own strength and health, the continued maintenance of that vitality and strength is a clear common good, although, as societies become more complex and differentiated, there may be disagreement about what constitutes social and political 'health' and how it may best be ensured.[64]

I would strongly caution against such interpretations, which open up the problem of a population becoming more than the sum of its parts; an issue discussed above in section 2.2. Even so, Dawson and Verweij are right that this sense of distribution amongst individuals within a public has an important bearing in many understandings of public in the context of public health, and thus it is important at least to be aware of it.

The third aspect of the population approach that is raised is more attitudinal.[65] It is hypothesised that we have two populations with equal aggregate health, and now also equal health distribution. It is then suggested that if one population's members aim to be healthy, whereas the other's members do not take such care and are just lucky to be in the situation they find, the former is healthier than the latter. Again, this arguably works with something of an equivocation concerning the term 'health' itself – the populations can only be of equal health but with one healthier than the other if we have two senses of health at play – but the

---

[63] This is not to deny that there may not be such a coincidence (i.e. that healthier societies in this sense are also better in some important, independent sense). The point is that it risks obscuring the reasons underpinning these judgments.

[64] Geuss, *Public Goods, Private Goods*, p. 37.

[65] Verweij and Dawson, "The meaning of 'public' in 'public health'," pp. 23–24.

idea of a shared purpose certainly evokes issues crucial to the idea both of a public, and things being public.

And now to the second sense of public raised by Dawson and Verweij; of public as it connotes collective intervention. Key here is the cooperation of individuals in pursuit of health benefits, at times when it is unclear exactly which individuals will be the direct beneficiaries. Three manners of public participation are proposed.[66] One entails participation in health promoting or protecting activities, such as taking part in vaccination programmes or practising 'safe sex'. A second is where individuals safeguard their own health, for example by eating a 'healthy diet'. Here, although in contrast with the first, the acts taken individually are self-regarding, as members of a public the aggregate effect will be clear on the group taken together. Finally, there are measures where the collective nature of the activity itself increases the chances of improving health. An example given is collective efforts to reduce smoking: this can make a significant change to the conditions, the human environment, and help people reduce their tobacco intake. These further thoughts on the meaning of public are important to consideration of arguments raised in 'public health ethics'. Although they do not all work within the framework I advocate in this chapter, their influence in wider analysis makes it crucial to engage with them.

2.5   Conclusions on public

This chapter has considered 'the public', 'public' as an adjective, and 'public' as it features within arguments on public health. The framing of public, in particular as it contrasts with private, sets up a hollow but important conceptual model, which we will be able to fill following analysis in political theory. What we find to fall within the 'private sphere' may be described as within the bounds of legitimate liberty; of politically (and legally) unfettered freedom. This sits beside what is 'public', which rules out or limits the freedom to act in various ways. This concept of public/private necessarily falls within a liberal political paradigm (broadly conceived), and thus may seem unattractive to some theorists. Nevertheless, as well as being an appropriate frame for discussion of normativity in common law jurisdictions and beyond, it is naturally suited to normative engagement with a concept labelled 'public health'. It leaves us in a position of having to engage with further concepts, perhaps most notably the public interest. However, conceiving of things

---

[66] *Ibid.*, pp. 25–27.

that are public as game for external regulation offers a core concept in analysis of questions of what makes health public.

The next chapter follows naturally from the discussion of Dawson and Verweij's paper, and considers different understandings of 'public health'. It is therefore well to end here with a salient warning voiced in Dawson and Verweij's conclusion, which reaffirms concerns that have emerged throughout the opening chapters of this book:

> Calling something a public health problem often serves implicit normative political purposes. This provides grounds for caution in thinking about the concept of 'public health' and public health activity. In ethical reflection, normative arguments and value statements should be made explicit, not disguised in seemingly descriptive terms.[67]

To discuss the public is to raise political ideas. Furthermore, we have seen in Chapter 1 that usefully to raise the idea of health is to invoke normative ideas. So in 'public' and 'health' we have quite separately normative terms. It is probably partly for this reason that they each imply such different things to different people. This has clear implications for how 'public health' itself might be variously understood or evaluated. The following chapter considers the different 'faces' of public health. This will allow us in the remainder of Part I to reflect on the interplay between the faces of public health in the analytic enterprise undertaken by those interested in public health law and ethics, and in the policy-making of the State given purported public health concerns.

[67] *Ibid.*, p. 29.

3 The seven faces of public health

3.1 Introduction

Having considered in Chapters 1 and 2 the meanings of 'health' and 'public', it is now possible to come to definitions of 'public health' itself. As above, I will set out my reasons for preferring particular definitions: in short, I think it is most usefully taken to refer to instances where there are known but not individually identifiable people whose health is affected by a policy or practice, or used as a shorthand in reference to *facts* about people's health within or between populations. Nevertheless, it is also important to consider and keep in mind other prevalent understandings that feature in academic, professional, and public discourse. Public health has such varied meanings that its uncritical or uncontemplated use in debate can lead to obscure arguments. Although these are easily overcome through clarification, the plurality of meanings of 'public health' itself, as well as those of 'public' and 'health', mean analysis is often more cumbersome than it might otherwise be.[1] As the salient questions for normative debates about public health are *political*, it will be unsurprising that the term 'public health' can itself come to be used as a powerful political device in social argument, and more narrowly it can be set up as something with a central mission, code, values, and perspective. I will discuss below the risk of allowing pre-analytic normativity to enter concepts of public health, where it looks like so doing will unduly direct the debate.[2]

This chapter presents in detail what I call 'the seven faces of public health'. I hope clearly to distinguish seven separate categories of

---

[1] Cf Lawrence O. Gostin, *Public Health Law and Ethics: A Reader* (Berkeley: University of California Press, 2002), chs 1 and 2; Wendy Parmet, *Populations, Public Health, and the Law* (Washington: Georgetown University Press, 2009), pp. 7–9; Jean McHale, "Law, regulation and public health research: a case for fundamental reform?", *Current Legal Problems* (2010) 63, 475–510.

[2] This is an issue I have addressed elsewhere: see John Coggon, "Does *public health* have a personality (and if so, does it matter if you don't like it)?" *Cambridge Quarterly of Healthcare Ethics* (2010) 19:2, 235–248.

meaning that are applied to public health throughout the literature. It is worth stressing that more than one of the following senses may quite reasonably feature in the same argument.[3] Equally, the divides I draw are not always perfect. However, each bears separate discussion because of its independently important focus. Without drawing the following distinctions, important insights can be lost: the inevitable overlaps are the necessary price of a sufficiently complete taxonomy. My 'methodological' aim is ambitious: through a conceptual analysis I seek to provide a comprehensive classification for the different definitions of public health. At the very least, the chapter shows quite how lacking in specificity the term 'public health' is in the abstract, and thus how important it is for analysts to be clear in what they are addressing when claiming to speak about public health issues. Where I concede that there is overlap, I nevertheless maintain that overall there is insuperable contradiction between understandings that renders impossible the satisfactory establishment of anything approaching a single, unifying definition.[4] Some of the faces of public health require quite detailed analysis. Prior to engaging in greater depth with them, I provide here a summary of the distinct things that protagonists 'do' with public health, or mean when employing the term. The summary is followed in the rest of the chapter with critical exploration.

3.1.1   The seven faces of public health

1. *Public health as a political tool*: in this sense 'public health' is used as an important end, denoting (supposedly) strong or compelling reasons for formulating policy. Here the term may be seen to imply a social mission, a social theory, or a naturally good concept. It entails what are taken to be necessary goods, and is thus cited as an important reason for acting.
2. *Public health as government business*: as a function of government, public health may be understood narrowly as relating to the competence or responsibility of specific health agencies, widely as any governmental power that affects health, or somewhere between these extremes.

---

[3] See also Mark Hall, "The scope and limits of public health law", *Perspectives in Biology and Medicine* (2003) 46:3, S199–S209.

[4] This contrasts starkly with Wendy Parmet's conclusions on what she labels the "myriad meanings of public health": Parmet suggests that certain shared features are amongst the distinct understandings that she reviews: "Most important, these definitions each stress that the focus of public health is on the health or well-being of people, not individuals." Parmet, *Populations, Public Health, and the Law*, p. 9.

3. *Public health as the social infrastructure*: in this sense public health is taken to represent society's organisation (both political and systematic but e.g. in voluntary codes) in respect to health issues, accommodating deferred or assumed non-State responsibility for health that nevertheless may be described as public in character.

4. *Public health as a professional enterprise*: public health refers here to professional approaches. Again this may be more or less narrowly conceived, relating, for example, to the scope of a professional's practical competence (e.g. his work for a particular government department), to the nature of expertise that a professional has, or to his work's being health-related.

5. *Public health as blind benefit/harm*: public health may be used as a qualifier to represent probable benefits or harms within a population. It may be used, for example, to denote instances of certain harm where the specific identity of those harmed is unclear – e.g. "alcohol consumption causes public health problems" – or instances where *ex ante* the ultimate beneficiaries of a policy are not known – e.g. in regimes that make the wearing of seatbelts compulsory.

6. *Public health as conjoined beneficiaries*: here 'the public' has moral, 'solidaristic' connotations encapsulated in John Donne's phrase "no man is an island". As members of the public, any individual health harm or benefit is also a public health harm or benefit as individuals are part of a community. On this view people have a normative reason to protect their and others' health, and there are no 'purely self-regarding' actions.

7. *Public health as the population's health*: this final use of public health is a non-normative alternative to number 6. Here it refers to the health of a population, either in aggregate or by reference to distribution. It is non-directive: it does not imply that action should be taken, but is just a presentation of fact.

None of the above is without merit or flaw, and as each face of public health features in debate, it would be futile either to deny or ignore them, or to claim that public health 'really' only has one of the above meanings. Whilst Part II offers scrutiny of the types of normative models that house or allow evaluation of the things these different perspectives imply, the remainder of the current chapter will develop each of the seven faces of public health.

One point that bears strong iteration is that whichever meaning of public health is advanced in any situation, it will often be the case that there are obscure connotations to what *health* itself means.[5] Whether health has a narrow definition, relates to all of well-being or welfare, or is a scientific measure of some phenomenon whose normativity is explicitly stated, there will be problems in this regard in much literature on public health. Thus, if two commentators choose to adopt a commonly cited definition of public health, such as "the science and art of preventing disease, prolonging life and promoting health through organised efforts of society",[6] it does not follow that they are both speaking to the same concepts. They may differ radically in their ideas about the meanings of health and disease.

3.2   The seven faces of public health in detail

3.2.1   Public health as a political tool

In some arguments and documents we find public health deployed as something political; as some sort of a normative driver. Quintessentially, we may look to the US Institute of Medicine's (IOM) interpretation of its own definition of public health:

> Public health is what we, as a society, do collectively to assure the conditions in which people can be healthy. This requires that continuing and emerging threats to the health of the public be successfully countered.[7]

The stated 'requirement' in the second sentence does not straightforwardly follow from the content of the first (which some readers may take it to do). Without doubt, many defensible premises may require that threats to health be countered through collective efforts. But strictly, 'public health', as expressed here, can not be said to require it. Nevertheless, this manner of approach to defining public health has found wide appeal, and is clearly reflected in the works and publications of eminent professionals, government bodies, advisory and policy bodies, and leading academics. Rather like Daniels' simultaneous appeal

---

[5] This observation is common to many critiques in public health law and ethics; see for example: Alan Cribb, *Health and the Good Society-Setting Healthcare Ethics in Social Context* (Oxford University Press, 2005), ch. 2; Stephen Holland, *Public Health Ethics* (Polity: Cambridge, 2007), ch. 5; Madison Powers and Ruth Faden, *Social Justice: the Moral Foundations of Public Health and Health Policy* (Oxford University Press, 2006), pp. 16–18; Parmet, *Populations, Public Health, and the Law*, p. 7; McHale, "Law, regulation and public health research".

[6] Donald Acheson, *Public Health in England* (Cmnd. 298), (London: HMSO, 1988).

[7] Institute of Medicine, *The Future of Public Health* (Washington DC: National Academy Press, 1988), p. 1.

to non-normativity and concession to a need for it in his understanding of health,[8] there risks here being an 'overclaim' of 'the scientific' – the morally neutral – in support of strong claims against States and individuals.

Public health here, perhaps tacitly, if not with deliberate opacity, becomes used as a concept with intrinsic politically normative characteristics. And these relate not simply to the 'philosophy' of people working as public health professionals, but imply some sort of political agenda; something that law and ethics ought to be fed by, rather than something whose normativity they ought to feed.[9] Conceptually this is not problematic. But if public health requires us successfully to counter continuing and emerging threats to people's health, it must not do so at all costs (and to be clear, as far as I am aware, neither the IOM, nor others alluded to in the previous paragraph, suggests otherwise). We can compare the rhetorical and perceived normative force of public health in this guise with the maxim "the health of the people is the highest law".[10] Although this sounds like a worthy dictum, it can not go unqualified unless health is to become so broad a category that it makes little sense using it as a limiting term.[11] Thus, for example, Lawrence Gostin and Lesley Stone, in their consideration of the entrenchment of public health in its normative guise, do not hold that health is necessarily the *highest* law, but rather that it is, more modestly, "an important societal goal".[12] Even so, they argue that the "public health community takes it as an act of faith that health must be society's overarching value",[13] and suggest that health is "a salient public value" because of two "interrelated theories":[14]

1. *A theory of human functioning* – health is a foundation for personal well-being and the exercise of social and political rights; and

---

[8] Daniels is a well-known advocate of Christopher Boorse's 'naturalist' conception of health. Nevertheless, as discussed in Chapter 1, Daniels argues in favour of "a modest form of normativism" in understandings of disease, and by implication health: see Norman Daniels, *Just Health: Meeting Health Needs Fairly* (Cambridge University Press, 2008), p. 42.

[9] See further Wendy K. Mariner, "Public health and law: past and future visions", *Journal of Health Politics, Policy and Law* (2003) 28:2–3, 525–552.

[10] Or *salus populi est suprema lex.*

[11] Contrast the thesis advanced in Parmet, *Populations, Public Health, and the Law*; see also Powers and Faden, *Social Justice*, p. 17.

[12] Lawrence O. Gostin and Lesley Stone, "Health of the people: the highest law?", in Angus Dawson and Marcel Verweij (eds.), *Ethics, Prevention, and Public Health* (Oxford University Press, 2007), p. 60.

[13] *Ibid.*, p. 66.   [14] *Ibid.*

2. *A theory of government* – governments are formed primarily to achieve health, safety, and welfare of the population.[15]

Chapter 1's analysis of different conceptions of health demonstrated why formulations such as this are more troublesome than they seem on first reading. As I will argue below, it is unlikely that health is something that can meaningfully be conceptually separated from welfare. And even if it can form a discrete category of welfare, it is not clear what is particularly special about health as contrasted with other welfare matters, suggesting the importance of not privileging some aspects of welfare if this comes at the cost of significant others.[16] As positive concepts of health play more significant and forceful roles in public debate and policy outputs, this point only increases in importance.[17]

To be clear, the problem I raise here is not the 'social mission' implicit – sometimes explicit even – in the works of influential authors such as Gostin.[18] It is that by making *public health* itself into an intrinsically normative enterprise, we risk loading the weight of argument.[19] By way of illustration, consider the position developed by the Nuffield Council on Bioethics in its report *Public Health – Ethical Issues*.[20] Public health is advanced as something that draws society together through government's organised effort to realise various 'public health goals', including the reduction of health inequalities, the reduction of the health risks citizens can impose on each other, and improvement of citizens' capacity to live healthily.[21] Although the Nuffield Council urges that public health is informed of these goals by a 'stewardship model' of government, it appears rather that the selection and articulation of this political philosophy is informed 'by' public health. In essence the argument seems to run as follows: public health demands a commitment to things such as health equality; therefore we need to direct ourselves – through law, if necessary – to achieve this and the other ends 'of' public

---

[15] *Ibid.*

[16] Cf James Wilson, "Not so special after all? Daniels and the social determinants of health", *Journal of Medical Ethics* (2009) 35:1, 3–6; Norman Daniels, "Just health: replies and further thoughts", *Journal of Medical Ethics* (2009) 35:1, 36–41.

[17] See Cribb, *Health and the Good Society*, ch. 1.

[18] Gostin famously includes a strong "objective" in his definition of public health law: see Lawrence O. Gostin, *Public Health Law: Power, Duty, Restraint* (2nd edn) (Berkeley: University of California Press, 2008), p. 4. See also his and Lesley Stone's view, cited above in this section, that the "public health community" has a shared perspective on society's "overarching value".

[19] See Coggon, "Does *public health* have a personality?".

[20] Nuffield Council on Bioethics, *Public Health – Ethical Issues* (London: Nuffield, 2007).

[21] See *ibid.*, ch. 2, especially pp. 25–26.

health. A 'classical Millian' interpretation of liberalism is discussed, and deemed inadequate because of its consequences, which are seen to be insufficiently potent in response to supposed imperatives relating to health. The report presents a clear list of apparently desirable ends, which seem to come directly 'from' public health, and only secondarily seeks a means of packaging these within what is contrived to be a normatively defensible political framework. It is not clear that such an approach is the most salient; it essentially makes a political theory of public health, rather than make more narrowly defined public health practices subject to the normative constraint of an independent political theory.[22] Even if this is not considered crucially damning, or the Report is given an alternative reading,[23] there are two sorts of questions to ask here. First, can we weigh all competing concerns satisfactorily if we put such a focus on health; does health require such prominence, and do we benefit from giving it this? (We may well be able to come up with a response; simply, it is important to do so.) Second, is public health in this sense *really* part of a normative theory, or is it in fact an entire normative theory in and of itself? If the latter, why label it 'public health'? (Again, these questions may be answered, but they must be if satisfactory debate is to take place.)

Conceptually, there is no difficulty with devising a conception of public health that is value-heavy or otherwise putatively normative. But when the values are considered necessary aspects of a *political* model, it is important to be clear about how and why this is the case.[24] Otherwise, we can not duly test that model. If someone asked "would you like it if everyone were healthy", an immediate response might just be a straightforward "yes". But a considered response demands a search for more information: "It depends what that would entail." Only with a complete picture can we assess the desirability of a policy. This fairly simple point is made, for example, by Matti Häyry, in relation both to the

---

[22] For more detailed analysis of the Nuffield Council's proposed model, see John Coggon, "Harmful rights-doing? The perceived problem of liberal paradigms and public health", *Journal of Medical Ethics* (2008) 34:11, 798–801; Angus Dawson and Marcel Verweij, "The steward of the Millian State", *Public Health Ethics* (2008) 1:3, 193–195; Tom Baldwin, Roger Brownsword, and Harald Schmidt, "Stewardship, paternalism and public health: further thoughts", *Public Health Ethics* (2009) 2:1, 113–116; John Coggon, "What help is a steward? Stewardship, political theory, and public health law and ethics", *Northern Ireland Legal Quarterly* (forthcoming 2012).

[23] See Baldwin *et al.*, *ibid.*, p. 116: they claim that whilst the model "has clear normative anchoring" it is not "the heart of a comprehensive moral theory, nor does it attempt to be the last word on the question of 'what is a robust normative theory for public health ethics?'".

[24] Cf e.g. Clare Bambra, Debbie Fox, and Alex Scott-Samuel, "Towards a politics of health", *Health Promotion International* (2005) 20:2, 187–193.

means and ends 'of' public health. Häyry suggests that an emphasis, for example, on disease reduction is ostensibly attractive, but its achievement in some cases will come at the cost of losing alternative, perhaps more important, values than good health.[25] Outside of a 'health theocracy', showing simply that a policy advances people's health is an insufficient ground on which to judge it acceptable.[26] Crucial knowledge lies in understanding the very nature of the political system that guides our actions – where we are not free, or fully free to guide them ourselves – towards healthier lives. We need to understand the benefits, but must also see the potential costs.

3.2.2   Public health as government business

Public health may have a different sort of normative content. Rather than being something that speaks a political ideology to legislators, policy-makers, and citizens, it may hold practical normativity, denoting the output of government policy. Here, the meaning may be said to relate to the State's 'stewardship' responsibility,[27] and the governmental functions associated with this. Thus, measures taken by non-governmental bodies, even if they target and benefit 'statistical people' rather than *ex ante* identifiable individuals, are not public health measures (with the possible exception of such bodies' performing such tasks through formally deferred or shared competence[28]). When breaking this down, there is a continuum open to us that demonstrates quite how broad

[25] Matti Häyry, "Public health and human values," *Journal of Medical Ethics* (2006) 32:9, 519–521.

[26] On the idea of a 'health theocracy', see Chapter 8, section 8.4; note also the need to account for 'health-health tradeoffs': see Cass Sunstein, "Health-health tradeoffs", *University of Chicago Law Review* (1996) 63:4, 1533–1571.

[27] Note that I use the term 'stewardship' advisedly: Coggon, "What help is a steward?".

[28] For present purposes, substantial engagement with "public-private paternerships" would not repay the attention it would warrant. We can take it for the purposes of the immediate discussion that the "private" aspect is only ostensibly a distraction from the public – i.e. State – function. For a brief overview of salient issues concerning public-private partnerships, see Michael Reich, "Public-private partnerships for public health", *Nature Medicine* (2000) 6:6, 617–620; Declan Gaffney, Allyson Pollock, David Price, Jean Shaoul, "The politics of the private finance initiative and the new NHS", *British Medical Journal* (1999) 319, 249–253; Peter Davies, "Is this the end of the road for the PFI?", *British Medical Journal* (2010) 341, 176–177. I note that in English legal practice, this question has not been straightforwardly settled: see *YL* v. *Birmingham City Council* [2007] UKHL 27. This is unimportant for the purposes of the current analysis, though attention is drawn in this case to Baroness Hale's dissenting speech (with which Lord Bingham concurred). See also Mark Elliott, "'Public' and 'private': defining the scope of the Human Rights Act", *Cambridge Law Journal* (2007) 66:3, 485–487.

public health may be, and why seeking to draw a boundary around it may be an impossible task, a task that calls for arbitrary distinctions, or one that involves an incomplete analytic focus. In seeking to limit the term non-arbitrarily, two noted approaches warrant consideration: the first is Richard Epstein's; the second Mark Rothstein's. It should be stressed that whilst each position stems from its own concern, there is a shared belief about the *necessary* implication of public health generally denoting a State's *coercive* powers, rather than any less invasive regulatory mechanisms.

Richard Epstein writes as a proud advocate of what is often labelled (one senses sometimes pejoratively) the 'old public health'.[29] His argument is partly an empirical one, and not one that is convincingly made.[30] He believes that the 'new public health' actually does more harm than good, suggesting that widespread health losses naturally follow the "social welfarist" measures that are necessarily entailed by – or more accurately that entail – positions that push for greater State intervention designed to improve the health of its people. But there is also, it seems, a more ethereal issue. I use the word "ethereal" as it is not even clear that it is a matter of principle: at best it may be labelled pedantic, although it seems really to be a claim to ownership of the term 'public health'. Specifically, Epstein's preference is for an expression that relates to a "limited set of ends" that bear on specific sorts of threats (perhaps best described as 'external threats') to health: things "such as the spread of *communicable* diseases or public nuisances like widespread pollution".[31] Part of his categorisation relies on a denial of the social determinants of health thesis: an empirical claim about his (and, by hypothesis, everyone's) being "at [no] greater risk for [e.g.] obesity because an increasing fraction of [his] neighbors are obese".[32]

We are also invited to reject the soundness of imagery associated with public health's being given a wider remit than the 'old public health' suggests is due. Epstein believes that it implies the wrong things about

[29] Richard Epstein, "Let the shoemaker stick to his last: a defense of the 'old' public health", *Perspectives in Biology and Medicine* (2003) 46:3, S138–S159; Richard Epstein, "In defense of the 'old' public health", *Brooklyn Law Review* (2004) 69:4, 1421–1470.

[30] See Lawrence O. Gostin and M. Gregg Bloche, "The politics of public health: a response to Epstein", *Perspectives in Biology and Medicine* (2003) 46:3, S160–S175; William Novak, "Private wealth and public health: a critique of Richard Epstein's defense of the 'old' public health", *Perspectives in Biology and Medicine* (2003) 46:3, S176–S198. A thoughtful analysis that may be used to help test Epstein's theory is found in Sunstein, "Health-health tradeoffs". See also Chapter 7, and Chapter 8, section 8.2.

[31] Epstein, "In defense of the 'old' public health", at 1425.

[32] *Ibid.*, at 1462.

putatively[33] socially determined ill health. He believes that the term 'public health' denotes the legitimacy of coercive State intervention, ostensibly justified as part of its police power. Thus he argues:

[D]esignating obesity as a public health epidemic is designed to signal that state coercion is appropriate when it is not. Education and persuasion, yes; but private institutions and foundation can supply these things without government coercion and even without government guidance and warnings over what personal health targets should be and how they are best achieved.[34]

And he goes on to assert that:

The language of epidemic suggests the need for a vigorous response akin to that of quarantine. Yet the best course would be to weaken the public safety net that induces harmful individual behaviors in the first event, and to replace it with a system of tailored disincentives that do not encroach on individual liberty.[35]

We might want to question this approach. Even if there is truth in the claims about the inherent connotations of the term, there is no reason that sound and reasonable definitions can not provide clarity on the question, stating clearly that "public health is not just about coercion". To retort, as a defender of Epstein's approach might, "but that would not be public health" would just be dogmatic. There is no evident reason that public health need denote the State's use of its coercive powers, rather than less intrusive regulatory measures,[36] or that terms such as 'epidemic' can not harmlessly be used with a bit of metaphorical flair. Even so, we may take from Epstein the most narrow understanding of public health as governmental power, or the legitimation of this. This account claims that it necessarily refers to coercive police powers, and thus legitimately only speaks to a small number of health issues that may give rise to coercive State interventions such as compulsory vaccination or quarantine policies.

In similar vein, but without the same attachment to political libertarianism, Mark Rothstein famously defends what might be labelled a 'jurisdictional approach' to public health. On his view, there are compelling reasons to limit the focus to the competence purely of formal public health agencies' legal authority. These reasons are essentially pragmatic: if we limit what is meant by 'public health', 'public health interventions' narrowly conceived will, Rothstein suggests, be more

---

[33] In fact on Epstein's account non-existent.
[34] Epstein, "In defense of the 'old' public health", at 1462–1463.
[35] *Ibid.*, at 1463.
[36] Gostin and Bloche, "The politics of public health: a response to Epstein", at S172–S173.

efficient and effective, and will receive greater popular support. (It should perhaps be mentioned that the argument is underpinned by a sense that public health measures on this count, whilst not necessarily coercive, will often entail the use of coercive governmental power: given the inherently controversial nature of this, it is suggested, the limiting narrows the risk, or perception of risk, of nefarious governmental acts in the name of public health (e.g. eugenics or morally reprehensible research on human subjects). Noting this, we should be clear too that the US context, to which Rothstein speaks, provides greater reason to accept his perspective than exists, for example, in the UK, where the idea that universal access to necessary healthcare is a good thing does not meet with comparably entrenched cynicism, and where 'public health' does not automatically lead to popular associations with "health care for the indigent".[37]) In Rothstein's argument, the narrowing of public health is achieved by holding that "[t]he term 'public health' is a legal term of art, and it refers to specifically delineated powers, duties, rights, and responsibilities".[38] By contrast with Epstein, this is explicitly not a denial that ill health is caused by many remediable social ills, or an argument that they ought not to be remedied; it is rather about what can reasonably fall under "the mission of public health".[39] Rothstein "oppose[s] the use of the term 'public health' as an open-ended descriptor of widely divergent efforts to improve the human condition",[40] suspecting that labelling a matter a public health issue will not help to fix it. We might contrast this with the observations made of public health used as a political tool, discussed in section 3.2.1, where I noted its use to obscure normative arguments because of its apparently *un*controversial nature. Possibly this difference of sense about rhetorical impact between me and Rothstein is due to differences between the UK and the US. Anyway, by only permitting public health to relate to specific governmental competences and the actions of designated officials acting in accordance with these, Rothstein hopes to provide an analytic framing that permits realistically bounded scrutiny, and reasonably bounded areas of State action. The type of competences relates to serious threats to the public, rather than health promotion or healthcare.

---

[37] Mark Rothstein, "Rethinking the meaning of public health", *Journal of Law, Medicine and Ethics* (2002) 30, 144–149, at 147. Note that Rothstein claims that whilst his definition is not exclusively for the US, it is "especially appropriate for the United States": Mark Rothstein, "The limits of public health: a response", *Public Health Ethics* (2009) 2:1, 84–88, at 84.

[38] Rothstein, "Rethinking the meaning of public health", at 144.

[39] *Ibid.* Though note the comments in section 3.2.1 about the nature of the mission on many accounts, and its logical entailments.

[40] *Ibid.*, at 147.

There are various reasons to question the value, if not the validity, of this approach. Rothstein is clear that he does not see wide issues affecting health, from income inequality to warfare, or poor education to unresponsive government, as unimportant.[41] Rather, he thinks that the breadth of these issues is beyond the expert competence of public health professionals. This, coupled with concerns about State powers being abused in the name of public health, speaks against a broader definition than he permits. However, his final portrayal of public health remains somewhat question-begging, or built on mere assertion. This may be attributed to the fact that Rothstein still looks for *the* mission and *the* role of public health.[42] Seeking *the* mission is likely to be fruitless, given the range of possible contenders. And whilst I share the view that in many ways public health can become so broad as to include almost everything, I see this as a logical consequence of the concerns and issues raised by a focused analysis on what it *might* mean. In other words, whilst broader conceptions may be the "creation of academics",[43] it does not follow that they are redundant. Rather, it may be that a concern for, dissection of, or critical engagement with public health necessarily leads to widely encompassing ideas. Cordoning off the important issues that have not 'traditionally' been labelled as public health matters does not make them go away (as Rothstein recognises). There is no obvious reason for a State to assume only the public health responsibilities entailed by its specifically labelled public health departments, unless it has the wider commitments that Rothstein fears will be politically contentious. Thus it is not clear what good really comes from following Rothstein's definition.

There is a probable root cause of this problem, which when considered as follows applies to analysts of views both similar and distinct to Rothstein's. Even if it were true that something that can be, or has been, labelled 'public health' existed in a sufficiently meaningful manner, with a single, coherent purpose, it does not follow that the term is now actually or most usefully kept just for this one thing. It may be the case that wider definitions are due to academics[44] (and that this is in some sense bad). But even if, for the sake of argument, we take it that Rothstein is right about the purposes 'of' public health, surely what is more important is *our* (whoever 'we' may be in a given instance) purposes. If an analyst wants to consider all the things that Rothstein agrees

---

[41] Rothstein, "The limits of public health: a response", at 86.
[42] *Ibid.*, at 84.   [43] *Ibid.*, at 87.
[44] *Ibid.*

are important but believes are without the remit of public health, that analyst provides coherent reason for assessing these things all together, and it is not a stretch of language to label this a 'public health analysis', it is not clear why he should not do so. Rothstein's arguments principally provide a pedantic terminology, with an insufficiently compelling group of reasons to adopt it. It does not narrow the scope of practical concerns, and it is not clear how the issues that he considers *do* fall under public health can usefully be analysed without an assessment of the wider, 'non-public health' context. (Indeed, given how strongly informed his perspective is by prevalent political norms (in the US), it *must* be the case that the assessments of public health in his narrow sense require governmental awareness of the wider context, and analysts able to engage with that wider context.)

Finally, the very narrow understandings of public health considered in this section are well considered alongside a wider construction, but one which is still limited just to the government's actions and powers. It may be argued that there is good reason to use 'public health' as a reference to competences beyond those of State agencies that are formally charged with 'public health powers', yet limit it – possibly because of an inference from the term 'public' – to government functions, rather than those of private or non-governmental bodies.[45] Many things bear on people's health, and are targeted through State policy. Possibly an analyst would seek the proviso that the policy be purposefully targeted at improving health, as opposed to measures that have an 'incidental effect' on health.[46] This will likely boil down to a matter of analytic preference, but it is not clear that the initial purpose of policy need have had explicit reference to health for it reasonably to be treated as a public health policy in the sense expressed in this section.[47] For example, if we suggest that a State authority that claims responsibility for controlling health-related behaviour thereby serves a public health function, we might find that the criminal regulation of the transmission of sexually transmitted diseases represents a matter of public health in the current sense. This could hold notwithstanding its not falling within the competence of the Department of Health, and even if the legal underpinning

---

[45] As is discussed, although rejected, in Marcel Verweij and Angus Dawson, "The meaning of 'public' in 'public health'", in Angus Dawson and Marcel Verweij (eds.), *Ethics, Prevention, and Public Health* (Oxford University Press, 2007), p. 25.

[46] For example, in discussion of interpretations of the IOM's definition of public health, considered above, Parmet suggests that "tax cuts enacted for reasons that have nothing to do with the health of a group may not, after all, be a public health activity": Parmet, *Populations, Public Health, and the Law*, p. 8.

[47] See further Chapter 4.

to the regulation is a nineteenth-century statute passed to protect people from criminal harms.[48] Equally, environmental regulation could relate to public health.[49] So could traffic regulation.[50] And so could countless other areas of State competence. Any law or legally instituted measure that positively affected people's health, which may simply be read as protecting them from harm, or even *the risk* of harm, would seem potentially to be a public health measure. Although Rothstein is right that this opens up an enormous scope to public health, it is not clear why this should cause conceptual or analytic difficulty. It is anyway artificial to exclude what analysis tells us falls within the fold simply because it is awkward. As a governmental matter, protection of health clearly can not be studied only to the extent that *the study* is convenient. However we label the totality, the narrowly conceived 'public health' capacity of government will need to be assessed within the context of the whole of the State's policy, and its wider commitments.

Ultimately a fully extensive theory will be required, and it can hardly be impracticable to devise, unless we place ourselves in the position where we believe that we are not equipped to assess the State and its responsibilities and duties. As 'health' or 'public health' arise increasingly in discussions of departments other than those whose stated competence relates to health, where public health as a governmental matter is being considered, it is best not to limit the scope by government department.[51] We might note that a defender of this face of public health, even at its most limited (i.e. as Epstein sees it), might not argue that his definition is the only one available. Mark Hall, for example, argues that public health can have two connotations. The first is analytic, and

[48] The statute alluded to is the Offences Against the Person Act 1861. Recent criminal jurisprudence has seen the conviction of defendants for reckless non-disclosure of their HIV status and subsequent transmission through sexual intercourse, prosecuted under s. 20 of the Act: see *R* v. *Dica* [2004] EWCA Crim 1103; *R* v. *Konzani (Feston)* [2005] EWCA Crim 706. It should be noted that in a review discussing both cases, Matthew Weait *contrasts* the use of criminal law with taking a public health approach. His position is therefore that criminalisation does *not* represent a 'public health measure' (for the reason that rather than share the responsibility for health, it imposes a duty unduly on particular parties). See Matthew Weait, "Knowledge, autonomy and consent: R. v Konzani", *Criminal Law Review* (2005) 763–772. Weait's perspective is valuable, but does not undermine the claim that this approach *may* be seen as a face of public health, as described in the current section.

[49] See e.g. Environmental Protection Act 1990, ss. 33 and 79(1); Water Resources Act 1991, s. 85.

[50] See e.g. Road Traffic Act 1988; Road Traffic Act 1991.

[51] For a comical representation of the need for a more extensive range of departments responsible for public health see James Landale, "Whitehall turf war saves cows' hides", *BBC Online News* (25 November 2009), available at http://news.bbc.co.uk/1/hi/uk_politics/8379759.stm. This documents a dispute between Whitehall departments over an issue that might be viewed as an agricultural, environmental, or a

relates to the work done, for example, by epidemiologists. The second, however, is a legal definition, and this, it is argued, ought to be kept narrow to maintain its association with the special State powers considered above, leaving other 'health issues' to be dealt with by alternatives to governmental public health.[52] Whilst I still see no particular need to infer – or maintain – the association with police powers when discussion relates to government, this dual approach is worth noting.[53]

3.2.3   *Public health as the social infrastructure*

Some would relate public health to the social infrastructure as a whole, rather than that relating just to government. This understanding again draws from the nature of public action rather than ideas of the health of the public (though we could clearly see the term used harmoniously in both senses).[54] Whilst we might say that paradigmatically *public* health problems will be the concern of, and responsibility of, the State, we might also take the view that there are necessary and legitimate roles for deferred or assumed non-State responsibility for health that have a properly described public aspect to them. And these too may therefore be included in a definition of public health. Equally, 'organs' of the State other than the government may be included here: for example, the courts in their interpretation of the scope and effect of Article 8(2) of the European Convention on Human Rights, which, *inter alia*, affords the State the power to limit individuals' right to respect for private and family life in the interests of the protection of health. In Chapter 5, we consider Gostin's definition of public health law. For now, we can just refer to part of it:

public health matter, depending on perspective: the Department of Health gave funding to a project researching the positive health and environmental effects of significantly reducing livestock numbers. The Department of Health and Department of Energy and Climate Change apparently received the report positively, though did not ultimately endorse it, following criticism from the main opposition party as well as the Department for Environment, Food and Rural Affairs.

[52] Hall, "The scope and limits of public health law".

[53] In relation to this and the next face of public health, consider also the perspectives explored in Linda Marks, Sally Cave, and David J. Hunter, "Public health governance: views of key stakeholders", *Public Health* (2010) 124, 55–59; Nan D. Hunter, "'Public-private' health law: multiple directions in public health", *Journal of Health Care Law and Policy* (2007) 10, 89–119; Roger S Magnusson, "Mapping the scope and opportunities for public health law in liberal democracies", *Journal of Law, Medicine and Ethics* (2007) 35:4, 571–587.

[54] See Verweij and Dawson, "The meaning of 'public' in 'public health'", especially pp. 25–27.

Public health law is the study of the legal powers and duties of the state, in collaboration with its partners (e.g., health care, business, the community, the media, and academe), to ensure the conditions for people to be healthy (to identify, prevent, and ameliorate risks to health in the population) ...[55]

Although Gostin here is defining public health *law* rather than just public health, his definition, encapsulating the role of the State and its "partners", rather than just the government, captures the breadth of this face of public health.

It works from a conception in which the human environment – both built and social – creates the conditions of public health: i.e. it contains an implicit reference to 'man-made' health-determinants and their alterability. So, critiques employing this perspective are often concerned with the way in which social factors – factors that can be changed – predictably determine people's health.[56] Public health can then denote the interventions or activity that shape and sustain that environment. Daniel Goldberg provides a good example in this regard, in a critique of Rothstein's argument discussed in the previous section. Goldberg defends what he describes as "a model of public health that involves sustained attention to the social determinants of health".[57] He fears that Rothstein's preferred model is limited by the wrong factor: political possibility. This, Goldberg argues, ignores the issue of causation in public health. Practical matters of government ought not, he suggests, to obscure the actual situation that avoidably leads to subdesirable levels and distribution of health within society. He finds it "fair to question the utility of public health practices and policies that are expressly intended to avoid addressing or ameliorating the root causes of poor health".[58] It is worth noting in response to this, that whilst Goldberg makes a good case about causation of poor health, a narrow conception such as Rothstein's (as opposed, for example, to Epstein's[59]), is not advanced in such a manner that it *does* preclude, let alone *avoid*, the causes of ill health.[60] In his argument, Goldberg

---

[55] Gostin, *Public Health Law – Power, Duty, Restraint*, p. 4.

[56] See Michael Marmot, *Status Syndrome: How Your Social Standing Directly Affects Your Health and Life Expectancy* (London: Bloomsbury, 2004).

[57] Daniel Goldberg, "In support of a broad model of public health: disparities, social epidemiology and public health causation", *Public Health Ethics* (2009) 2:1, 70–83, at 70.

[58] *Ibid.*, at 72.

[59] Epstein, "In defense of the 'old' public health".

[60] A point restated in Rothstein's response to Goldberg's critique: Rothstein, "The limits of public health: a response", at 87. Note also Goldberg's sympathy with Rothstein's concern about governmental overreach of power: Goldberg, "In support of a broad model of public health", at 70.

seems to be seeking to claim some manner of ownership over the term public health itself. This is unsurprising if we note that, like Rothstein but with different effect, Goldberg looks to the analytically inherent normative purposes of public health (as he sees it). As such, this interpretation of public health assumes what these imputed purposes recommend.

The extent to which this meaning of public health holds sway in debate may be contested. However, it is alluded to in the Report of the Nuffield Council:

The political, regulatory and economic environments in which people live establish a setting that has a considerable influence on the extent to which they are able to lead healthy lives ... The term 'public health' is generally used to refer to efforts made to improve that setting ...[61]

This face of public health, then, may be considered to be one of considerable importance, notwithstanding its raising the practical objection that it includes too much to be useful or even usable. If public health is the social infrastructure *and* the means to make this more conducive to good health, and even if it is a normative model in the sense that it 'thinks' that we should drive towards a healthier society, it may still allow for health to be set aside for other goods. It is important to acknowledge that the more directive this understanding is, the closer it becomes to a conception within the first face of public health, until the two melt into one. It should be noted too that the meaning of 'health' under this conception is not settled: two protagonists may adopt this meaning of public health, and even accept some normative commitment as intrinsic to it, yet disagree about what the health aspect entails. The sorts of things that will be considered crucial to the achievement, or even success, of public health on this understanding will include a (sufficiently) clean environment, controlled limits to risky and harmful behaviour, good education, and access to preventive and remedial healthcare. The social infrastructure may be observed, and even controlled, in large part by government, but voluntary codes and behaviour will also be key to public health.[62]

---

[61] Nuffield Council on Bioethics, *Public Health – Ethical Issues*. (London: Nuffield, 2007), p. xv.

[62] In regard to this understanding of public health, it is worth noting again the discussion of the second sense of 'public' outlined by Verweij and Dawson, "The meaning of 'public' in 'public health'," pp. 25–27, and raised in Chapter 2, section 2.4.

3.2.4   Public health as a professional enterprise

The fourth face of public health relates not to political norms, mechanisms, or competences, but instead takes the more practical approach of looking to what public health professionals do. Public health in this sense is a professional enterprise. Without more, we may note two things that might be viewed as problematic with this approach. First, it may be seen to entail circularity: to know what public health is, we simply ask who 'does it', and define it by reference to that. Second, depending on how widely we consider something to be a public health issue, we may end up making so many people into public health professionals that it becomes a meaningless term.[63] For example, when a worker in a supermarket asks an apparent minor to prove his age when he attempts to buy alcohol, does that create a role of public health worker? Are 'bouncers' who limit and control harm caused through violence public health workers? When teachers educate children – in accordance with a formal curriculum, or even informally – about personal hygiene, 'safe sex', 'drug abuse', and 'responsible drinking', are they public health workers? Answers to these questions may vary, but, for some people at least, positive answers to any of them will imply that the net is cast too wide, and the term 'public health' (and *ipso facto* 'public health professional') has become meaningless. So, is there a way to avoid an unattractively large scope and problems of circularity *without* arbitrary narrowing stipulations?

One natural approach would be to limit public health as a professional competence by reference to *expertise*, and even further still by the approach taken by types of experts. It is useful to start this consideration with Geoffrey Rose's influential paper "Sick individuals and sick populations".[64] As its title suggests, the paper distinguishes two approaches that may be taken in understanding ill health, and the potential value in so doing. In Rose's words:

I find it increasingly helpful to distinguish two kinds of aetiological question. The first seeks the causes of cases, and the second seeks the causes of incidence. 'Why do some individuals have hypertension?' is a quite different question from 'Why do some populations have much hypertension, whilst in others it is rare?'. The questions require different kinds of study, and they have different answers.[65]

---

[63] See also Stephen Holland's discussion of health promotion: Holland, *Public Health Ethics*, particularly pp. 101–103.

[64] Geoffrey Rose, "Sick individuals and sick populations," *International Journal of Epidemiology* (1985) 14:1, 32–38.

[65] *Ibid.*, at 33.

Without looking at populations, an understanding may be reached of why some people suffer a condition such as hypertension when others do not, but not – in Rose's words "the most important public health question"[66] – what "mass influence" acts on whole populations: for example, to tell us why hypertension is common in one population and absent in another. The "population approach" permits investigations in causation that allow associations validly to be drawn, for example, between some aspect of our diet and some condition. It permits links that simply can not be made when individuals are studied alone. Rather than look at an individual, a population can be compared with itself as it changes over time, or with other populations.

Rose goes on to note a difference in practical approach given knowledge from the population perspective, in contrast with the individual perspective. Whereas with individuals health professionals would concern themselves only with those who are sick or at high risk of sickness, with populations general measures are taken. Rose discusses two population approaches: the "traditional 'public health' form" targets the environment; the "modern form" targets "society's norms of behaviour"[67] (thus we see the link to Goldberg's analysis, and the third face of public health). As Rose notes, the individual and the population approach each has its drawbacks. But the relevance of his categorisation here is that it provides a specific means of categorising public health by reference to a professional approach. If we consider public health to be something 'done' by certain experts, then we could say it is those who have a specialist interest in health, and who take a population approach to their work.

At its most basic, we could see public health on this understanding as relating to the scientific aspect of its professionals' work. Public health practitioners need not be committed to any particular values or overall mission; rather, they are defined by their employment of a particular scientific methodology or approach. As we have seen, however, some commentators imply the possession of an intrinsic value-base that is defining of a public-health professional.[68] It is important to remain aware of this, but in the abstract, I see no reason for it to be a necessary conceptual stipulation. It would, at the very least, lead to some tenuous or counter-intuitive conclusions. Petr Skrabanek, for example, would not have been considered a public-health professional because of his libertarian viewpoint, and powerful scepticism in regard to preventive

---

[66] *Ibid.*, at 34.   [67] *Ibid.*, at 37.
[68] Gostin and Stone, "Health of the people: the highest law?", p. 66.

medicine, notwithstanding his undoubtable scientific expertise in this area.[69]

If this understanding of public health is to be cogent, it may be thought that whilst we do not want to consider every health-affecting member of the social infrastructure as 'doing public health', limiting it to those with the expertise just described may be too narrow. Public health workers may include those who *implement* public health measures, without having any special expertise. Yet, as we have seen, if being operative in the implementation of a public health measure or strategy is taken as sufficient to qualify someone as a public health worker, teachers, bouncers, and supermarket checkout assistants will also meet the criterion. And we can imagine that there is likely some muddiness in a dividing line relating to professional competence where expertise is contrasted with simple practice. However, it may be that public health on this understanding can have its limits drawn by reference to a model described by Griffiths, Jewell, and Donnelly,[70] and endorsed by the UK's Faculty of Public Health as the "three key domains of public health practice".[71] The authors contend that "public health is everybody's business" and that a wide range of skill and contribution is needed for public health programmes to work. The definition *they* choose for public health would fall under the previous categorisation made in this chapter: they see it as an enterprise that engages all of society, with a strong role for the government and community.[72] However, having given this – as we have seen – broad definition of public health, the authors suggest it can become "more manageable if conceptualized within the model of three domains of practice".[73] Importantly, this model is still vastly broader than, for example, Rothstein would accept under the heading 'public health'. As well as workers in the National Health Service, they include those in education and employment, and, given the concern with social determinants, looking at the built environment and engagement with individuals and families. And they are concerned too with environmental issues more widely; matters such as ensuring there is clean air and water, and having the means to deal with

---

[69] See Petr Skrabanek and James McCormick, *Follies and Fallacies in Medicine* (Glasgow: Tarragon Press, 1989); Petr Skrabanek, *The Death of Humane Medicine and the Rise of Coercive Healthism* (St Edmundsbury Press: Bury St Edmunds, 1994). See also James McCormick, "Death of Petr Skrabanek", *The Lancet* (1994) 344, 52–53.

[70] Sian Griffiths, Tony Jewell, and Peter Donnelly, "Public health in practice: the three domains of public health", *Public Health* (2005) 119, 907–913.

[71] See www.fph.org.uk/what_is_public_health.

[72] Griffiths, Jewell, and Donnelly, "Public health in practice: the three domains of public health", at 908–909.

[73] *Ibid.*, at 910.

environmental disasters.[74] The three overlapping domains are health protection, health improvement, and health service delivery and quality. Expertise will vary between professionals in each domain, but the expertise that each domain requires helps define who may be given the broad label of 'public health professional'.

Although this understanding of public health may seem in some senses contrived – after all, the authors whose work is used to give it flesh do not claim the definition – there is value in making this separate categorisation that works from professional competence rather than relating either to people's health status or to the overall framing of directed action: 'public health professionals' are often referred to, suggesting that 'public health' is something in which one can have expertise. However, there will often be a necessary coincidence between the nature of a State's infrastructure for responding to health issues, and the manner of professional who can be said to be working in public health, even though the two need not be co-extensive. When considering this understanding of public health, it is thus worth highlighting a problem that it raises in not dissimilar manner regardless of whether or not public health is treated as an intrinsically normative enterprise. In a context of 'real politics', public health as a professional enterprise may become sullied when twisted to fit the agendas of political actors whose motivations are not entirely 'on message'. Real world considerations, accounting for distinct and sometimes questionable or cynical political agendas, may mean it is better to keep public health separate from practically grounded political systems, especially if those working in public health are to be seen as having some sort of moral integrity.[75]

It should finally be emphasised that taking this understanding of public health would subject an analyst to a charge of circularity in the same manner as a definition according with Rothstein's preferred conceptualisation. Even so, such a definition may find attraction or use, not least as public health is a subject in which many graduates now specialise. As Rothstein suggests, whether speaking purely to limited government competence, or more widely, there is a shared range of relevant expertise that comes to the fore as essential in a public health curriculum: his list covers health promotion, health education, health policy, health services, health research, health law, epidemiology, biostatistics, toxicology, sanitation, occupational and environmental health services, and essentially anything else that might be relevant.[76] For him,

---

[74] *Ibid.*

[75] Jeffrey P. Kahn, "Why public health and politics don't mix", *American Journal of Bioethics* (2007) 7:11, 3–4.

[76] Rothstein, "Rethinking the Meaning of public health", at 147–148.

subsequent engagement defines whether the skills acquired are used in public health, but we can see how someone might put it differently, and describe professionals deploying these skills in their work as engaging in public health. It is interesting to note that Gostin, who we have seen is far less reserved than Rothstein about the scope of public health, nevertheless also seems to adopt a cautious tone when contemplating the range of expertise in public health:

> The problem with an expansive view is that public health – as a field, as a mandate – becomes limitless, as almost everything human beings undertake affects public health. By this account, public and private activities across a wide spectrum are the work of public health. To many, this all-inclusive notion of public health is counterproductive. First, by defining itself so widely, the field lacks precision. Public health becomes an all-embracing enterprise bonded only by the common value of societal well-being. Second, by adopting such a broad array of behavioral, social, physical, and environmental interventions, it lacks a discrete expertise. The public health professions consequently incorporate a wide variety of disciplines (e.g., occupational health, health education, epidemiology, and nursing) with different skills and functions.[77]

For this face of public health to be conceptually robust, we need some gauge that reasonably delimits what a non-arbitrarily defined group of people do. Although their work focuses on the health of a public, the focus here is likely to be more on the nature or method of professional approaches, than the social or political infrastructure within which some people work.

3.2.5   Public health as blind benefit/harm

A celebrated theme in much of the literature on public health draws on the fact that its 'population approach', whilst affording knowledge of causation where otherwise it would be obscure (because, for example, it permits greater understanding of the effects of social status on health), can lead to recommendations that can not be said with certainty to confer a 'direct' benefit on any specifiable individual.[78] For example, a policy that leads to a reduction in alcohol consumption may demonstrably reduce the incidence of cirrhosis of the liver amongst a closely estimable number of people within a population, yet it is unclear which specific

---

[77] Lawrence O. Gostin, "Public Health, Ethics, and Human Rights: A Tribute to the Late Jonathan Mann," *Journal of Law, Medicine and Ethics* (2001) 29, 121–130.

[78] See the discussion in section 3.2.3, above. Note, the word 'benefit' here is used presumptively: i.e. it relates to 'health benefits', and does not confer a sense that the 'health benefit' is compelling, or that the net good of a policy is highest when the net level of health benefit is maximised.

individuals make up the number. This 'public health benefit' highlights the fact that *members* of the public have benefited, but we are blind to their individual identities. The beneficiaries here are real people, but our blindness asks that we refer to the public health aspect of the intervention; it highlights what is in each person's case a probabilistic benefit. And just as it can relate to people, so this blindness can also be deployed in reference to things, environments, activities, or behaviours; for example, cigarettes, contaminated workplaces, 'black slope skiing', or dietary habits.[79] In this sense, 'public health' may baldly be stated as a presumptive reason against, for example, someone eating something that might be harmful, or his undertaking some risky act. Sometimes, it should be added, the beneficiaries *can* be identified *ex post*: for example, someone who survives a road traffic accident, or who comes out of it better off, because he wore a seatbelt may be positively identified as a beneficiary of a public health measure (i.e. the mandatory wearing of a seatbelt).[80] This manner of approaching public health forms a central focus in Rose's analysis of the 'population approach' (discussed above). It still raises practical difficulties now, as it did at the time Rose wrote his celebrated paper. Convincing people to change the norms according to which they live for uncertain or indirect benefit can be hard: with regard to smoking, the tide seems to have turned (in the UK, and elsewhere in the 'developed world'[81]), but there is seen to be a formidable task – for those who think it worthwhile – in changing attitudes to alcohol consumption.[82] Anyway, this face of public health, as a watchword for 'probabilistic', 'statistical', or 'indirect' benefit is central to many arguments in this area.[83] Given its less controversial standing,[84] it requires less critical scrutiny than the other faces of public health.

---

[79] Cf Verweij and Dawson, "The meaning of 'public' in 'public health'"; Parmet, *Populations, Public Health, and the Law*, p. 8.

[80] Unnecessary complications can be thrown in here: questions such as whether he would have been wearing the seatbelt were the law not instituted. They need not concern us, as it may simply and without a stretch be hypothesised that some people would not wear seatbelts but for the law, and that some of these particular people will be spared injury for doing so.

[81] Howard K. Koh, Luk X. Joossens, and Gregory N. Connolly, "Making smoking history worldwide", *New England Journal of Medicine* (2007) 356:15, 1496–1498.

[82] See House of Commons Health Committee, *Alcohol: First Report of Session 2009–10 – Volume I*, HC 151-I (London: The Stationery Office, 2010); British Medical Association Board of Science, *Under the influence – The damaging effect of alcohol marketing on young people* (London: BMA, 2009).

[83] See also Verweij and Dawson, "The meaning of 'public' in 'public health'", p. 26.

[84] I.e. any controversy relates to substantiating the term 'benefit', rather than accepting the principle as described.

3.2.6   Public health as conjoined beneficiaries

Public health as blind benefit may be developed further, and used in a more abstract, 'solidaristic' sense. This face of public health is found when the term is used to point towards health effects within a population, conjoined importantly with a sturdy normative claim that as members of a shared system – a public – no one is separate from the rest; in other words, that health is shared. This idea underscores a denial of the notion that there can be any purely self-regarding harms to persons,[85] and, if plausible, finds its voice in Wendy Parmet's claim that there is a qualitative distinction between the "health of people" or "populations" on the one hand, and that of "individuals" on the other.[86] This face of public health differs from that described in the previous section as "blind benefit" by assigning *ex ante* a normative significance to the group, public, or population under discussion. In Parmet's analysis, to be clear, this normativity is derived from the *internal* dynamics of a population, and the necessary associations and interrelations entailed in its being a population, rather than because of any commitments to, for example, national identity. She is not interested in "reifying or privileging the health of any particular pre-set group of people".[87] Rather, the normative questions derive from the necessary "interdependence of health within a population".[88] Ronald Bayer and Amy Fairchild seem to work from a similar understanding of public health when they describe "the tension between [individual] autonomy and public health perspectives".[89] Their disapproval of a dominant individualism is substantiated by claims about the "collective", "common", and "public good" that individuals *qua* members of the public may, possibly coercively, be steered towards protecting either by or for the public health. Where we find 'public health' either presenting this position, or being placed within a wider communitarian framework that it is said to complement,[90] we see it as referring to a system of shared benefit. Considered in this way, we are not far from needing to articulate a

---

[85] This face of public health is strongly hinted at in Parmet's specific discussion of the 'population' perspective generally, and most notably in her references to Lemuel Shattuck and John Donne: see Parmet, *Populations, Public Health, and the Law*, pp. 13–19, especially at 13–14.

[86] *Ibid.*, p. 8.

[87] *Ibid.*, p. 19.

[88] *Ibid.* On Parmet's understanding, a population is necessarily "contingent, constructed, and relative" (p. 18).

[89] Ronald Bayer and Amy Fairchild, "The genesis of public health ethics", *Bioethics* (2004) 18:6, 473–492, at 489.

[90] Amitai Etzioni, "Public health law: A communitarian perspective", *Health Affairs* (2002) 21:6, 102.

political theory through which to assess any proposed public health models. This clearly may bring us back towards public health as a normative model.[91] The distinction here, however, is with the focus not on public health serving as a political model or theory, as discussed above, but as a more descriptive reflection of the nature and dynamics (including the normative dynamics) of health within groups of people. That is to say, rather than a 'tool' in political discourse, it is a statement of (putative) normative fact.

Such arguments suggest that one individual *qua* member of the public benefits when another is healthier, because both are members of that public and both share an interest in that public being healthy.[92] This belief may only be presumptive: i.e. the conception may only recommend the healthier public where all else remains equal, or at least where there are not sufficient costs that would tip the balance the other way. When this sense of public health is found, the effects of an individual's actions may be highlighted to express moral disapprobation. It is important, therefore, to be aware of normative – or even just prejudiced – perspectives to which it may give gloss. Some practices may carry equivalent risk factors, yet one be deemed ill and the other not. A prominent and well publicised example is that of David Nutt's comparison between the risks of horse riding and use of the drug ecstasy.[93] That both activities carry the same statistical risk of harm may suggest that they are equal public health problems, in the sense considered in this section. If it is argued that one is a public health problem and the other not, it seems that reasons are needed to substantiate the claim (which is not to deny that such reasons may be presented).

Whilst I caution against too much of ethical relevance being taken as implicit with regard to the distribution of health, and the population's general attitude,[94] these may tolerably feature in a concept of public health. However, we should completely reject a concept of a healthy public that takes the public not to be a collection of people, but holds also that it is some sort of *organic* entity in its own right. I have argued that this approach to the public is problematic.[95] It bears repeating, because when analysts do talk about a 'healthy public' in this sense, they are doubly misleading: not only are they referring to some meta-entity

---

[91] I.e. as described in section 3.2.1, above.

[92] See Richard Mohr, "AIDS, gays, and State coercion", *Bioethics* (1987) 1:1, 35–50. (Mohr is critical and dismissive of this understanding of public health, describing it as "the medical model of society".)

[93] This widely reported discussion led to David Nutt being sacked as a drugs adviser to the government. See Dominic Casciani, "Profile: Professor David Nutt", *BBC Online News* (30 October 2009), available at http://news.bbc.co.uk/1/hi/uk/8334948.stm.

[94] See Chapter 2, section 2.4.   [95] See Chapter 2, section 2.2.

whose abstracted nature renders it pointless in applied theory, they are also bouncing off an easy – and for the purposes of argument, simplistic – equivocation in the term 'health'. If the public is more than the sum of its constituents, then its health is not going to be recognisable as a similar concept to a concept of health that can relate to people. This point is made by Richard Mohr:

> No literal sense exists in which there could be such a thing as a public health. To say the public has a health is like saying the number seven has a color: such a thing cannot have such a property. You have health or you lack it and I have health or lack it, because we each have a body with organs that function or do not function. But the public, an aggregate of persons similarly disposed as persons, has no such body of organs with functions which work or fail.[96]

Although some conceptions of health relate, for example, to autonomy,[97] and it is conceivable that both people and publics can have greater or lesser autonomy, even in this case there is no obvious correspondence between the aggregated health of individuals and the 'health' of the public. A healthy public in this sense is metaphorical; whatever we mean by 'health', it is better to reserve the term 'healthy' for entities that are not just figuratively 'organic'. This clearly does not preclude exploration, evaluation, or statement on how good – in a whole range of senses – a public, or a political community, is. Simply, the sixth face of public health should relate to the health of people considered together; it should not relate to some abstracted conception of the public and *its* supposed health.[98]

3.2.7   Public health as the population's health

Under this heading, public health denotes the health of the, or a, public. This is not to be understood in too abstract a sense; it does not imply the 'solidaristic' claims entailed in the understanding just discussed. Rather, on this count 'the public' is taken to be a number of individuals, considered collectively because of some common identifying feature; this may, for example, be geographical or professional. And the public's

[96] Mohr, "AIDS, gays, and State coercion", at 47. (My thanks to Timothy Murphy for initially drawing my attention to this quotation.) Note: Mohr does not object to what he labels "metaphoric senses of public health" provided these are legitimate (and he gives the terms of legitimacy as relating to public goods in the sense used by economists).

[97] For example: David Seedhouse, *Health: The Foundations of Achievement* (2nd edn) (Chichester: John Wiley & Sons, 2005).

[98] As well as referring back to Chapter 2, it is well to draw attention again to Bruce Jennings, "Public health and civic republicanism", in Dawson and Verweij (eds.), *Ethics, Prevention, and Public Health*, pp. 54–55.

health is the aggregate health of the people it comprises, informed possibly by further data, relating for example to the distribution of health. However, it is important to stress that this conception does not entail any normative stipulations. The measure it offers is ultimately to be considered as empirical or scientific rather than necessarily attaching to any action-guiding judgement. We may be interested to know how health is distributed throughout a population, but public health as the health of a population does not tell us, for example, that health states should be equal, or that radical variations in health are a matter of indifference. This conception has received some critical attention,[99] and is prevalent in the literature. In many cases this seems due to an ease of familiarity. (Note too that in some cases 'population health' is the term used for what I describe in this section.[100])

Perhaps the most telling example of the attractiveness of this face can (ironically) be taken from Rothstein. As we have seen, he urges and claims a faithful commitment to his own tight terminology, yet in practice his own usage does not accord absolutely with his recommendations. He rejects the idea that "public health" is anything but a legal term of art, explicitly pleading that it is not "even the 'health of the public'".[101] Yet in the very introduction to his original paper, he vacillates between meanings within a single sentence:

Outbreaks of new diseases, as well as changing patterns of population growth, economic development, and lifestyle trends all may threaten public health and thus demand a public health response.[102]

Unless Rothstein fears that disease, etc. threaten the State's jurisdiction, which seems a perverse reading, he must accept the potential for this being a sound use of the term 'public health' beyond his narrowed scheme. This highlights how intuitive or easy the meaning is to adopt, even when an analyst is forcefully seeking to offer a different definition. The ease of adoption is something that should be embraced. It is important to the application of analysis to have a non-political conception of public health to provide the context and setting of our attention.

On this understanding, simply looking to the health status of individuals within a population does not tell us what should be done. A wider,

[99] See especially Verweij and Dawson, "The meaning of 'public' in 'public health'", pp. 22–25.
[100] See e.g. Nuffield Council on Bioethics, *Public Health – Ethical Issues*, p. xv. Cf David Kindig and Greg Stoddart, "What is population health?", *American Journal of Public Health* (2003) 93:3, 380–383.
[101] Rothstein, "The limits of public health: a response", at 86.
[102] Rothstein, "Rethinking the meaning of public health", at 144.

considered, complete political theory is what tells us that. We need the objective public health measures in order to make meaningful application of theories. Employing the findings of analysts taking the 'population approach', we can compare populations as they develop over time, or with other populations, and gain an idea of what is possible. If we are to make an informed assessment of the implications of (not) making health public in regard to a given matter, we need to know about the health of members of the society we are examining.

We should accept the conceptual force of this understanding requires some delimiting. We have considered in Chapter 2 various meanings that may be given to the word 'public', and focused particularly on what is most useful to us in critical analysis of claims related to public health. When public health is used as a catch-all term, simply referring to the health status of members of a given population, it markedly does not follow that all health-related issues are public in a political sense; i.e. it does not entail that they are a *shared* (as opposed to overlapping) concern. If within a population we find a prevalence of some unhealthy condition, it would not follow that this had been 'made public'.

3.3   Conclusions

We have considered in this chapter what I take to be the seven faces of public health. It is important when using the term 'public health' in any instance to think about its potential connotations, how these fit into a wider scheme, and what that implies. As suggested in conclusion to Chapter 2, this array of faces may be attributable to the hotly contested political, moral, and legal matters that seem to be raised by the ostensibly simple notion of just *having* something called 'public health'. It is, I hope, clear that a field imbued with purpose and personality can be an unhelpful analytic and conceptual tool when we want to define and assess norms. Simply, if we are concerned with the public aspects of health, in finding out what these are, assessing them, and working out what we may do as a practical upshot of our conclusions, we face an enormously wide frame of analysis. And we will, as a matter of practice, work in accordance with this frame, even if we do not like labelling it 'public health'. The most trenchant libertarian needs to engage with and respond to the widest conceived 'public health issues', even if his preference is to think "that's not public health, it's something else". Equally, there is no 'victory' in claiming that a definition – however well established it is – *means* anything that of itself directs us authoritatively. "Public health" baldly stated does *not* mean that governments must institute some policy, that any rights in fact exist, or that any action is necessarily legitimate. To substantiate such contentions, well-reasoned argument is needed. No one owns the label 'public health', and it should not be used as a substitute for nuanced political, moral, or legal argument. If an adopted definition binds its users to pre-analytic commitments or truths, it is best to be aware of these, and in considered debate, inasmuch as is possible, to state them or rethink and leave them outside the definition. It can be observed that none of the faces of public health necessarily – far less conclusively – tells us what makes health public. If we agreed on what health was and what made it public, it would be easier first to work out what we should be doing, and second to overcome concerns about governmental under- or overreach, unmet duties, and other such issues. This very contention, however, is conceptually, as well as normatively, quite a mess. To tidy it up, we do not need to know the 'true' meaning of public health. Rather, we need to acknowledge its varied senses, and perhaps allow these to inform sound political understanding and theory that *can* guide governance as it relates to health *and* to other things. In other words analysts and policy-makers need a theory to strip apart the shared from the non-shared aspects of ourselves, our lives, and our health: to ascertain to what degree my health or health-affecting behaviour is your business. This will be the focus of Parts II and III, but first, to finish off our conceptual analysis, there are two short chapters considering public health policy and public health law and ethics.

4   Public health policy

4.1   Introduction

Although it only requires a short chapter, the idea of 'public health policy' does warrant a discrete consideration in preparation for wider critical evaluation as, especially given the great variety of meanings established of public health, it may be variously understood. In the sort of analysis I undertake in this book, and that which we find more generally in the public health and public health law and ethics literature, it is best to adopt a very broad definition of public health policy. This is a strength for present purposes, but as it may be considered a weakness, it is crucial to explain why I advocate this position. In so doing, I draw from some observations and conceptual proposals found in the Nuffield Council on Bioethics' report on public health and ethics.[1] First of all, I will explore what might be meant by policy.

4.2   The nature of policy

The current book's concern is primarily with issues that are most naturally defined as 'public policy' matters, although, given the potential confusions we have seen regarding the term public, it is most useful not even to be that restrictive with a definition. In other words, concerning questions of policy broadly, and public health policy more specifically, we profit most from taking as wide and inclusive a perspective as possible.[2] Even so, we must be aware of the potential implications of describing something as policy, *a* policy, or particularly *the* policy of government or some agency. There is bound to be some subjectivity in discovering these: to an extent commentators will see policy where they

[1] Nuffield Council on Bioethics, *Public Health – Ethical Issues* (London: Nuffield, 2007).

[2] See also the inclusive discussion of both "public" and "private" public health "interventions" and "programmes" in Marcel Verweij and Angus Dawson, "The meaning of 'public' in 'public health'", in Angus Dawson and Marcel Verweij (eds.), *Ethics, Prevention, and Public Health* (Oxford University Press, 2007), pp. 25–26.

choose.[3] It is useful to consider policy as relating to the output or the outcome of considered decision-making by an agent or agency: the output is what is 'delivered', be that e.g. money, goods, services; the outcome, is the final impact.[4] This understanding of policy includes omissions to act, and it includes considerations that are apart from the purposes that a third party may ascribe to the policy: the deliberations that lead to the policy do not circumscribe its 'policy effect'. However, 'policy' may also be used to relate to the principles or goals of an agent or agency; its contemplated purpose, as opposed to a purpose fictitiously ascribed to it or based on foreseen but undesired consequences.[5] Although often in the context of critical analyses of public health we will find ourselves focused on government or State policy, we may need also to concentrate our attention on the policies of 'private' actors. For example, we may want to study producers of foods who engage voluntarily in a 'traffic light system' on their products' labels,[6] or supermarkets instigating a specific pricing policy – such as running a 'loss leader' on alcoholic drinks – in a manner that may be argued to harm public health.[7]

Public policy may be viewed as a (perhaps presumptively legitimate, but, from a constitutional perspective, possibly worrying) gap-filling exercise, performed by the executive in order to complete the legislative picture, and bringing government "closer to the people".[8] As Geoff

---

[3] Brian Hogwood and Lewis Gunn, *Policy Analysis for the Real World* (Oxford University Press, 1984), p. 23; Michael Hill and Peter Hupe, *Implementing Public Policy: Governance in Theory and Practice* (2nd edn) (London: Sage, 2009), p. 5.

[4] Here my categorisation follows Hogwood and Gunn, *Policy Analysis for the Real World*, pp. 16–18.

[5] For example, a government will be able to foresee that a number of fatal accidents will eventuate on the public roads within its jurisdiction, some of which could, with more restrictive or better policed laws, be prevented. At the start of a year, a government may know in advance that, say, there will be 400 deaths on the roads. It does not follow that it can meaningfully or usefully be said that it is government policy that 400 people die on the roads annually. This idea of purpose in itself raises no excuse or justification for the policy position. It just speaks to a *further* use of the term.

[6] On which see the (UK) Food Standards Agency webpage: www.eatwell.gov.uk/foodlabels/trafficlights.

[7] See, for example, British Medical Association Board of Science, *Under the influence – The damaging effect of alcohol marketing on young people* (London: BMA, 2009), p. 6, and note more generally the widespread concern that cheaply available alcohol has created, with calls for legal measures to ensure minimum pricing: see especially House of Commons Health Committee, *Alcohol: First Report of Session 2009–10 – Volume I*, HC 151-I (London: The Stationery Office, 2010), available at www.publications.parliament.uk/pa/cm200910/cmselect/cmhealth/151/151i.pdf; Jacqui Wise, "MPs criticise government for ignoring doctors' advice on alcohol", *British Medical Journal* (2010) 340:c136; Laura Williamson, "Scotland: leading the way for alcohol policy in the United Kingdom?", *Journal of Bioethical Inquiry* (2009) 6(3): 265–266.

[8] These mark the final two of five points mapped by Theodore Lowi in developments of understanding of policy: Theodore Lowi, "Law vs. public policy: a critical exploration", *Cornell Journal of Law and Public Policy* (2003) 12, 493–501, at 499–500.

Edwards puts it, "[i]n public administration, policies establish a framework for making decisions where a discretion is to be exercised under legislation".[9] For our purposes, such a perspective is too narrow. We do well to consider all manner of political (and legal) normative frameworks to be describable as policy. Brian Hogwood and Lewis Gunn provide a taxonomy of what policy can mean, before offering what they consider to be the crucial aspects to a definition that they take into their analysis.[10] These aspects are tenfold,[11] and lead to a tentative defining of public policy:

Any public policy is subjectively defined by an observer as being such and is usually perceived as comprising a series of patterns of related definitions to which many circumstances and personal, group, and organizational influences have contributed. The policy-making process involves many sub-processes and may extend over a considerable period of time. The aims or purposes underlying a policy are usually identifiable at an early stage in the process but these may change over time and, in some cases, may be defined only retrospectively. The outcomes of policies require to be studied and, where appropriate, compared and contrasted with policy-makers' intentions. Accidental or deliberate inaction may contribute to a policy outcome. The study of policy requires an understanding of behaviour, especially behaviour involving interaction within and among organizational memberships. For a policy to be regarded as a 'public policy' it must to some degree have been generated or at least processed within the framework of governmental procedures, influences and organizations.[12]

Michael Hill and Peter Hupe, concerned with the implementation of public policy, draw from Hogwood and Gunn's analysis. Their summary provides a good understanding of what may constitute policy:

[Hogwood and Gunn] identify the following elements in the use of the term 'public policy'. Although policy is to be distinguished from 'decision', it is less

---

[9] Geoff Edwards, "Clarifying the status of policy", *Australian Journal of Public Administration* (2000) 59(2), 109–114, at 110.

[10] See Hogwood and Gunn, *Policy Analysis for the Real World*, ch. 2. Ten uses of the word policy are briefly explored on pp. 13–19: taken from Hogwood and Gunn's subheadings, they are 'policy' as: a label for a field of activity; an expression of general purpose or desired state of affairs; specific proposals; decisions of government; formal authorisation; a programme; output; outcome; a theory or model; and a process.

[11] Again, to provide a list taken from the authors' subheadings, from *ibid.*, pp. 19–23, policy: is to be distinguished from 'decision' (because it is "larger than a decision", because understanding a policy often requires a consideration of a series of decisions, and because the study of a policy will tend to require examination of multiple actors, rather than *a* decision-maker); is less readily distinguishable from 'administration'; involves behaviour as well as intentions; involves inaction as well as action; has outcomes which may or may not have been foreseen; is a purposive course of action but purposes may be defined retrospectively; arises from a process over time; involves intra- and inter-organisational relationships; (*public* policy) involves a key, but not exclusive, role for public agencies; is subjectively defined.

[12] *Ibid.*, pp. 23–24.

readily distinguishable from 'administration'. Policy involves behaviour as well as intentions, and inaction as well as action. Policies have outcomes that may or may not have been foreseen. While policy refers to a purposive course of actions, this does not exclude the possibility that purposes may be defined retrospectively. Policy arises from a process over time, which may involve both intra- and inter-organizational relationships. There is a difficult issue here about what is exactly meant by public, since private actors may participate in all aspects of public policy-making. Thus, Hogwood and Gunn say, 'Public policy involves a key, but not exclusive, role for public agencies' (1984: 23). The implication of 'key' may be seen in the extent to which the involvement of government legitimizes the action.[13]

Whilst this summary provides a useful springboard, one minor qualification should be given. Where Hogwood and Gunn's focus is on *public* policy, whilst public (i.e. governmental) agencies are said not to have an exclusive role, policy "must at least have been partly developed *within* the framework of government".[14] Whether we should accept this condition depends on what it means to be "within the framework of government", but for the purposes of allowing as broad as possible normative analysis of 'public health issues', we do well not to construe it too tightly. Hogwood and Gunn themselves permit that such incorporation may only require a public agency's authorisation: provided we allow that this can be as extensive as meaning the 'private' actor does not contravene what the public agency knows about and permits, there is no problem. And if that is a stretch, it is a stretch worth making. Given potential for incoherence or even straightforward uncertainty, we need also to be able to accommodate anomalous or *possibly* unlawful policy in our assessments. Although our focus is on 'public health policy', we are not always or only concerned with 'public policy'. It is worth stressing, therefore, that from finding something to be a public health policy, we require further steps before we can take it that it is good, legitimate, lawful, governmental, or warranted. It is worth iterating Hogwood and Gunn's conclusion that, notwithstanding their giving a definition, (public) policy is susceptible to numerous contradictory definitions, and thus it is best to be clear on how it is understood in a given circumstance.[15]

A final observation of Hill and Hupe, who bear in mind a range of possible understandings of public policy, should be noted:

---

[13] Hill and Hupe, *Implementing Public Policy*, p. 4.
[14] Hogwood and Gunn, *Policy Analysis for the Real World*, p. 23 (emphasis in original).
[15] *Ibid.*, pp. 30–31.

What, in general, is striking about the definitions of public policy indicated here is the purposive character public policies are expected to have, and the way in which they are expected to be related to (societal) problems. For implementation theory and research, this means that contextualization is important; 'implementation' is always connected to specific policies as particular responses to specific problems in society.[16]

The current work is not, and does not claim to be, an engagement in implementation theory. Nevertheless, applying to our analysis of public health the broad conception of policy that can be taken from the excerpts quoted, we see a definition that houses a wide range of measures, coming from a whole variety of sources, including Parliament, the government, judicial statements, professional regulatory codes, and the practices of 'private' bodies and actors. Public health policy may include complete but deliberate omissions to institute any measure in order to effect some end considered to bear on public health.[17] Equally, *we* may judge something to be a public health policy, or at least a policy that bears on public health, even if it was not instituted with such a conceptualisation in mind.

4.3   Regulation and public health policy

Having achieved the preliminary matter of determining that policy is to be used as a term to refer to purposeful matters of some agent or agency, or to the outcome (positive or negative) of measures instituted by an agent or agency (in each case including but not limited to government), let us now focus more closely on public health policy. There may exist a view that policies, in the end, equate with rules, perhaps even coercion, whether they are based in 'hard law' or 'soft law'. It is better to take a wider perspective, and note that whilst coercion is an important aspect of policy, it forms only a part – in the main, a fairly small part – of the possible approaches that may be taken.[18] Within a liberal paradigm, coercive measures tend to occupy a great amount of debate, but the nature of coercion is quite complex.[19] Furthermore, there may be matters of uncontroversial moral concern that still remain without

---

[16] Hill and Hupe, *Implementing Public Policy*, p. 5.

[17] As the Nuffield Council says: "Any policy, including a policy to 'do nothing', implies value judgements about what is or is not good for people, and requires justification" (Nuffield Council on Bioethics, *Public Health – Ethical Issues*, p. xvi).

[18] Chris Bonell, Martin McKee, Adam Fletcher, Paul Wilkinson, and Andy Haines, "One nudge forward, two steps back", *British Medical Journal* (2011) 342:d401, 241–242.

[19] Grant Lamond, "The coerciveness of law", *Oxford Journal of Legal Studies* (2000) 20:1, 39–62.

the State's competence for ('competing') principled reasons, such as a perception that it is good that people be free to make moral choices for themselves, even when there is a risk they will decide wrongly,[20] or straightforward practical ones, such as complete or practical unenforceability negating the value of regulation.[21] Equally, there may be matters whose 'value-base' is greatly contested, but on which the State nevertheless does hold a competence.[22] In dealing with such issues, complexities may further recommend a more nuanced approach than either ban, coerce, or permit. The Nuffield Council provides a helpful conceptual presentation that assists here, in what it labels the "intervention ladder":

The range of options available to government and policy makers can be thought of as a ladder of interventions, with progressive steps from individual freedom and responsibility towards state intervention as one moves up the ladder. In considering which 'rung' is appropriate for a particular public health goal, the benefits to individuals and society should be weighed against the erosion of individual freedom. Economic costs and benefits would need to be taken into account alongside health and societal benefits. The ladder of possible policy action is as follows:

Eliminate choice. Regulate in such a way as to entirely eliminate choice, for example through compulsory isolation of patients with infectious disease.

Restrict choice. Regulate in such a way as to restrict the options available to people with the aim of protecting them, for example removing unhealthy ingredients from foods, or unhealthy foods from shops or restaurants.

Guide choice through disincentives. Fiscal and other disincentives can be put in place to influence people not to pursue certain activities, for example through taxes on cigarettes, or by discouraging the use of cars in inner cities through charging schemes or limitations of parking spaces.

Guide choices through incentives. Regulations can be offered that guide choices by fiscal and other incentives, for example offering tax-breaks for the purchase of bicycles that are used as a means of travelling to work.

Guide choices through changing the default policy. For example, in a restaurant, instead of providing chips as a standard side dish (with healthy options available), menus could be changed to provide a more healthy option as standard (with chips an option available).

---

[20] Classically this idea may be attributed to the manner of liberalism defended in John Stuart Mill, *On Liberty*, Edward Alexander (ed.) (Peterborough, Ontario: Broadview, 1999 [1859]). In the context of regulation theory specifically, see also Roger Brownsword, "So what does the world need now? Reflections on regulating technologies", in Roger Brownsword and Karen Yeung (eds.), *Regulating Technologies: Legal Futures, Regulatory Frames and Technological Fixes* (Portland, OR: Hart Publishing, 2008), p. 41.

[21] Anthony Ogus, "Regulation revisited", *Public Law* (2009), 332–346, at 344.

[22] A review of the relevant arguments is provided in Part II.

Enable choice. Enable individuals to change their behaviours, for example by offering participation in an NHS 'stop smoking' programme, building cycle lanes, or providing free fruit in schools.

Provide information. Inform and educate the public, for example as part of campaigns to encourage people to walk more or eat five portions of fruit and vegetables per day.

Do nothing or simply monitor the current situation.[23]

Taking the intervention ladder as a conceptual tool need not commit us to any pre-analytic assumptions, such as that doing nothing requires no justification, eliminating choice will always be the most controversial intervention, or that there is any sort of ordinal ranking corresponding with the position on the ladder. Rather, it presents, in a useful and concise manner, the range of approaches that may be taken in regard to public health policy. (Inasmuch as there is no evaluative ordering in the Nuffield Council's list, the metaphor of a ladder may seem unfortunate: perhaps it is, though I see no compelling reason to believe that being at the top (or bottom) of a ladder is always, even presumptively, best.)

As it contrasts with the rich scholarship in regulatory theory, this analysis might seem rather crude, but it may usefully be tied with crucial aspects of regulation that offer good reason both to take policy as a wider conception than 'law', and to recognise the scope for governmental involvement and interference in the way we live our lives. By denying that the different levels of intervention are lexically ordered, we are not constrained by the presumptive underpinning associated with Ian Ayres and John Braithwaite's "enforcement pyramid", which suggests that first should come advice or persuasion, then mild sanctions such as warning letters, and then more punitive sanctions through civil and criminal penalties, then licence suspension, and finally revocation.[24] Although the pyramid's content may vary from context to context, this move from least restrictive to most coercive is general. In practice, more usefully responsive regulation will be much more nuanced than the regulatory pyramid – or the intervention ladder – make apparent.[25] As Anthony Ogus puts it, "'better regulation' has to be based on a better understanding of behavioural responses to regulation".[26] Although it is not the purpose of this book to develop a theory of regulation, I hope that the strengths and shortcomings of different regulatory measures

---

[23] Nuffield Council on Bioethics, *Public Health – Ethical Issues*, p. 42.

[24] See Ian Ayres and John Braithwaite, *Responsive Regulation: Transcending the Deregulation Debate* (Oxford University Press, 1992), ch. 2, especially pp. 35–38.

[25] For a framework that could usefully be drawn into analysis, see Robert Baldwin and Julia Black, "Really responsive regulation", *Modern Law Review* (2008) 71:1, 59–94.

[26] Ogus, "Regulation revisited", at 346.

may be accounted for when distinct interventions are considered in the name of 'public health policy'. It is useful in this regard to summarise some important aspects of Robert Baldwin and Julia Black's overview of key regulatory approaches, and to note some of the weaknesses they highlight. First, with regard to 'responsive regulation', they note that a more subtle approach than "step by step escalation" up the pyramid (or for our purposes, we might say the ladder) is often required.[27] Furthermore, such escalation may often simply be impracticable.[28] Even the wider conceived 'smart regulation', which looks beyond state-controls, suffers for its sharing many of the shortcomings of the "escalation process".[29]

We may imagine that 'risk-based regulation' is more appropriate to public health policy. This "offers an evidence-based means of targeting the use of resources", and thus "differs from 'pyramidic' approaches by emphasising analysis and targeting rather than a process of responsive escalation".[30] According to the Nuffield Council, the evidence base that should underpin decisions on public health policy seems naturally suited to this manner of regulation.[31] A shortcoming of the risk based approach is that it operates within constrained rationalities that will potentially be subject to problems politically, practically, and legally, and may be insufficiently adaptable to unfamiliar new or developing risks.[32] When policy-makers and analysts are considering the appropriate policy in a given situation, it is important to account for the subtleties of context, to allow for constraints on the capacity to control behaviour, and to be aware both of the range of approaches available and the problems inherent in them.

4.4   Conclusions

We tend to use the word policy in reference to a specific regulatory measure. However, it may refer also to the outcome of measures. It may find itself in both positive and negative forms, each opening itself up to critique and possible need for normative justification. As well as considering the *target* of policy, we are concerned with the source of the policy, and, in analysis, its legitimacy as such a source. As well as wanting to know what makes health public – what makes it a shared concern – we need to know what makes an agent or agency a public actor in a given

---

[27] Baldwin and Black, "Really responsive regulation", at 62.   [28] *Ibid.*, at 64.
[29] *Ibid.*, at 65.   [30] *Ibid.*, at 66.
[31] See Nuffield Council on Bioethics, *Public Health – Ethical Issues*, ch. 3.
[32] Baldwin and Black, "Really responsive regulation", at 66.

instance: what legitimises his, her, their, or its institution of a measure. In some circumstances, we may be very concerned with the actual purposes given to a policy by its creator. However, more generally we will be interested in the outcome, rather than just the intended consequences of the policy-maker. Thus, health need not have been a stated, or even contemplated, reason or justification underpinning the institution of a relevant policy. When considering policy responses to purported public health issues, and especially purported public health *problems*, we will tend to see reference to the need for 'public health measures' or 'public health interventions'. These will take the form of processes that can be mapped onto the intervention ladder as (potential) policy. It will tend to be the case that public health measures or interventions are explicitly designed with the amelioration of health in mind, through coordinated and directed efforts. Plainly such efforts may be transposed onto some of the definitions of public health itself. However, it is clearer analytically to refer to undertaking such measures as instituting public health interventions, rather than 'doing', or being a logical and necessarily good aspect 'of', public health.

5   Public health law and ethics

5.1   Marking out fields without boundaries?

This chapter addresses questions of what we should take 'public health law' and 'public health ethics' to mean. I will consider each, but first it is worth addressing the question of "coherence anxiety", which seems necessarily to obstruct analysts claiming to focus their attention in these areas.[1] "Medical law",[2] "health care law",[3] "health law",[4] and "public health law",[5] have all for some time been cordoned off into discrete but unconventional areas of analytic focus.[6] All of them can be seen to fall under the wider umbrella of bioethics, which has been defined as "the study of ethical, social, legal, philosophical and other related issues arising in health care and the biological sciences".[7] We can allow too that they may be about more than just study; that as well

---

[1] Cf Theodore W. Ruger, "Health law's coherence anxiety", *Georgetown Law Journal* (2008) 96:2, 625–648; Keith Syrett and Oliver Quick, "Pedagogical promise and problems: Teaching public health law", *Public Health* (2009) 123, 222–231.

[2] As conceived, for example, by Margaret Brazier and Emma Cave, *Medicine, Patients and the Law* (4th edn) (London: Penguin, 2007); J. K. Mason and Graeme Laurie, *Mason & McCall Smith's Law and Medical Ethics* (8th edn) (Oxford University Press, 2010).

[3] As conceived, for example by Jonathan Montgomery, *Health Care Law* (2nd edn) (Oxford University Press, 2002); Jean McHale and Marie Fox, *Health Care Law – Text and Materials* (2nd edn) (London: Sweet and Maxwell, 2007).

[4] As described, for example, by Tamara K. Hervey and Jean V. McHale, "Law, health and the European Union", *Legal Studies* (2005) 25:2, 228–259.

[5] As conceived, for example, by Lawrence O. Gostin, *Public Health Law: Power, Duty, Restraint* (2nd edn) (Berkeley: University of California Press, 2008); Syrett and Quick, "Pedagogical promise and problems".

[6] On the distinct nature of medical law as an area of legal practice and study, see Kenneth Veitch, *The Jurisdiction of Medical Law* (Aldershot: Ashgate, 2007). Veitch examines, inter alia, the means used by scholars to demarcate medical law as a legal sub-discipline, highlighting in particular the role of ethical argument in medical law and the claiming of expertise over particular social issues.

[7] This is the definition provided in Art. 2 of the constitution of the International Association of Bioethics, available at www.bioethics-international.org/constitution.html.

as developing theory, they may be concerned with policy-making.[8] The upshot is that we find a peculiar approach to formulating a discipline. Rather than drawing boundaries in accordance with categorically distinct doctrines – such as tort, contract, crime, human rights – a doctrinally irrelevant common nexus, namely health, binds together different disciplines, and different approaches from within disciplines.[9] Health-related matters are key. Given this, public health law might include *any* form of law that bears on health. There is a lack of orthodoxy to this approach.[10] For it to be worthwhile, one has to accept the claim that health itself is sufficiently important that it warrants attention from a doctrinally disparate perspective. And notably, health law and public health law seem to open themselves up to 'coherence problems' that need not apply to medical law – i.e. the law governing medical practice – and perhaps also healthcare law.

Even if health is a contested concept, however, it arguably *is* worthy of privileged treatment, and it is such in a manner both for those who consider it to be of fundamental importance, and for those who consider that it ought not to be of any (or of no more than very limited) concern of the State. Possibly we should also add the practical consideration that as many people *think* they are interested in public health law, this gives sufficient reason to focus on it, notwithstanding any scepticism about its naturally forming a coherent system of study. Public health commitments are becoming of relevance and interest in both public and academic debate.[11] Those who think health ought to be a priority might share Lawrence Gostin's view that its special importance makes it a proper focus of study and policy formulation:

The health of individuals, families, and communities has deep, intuitive meaning. So much of what we aspire to be as individuals or as members of society relies on health. Our shared intuitions about the value of health manifest themselves in public and political concerns. The media widely reports threats to the public's health, such as a traveler with multi-drug resistant tuberculosis, E-coli from contaminated spinach, miners' deaths, unsafe children's

---

[8] Ruth Chadwick, "Defining Bioethics", *Bioethics* (2007) 21:2, ii.

[9] To be clear, there is a risk of making too much of the 'coherence' of 'traditional' legal sub-disciplines. As Peter Cane says in reflections on the conceptual basis of tort law, "[t]he boundaries of a legal subject are not set by divine prescript but by the custom of lawyers. The law of torts as a separate legal subject is largely a product of the systematising activities of academic lawyers in the past hundred years or so". He goes on to describe tort law conceptually as "disorganised and ramshackle". Peter Cane, *Atiyah's Accidents, Compensation and the Law* (6th edn) (Cambridge University Press, 2004), pp. 25–26.

[10] Ruger, "Health law's coherence anxiety".

[11] See Nuffield Council on Bioethics, *Public Health – Ethical Issues* (London: Nuffield, 2007); Syrett and Quick, "Pedagogical promise and problems".

toys, and dangerous pharmaceuticals. Election years predictably spur new, or refashioned, proposals for health care reform. And there remain enduring, intractable health hazards, such as tobacco, obesity, motor vehicle crashes, and endemic diseases such HIV/AIDS.[12]

In contrast with the thrust of Gostin's work, others may be concerned that health is used as a cover for State tyranny. For these, a focus on measures ostensibly legitimised by their relationship to health protection or promotion is necessary in order to expose instances of the State acting without its competence. "The roads to unfreedom are many" writes Petr Skrabanek. "Signposts on one of them bears the inscription HEALTH FOR ALL."[13]

Whether we are more sympathetic with the perspective of Gostin or Skrabanek, or remain equally unconvinced by both, they highlight two distinct and important reasons why public health law and ethics may be important areas of study: either because 'we' do have an idea of what health is, and do think it is of sufficient importance that it warrants this level of focus; or because we see that health is used as such a special form of justification, and with such special force in social and political reality, that it demands critical attention. I consider health – even if it remains undefined – to have become a matter of sufficient importance, interest, and effect that it provides a body of work that merits examination in its own right. I am simultaneously sympathetic with, and not put off by, the charge of 'coherence anxiety'[14] that might be levelled at an analyst who claims to work in public health law and ethics. As Theodore Ruger suggests:

Health law flunks most of the classical attributes of field coherence. It is a mishmash of various legal forms, applied by divergent and often colliding institutions, and has developed much more often through external pressures and even historical accidents than from any determinate internal evolution or refinement. Yet it is hardly the only legal field that possesses these centrifugal features (the postmodern conception of constitutional law is another). And it would be surprising if all legal subjects fit the same off-the-rack model of coherence …

But this possible lack of a central core does not mean that health law lacks essential, or special, attributes worthy of study; nor does it mean that the field lacks an identifiable structure and architecture. Moving away from the conventional coherence paradigm need not resort to a focus only on minutely

---

[12] Lawrence O. Gostin, "National and global health law: a scholarly examination of the most pressing health hazards", *Georgetown Law Journal* (2008) 96:2, 317–329, at 317.

[13] Petr Skrabanek, *The Death of Humane Medicine and the Rise of Coercive Healthism* (St Edmundsbury Press: Bury St Edmunds, 1994), p. 11.

[14] Ruger, "Health law's coherence anxiety".

particularized analysis of given cases and doctrines. To say health law is messy is not the same as saying it is random; to say it is multifaceted and difficult to center on a parsimonious internal core is not the same as saying it defies all abstraction and generalization. Health law is a legal field shaped dramatically by external dynamics: the surrounding political and economic climate, interest group pressure from various organized actors, and institutional change and interaction among bodies that apply and shape the law.[15]

Public health law is not an area comparable with, for example, contract or criminal law, but is still a field worth tilling. As with the narrower fields of medical and health care law, its study offers great importance to ethical analysis. The questions and concerns of public health law are shared and developed in the broad bioethical literature, which therefore provides apposite points of reference for analysis and criticism, as well as reason to note that whilst public health ethics seems to raise new issues, sometimes there is a risk of simplistic repackaging of old arguments, or artificial fencing off of relevant arguments from an apparently adjoining field. In order to establish the boundaries of public health law and ethics the following sections provide consideration of workable definitions of each.

5.2   Public health law

We have seen how public health law is not a field of study comparable, for example, with human rights law. Given the understandings of public health that we have explored, it is to be expected that the breadth of measures that might constitute public health policies is so broad that it could almost include any area of law. Robyn Martin and Richard Coker discuss the historical difficulty of defining, and thus studying or teaching, public health law:

As a consequence of the paucity of scholarship on public health law, the focus and boundaries of public health law have been far from clear. British law schools which offer 'Health Law' programmes at undergraduate level have addressed almost exclusively issues pertaining to the treatment of the individual patient, issues that are easily identifiable and easily defined. Few health law programmes have ventured into the obscure and unbounded terrain of public health law because of difficulties of knowing where to start, what to include, what to exclude, and what constitutes the essence of public health law. Graduates of both law and public health programmes will probably have had little exposure to public health law, and so have very limited understanding of what law can do for public health, of how law can work for the benefit of public

---

[15] *Ibid.*, at 627–628.

health, of the limits of what law can achieve, or of the principles of human rights and ethics which are relevant to public health law.[16]

The boundaries of public health law may still be uncertain, but it is becoming a subject of specific focus.[17] Gostin provides perhaps the most influential definition:

Public health law is the study of the legal powers and duties of the state, in collaboration with its partners (e.g., health care, business, the community, the media, and academe), to ensure the conditions for people to be healthy (to identify, prevent, and ameliorate risks to health in the population), and of the limitations on the power of the state to constrain for the common good the autonomy, privacy, liberty, proprietary, and other legally protected interests of individuals. The prime objective of public health law is to pursue the highest possible level of physical and mental health in the population, consistent with the values of social justice.[18]

As with some of the definitions of public health, we see that Gostin's classification of public health law is extremely broad. It focuses on State responsibilities and powers, including those that are deferred, and it looks both at removal of risk to, and improvement of, health. As well as its breadth, an interesting contrast between this definition of public health law and, for example, a definition of tort law, is the agenda implied in public health law. Perhaps this is unsurprising: throughout his career Gostin has been a pioneer.[19] Just as some definitions of public health imply a purpose, so does Gostin's definition of public health law. It is arguably strange to think of an area of law as having an objective for its students (and practitioners).[20] When I meet tort lawyers at conferences, I do not presume without more that they are in favour of distributive over retributive justice (or vice versa, or any other ideological

---

[16] Robyn Martin and Richard Coker, "Conclusion: where next?", *Public Health* (2006) 120, 81–87, at 81.

[17] Note that 'welfare law' is of much longer standing even than the upsurge in 'public health law' seen in the Victorian era. Ironically, it was the legal changes to welfare law at that time that have led to its becoming obsolete, whilst public health law as it is widely conceived today assumes a strength and air of novelty that is perhaps less deserved than some accept. For a socio-legal historical analysis, see Lorie Charlesworth, *Welfare's Forgotten Past* (Abingdon: Routledge, 2009).

[18] Gostin, *Public Health Law – Power, Duty, Restraint* (2nd edn), p. 4.

[19] For an autobiographical reflection, see Lawrence O. Gostin, "From a civil libertarian to a sanitarian", *Journal of Law and Society* (2007) 34:4, 594–616. And for an example of Gostin's current practical work, see Lawrence O. Gostin, Mark Heywood, Gorik Ooms, Anand Grover, John Arne Røttingen and Wang Chenguang, "National and global responsibilities for health", *Bulletin of the World Health Organization* (2010) 88:10, 719–719A.

[20] Contrast Roger S. Magnusson, "Mapping the scope and opportunities for public health law in liberal democracies", *Journal of Law, Medicine and Ethics* (2007) 35:4, 571–587.

position). So it may be strange to suppose that if I meet a colleague who is a 'public health lawyer', I take for granted that he is committed to the improvement of health through organised mechanisms instituted by the State. The definition of bioethics presented above referred to the study of matters related to biological science and healthcare. The definition of public health law as something that has a "prime objective" carries a directive content that bioethics does not. This is problematic and may be sufficient reason to qualify acceptance of Gostin's definition. No doubt Gostin does not seek to be exclusive, but it is important to accept the sceptical voices, and the certain but contradictory ones, in their critical input into debate. (And then it is important to decide which of the *views* to accept, but inclusion is required first.)

As a matter of academic evolution, public health law is establishing a stronger identity in the mindset of legal analysts. Health law textbooks in the UK have not overlooked public health, and will likely take an increased focus on it.[21] Jonathan Montgomery argues for the great importance of avoiding "an approach which begins from the work of doctors and works outwards".[22] The problem with that approach is that:

It sees the clinical interaction between doctor and patient as the paradigm. This view influences both the content of the subject, individualizing its focus, and its underlying conceptual coherence, emphasizing the application of ethical principles.[23]

Montgomery defines (what he labels) 'health care law' "in terms of the United Kingdom's international obligations to tackle health problems and ensure that citizens have access to the health care that they need".[24] His view finds its logical grounding in the shift in emphasis in the State's health policy, and the importance of taking a more wide-ranging perspective:

This means that the subject of health care law is wider than medical law. It embraces not only the practice of medicine, but also that of the non-medical health care professions, the administration of health services and the law's role in maintaining public health. It also means that the concept of 'law' in this context must be examined carefully. Legal rules in a strict sense, as developed by Parliament and the courts, are not the only type of binding norm that is relevant to health care law.[25]

---

[21] Contrast with the position around fifteen years ago, reported in Margaret Brazier and John Harris, "Public health and private lives", *Medical Law Review* (1996) 4:2, 171–192, at 173.

[22] Montgomery, *Health Care Law*, p. 1.   [23] *Ibid.*

[24] *Ibid.*, p. 2.   [25] *Ibid.*, p. 4.

In line with this view (and noting that some may interpret 'medical law' in accordance with Montgomery's definition), it is fundamental not only to consider 'hard' law, or indeed law designed to improve health, when studying public health law. Policies, regulations, case law, default positions, and professional and social mores are all potentially relevant to analysis. Even if a non-directive definition of public health were adopted, the *context* of law is crucial to an evaluation of it. An analysis, for example, of a governmental failure to allow needle exchange programmes for drug users in prisons would be hollow if only statute and case law were to be looked at.[26] Legal measures will be relevant, but so will other governmental policy, the practices in other jurisdictions, social practices, and even perhaps expectations in the jurisdiction under analysis.

The rationale of this perspective underpins the view taken in J. K. Mason and Graeme Laurie's medical law textbook. They also consider the need to reappraise established paradigms from medical law and ethics, looked at in the light of public health concerns:

Public health measures tend to fall into two overlapping categories: health promotion and/or disease prevention and control … [W]hen our state of health becomes beyond our control, and most particularly, if our state of ill health becomes a threat to others, then the time for individual action has passed and it may be necessary for government to step in to institute measures to protect the community, even when this might entail threats to the rights of the immediately affected individual. The important relationship, then, is no longer that between doctor and patient but rather that between patient and state and the many actors in between. The role of the law in this sphere is to police the boundaries of this relationship and to ensure that every reasonable justification is offered to support state action that encroaches on individual rights. Even so, as we shall see, the health interests of the community can sometimes be so strong – or threat to its health so great – that even compulsory action against the bodily integrity and freedoms of individuals can be defended.[27]

Public health law as described before is clearly not the primary focus of Mason and Laurie's book. However, there is an interesting paradigmatic constraint in their reformulation to the relationship "between *patient* and state". In many instances, the relevant party will not be identifiable as a patient. Public health law focuses on matters without the doctor-patient paradigm, and in the vast majority of cases it is better considering the State-individual, or State-citizen relationship.

---

[26] See *Shelley* v. *United Kingdom* (2008) 46 EHRR SE16, and John Coggon, "Public health, responsibility and English law: are there such things as no smoke without ire or needless clean needles?", *Medical Law Review* (2009) 17:1, 127–139.

[27] Mason and Laurie, *Mason & McCall Smith's Law and Medical Ethics*, p. 29.

Jonathan Herring, without providing a formal definition of public health law (though acknowledging the expansion of the meaning of public health itself), recognises the increased scope of legal analysis of public health:

[A]ctions which can be said to be public health issues could include things like the provision of recreation and park facilities which might never have been included in earlier understandings of the term [public health].

But the key issue in public health is the role the Government should play in some of the major public health issues: smoking; obesity; and alcohol misuse, for example. Should the Government be actively seeking to prevent unhealthy life-style choices or is that too interventionist and rather should the Government's role be to encourage and enable people to live more healthily? ...

There are two issues here. The first is practical. There is a limit to what the Government can do in some areas. Programmes of vaccination and sanitation can be relatively easy to implement. But even if the Government wanted to force everyone to eat five portions of fresh fruit and vegetables a day that would be almost impossible to implement. Second is the theoretical issue, which concerns the extent to which it is the role of the Government to influence people's life style choices.[28]

And beyond textbook definitions, Tamara Hervey and Jean McHale, considering what they label health law, and distinguishing it from public health law, map the distinctions in focus in a manner similar to that suggested here. Reflecting on public health law, they say:

Public health law is concerned with the regulation of risks to the health of the population. Public health interfaces with human rights considerations, notably in areas such as mental health and disease transmission. The very essence of public health law is that containment of many threats to public health within one jurisdiction is problematic. There is therefore an international dimension to the discipline as whole.[29]

This emphasis on international issues and the role of risk provides a helpful final focus when establishing the scope of public health law, and the matters that might be studied under its name. As noted when considering public health, many policies will offer probable benefits rather than certain ones. Assessment of the probable harms attached is thus necessary.

Having considered the different approaches that might be taken to formulation of public health law as a field of study, I suggest the following definition: *public health law entails those aspects of law, policy, and regulation that bear on the health status (howsoever understood) of their*

---

[28] Jonathan Herring, *Medical Law and Ethics* (Oxford University Press, 2006), p. 511.
[29] Tamara K. Hervey and Jean V. McHale, "Law, health and the European Union", *Legal Studies* (2005) 25:2, 228–259, at 234.

subjects. Thus public health law enjoys (or suffers) the broadest of scopes. However, public health law itself is to be distinguished from two further things: first, the *study of public health law*, which refers to the evaluation of legal, policy, and regulatory measures (or non-measures) that have or would have effects on the health of subjects; second, *practices relating to public health law*, which entail the advancement or attempted advancement of measures directed to the alteration of health.

On this count public health law itself is not a directive field. Its study does not require a particular normative commitment: a radical libertarian lawyer may be a student of public health law just as a 'sanitarian lawyer' may be.[30] A student of public health law may be interested in measures that have come about without consideration of health.[31] Conduct described as public health practices will be of relevance to the study, but so also may be laws that affect health, yet have developed on the back of other considerations. Public health law is open to sufficient interpretation that, in effect, it covers any measure that may be of relevance to a legal scholar who is interested in health issues.[32] The level to which an argument claiming to be about public health law is convincing will ultimately be a matter that can be stretched, and possibly stretched too far.[33] The analysis in the following chapters of this book will shed some light on where the boundaries – hard to draw in principle – might lie. I do not doubt that we can usefully study something called 'public health law', but its scope is so broad and its concerns so varied that it seems to be subsumed by wider debates about the nature and basis of law more generally.

5.3   Public health ethics

In similar vein to public health and public health law, public health ethics has disputed connotations. Like public health law, it is developing as a field in its own right. Seeking to distinguish public health ethics from medical ethics, Ronald Bayer and colleagues, in the introduction to their book on public health ethics, say:

Because of the individualistic orientation of medical ethics, the concepts of autonomy and negative rights of the person (the right not to be harmed) have tended to predominate in that field. In public health ethics, by the very nature of the problems and policies with which it deals, there will tend to be

---

[30] The label is derived from Gostin, "From a civil libertarian to a sanitarian".
[31] See Chapter 4.
[32] Given disagreements about what health itself means, one scholar may of course fail to recognise what another scholar posits as 'really' being public health law.
[33] Cf Syrett and Quick, "Pedagogical promise and problems", especially at 226–227.

more emphasis on the interests and health of groups, the social justice of the distribution of social resources, and the positive or social/human rights of individuals. When social interests and the interests of individuals come into conflict, then there will be a conflict between medical ethics and public health ethics.[34]

The rise of 'public health ethics' has been astounding, but it is important when discussing a field such as this not to lose sight of what ethics itself is about. Inasmuch as it relates to normative argument, we should be wary of positions that suggest the possibility of wholly detachable 'spheres' of ethics, each with its own distinct underpinning, and the chance for conflict or incompatibility between them. Purely theoretical moral critiques can afford to entrench themselves in particular moral universes where all things need not be considered. Action-guiding philosophy, however, *is* grounded. Public health ethics is necessarily connected to something below the ether: the public; people. A theory of public health ethics must be commensurate with (ideally logically entailed by) a broader ethical system that explains the relationships between members of a polity. If there is a 'clash' with public health ethics and, for example, medical ethics, this means that there is something wrong with (at least) one of the ethical systems.[35]

Just as I describe a field called public health law, notwithstanding its doctrinal coherence being of secondary importance to its focus, so I accept the utility of engaging in discourse under the name of public health ethics. However, public health ethics must not be considered as a truly isolated focus. It is of extreme importance to stress that drawing boundaries around it as a critical exercise is artificial. Population approaches, the call to political philosophy, or other apparently distinguishing features may suggest novel (or at least, relatively rarer) perspectives, but they do not in truth make public health ethics new, or analytically distinct from social normative theory as it has existed for millennia. Flaws in thinking that have 'evolved' within bioethics – for example unworkable 'autonomy' paradigms – cause unease amongst many theorists,[36] and designing a discipline called 'public health ethics'

---

[34] Ronald Bayer *et al.*, "Introduction: ethical theory and public health", in Ronald Bayer, Lawrence O. Gostin, Bruce Jennings, and Bonnie Steinbock (eds.), *Public Health Ethics – Theory, Policy, and Practice* (Oxford University Press, 2007), p. 4.

[35] John Coggon, "Does *public health* have a personality (and if so, does it matter if you don't like it)?", *Cambridge Quarterly of Healthcare Ethics* (2010) 19:2, 235–248.

[36] See for example, Onora O'Neill, *Autonomy and Trust in Bioethics* (Cambridge University Press, 2002); Willard Gaylin and Bruce Jennings, *The Perversion of Autonomy: Coercion and Constraints in a Liberal Society* (2nd edn) (Washington DC: Georgetown University Press, 2003); Margaret Brazier, "Do no harm – do patients have responsibilities too?", *Cambridge Law Journal* (2006) 65:2, 397–422.

is seen as a means to start afresh; to develop and appraise our paradigms with a better idea of all that is important.[37] We must be careful that this does not lead to a simplistic repackaging exercise. Where poor conceptions exist, they should be disassembled altogether, not left floating in their own 'sphere' of ethics whilst we push forward elsewhere.[38] Rather, public health ethics, if it is to be useful, requires a sense of 'self-awareness' from its commentators, and their recognition of the nature, value, and scope of ethical discourse.

Although ethics generally, and public health ethics specifically, need not be taken to relate to a critical enterprise, for the purposes of analysis, and the useful grounding of norms that may bear on practice, I suggest that it is this more philosophical enterprise that should concern us.[39] I therefore take public health ethics to refer to *the critical ethical evaluation of questions concerning possible, actual, and proposed public health measures*. The 'professional ethics' of public health practitioners may also be referred to as public health ethics and may seem to draw from 'its own' particular principles.[40] But simply knowing that some professional code says something is no more useful than knowing that 'the law' says something.

5.4   Conclusions

Public health law and ethics describe two broad fields of study. The above analysis presents starkly their vast scope, and this feeds a sense that they are not well thought of as 'closed' or 'bounded' areas of study or practical theory. The subject matter of each covers all manner of social issues. With health as the common thread throughout the arguments, rather than a professional practice such as medicine or a disciplinary approach such as tort analysis, we find that almost anything can at least presumptively be of interest to a scholar in public health law and ethics. As suggested in Chapter 3, public health law and ethics may be viewed as such wide-spanning subjects that they become unappealing to some scholars. This is a conclusion that must be accepted.

---

[37] Angus Dawson and Marcel Verweij, "Public health ethics: a manifesto", *Public Health Ethics* (2008) 1:1, 1–2; Angus Dawson, "The future of bioethics: three dogmas and a cup of hemlock", *Bioethics* (2010) 24:5, 218–225.

[38] Coggon, "Does *public health* have a personality?".

[39] Contrast Bruce Jennings, "Frameworks for ethics in public health", *Acta Bioethica* (2003) IX:2, 165–176.

[40] *Ibid.*

However, the issues that public health law and ethics would put under the spotlight are of considerable importance, and need to be debated. Rather than worry about finding or securing the boundaries of these fields, we are better directed to understanding how best to frame and undertake the specific normative analyses that are found to fall within them.

6   Conclusion to Part I

While health is considered to be of such high concern that we should specifically consider the law that does, might, and should relate to it, (public) health law and ethics break down where and to the extent that this central concept is either many things, or an uncertain thing. This raises difficulties. If of necessity policy-makers must embrace a value-laden concept of what is good for us, there is going to be radical disagreement about the concept, and thus of what founds appropriate political measures. We need to respond to this in analysis and public debate. Health-based laws and policies relate to those aspects of health that are deemed to be a shared concern, and thus on which effective value-claims must be made. Above I reviewed some of the key aspects of the literature on the philosophy of health, and clearly there is a wealth of alternative definitions that we must be aware of as we approach analyses of public health.

It is arguable that public health, and public health law and ethics, may in some senses be the logical culmination of normative concepts of health. But if we are to advance useful analyses, or develop defensible policies, looking for conclusive political answers *within* 'public health' is going to be fruitless. The term 'public health' juxtaposes two widely contestable, distinctly normative terms, and has become in many instances usurped as a 'tool' in political, legal, and ethical argumentation. We have seen how it can serve as something that *drives* rather than is *driven by* wider normative considerations. This is not to say that in its different guises it reflects bad or useless things. But there is, quite simply, too much going on conceptually. The term 'public health' often affords a good shorthand, provided its contextualised meaning is clear, but as a concept it is less illuminating and limiting than some may think or hope. We can turn recognition of this to our advantage, by considering a positive point: there is much in the concepts of health and of public that can help us to develop practically useful ethical, legal, and political analyses. Ultimately, it does not matter so much what 'public health' means. What is important is the overall framing of our social interactions. To know how purported 'public health issues' fit into this, we need arguments that lead to an idea of what health is taken to mean in a given instance, and what would make it public.

Part II

Evaluating evaluations: making health public
Introduction to Part II

In Part II my focus is on the nature of analysis in a political sphere, and the views that have been presented by other theorists working in public health law and ethics. I do not aim or claim to offer a comprehensive presentation.[1] Rather, I hope to offer a good representation of the array of arguments that can be found in this area of policy and academic study. My analysis works in part as a hint to a broader depiction of accounts in public health law and ethics, in part as a means to demonstrate quite how wide-ranging and fundamentally opposing distinct accounts can be, in part to show what they share, and primarily as a device to allow the reader to contextualise politically these and other arguments about public health issues. By focusing on the political aspects of the questions, we bring to the fore the nature of and need for a relevantly *all things considered* approach to policy questions, drawing out the germane normative concerns and the important competing issues that sit alongside health matters, which may be obscured if our focus is narrowed by a central endeavour in public health. In other words, my approach allows us to study public health without losing sight of the other things that matter in human society. My purposes in this Part are twofold. First, in Chapter 7, I present the basis for recognising that our concern is necessarily *political*. Second, in both Chapters 7 and 8, I consider key arguments from the broad range of ideas that underpin approaches to politics and policy, allowing us to understand why disagreement is so profound, and why overcoming it may prove so difficult, especially if *moral* consensus is thought necessary.

---

[1] I suspect that such an endeavour would be ill fated, but readers interested in good and much broader presentations of the literature than I can offer in Part II are directed to: Dan Beauchamp and Bonnie Steinbock (eds.), *New Ethics for the Public's Health* (New York: Oxford University Press, 1999); Lawrence O. Gostin, *Public Health Law and Ethics – A Reader* (Berkeley: University of California Press, 2002); Ronald Bayer, Lawrence O. Gostin, Bruce Jennings, Bonnie Steinbock (eds.), *Public Health Ethics: Theory, Policy, and Practice* (Oxford University Press, 2006); Lawrence O. Gostin, *Public Health Law and Ethics – A Reader* (2nd edn) (Berkeley: University of California Press, 2010); Michael Freeman, *The Ethics of Public Health*, vols. I and II (Aldershot: Ashgate, 2010).

7 Analysis in the political realm

7.1 Introduction

The core question of this book is *what makes health public?* My base contention is that this question must be prior, and its answer central, to any endeavour in public health law and ethics. And more practically, its answer supports all claims about the defensibility of any progression in the name of, or conservatism against, proposed public health policy. "What makes health public?" is necessarily a political question, whose proper answer is therefore also political. This may seem a statement of the obvious, but it bears such blunt presentation. Recognising the home of our debate as a political one is key to recognising the sorts of ideas that are (and are not) relevant. This manner of approach shares its rationale with Bernard Williams' exploration of political freedom, and the premium he places on situating its investigation in a political (as opposed, e.g., to a metaphysical) context: in Williams' words: "we must take seriously the point that because it [i.e. political freedom] is a political value, the most important disagreements that surround it are political disagreements".[1] In Part I, I presented seven distinct meanings of public health that find themselves in the literature and in discussions ostensibly on the subject. Their wide variation reinforces any pessimism about finding some unitary definition that everyone has 'in fact been meaning'. It is thus unhelpful to descend into dogmatism about 'what public health is or isn't', or to use such claims as the basis of normative argument. Giving 'public health' a kind of activist role in our deliberations on the best shaping of society is problematic. It is preferable to work out first what society should be about, and allow that to direct our conclusions on how this means, inter alia, public health policies and practices should be. This all amounts to an enterprise in politics, and demands consideration as such.

---

[1] Bernard Williams, "From freedom to liberty: the construction of a political value", *Philosophy and Public Affairs* (2001) 30:1, 3–26, at 5.

In Chapter 2, where we focused on the meaning of public, I followed Bruce Jennings and distinguished 'overlapping concerns' and 'shared concerns'.[2] Overlapping concerns simply refer to matters that affect many or all people. For example, the functioning of the human heart is an overlapping concern; it is something that is relevant to everyone. Health, however it is understood, is an overlapping concern; it is something of relevance to each of us. This is something we can take *ex ante* to be true. It does not of itself mean that we should value each other's health, prioritise it, or even care about it. It just means it is something that affects each of us. *Shared* concerns, by contrast, present themselves where something about one person is, in crude terms, the business of everyone else. Within private relationships, concerns can also be shared. A couple will often share many of their personal concerns, health-related and otherwise. But this idea of sharing is distinct. What we need to find, if public health ethics is to come to anything, are concerns that are shared with *everyone* (within a political community); we need to know, for example, why *my* drinking alcohol might be *yours and everyone else's* business. The current chapter looks at this question. To derive an understanding of political community, I contrast political and moral philosophy, and consider arguments about anarchism and the State. The arguments demonstrate how the political normativity in a community may be related to, and contrasted with, moral and legal normativity. As there is a danger of being 'divided by a common language' on these matters – e.g. what one person calls 'political philosophy' another may call 'legal philosophy' – the first half of the chapter explains how I distinguish moral, political, and legal spheres of thought. The second half sharpens the distinctions through critical analysis of arguments about political authority. Finally, I consider how we should approach paternalism and the 'population perspective', which feature with increasing prominence in debates in public health law and ethics.

7.2   Three spheres of normative discourse: moral, political, and legal

7.2.1   *Distinguishing the moral and the political*

Christopher McMahon succinctly captures the need for a normative and analytic realm separate to morality when he writes: "political society is a peculiarly human phenomenon".[3] The "*raison d'être* of political

---

[2] Chapter 2, section 2.2.
[3] Christopher McMahon, "Autonomy and authority", *Philosophy and Public Affairs* (1987) 16:4, 303–328, at 325.

society", he says, "is to overcome the mutual frustration of moral purposes which ensues when autonomous moral agents follow their own conceptions of the public good."[4] Taken at face value, perhaps at this stage without too much concern for the substance of the words "moral" and "public", this sums up why we do well to look at a political realm, and consider its upshots. Defining 'the political' in a sufficiently broad sense that it captures the sorts of things it seems to need to, yet in a sufficiently narrow sense that it forms a coherent classification, is not easy. It is therefore helpful to work from Thomas McPherson's rough categorisation, which distinguishes the focal points of political and moral philosophy. This makes it possible to contrast them not just by reference to what they *are*, but also by reference to whom they address and what each allows us *to do*:

Morality, it would commonly be said, is concerned with 'personal relations'. (This is in no sense meant as a *definition* of 'morality'.) Politics is concerned with the State and with our relations to the State and its to us – in the liberal tradition with how to achieve peace and security and our interests, and with how to achieve 'more commodious living'.[5]

It is important to emphasise McPherson's reference to "the liberal tradition", as it is in this tradition that the analysis of the current book is applicable.

In approaching political liberalism, I consider it important to draw from three very distinct perspectives. The first is hinted to in McMahon's paper, quoted above, and is at least implicit in the works of theorists as ostensibly diverse as John Rawls and Robert Nozick.[6] On McMahon's account, it is analytic that a community of morally perfect beings would require no externally decreed law; for him, 'the moral' speaks to ideal type agents in an ideal type community. This sort of view is more controversial than some analysts seem to allow. What may very loosely be labelled the 'Kantianism'[7] of much contemporary political liberal theory

---

[4] *Ibid.* Note that McMahon's reference to "the public good" in this quote is to a carefully argued account, developed and described in the paper. The detail of some of this will be considered below (section 7.3), but the less defined characterisation serves for present purposes.
[5] Thomas McPherson, *Political Obligation* (London: Routledge and Kegan Paul, 1967), p. 76.
[6] John Rawls, *A Theory of Justice – Revised Edition* (Oxford University Press, 1999); Robert Nozick, *Anarchy, State, and Utopia* (Oxford: Blackwell, 1974).
[7] As in the sense meant by Raymond Geuss, when he says "A strong 'Kantian' strand is visible in much contemporary political theory, and even perhaps in some real political practice": Raymond Geuss, *Philosophy and Real Politics* (Princeton and Oxford: Princeton University Press, 2008), p. 1. It should not be taken to imply that everyone who falls under this heading is a Kantian, or even 'neo-Kantian': indeed, whilst

hearkens to a final situation (albeit most probably unrealisable on any account) wherein rational moral perspectives converge on an ideal that is a unitary, comprehensive, and preclusive view of the right. In this sense, politics and law may be viewed as necessary encumbrances, introduced to make up for the shortcomings in people – both their epistemic and practical failures in rational agency – in order to allow harmonious and soundly coordinated society, with a minimum of moral infringements, based on what people *should* agree to (and apparently *would* agree to if only they were what they simultaneously are and are not!) given the fact that they will not, or can not, do so.

This 'Kantian' approach contrasts markedly with two alternative understandings of politics, political philosophy, and political inquiry presented by John Gray in *Two Faces of Liberalism* and Raymond Geuss in *Philosophy and Real Politics*.[8] Their respective approaches are importantly different, but both share a strong commitment to engagement with historical and 'real world' contexts, and each grounds his philosophy in the Hobbesian tradition. In both books, there is a tangible sense of weariness about the state of much current political theory. For Gray, it is not wrong that philosophical inquiry should be – in some sense – a pursuit of an ideal. Rather his concern is with the plausibility of claims advanced or rooted in the Kantian or Lockean tradition. In contrast with these, he seeks to draw truths about morality from the way it is evidenced in the world, and seeks to ground good political purposes against this world, as we find it. To explain his perspective, Gray distinguishes two "faces" of philosophical inquiry into political liberalism and their accommodation of morality: in the first sense it is "the search for a rational consensus on the best way of life";[9] in the second it is "the search for terms of peace among different ways of life",[10] "the pursuit of *modus vivendi* in a more plural world".[11] He derides the former as ill-fated, standing in the face of the evident moral 'dissensus'[12] that exists in human societies, and always has and always will. Gray seems

---

attributing this Kantianism to Rawls, Geuss allows that Rawls may be better compared with Hegal than Kant: see p. 89. Compare John Gray's equivalent bugbear, which he labels "the ideal of rational consensus": John Gray, *Two Faces of Liberalism* (Cambridge: Polity Press, 2000), p. 1.

[8] Gray, *ibid.*; Geuss, *ibid.* See also Bruce Jennings, "Autonomy and difference: the travails of liberalism in bioethics", in Raymond Devries and Janardan Subedi (eds.), *Bioethics and Society: Constructing the Ethical Enterprise*, (New York: Prentice Hall, 1998).

[9] Gray, *ibid.*, p. 1.   [10] Gray, *ibid.*, p. 2.

[11] Gray, *ibid.*, p. 1.

[12] This term is not Gray's, but used by Madison Powers, "Bioethics as politics: the limits of moral expertise", *Kennedy Institute of Ethics Journal* (2005) 15:3, 305–322, e.g. at 319.

to take the *truth* of moral pluralism to be an empirical fact about the human world. Some theorists may dispute the strength of his evidence in the sense of its offering what might be called a 'metaphysical' or 'ontological proof about morality'.[13] However, the *'practical* truth' of his position is beyond doubt. Given the fact of competing moralities, *modus vivendi* provides that the role of politics is the pursuit of "compromises amongst incompatible claims",[14] resulting in "a liberal philosophy in which the good has priority over the right, but in which no one view of the good has overall priority over all others".[15] And this in turn gives Gray a clear view of the role of the theorist:

> The task of political philosophy is not to give practice a foundation. It has never had one in the past, yet somehow the human species has stumbled on. The aim of political philosophy is to return to practice with fewer illusions. For us, this means shedding the illusion that theories of justice and rights can deliver us from the ironies and tragedies of politics.[16]

Thus, in Gray's analysis we see a purpose; an ideal to be pursued. He is concerned not about any and all politics or political systems, but specifically with political liberalism. Properly understood, his argument goes, this is a good thing that we should aim towards; it is a sound ideology. Even so, it is harnessed to realities that exist as historical facts about people and the world, rather than ones drawn from theoretical abstractions about hypothetical, unitary, moral society. It is good because it is good for humans, and demands our attention because it speaks to the grounds on which we can harmoniously associate. It is a politically, rather than morally, normative theory, entrenched in an understanding of the human good as true, but plural and contradictory. Thus as analysts our practical concern is not with discerning what is good or right for hypothesised rational beings, less still with forming institutions based on *their* supposed rights; rather it is to study the means of peaceful coexistence of people with distinct moralities, because *that* should be everyone's aim.

---

[13] The impossibility of gaining 'rational proof' of the truth of distinct theories serves, for example, as a fundamental premise in Matti Häyry, *Rationality and the Genetic Challenge – Making People Better?* (Cambridge University Press, 2010). Häyry does not claim that the coexistence of conflicting moralities demonstrates their 'actual' coexistence; rather, his position is that the impossibility of *disproof* leaves each with some sort of legitimate claim to be taken equally seriously. As a methodology, it is not clear how far Häyry's approach can take us: see Matti Häyry, "Can arguments address concerns?", *Journal of Medical Ethics* (2005) 31:10, 598–600; John Coggon, "Confrontations in 'genethics': rationalities, challenges and methodological responses", *Cambridge Quarterly of Healthcare Ethics* (2011) 20:1, 46–55.

[14] Gray, *Two Faces of Liberalism*, p. 133.   [15] *Ibid.*, p. 135.

[16] *Ibid.*, p. 139.

We may contrast both Gray's and the 'Kantian' approach with that of Raymond Geuss, who is not an idealist.[17] His concern is not with what the *ends* of our political theories, institutions, and systems should be, or anyway in unifying these things to one particular end such as *modus vivendi*. Rather, his argument is methodological. Geuss does allow for a real, albeit unstable, understanding of 'the good' as a motivating factor in politics, and allows that its role be labelled "ethics":[18]

Political actors are generally pursuing certain conceptions of the "good," and acting in the light of what they take to be permissible. This is true despite the undeniable fact that most human agents most of the time are weak, easily distracted, deeply conflicted, and confused, and that they therefore do not always do only things they take to be permissible. One will never understand what they are doing unless and until one takes seriously the ethical dimension of their action in the broadest sense of that term: their various value-judgments about the good, the permissible, the attractive, the preferable, that which is to be avoided at all costs.[19]

This view of ethics is important to gain an understanding of politics, but it is only a *part* of its understanding, and clearly gives no credence to the idea that politics in fact can be traced to a single, coherent, moral theory.[20] Indeed Geuss objects in the strongest terms to the idea that politics is "applied ethics" in the sense that analysis should or meaningfully can start with an ideal theory. He is clear that beginning a political analysis by creating in abstraction a 'good political actor', existent only in the universe of 'pure ethics', and *then* considering historical reality when it comes to application, gets things wrong. Instead, he advocates "the realist approach to political philosophy",[21] which:

[I]s centred on the study of historically instantiated forms of collective human action with special attention to the variety of ways in which people can structure and organise their action so as to limit and control forms of disorder that they might find excessive or intolerable for other reasons. This is a historically specific study if only because the concepts of "order" and "intolerable disorder" are themselves variable magnitudes.[22]

His approach works with (non-morally) contingent and non-ideal understandings of 'the good', which he grants to be important and,

---

[17] For the purposes of *Philosophy and Real Politics*, anyway: in surplus to his project, he points the reader to his own politics, but unapologetically refuses to offer a positive alternative to the theories that he argues should be rejected in the book: see pp. 94–95. This is reasonable enough; his concern there is methodological, not ideological.

[18] In an "anodyne" sense, as Geuss puts it: *Philosophy and Real Politics*, p. 1.

[19] *Ibid.*, p. 2.   [20] *Ibid.*, pp. 2–6.

[21] *Ibid.*, p. 22.   [22] *Ibid.*

in some manner, fundamental, but without the richness or coherence to the different ways of life that Gray would protect in accordance with *modus vivendi*. For Geuss, politics is at base about power in real human society. It is not, or is only most peripherally, about ideal theories, and only then ever about them secondarily. Rather, analysts should first look at the world – at people, history, ethnography – and see what, why, and how they are; only second should we bring in theoretical concerns, and then only insofar as they are usefully applicable. Superficially, his project works in part through similar motions to Gray's: he works from and through the importance of historical understanding, and specifically draws out theories of rights and justice as being the tiresome, flawed, and regrettably dominant face of contemporary political philosophy. He differs from Gray by giving a profoundly low estimation of any forms of 'the good' in a sense that affords them – for want of a better term – any sort of moral or even 'practical' dignity. For Geuss, they are facts about the world; interesting from that perspective, and therefore to be learned from for those interested in politics, but only as part of the wide practical context in which politics 'happens'. Politics, on Geuss' account, *may* be about the advancement or refutation of an ideology; it may be normative in senses that appeal to people concerned about making the world a better place. But although it can exist for this amongst other things, it is too much to say that it *does* exist for this. Political theory is dependent on the study of people, and more specifically than this the relations of power (perceived and actual) between them. Political theorists need to understand how things are and have been, and limit their views on how things can and should be to those that fit within the context provided by this 'realism'.

To be clear, the sketches I have made of these three approaches are necessarily brief and thus rob nuanced philosophical works of a great deal of their strength and subtlety. But I hope my summaries suffice as background of the range of issues and arguments that need to be addressed when our analysis is considered in a political as opposed to a moral realm. I am interested in moral arguments, and the idea that a defensible basis be found for policy. Consideration of ideal moral theories is clearly informative in this regard. But I am at the same time minded that the application of any theory will be in the world as we find it, which does demand a prior understanding of that world and how it functions, including the divergence in views on 'fundamental' moral positions. It is therefore useful to go beyond the contrasts and draw from all of the three broad modes of inquiry, each of which is in its own way well described as 'political'.[23] Together they provide access to the sorts of insights needed in useful analysis of public health issues, and whilst they are contradictory approaches, we can coherently draw from the understandings each affords in a more singular methodology, provided we remain wise to the risk of contradiction. These insights allow us to see how useful normative analysis of public health is first and foremost a *political* matter, applicable to societies of humans (with all their frailties of body and of mind), and to recognise the better ways of approaching it as such. This is preferable to either constraining ourselves with irrelevant or partial debates in pure moral philosophy, or engaging in a morally vacuous exercise of social and anthropological descriptivism. Our political inquiry can accommodate concerns from all three perspectives, which may crudely be broken down as follows: *universalist ideal type*, based on claims of unitary liberal rationalism and the best means of protecting it in a community of substandard agents; *pluralist ideal type*, based on claims of equally legitimate, diverse, incommensurable accounts of the good and the best means of protecting them in a community; and *anti-ideal type*, based on amoral considerations of facts about the world and people and power relations.

7.2.2   On conducting analysis under the combined approach

The necessity of combining aspects of each of the three approaches is that the analytic concerns in public health ethics are themselves plural. To conduct evaluative analysis, we need some sort of normative yardstick. This may, for example, be drawn from a 'purely moral' account, such as one of the 'three classical approaches' in Western moral philosophy, typically presented under headings such as consequentialism, deontology, and teleology; or (though these are not quite the same things) utilitarianism, liberalism, and communitarianism.[24] Such ideal-

---

[23]   Cf Alan Cribb, "Translational ethics? The theory-practice gap in medical ethics", *Journal of Medical Ethics* (2010) 36:4, 207–210. Compare too the approach of Madison Powers and Ruth Faden, which combines concern for moral theory with concern for empirical reality: Madison Powers and Ruth Faden, *Social Justice: The Moral Foundations of Public Health and Health Policy* (Oxford University Press, 2006). See discussion of Powers and Faden's theory of public health ethics in Chapter 8, section 8.3. Consider also Häyry's reflections on the inapplicability of pure 'rational' argument: Häyry, "Can arguments address concerns?". Whilst Häyry seems to consider that this renders them practically useless, my own view is that used well they can effectively complement other sorts of argument.

[24]   See, for example, Stephen Holland, *Public Health Ethics* (Cambridge: Polity, 2007), especially chs. 1 and 2. Note Holland also engages with 'principlism': this is something considered in Chapter 8, but no further here. See also Bruce Jennings, "Frameworks for ethics in public health", *Acta Bioethica* (2003) IX:2, 165–176; Marc

type reasoning allows (in principle) for the creation of rationally defensible moral norms, that permit analysts to evaluate how good or right something is. And theories built within one of these models offer criteria for moral judgement or directivity. This is important in accounting for people's being held 'on the pain of consistency', or testing the 'rational coherence' of positions, arguments, and policies. But it can not do all that is needed. Although it can be both noble and productive to assume an idealist position, it often proves less than it might. It is largely a fiction to suppose that everyone really does subscribe to a specific understanding of any given moral principle, other than in a fairly sparse or bland abstract way. Given this, reasoning along the following lines is at best tenuous, and anyway over-simplistic:

We all believe moral principle x is a sound basis for policy. X implies y, so it is crazy that everyone doesn't also support all policies that would be based on y.

This is not about the 'principle of charity' in argument; giving the kindest reading to position of an analyst you are criticising.[25] It is about the actual nature of law and policy-making. Policy is formed on the back of compromise between positions. Claiming that a legislature can straightforwardly be held against the principle underpinning each policy on the pain of consistency is to misunderstand the nature of legislating (at least in liberal democracies as they exist over any significant amount of time). And though we may expect greater consistency in governmental, as opposed to legislative, policy, even then the final positions can and will only rarely be based on a singular, coherent morality.[26]

A different but equally important problem is that the 'we' in a "we all believe x" statement such as that presented above is nearly always used to simplifying or tendentious effect. Consider the following excerpt from part of Geuss' discussion of Rawls:

To whom is the "we" supposed to refer in Rawls's claim that "we" have the intuitive conviction of the absolute primacy of justice? Does "we" mean "all empirical human beings"? Then the claim that "we" think justice has priority is certainly simply false. Does "we" in a Kantian mode purport to refer to "all rational creatures ..."? To believe that Rawls's claim about "our" intuitions concerning the priority of justice in this sense is to subscribe to an extremely

Roberts and Michael Reich, "Ethical analysis in public health", *The Lancet* (2002) 359, 1055–1059.

[25] Cf Søren Holm, "If you have said A, you must also say B: Is this always true?", *Cambridge Quarterly of Healthcare Ethics* (2004) 13:2, 179–184.

[26] Søren Holm, "'Parity of reasoning' arguments in bioethics – some methodological considerations", in Matti Häyry and Tuija Takala (eds.), *Scratching the Surface of Bioethics* (Amsterdam: Rodopi, 2003).

strong, and highly implausible – that is to say, almost certainly false – thesis about the universal structures of human rationality.[27]

Arguments presented on the back of pure moral principle often sound very convincing, and are in many ways seductive. And it is my view that they have a good deal more to offer than Geuss seems to allow. But even so, he is surely right in the line of criticism quoted here. Much apparently compelling moral reasoning simply fails to account for its own fundamental contentiousness, working from blandly acceptable 'high principle', without regard to swathes of competing and intricate qualifications.

The point here is that pure moral reasoning can be granted a role, but it is insufficient alone to do all that is needed in an applicable normative inquiry. The normative yardstick we need must relate to political normativity. It is unclear that 'rational consensus' models of morality can dictate political normativity. Claims that "we think x" are often rather less forceful than they first appear. Moral pluralism and reasonable disagreement are at least 'practically true', and there are good arguments for allowing this *fact* to lessen practical demands made on purely abstract grounds. Geuss forcefully reminds us that we need to look at the world we are addressing, the nature of the people in it, and what is practically possible. And Gray reminds us that there are competing, incommensurable accounts of the good, and politics can be used to accommodate them, rather than to eradicate all but one. Whilst Gray's case is not 'proven' in some rationally conclusive sense (likewise, of course, the 'rational consensus' view), it has sufficient appeal that, in combination with the concerns attributed to Geuss, it gives us reason to look for a different manner of normativity than that found in a singular account of pure morality. We have to look beyond idealised models, even as we allow them to inform our normative conclusions.

Accounting for these three approaches, it is possible to see the following. If we have any concern with making the world a better place – in the current instance, in establishing imperatives relating to public health issues – or even the more modest concern of understanding how good the world is in some regard, then we will, of necessity, look to ideal accounts. But we also need to consider the practical context of our evaluations. This means recognising the shape and scope of the relevant community.[28] The political community is not the abstract moral

---

[27] Geuss, *Philosophy and Real Politics*, p. 85.

[28] Jonathan Wolff, "Harm and hypocrisy – Have we got it wrong on drugs?", *Public Policy Research* (2007) 14:2, 126–135; Jonathan Wolff and Avner de-Shalit, *Disadvantage* (Oxford and New York: Oxford University Press, 2007), introduction; and chs. 8–11.

communities that we encounter in parts of the literature; political communities are often established by reference to criteria that are morally questionable. There is geographical bounding,[29] and becoming a political 'agent' is something generally achieved in contemporary liberal societies by being a born and living member of the human species,[30] rather than by reference to rationally coherent moral criteria. Moral theories, by contrast, will tend to limit the numbers of humans who are due recognition as rights-holders,[31] or open the doors of concern to many other animals too.[32] (The exception, of course, is found in 'natural law' theories that ascribe moral importance to agents by simple virtue of their being human.[33]) To some theorists, speaking from a moral perspective, this political framing will seem arbitrary, uninteresting, or immoral, and thus not in itself defensible.[34] I am more than a little sympathetic with that. Especially as regards transnational obligations to other humans, I am most concerned not to justify 'moral inertia' behind claims about real world limitations to what we can and should do. By working within a predefined political community, it will be argued by some that I concede too much. But conducting analysis within a political frame need not be quite so deterministic as to preclude

[29] See, for example, Christopher Wellman, "Liberalism, samaritanism, and political legitimacy", *Philosophy and Public Affairs* (1996) 25:3, 211–237; David Copp, "The idea of a legitimate State", *Philosophy and Public Affairs* (1999) 28:1, 3–45.

[30] The nature of this claim is a source of considerable contention, and I visit it in detail below, both in this part, and in Part III. Note especially the discussion of Ngaire Naffine, "Who are law's persons? From Cheshire cats to responsible subjects", *Modern Law Review* (2003) 66:3, 346–367.

[31] According, for example, to 'personhood theories', which attach special status to those able to exercise specific mental capacities; see, for example, John Harris, *The Value of Life* (London: Routledge and Kegan Paul, 1985); James Griffin, *On Human Rights* (Oxford University Press, 2008).

[32] On deontological or utilitarian grounds: see e.g. Alasdair Cochrane, "Animal rights and animal experiments: an interest-based approach", *Res Publica* (2007) 13:3, 293–318; Peter Singer, *Animal Liberation* (2nd edn) (London: Pimlico, 1995). With much contemporary thought directed towards "posthuman" and "transhuman" futures, it is probably also worth considering the pre-emptive arguments of philosophers concerned that normative protection is due to non-human animals of species as yet unknown: see e.g. John Harris, "Taking the 'human' out of Human Rights", *Cambridge Quarterly of Healthcare Ethics* (2011) 20:1, 9–20.

[33] See e.g. John Finnis, *Natural Law and Natural Rights* (Oxford University Press, 1980). Note I purposefully do not consider human rights – at least as jural constructs – to classify as an exception in this regard. The scope of human rights – i.e. who counts as a rights-holder in any given moment – is a rather haphazard matter, and the appeals to 'universalism' that seem intrinsic to human rights are so qualified (no doubt in most cases justifiably) that it is implausible to suggest that they offer a coherent *moral* account that applies to all and only born, living humans. Human rights are discussed in Chapter 8, section 8.3.

[34] See e.g. Iain Brassington, *Public Health and Globalisation – Why an NHS is Morally Indefensible* (Exeter: Imprint Academic, 2007).

positive advances; rather, it is our practical normative start point, and it is folly to argue as if it were not.[35]

7.2.3   Parallel concerns and arguments

I hope the foregoing discussion allows the reader to understand what I take 'political' to mean, and see how it is the important locus for inquiry into public health issues. It grounds itself in a different manner to (what I label) morality, gives distinct reasons for understanding the size, nature, and scope of a community, and thus gives its own answers to questions of who is owed what, and thus what claims may be made between agents. As a final note on 'the political' as the normative category that should ultimately concern us, it is instructive to mention that my approach, at least when described as broadly as it is here, is not unique or novel. Without seeking to be exhaustive, we can see it reflects concerns expressed in, and shares many of its most important features with, (some) critiques based in feminist theory,[36] human rights theory,[37] and arguments derived from contemporary theories of civic republicanism.[38] These allusions are not supposed of themselves to lend support to my approach's superiority (another analyst could point as quickly to approaches that disregard the concerns that I consider salient). Rather, they exemplify in alternative terms the manner of normative concern that leads me to what I label the political, in contrast with the moral. In this regard, one argument that does bear more explicit comparison is the parallel reasoning of Madison Powers in his paper "Bioethics as politics".[39] Powers is also wary of the plurality of 'fundamental' and irreconcilable moral perspectives that abound in the critical literature, as well as with separate questions of political philosophy, relating to which matters of moral concern are the proper subject of governmental intervention. Powers focuses on Isaiah Berlin's reference to the "ancient

---

[35] So, for example on the question of transnational obligations, I betray no great pessimism or undue resignation by saying we need to look at the world we find, rather than make detached claims about universalism and ignore any theories that appear to make concessions against that. A productive approach to such issues is: Lawrence O. Gostin and Allyn Taylor, "Global health law: a definition and grand challenges", *Public Health Ethics* (2008) 1:1, 53–63.

[36] See e.g. Françoise Baylis, Nuala Kenny, Susan Sherwin, "A relational account of public health ethics", *Public Health Ethics* (2008) 1:3, 196–209.

[37] See e.g. Andrew Vincent, *The Politics of Human Rights* (Oxford University Press, 2010).

[38] Bruce Jennings, "Public health and civic republicanism", in Angus Dawson and Marcel Verweij (eds.), *Ethics, Prevention, and Public Health* (Oxford University Press, 2007).

[39] Powers, "Bioethics as politics: the limits of moral expertise".

faith" – the view that single objective answers to normative questions in principle exist and thus that the questions can be answered harmoniously[40] – which we may relate to the 'Kantianism' described above.[41] Powers, like Berlin, is sceptical of the truth of the "ancient faith", and appeals also to "an empirically based assessment of the depth of dissensus in the public realm".[42] He goes on to make the compelling suggestion that "those who doubt the plausibility of the Ancient Faith have good reason to suppose that the plurality of morally eligible options enlarges rather than contracts the scope of reasonable disagreement".[43] Furthermore, Powers contends, this level of disagreement is reflected as far again in questions concerning proper (political) government as they do "private virtue".

Insofar as this is true, we are faced with political conflict in the very sense that we find incompatible or combating moralities at once making competing claims. I take from this that resolution or compromise will of necessity have to be found through *political* rather than *moral* theorising and practice. That the *status quo* demands a response that of necessity will not satisfy the more 'puritan' moral philosophers is probably a truism. But for practical answers to be met – for anything, ethics or otherwise, to be 'applied' – we must engage with a world in which competing moralities exist, and where alternative concerns to moral ones also press on political decision-makers (those with power, in its various senses, as is considered so important by Geuss[44]). The analysis of public health issues must take place against, or better still within, this *political* context. Practical questions concerning public health *are* political questions. They are not purely moral, and can not be resolved by simple reference to moral criteria.[45] Powers is right to suspect that

---

[40] See Isaiah Berlin, "Political Ideas in the Twentieth Century", in Isaiah Berlin, *Four Essays on Liberty* (Oxford University Press, 1969).

[41] Given Berlin's great influence on the work of John Gray, this applies in particular to him, and the reasoning that leads to my accounting for his claims about political philosophy. As well as *Two Faces of Liberalism*, see John Gray, *Isaiah Berlin* (Princeton University Press, 1996). Much of the analysis in *Two Faces of Liberalism* seems to be drawn from arguments presented in this earlier book.

[42] Powers, "Bioethics as politics: the limits of moral expertise", at 319.

[43] *Ibid.*, at 320.

[44] As noted above in the core text, power is Geuss' central concern in political philosophy. In making it so, he allows the term a very broad meaning, covering all sorts of power (perceived and actual) that humans may exercise, or threaten to exercise, over each other: see Geuss, *Philosophy and Real Politics*, pp. 26–28.

[45] This may be criticised as being conservative (in a pejorative sense), against the more 'pure' concerns of an uncompromising moral theorist. We visit such concerns in the discussion of anarchism in section 7.3, below. We should note too that the charge of 'conservatism' would be an odd one in the very real sense that the approach I advocate

(bio)ethicists (*qua* 'specialist' moral philosophers) are not the ones to provide the answers that we need. Indeed the central argument of this book is that this is necessarily true. It is political inquiry that can explain the filtering of what would otherwise be uncoordinated brute power. Politics describes the centralising of authority, and the formation of the necessary institutions and practices to allow the society it speaks to to cohere, sustain, and indeed imagine itself.[46] It is through political theory that we can establish how one person's actions are the practical concern of another; how we establish that they are of sufficient concern that the mere (if also profound) fact of his having acted (on some count) immorally warrants some manner of response; and how we express the establishment of norms and institutions that restrict an agent's freedom to do wrong or bad in the first place (and in so doing, limit the import of his freedom to do right or good). It is on the basis of *politics*, and the considerations to which it gives rise, that we formulate concrete notions that can guide us in assessing imperatives that are advanced in the name of public health. Useful normative understandings of public health issues necessarily come from an assessment of political questions; looking simply to moral theories that can not map onto a regulated society of people is of no use.

7.2.4   The legal

A liberal political society requires the assurance of minimum standards of conduct; the limitation of practical freedom and the institution of defensible means of ensuring compliance. This necessarily calls for the articulation and defence of legal mechanisms. The legal, on this count, may be considered as a *part* of the voice of politics. We saw in Chapter 4 the importance of looking beyond accounts of law and policy as a simplistic triad of enforce, prohibit, or allow. Politics finds its voice in laws, regulations, policies, and even less tangible things such as conventions and common practices. 'The law' baldly stated may be seen as the bedrock to these different outputs, but it is not the whole, and all parts are geared *instrumentally* in pursuit of the ends of the political. When we question the legitimacy of a measure, for example a proposal

---

would *conserve* less rather than more: a theorist who sits on the sidelines with a sense that right is on his side, but with no concern for its actually changing anything, is in passive cahoots with the *status quo* he derides. The 'conservatism' of the theorist willing to engage with political reality, in contrast, is what makes him in reality the progressive actor.

[46] See Chapter 2, section 2.2.

to ban smoking tobacco in cars carrying children,[47] our interest will be in the *political* legitimacy of that measure. This is not to deny that some analysts will take their test of legitimacy from a more positivist legal framing, or at least begin committed to an existing source of law: for example, a State may have a written constitution, and the legitimacy of the measure may be held up against that. This manner of inquiry is valuable. It is of notable value when practical questions are raised about the possibility of instituting some new measure. In England, for example, there may be real concern if a proposed statutory regulation seems likely incompatible with obligations enshrined in the Human Rights Act 1998.

Public health law and ethics will contain theorists who limit their interest to the bounds of existing legal norms. This is fine, but it is only a part of the whole inquiry. More interesting to many analysts who see reference, for example, to the constraining or liberating aspects of human rights, will be critiques built around an argument that human rights themselves are *rightly* constraining. For the purposes of the description here, the defence of a practically effective human rights framework will be political. For analysts investigating the question "what makes health public?" a critique of an existing legal situation in light of prevalent or preceding legal norms will not do all that is required. First there is the trite point: "just because it's legal, doesn't mean it's right." But more fundamentally, the investigation is into the nature of health, and then a development of our understanding of the boundaries of responsibilities, claims, and so forth that relate to health. If sound progress is to be made, or conservatism to be defended, we need to know more than what happens; we need to know how and why it should be so. The law is hugely informative, and it is a blinkered theorist who ignores it because "it's nothing to do with morality". It is informative for what it 'says', and also instructive for what it does, and can do. Even a theoretical critique of public health issues requires some practical grounding, and part of that grounding is in law. This is true in two senses.

The first is about context. If we want to know what is practically realisable, we need a good understanding of what is, amongst other things, legally feasible. It is in part for this reason that the impressively broad analysis in Lawrence Gostin's textbooks is so valuable.[48]

---

47 Terence Stephenson [President of the Royal College of Paediatrics and Child Health], "Ban smoking in cars with children", *BBC Online News* (17 June 2009), available at http://news.bbc.co.uk/1/hi/health/8079357.stm.
48 Lawrence O. Gostin, *Public Health Law: Power, Duty, Restraint* (Berkeley: University of California Press, 2000); Lawrence O. Gostin, *Public Health Law: Power, Duty, Restraint* (2nd edn) (Berkeley: University of California Press, 2008).

In some abstracted discussions, it may be useful to make lofty points about what would be best for society, but if we seek to effect change, we need to know what is possible not just in principle, but in practice too. Knowledge of the law helps this, and an understanding of regulation in any given jurisdiction must be integral to sound arguments in favour of legal change, whether that is to improve people's health, or something else. If we remind ourselves that part of analysis of public health as a science is environmental, and much of it relates to the social environment, then it becomes overwhelmingly apparent that the law provides a crucial part of the context – the social environment – that requires examination.[49] To be clear, this does not mean that the law as it exists anywhere necessarily provides a *good* part of the context, or a context that wants in its entirety to be preserved. Simply, it is 'there', and must be accounted for.

The second sense in which law is important, derives from the point already outlined above relating to the law as part of the voice of politics. A political theory will help us to understand certain 'truths' about how society should function: what ends it should pursue; what values underpin it. In order to translate that theory into practical action, various sorts of understanding are needed. In the context of public health policy, scientific understanding is crucial. Effective measures are what we are concerned with. Similarly, legal understanding, and understanding of regulatory theory and practical policy more generally are needed if sound means of addressing problems are to be reached.

It is for these reasons that legal scholarship is so important to debates on public health issues, in unpacking both practical and theoretical problems. The political debate remains central to this book's core question. But like the moral, the legal considerations are not therefore ignored. Law, regulation, and policy will form the final expression of the imperatives (both liberating and constraining) that we draw from whichever political theory we prefer. And to be effective, the bounds of practicability must be understood: for example, what prohibitions could effectively be enforced, what behaviours can pragmatically be monitored? Investigation of such questions is crucial.

7.2.5   Conclusion on the three spheres of normativity

In the first half of this chapter, I have started to establish how meaningful normative discussions on public issues begin when we start discussing

---

[49] Wendy Parmet, *Populations, Public Health, and the Law* (Washington: Georgetown University Press, 2009).

issues in political philosophy. If we distinguish moral, political, and legal arguments, it helps us to uncover what is going on here. The three may be considered under one heading, but that obscures important distinctions in the upshot of their exploration. Furthermore, by separating them, we see more clearly the nature of the conceptual, and ultimately practical, inquiry that is undertaken when we place public health under the spotlight. I have embraced this separation, and would note particularly the structured and formalised nature of a political community, as contrasted with a more ethereal collective that might be described as a moral community. In a political community, the practical nature and import of normative concerns is qualitatively distinct to those in a moral community. In contrast with some moral theories, a defensible political theory can account for compromise between competing positions, and need not speak to every matter of moral concern. A plurality of competing and contradictory moral theories can be sustained within one system of political liberalism, sometimes in whole, and often in great part. A concept of the State provides a particular source of normative concerns, and distinct subjects to those addressed by moral theory. Morality – and moral arguments – may inform our positions about law and policy, but politics can be non-ideal in a way that morality can not be.

For the purposes of the current work, 'the law' is conceived as part of the output of political positions. This contrasts with how matters are framed in many texts on jurisprudence, where law is conceived in a similar manner to what I call 'the political'. I hope this distinction can be viewed as the terminological one that it is, rather than some 'territorial' analytic claim. Works in jurisprudence are of great relevance here; it is just most useful to consider 'the law' to be part of the State's mechanisms for promoting and protecting various norms, and conceive of the interesting evaluative discussions under the heading of political philosophy. Finally, the reader is reminded of the discussion in Chapter 4, where we saw how legal measures form only part of a wider scheme of possible instruments that the State may use to realise the claims and obligations entailed in its underlying political philosophy. The defensibility (or otherwise) of law and policy will come back to the political questions. Morality may inform the normativity of our political system; the legal possibilities will inform, in part, what is practically realisable. But the ultimate area of analytic interest is the political argument.

When I say something is made public, I mean that it becomes a practical matter of shared concern amongst a political community understood as being answerable to one another, with this 'answering' mediated through the State, in accordance with its laws and policies.

Put another way, making a matter public means bringing it into the realm of the political, and, in the practical senses that this may imply, making it a shared responsibility. How the underpinning is established, and what its implications are, will vary between different States and different theories. The remainder of Part II is devoted to establishing how things generally, and health specifically, may be made public. In order to do this, it is necessary to consider how and why health could enter the political sphere in the first place; why accept that there should be any body called the State, claiming or denying practical authority to ensure the proper sharing of, inter alia, health concerns?

7.3   Anarchism, morality, and politics

7.3.1   Developing the political context

There are many layers to political disagreement, with contestations over ideological as well as empirical claims. There are disputes about the scope of the public – about who is in and who is out – and how much each person is 'his brother's keeper'. There are foundational issues concerning the basis and import of political authority, the relationship (if any) between political authority and political obligation, and the relationship (if any) between moral and political philosophy. In the current section, I present no attempt at final resolution to these debates, but rather introduce the terms on which they present themselves. This will allow the reader to recognise the foundational problems in public health law and ethics, and to see the bases of different positions explored explicitly in this book, as well as positions that feature elsewhere in the literature. It will also expose the need to account for a particular perspective – often labelled the 'population perspective' – in assessments of public health. We will come to this issue towards the end of the chapter.

In its report *Public Health–Ethical Issues*, the Nuffield Council on Bioethics invites its readers to imagine a spectrum of political positions spanning from libertarianism to extreme collectivism or contractarianism.[50] This idea is instructive, but with a small modification it becomes a much more powerful heuristic. We learn more about the significance of making health public if we begin from the very extreme

[50] Nuffield Council on Bioethics, *Public Health – Ethical Issues* (London: Nuffield, 2007), pp. 13–14. An alternative way of describing this is a spectrum from libertarianism to interventionism: Karen Jochelson, *Nanny or Steward? – The Role of Government in Public Health* (London: King's Fund, 2005), p. 4.

of individualism: not libertarianism, but *anarchism*. With anarchism, there is no overarching political framework: no political community, no public. By understanding why anarchism might and might not be attractive, we gain greater insight into if, why, and how we should make things public. There is a further advantage to this approach. A 'liberty bias' ('liberty' here meaning freedom from political constraint) is often discerned in the literature and policy documents,[51] in reflection of normative claims that liberty is the natural default, given a supposed start point in a 'state of nature' and claims that any interference with it requires justification. For some analysts this is inherently and factually problematic.[52] For others it reflects the way things should be.[53] However, allowing libertarianism to sit at the end of the spectrum is necessarily question-begging, ignoring as it does the question of philosophical anarchism. Furthermore, depending how liberty is measured, and what reasons there are for shunning anarchism, it is not clear without argument either (contentiously) that libertarianism is the most liberty-friendly political doctrine,[54] or (less contentiously) that, having shunned anarchism, the following legitimate political steps can take us only as far as libertarianism.[55] By unpacking some of the arguments surrounding anarchism, and establishing why and how a political community is a good thing, we address some of the often unargued presumptions that are taken to support the libertarian position as being the one from which any deviation requires justification. This does not remove the 'burden of proof' from other parties, but rightly places it as

[51] See Angus Dawson, "Political philosophy and public health ethics", *Public Health Ethics* (2009) 2:2, 121–122; James Wilson and Angus Dawson, "Giving liberty its due, but no more: Trans fats, liberty, and public health", *American Journal of Bioethics* (2010) 10:3, 34–36.

[52] George Klosko, for example, suggests that taking the 'state of nature' as our default, and out of whose way we must find justification, simply provides the wrong start point, ignoring as it does the *fact* that individuals are *already* members of – and beneficiaries of – societies: George Klosko, "The natural basis of political obligation", *Social Philosophy and Policy* (2001) 18:1, 93–114. See also the critique of simplistic accounts of Millian liberalism in Angus Dawson and Marcel Verweij, "The steward of the Millian State", *Public Health Ethics* (2008) 1:3, 193–195.

[53] Emphatically we might consider here Robert Paul Wolff, *In Defense of Anarchism* (with a new preface) (Berkeley: University of California Press, 1998). And in the context of public health, the forceful advocacy of libertarian thinkers such as Richard Epstein, "In defense of the 'old' public health", *Brooklyn Law Review* (2004) 69:4, 1421–1470.

[54] Contentiously in part because libertarianism is not, of course, just one thing, and in part because it depends what is meant by liberty. Even so, I find most persuasive Samuel Freeman's arguments concerning the nature of many conceptions of libertarianism and the priority they afford not to liberty, but to property: see Samuel Freeman, "Why libertarianism is not a liberal view", *Philosophy and Public Affairs* (2001) 30:2, 105–151.

[55] As influentially argued in Nozick, *Anarchy, State, and Utopia*.

weightily on the libertarians arguing about public health law and ethics as it does on their contenders.

Before engaging further, it is important to note one caveat: the broad brush strokes here can not paint every account that labels itself 'libertarian', 'anarchist', and so forth. This is a necessary price to pay for the purposes of the current analysis (and a concession made in other such analyses in the political philosophy literature). Thus, whilst I do not claim to speak to every school of thought, let alone every understanding within a particular doctrinal approach, I hope that the discussion is useful in illuminating the core concerns that require response in any analysis of or in public health law and ethics. I present my thoughts through a series of contrasts that arise when theorists seek to ground a defensible policy position against the backdrop of political theory. When considering the nature of the State – typically conceived as a geographically bounded structure, comprising a legal system and a government that can give authoritative commands, employ coercive measures to ensure compliance, and mediate conflicts between aggrieved parties in its citizenry and on its territory – various questions arise concerning legitimacy and conflicts with the demands of morality. Let us look at these, to see how they assist analysis as it bears on public health.

7.3.2   Politics: moving beyond the noble fools versus the brutes who would sell their own grandmothers

At the root of disputes in political philosophy, it might be argued, we face and need to overcome the practical dilemma caricatured in the conflict between perspectives in deontological ('rights based') and consequentialist ('utilitarian') ethics; between protagonists who are committed to the view that there are such things as side-constraints – what might be labelled 'basic rights' – and protagonists who see such things as undue interferences with good outcomes or policy. The two sides of the debate may be presented in the unkind light cast upon them in the heading to this section. The person who defends rights until the bitter end is taunted for doing so even if society is bound therefore to reach (unsurprisingly enough) a bitter end. And his opponent is derided for defending a system where a consequentialist calculation can allow that some great personal evils are justified, or even mandated, when the greater good dictates.

Against this backdrop, efforts in political theory generally, and political liberalism specifically, may be conceived as attempts at harmoniously reconciling these two broad perspectives.[56] Perhaps in classical philosophy, this reconciliation was achieved with a more natural symbiosis of moral and political concerns: 'communitarian virtue ethics', or 'civic republicanism', naturally treat moral and political communities as one and the same thing, drawing from a single source of normativity.[57] In contrast, political liberalism as it is found in much contemporary theory may be seen as a phenomenon born following the divorce of politics and morality. This is the view of Thomas McPherson, who draws a clear analytic distinction between political and moral philosophy,[58] but notes that historically the divide was not comparably stark:

> The Greek philosophers did not distinguish as sharply as we do between morals and politics: [for them,] man is a social and political animal, and the good life is only to be lived in society and, moreover, in political society.[59]

Over time this perspective changed, argues McPherson, perhaps markedly since Machiavelli, leading to our now having separate spheres

---

[56] Although these matters do not 'begin with' John Stuart Mill, the point I am making in this section is clearly reflected in the debates over the (arguable) inconsistencies between Mill's utilitarianism and his political liberalism: for an attempt at refutation of the charge of inconsistency, through reconciliation of the apparently discordant theories, see David Brink, "Mill's deliberative utilitarianism", *Philosophy and Public Affairs* (1992) 21:1, 67–103.

[57] Thus in public health ethics there are cogent communitarian accounts. Some are heavily influenced by classical theory: e.g. Jennings, "Public health and civic republicanism"; Bruce Jennings, *Civic Health: Political Theory in Public Health and Health Policy*, (forthcoming) (though note that Jennings' account entails developments taken from liberal political theories in the line of John Stuart Mill and Isaiah Berlin). Other communitarian ethics also draw from this manner of perspective, such as 'relational' accounts in feminist theory: e.g. Baylis, Kenny, and Sherwin, "A relational account of public health ethics". I sense (and only time will tell whether I am right to do so) that republican models will become increasingly prominent in bioethics generally, and in public health ethics particularly. Richard Ashcroft hints at the same when referring to "untapped resources in political philosophy" in his inaugural lecture "The Republic of Health" (London, 19 May 2010). Rather than defend against the caricature of sinister paternalism, personified in the wrong-headedly benevolent doctor of late-twentieth century bioethical 'narratives', increasing interest will focus on shared responsibilities; what citizens (*qua* patients *and* non-patients) owe themselves and each other. I do not claim to be the first to hint towards this manner of thinking: compare, for example, the review and argument presented in Ronald Bayer and Amy Fairchild, "The genesis of public health ethics", *Bioethics* (2004) 18:6, 473–492; H. Martyn Evans, "Do patients have duties?", *Journal of Medical Ethics* (2007) 33:12, 689–694. Consider also the arguments and reflections in Margaret Brazier, "Do no harm – do patients have responsibilities too?", *Cambridge Law Journal* (2006) 65:2, 397–422, against the backdrop of Brazier's works as a key pioneer in English medical law, and the great work she has done in advancing the rights of patients.

[58] Notwithstanding his observation that "Ethical philosophers and political philosophers tend to be the same people": Thomas McPherson, *Political Obligation* (London: Routledge and Kegan Paul, 1967), p. 76.

[59] *Ibid.*

of morality and politics. At times there will be little or no difference between the two. But as a matter of fact (or perhaps a better word would be 'practice') *and* as an analytic truth, both in our discussions of morality and politics and in what we consider each to deem permissible or imperative, they differ.

It is instructive to explore how contemporary liberal political theorists try to overcome apparent disputes between moral and political norms. Whilst political liberalism, broadly conceived, may be an umbrella term covering (putatively) morally defensible political systems, the questions are more subtle, and reinforce the intuition to follow McPherson and acknowledge a formal distinction between morality and politics. As described in section 7.2, politics seems to be more about protection and/or optimisation of x good or rights given people's 'imperfect' conditions, or the imposition of amoral – or even apparently immoral – constraints in order to achieve a better (in x sense) situation. Political normativity, given its voice through the State's regulatory measures, is the necessary product of our manifest 'imperfection'. Granted this, we must make concessions in our understandings of sound political normativity that would not apply in a moral account that speaks only to and for 'pure moral agents'.

In doing this, we should note that it is common to distinguish obligations that respond to 'coordination problems' (e.g. which side of the road to drive on) and those founded on 'wrongs in themselves' (e.g. acts of wanton violence).[60] Some commentators distinguish these categorically, arguing that the coordination issues may be incumbent for moral actors, but are not themselves matters relevant to questions of political authority.[61] However, even if we limit our concern to moral wrongs in themselves, it is not clear that we can even 'in principle' achieve a post-political utopian society. As discussed above, whilst Christopher McMahon suggests that with moral perfection comes the manner of societal harmony that would allow political society to "wither away",[62] this seems to rely on the truth of there being a single, moral way of life; the end point of what John Gray describes as "the liberal project of a universal regime".[63] Gray, as we have seen, refutes the basis of this truth claim. If Gray is right, political harmony is needed in order to allow shared society to function, but is not a logical endpoint of a gradual

---

[60] See e.g. A. John Simmons, "The anarchist position: a reply to Klosko and Senor", *Philosophy and Public Affairs* (1987) 16:3, 269–279, at 275ff.

[61] See e.g. McMahon, "Autonomy and authority", at 326. See also Leslie Green, "Authority and convention," *The Philosophical Quarterly* (1985) 35:141, 329–346.

[62] McMahon, "Autonomy and authority", at 325.

[63] Gray, *Two Faces of Liberalism*, p. 2.

convergence on enlightened, rational morality. Here, the formality of the divide between morality and politics is necessarily stark. In Gray's words:

[Political] liberalism is not a partisan claim for the universal authority of a particular morality, but the search for terms of coexistence between different moralities. In this alternative view, liberalism has to do with handling the conflicts of cultures that will always be different, not founding a universal civilization.[64]

It is important to revisit this view not as an attempted knock-down argument in favour of the separability of morality and politics, but as a plausible argument in its favour. To reiterate the argument above, what Gray describes is at the very least a 'practical truth'.[65] This suggests that we may not presume that morality obtains in a unitary or universally applicable system. As Powers forcefully demonstrates, we do well to note alternative perspectives on morality and politics, and the probability of their being demonstrative of 'reasonable disagreement'.[66] However, to sidestep the epistemic questions about 'rational foundations' does not automatically allow us to skip theoretical questions about the formal separateness of morality and politics. To argue that they are separate formally, and not just practically, we need to consider *moral* objections to political authority, and assess how compelling these are.

7.3.3   Anarchism

If we are to test the idea that health may demand any binding obligations or meaningful freedoms, it is useful to consider the basis of anarchist objections to any form of political system. In rough terms, these may be based on one of two grounds. The first, more prosaic objection to political authority lies with the empirical claims of those whom Christopher Wellman labels "descriptive anarchists".[67] Descriptive anarchists disagree with "descriptive statists" about whether we should have a political system. But they do not do so on ideological grounds; rather they argue, contrary to descriptive statists, that *as a matter of fact* we will be better off without a State than with it. Their methodology

---

[64] *Ibid.*, p. 138.
[65] That is to say, our epistemic deficit here leaves us with two alternatives in rational discourse: go no further because 'we just can't know', or take it for what it suggests to be the case, and work from there: cf Becky Cox White and Joel Zimbelman, "Abandoning informed consent: an idea whose time has not yet come", *Journal of Medicine and Philosophy* (1998) 23:5, 477–499, at 482–484.
[66] Powers, "Bioethics as politics: the limits of moral expertise".
[67] Wellman, "Liberalism, samaritanism, and political legitimacy", at 229ff.

is consequentialist and their question is straightforward: which offers the better outcome, existence in the 'state of nature' or existence in the State? This is important to note in part as there is often a sense that apparently ideological positions in public health ethics are presented with reference to the strength of their practical consequences.[68] Note too, that an analyst may be a more specifically defined 'descriptivist'; for example, a 'descriptive small State libertarian'. What is crucial here is that his defence of a system is based on its conducing to the best outcome, rather than on claims about side-constraints against, for example, non-voluntarily accepted interferences.

Naturally enough, the alternative anarchist objection to the State lies in the pre-eminence of morality; objections of theorists that Wellman describes as "normative anarchists".[69] Here we find accounts based without regard to consequences, and instead rooted firmly in principle. A famous defence of normative anarchism is that presented by Robert Paul Wolff.[70] Wolff sees it as given that an insuperable individualism is inextricably linked to morality, which he takes to be the supreme source of normativity. He argues that:

The fundamental assumption of moral philosophy is that men are responsible for their actions. From this assumption it follows necessarily, as Kant pointed out, that men are metaphysically free, which is to say that in some sense they are capable of choosing how they shall act.[71]

From here, it is a small step that takes Wolff to his central and, as he sees it, conclusive contention, which he believes is fatal to any claim of political authority:

Every man who possesses both free will and reason has an obligation to take responsibility for his actions, even though he may not be actively engaged in a continuing process of reflection, investigation, and deliberation about how he ought to act …

The responsible man is not capricious or anarchic, for he does acknowledge himself bound by moral constraints. But he insists that he alone is the judge of those constraints.[72]

---

[68] For interesting contrasts in this regard, compare Ivan Illich, *Limits to Medicine – Medical Nemesis: The Expropriation of Health*" (London: Marion Boyars, 1995 [1976]); Epstein, "In defense of the 'old' public health"; Norman Daniels, Bruce Kennedy, and Ichiro Kawachi, "Why justice is good for our health: The social determinants of health inequalities", *Daedalus* (1999) 128:4, 215–251; and Lawrence O. Gostin and Madison Powers, "What does social justice require for the public's health? Public health ethics and policy imperatives", *Health Affairs* (2006) 25:4, 1053–1060.

[69] See also McMahon, who creates a similar distinction to Wellman's, but describes the positions as "consequentialist anarchists" and "libertarian anarchists": McMahon, "Autonomy and authority".

[70] Wolff, *In Defense of Anarchism*.

[71] *Ibid.*, p. 12.   [72] *Ibid.*, p. 13.

So Wolff's view is neither that people are morally free to do wrong – he recognises morality and its demands – nor that mutual cooperation is wrong, foolhardy, or unacceptable. Instead, he opposes the idea that *the State* has any business imposing duties on people. To deny people the physical freedom to do right (or wrong) is an unjustifiable infringement of their moral right (and duty) to do right of their own accord. And for people to accept the rule of others, "forfeit[ing] their duty unceasingly to weigh the merits of the actions which they perform", makes them "no better than children".[73] In a very different sense to that employed by Rousseau,[74] but with no less practical or rhetorical force, Wolff would force people to be free, or anyway refuse to recognise any right or liberty not to be free.

Wolff's position, then, is primarily based in normative anarchism. It is worth noting that in his acceptance of voluntary coordination, however, he also seems to appeal to a utopian vision (albeit in largely modest terms) that suggests descriptive anarchists/statists should think seriously about the upshot of everyone's ceasing to recognise the undue (merely 'de facto') legitimacy of the State. (Wolff makes the following claim, which I confess to find rather unsettling: "I personally would feel quite safe in an America where soldiers were free to choose when and for what they would fight."[75]) How convincing these utopian claims are, we might wonder. But they contrast interestingly with the third part of Robert Nozick's *Anarchy, State, and Utopia*[76] (Nozick, of course, argues for the legitimacy of a minimal State, rather than in complete opposition to its possible authority). The contrast is interesting in part because the bounds of permissible actions within their respective utopian visions are quite distinct: Wolff places a premium on moral freedom, whilst Nozick's primary concern seems to be freedom in relation to property (including of one's self).[77] In each case, a sceptical reader may be forgiven for thinking that the dice are loaded in favour of the outcome; that the inquiry into State legitimacy is doomed to its fate as the logical consequence of premises that themselves really ought to be the focus of inquiry and justification. In both books we are essentially told *x*, and then invited to join in an exploration of *not x*. It is

---

[73] *Ibid.*, p. 72.

[74] Indeed Wolff explicitly considers and rejects Rousseau's arguments as invalid: see *ibid.*, pp. 48–58.

[75] *Ibid.*, p. 80.   [76] Nozick, *Anarchy, State, and Utopia*.

[77] Although Nozick peppers his analysis with reference to Kantian moral philosophy, this distinction is no doubt due to Nozick's base contentions lying in Lockean theory, in contrast with Wolff's near exclusive reliance on an understanding of Kant's metaphysics of morality.

unsurprising that *not x* is incompatible with *x*, and what would be more useful (and interesting) is the proof of *x*.[78]

Wolff takes for granted that interference with individual freedom is categorically wrong. It is hardly surprising, then, that he goes on to find that such interference can not be justified![79] He presents political philosophy as "a dependent or derivative discipline" of moral philosophy.[80] And in so doing, he takes it as evident that concerns regarding the State are concerns with (exclusively) moral concepts, and the import of terms such as 'right' and 'duty' is adequately found in morality. If the supreme answers are *in* moral philosophy, and political philosophy is a part of moral philosophy, then coherence dictates that the two can not offer conflicting norms. And the ordering means morality does not just 'trump' politics; it wipes it back out of existence. In Nozick's case, he asserts various rights, which with some manner of modesty he admits he will not defend, and then presents the morally legitimate bounds of political authority given these. But almost exactly as in Wolff's case, we retain moral philosophy as the meaningful locus of inquiry, and political philosophy seems at best spare (or cripplingly subservient), and at worst non-existent. This point is worth emphasising. If politics is to mean anything, and warrant analysis in its own right, it is most odd to make it a redundant category. If we are persuaded, for example, of Wolff's or Nozick's position, this does not mean simply that we should not believe it plausible that politics and morality can serve each as (categorically) separate sources of normativity, with the likely upshot that their demands are not carbon copies of each other. It means that there is no political philosophy to be studied.

This contrasts, as we have seen, with the view of politics presented by Raymond Geuss, and of political obligation as developed by Thomas McPherson.[81] It is at odds, also, with Bernard Williams' conception of political philosophy, which he sees as qualitatively distinct from moral philosophy:

---

[78] With reference to Nozick, Raymond Geuss puts this criticism rather less kindly, though no less fairly, saying: "In the much-quoted first sentence of his book *Anarchy, State, and Utopia* he [Nozick] writes, 'Individuals have rights, and there are things no person or group may do to them (without violating their rights)' (p. ix). He then allows that bald statement to lie flapping and gasping for breath like a large, moribund fish on the deck of a trawler, with no further analysis or discussion, and proceeds to draw consequences from it": Geuss, *Philosophy and Real Politics*, p. 64.

[79] He does argue in defence of 'direct democracy', in a manner that seems inconsistent with the rest of his argument. James Sterba reports subsequently that Wolff himself renounces this line of argument: James Sterba, "The decline of Wolff's anarchism", *The Journal of Value Inquiry* (1977) 11:3, 213–217.

[80] Wolff, *In Defense of Anarchism*, p. 10.   [81] See above, section 7.2.2.

The idea of the political is to an important degree focused in the idea of political disagreement; and political disagreement is significantly different from moral disagreement. Moral disagreement is characterized by a class of considerations, by the kinds of reasons that are brought to bear on a decision. Political disagreement is identified by a field of application – eventually, about what should be done under political authority, in particular through the development of state power. The reasons that go into political decisions and arguments that bear on them may be of very various kinds. Because of this, political disagreement is not merely moral disagreement, and it need not necessarily involve it, though it may do so; equally, it need not necessarily be a disagreement simply of interests, though of course it may be.[82]

I do not here just cite some disagreement with Wolff's and Nozick's approach and expect this to serve as a refutation of their positions. However, Williams is surely right (i.e. it is analytic) when he goes on to argue that anarchism is not a political position in the sense of being able to speak to political problems or values.[83] It is hard to see how Wolff (or any normative anarchist) could dispute this. So, far from finding that political philosophy is derivative, dependent, or anything else in relation to moral philosophy, the normative anarchist talks it into and then back out of existence. Surely it is conceptually tenable (i.e. coherent) to deny the existence of politics. But it is also clear that many issues raised in debates that are framed as political still need to be addressed in a manner that this narrower category of moral philosophy is simply not equipped to address. Not least are the following contingent and practical points: the political community (Wolff might label it the 'de facto community') is not coextensive with Wolff's moral community; and the 'real world limitations' even amongst the best of us[84] require more grounded, practical responses through – for want of a term – political measures. There are 'de facto' members of the community who require consideration.[85] There are coordination problems, as explained above. And there are apparent imperatives to limit (even eradicate some) wrongs in themselves, within the imperfect communities we find. Public health as a political question by definition can not interest, or even be discussed with, the normative anarchist who claims these matters are based on misplaced assumptions and do not warrant, or are incompatible with, meaningful normative analysis. But for the rest, let us now move to consider reasons for invoking a realm of normativity

---

[82] Williams, "From freedom to liberty: the construction of a political value", at 6.

[83] Ibid., at 14.

[84] Granted everyone's inability, with the best will in the world(!), constantly to reason.

[85] For example, children: see further Part III.

distinct from the moral, and efforts to reconcile its justification and desirability.

7.3.4   Towards the State

In the previous section, I distinguished empirical and normative anarchism. The former remains of direct interest to an inquiry into public health, inasmuch as it looks to the effectiveness of a system rather than to its ideological underpinnings; an empirical anarchist may be compared with a 'healthy sceptic'. A normative anarchist, by contrast, will hold doggedly to idealised claims about the uncompromising demands of morality, in (generally implicit) conjunction with an empirical claim that all members of society unproblematically reflect the moral agents on which and for whom his moral theory is based. I shall continue to argue in this section that normative anarchism, in this way, speaks to too narrow a community, and ignores fundamental 'real world' considerations that should not be overlooked. We require, or so I contend, a political arena, both for critical inquiry and as an ultimate source of practical normativity. In section 7.2 I made the argument in support of political inquiry; now I will address questions of political authority.

7.3.4.1 Coercion and control   In examinations of the State's claims to legitimacy, a prominent concern that is raised – and seen sometimes as a paradox or contradiction – with political authority is the simultaneous appeal to moral duty (i.e. to citizens' obligations to do as the government requires because it is right that they do so) and the pre-emptive threat of coercive measures should citizens not fulfil their duty.[86] Whilst a monopoly on the rightful use of coercive force is often considered a defining feature of the legitimate State, it is also held up as the defining feature of its authoritative failure: how, it is asked, can an authority at once demand respect as an authority *and* threaten force if it is not followed?[87] If its citizens are morally cognisant, morally valuable agents, the State can not be said to respect them if it appeals to fear or apprehension rather than moral reasons. Given this, whether we are concerned with coordination problems or the prevention of wrongs in themselves, we are presented with the following, apparent conundrum: if the State's commands give independent and authoritative reasons for acting, why

---

[86] See e.g. Meir Dan-Cohen, "In defense of defiance", *Philosophy and Public Affairs* (1994) 23:1, 24–51.
[87] *Ibid.*

does it need coercion, and how can its threats not undermine its claims to authority?

Prior to engaging with ways these questions might be addressed, it is necessary to consider what coercion is, and how it relates to other possible manifestations of State power, because clearly every command of the State is not backed by a sanction. We saw in Chapter 4 the great range of policy approaches that may be employed individually or in combination to modify people's behaviour without resort to coercion. And in the context of justifications of authority, the need to focus on a more nuanced approach to regulatory theory is something Herbert Hart raises in his discussion of the relationship between law and morality. With regard to John Stuart Mill's arguments in *On Liberty*, Hart makes the point that:

This distinction between the use of coercion to enforce morality and other methods which we in fact use to preserve it, such as argument, advice, and exhortation, is both very important and much neglected in discussions of the present topic.[88]

In other words, there are more subtle mechanisms available than blunt coercion that may be used to change behaviour. This richer understanding of regulation (and less formal directive mechanisms) finds vogue too in Richard Thaler and Cass Sunstein's well noted discussions of "nudge paternalism",[89] and makes concerns about coercion seem more peripheral than much literature on political authority suggests would be the case. However, acknowledgement of this cuts in two directions. On the one hand, it recommends a wider focus to that raised by understandings that the State simply declares rules and threatens force if its declarations are not obeyed. On the other hand, it recommends a more acute wariness of other means of control that might be employed: it suggests we should not simply focus our inquiry on coercive policy, but rather consider the wisdom and basis of non-coercive measures too. Notwithstanding the anarchist objections raised by Wolff, we may need to worry not only about the surrender of liberty to coercive measures, but also its practical diminishment in the face of a centralised system of regulatory mechanisms. Briefly, coercion is a legitimate source of concern, but we should not treat it as the only exercise of the State

[88] H.L.A. Hart, *Law, Liberty, and Morality* (Stanford University Press, 1963), p. 75.
[89] Cass Sunstein and Richard Thaler, "Libertarian paternalism is not an oxymoron", *The University of Chicago Law Review* (2003) 70:4, 1159–1202; Richard Thaler and Cass Sunstein, *Nudge: Improving Decisions About Health, Wealth, and Happiness* (London: Penguin Books, 2009).

that repays critical inquiry in the face of concerns about the legitimate control of behaviour.[90] As Geuss puts it:

Perhaps, as Weber thought, the characteristic of modern states is that they have control over the threat to use certain kinds of concentrated force as their *ultima ratio*, but not all politics is, in its immediate phenomenal reality, about the control of violence. There are, after all, as Weber knew very well, other ways of coordinating human action apart from the use of force. So a more realistic understanding of what is at issue in politics in a wider variety of circumstances would connect it with attempts to provide legitimacy not simply for acts of violence, but for any kinds of collective action, such as deciding voluntarily to build a new road or change to a new unit of measurement … or for that matter any arrangements that could be seen as capable of being changed, controlled, modified, or influenced by human action. This will include institutions, patterns of distribution of access to resources, and other similar things.[91]

Furthermore, coercion itself is an ambiguous concept. Grant Lamond notes two things that are referred to in discussion of State coercion: there are coercive laws (meaning "that at least parts of 'the law' provide for the use of coercion"[92]); and coercive institutions contained within legal systems (meaning "agencies or officials charged with giving coercive effect to the law"[93]). Lamond makes clear why it is important not to conflate, or see necessary correspondence between the imposition of a sanction and the exercise of physical force. In his argument:

Neither the use of physical force nor the use of sanctions are ultimately reducible to one or the other. Instead they correspond to two distinct *modes* of coercion – which may be described as 'physical compulsion' and 'rational compulsion'. What is common to all modes of coercion, and what makes them instances of coercion, is the underlying notion of sufficient pressure being brought to bear by one person to *force* or *make* another person do as the first wills. Hence to be coerced into doing something is not to do it voluntarily: it is to do it against one's will. But there are different sorts of pressure which can achieve this, and it is *pressure* – not physical force nor sanctions – which is the key operative factor in coercion.[94]

Beyond their being different "modes", Lamond distinguishes physical and rational compulsion on two grounds. First, he suggests that only

---

[90] In the context of public health ethics, consider e.g. Stephen John's discussion of the government's approach to vaccination policy following the MMR scandal, and his cynicism of the underpinning threat of coercion, given the clear outcome that the government wanted to achieve: Stephen John, "Expert testimony and epistemological free-riding: the MMR controversy", *The Philosophical Quarterly* (2011), 61:244, 496–517.

[91] Geuss, *Philosophy and Real Politics*, p. 35.

[92] Grant Lamond, "The coerciveness of law", *Oxford Journal of Legal Studies* (2000) 20:1, 39–62, at 41.

[93] *Ibid.*   [94] *Ibid.*, at 43–44.

physical compulsion is irresistible, and second that rational compulsion can be relative to what is demanded in a way that physical compulsion can not (e.g. "a threat to damage a car might compel someone to move it, but not compel them to injure another person"[95]). Regarding these distinctions, Lamond is mistaken. He seems to trip up on a confusion of compulsion and attempts at compulsion, somehow allowing the latter only to relate to rational compulsion. To take his second distinction first, we see that it quickly collapses under scrutiny. An agent is given a reason or reasons, and is either compelled or not. The question of relativity is in this sense only a distraction. The force of reason, and its relativity, means that compulsion occurs or it does not, as is true with attempts at physical compulsion. Imagine you want me to sign a contract. You apply force to the arm of my non-writing hand. You are either strong enough to compel me to sign or you are not. Alternatively, you threaten to damage my car unless I sign. Either the strength of that reason is enough to compel me or it is not. The relativity bears on particular instances where coercion is attempted, but it does not distinguish the physical from the rational. Simply, some efforts at coercion – physical or rational – will succeed and others will fail. Equally, the idea that physical compulsion is irresistible whilst rational compulsion is not misses the point. If in fact I am able to defy your attempt at rational compulsion, that means that it was, simply, because the reasons you gave were not strong enough; it was not, after all, compulsion.[96] This is precisely as would be the case if you tried to compel me physically, but were not strong enough. Attempts at either sort of compulsion may be resisted more or less successfully in any given case.

Notwithstanding my disregarding Lamond's distinctions between the effects of the two forms of coercion, it is important to acknowledge that both modes exist, and to accept the force of his conclusion that:

---

[95] *Ibid.*, at 44.

[96] Lamond seems in his analysis to have caught himself out with something similar to the problem of there being two senses of "can" at play in arguments about consequentialism, the equivocation between which allows unfair condemnation: see Elinor Mason, "Consequentialism and the 'ought implies can' principle", *American Philosophical Quarterly* (2003) 40:4, 319–331. Mason distinguishes "can" meaning (something along the lines of) 'within the bounds of logical possibility' and "can" meaning (something along the lines of) 'with an agent's clear, informed, and concerted self-direction'. Although it is logically possible that I can beat a grand master at chess (i.e. I can do it in the first sense), it is not true that I can do it in the second sense; were I victorious, this would be a fluke. Bringing this back to Lamond, just because it is in principle possible that some agent would not be rationally compelled in a given instance does not prove that the particular agent who is being subjected to an attempt at rational compulsion could avoid being rationally compelled.

[T]he law is both more and less coercive than is ordinarily supposed. More coercive, because a far wider range of measures than physical force and sanctions can be used to coerce. Yet less, because rational compulsion can be achieved by the threat of disadvantages far removed from the use of physical punishments ...[97]

Although coercive measures will tend to be considered the most controversial, and thus we should recognise that coercion is not under issue in every instance, it does not follow that all non-coercive State acts are uncontroversial. We need to consider the exercise of coercive powers *and* other means of modifying, regulating, or controlling people's behaviour. This is especially the case if we reject anarchism, as this means not only that a State's positive policy must be defensible, but also that the State can be called to account for *failing* to introduce policy where it is needed. To test legitimacy, we need to see if there are grounds for believing that the State has the authority to direct people's behaviour, rather than just the brute power to do so.

So let us return to the challenge posed at the start of this section. Morality guides people's actions.[98] In a community whose members are considered to have moral value, moral insight, and moral understanding, appeals may be made to an account of morality as *the* source of normativity. Furthermore, echoing the thesis presented by Wolff that we considered above, it may be argued that the quintessence of acting morally is not simply doing the right thing, but engaging in moral reasoning and thereby doing the right thing for the right reasons.[99] Therefore, by seeking to assure the right or good through some superimposed normative system – i.e. a political system – we *undermine* both morality itself, and agents' status as moral agents. Meir Dan-Cohen, for example, describes politics as presenting a "disjunctive" view of authority, which, he claims, invalidates it:

"A request backed by a sanction" is an oxymoron. The case of authority, I maintain, is similar. "A norm backed by a sanction" presents an incongruity that the prevailing additive conception of authority ignores.[100]

---

[97] Lamond, "The coerciveness of law", at 62. Note, I have omitted the final clause from this quote. It reads: "... or the loss of fundamental rights". For our current purposes, we can not suppose the existence, less still assert the content, of fundamental rights, so leaving in these words would serve as a distraction. This does not damage the thrust or applicability of Lamond's argument to our current analysis.

[98] For present purposes, I straightforwardly presume this to be an empirical fact, without worrying about ontological claims concerning morality itself, or engagement with the internalism/externalism debate.

[99] As noted above, this is formed on the basis of Kantian moral philosophy: Immanuel Kant, *Groundwork of the Metaphysics of Morals*, ed. Mary Gregor (Cambridge University Press, 1998).

[100] Dan-Cohen, "In defense of defiance", at 29.

The "prevailing additive conception" is attributed in its most influential guise to Hart.[101] Dan-Cohen describes Hart's view as holding that threats of coercion are "separate but complementary" to the normativity of commands, employed because people's tendency to follow commands, or their reasons for so doing, vary. However, Dan-Cohen's central argument is that Hart's "additive conception" is flawed: "sanctions cannot be simply appended to antecedently and independently existing norms without affecting them".[102] The sanctions and the norms are "at odds with each other".[103] To illustrate, he takes the following example:

Consider a simple request such as "Please pass the salt." By making such a request A provides B with a reason ... to pass the salt. Now suppose that A expands on his request by adding the words "or else I'll break your arm." On the additive view, B is now presented with two reasons for passing the salt: the reason generated by the initial request and the reason created by the coercive threat. But this analysis is strikingly inadequate. Rather than leaving the first reason intact, the threat clearly seems to undercut the request and to supersede it: the reason that B had to pass the salt prior to the threat has been destroyed by A's threat.[104]

There seems to be a great deal of force to this argument. I seek specifically to respond to it as in doing so I hope to demonstrate clearly the need for recognising a political realm, and locating our normative analysis within it. In the current chapter I do not aim to go beyond this in order to present a knock-down argument in favour of political authority (though in Part III I will offer reasons for adopting a specific form of political liberalism). The discussion here will, however, lead to some consideration of discussions about the validity or otherwise of political authority. As I have argued, a normative anarchist will see no business in 'public health' as a political enterprise (though may be interested in scientific data relating to health); he will not accept that *anything* relating to health can be a public concern. For analysts willing to accept the

---

[101] H.L.A. Hart, *The Concept of Law* (2nd edn) (Oxford University Press, 1997).

[102] Dan-Cohen, "In defense of defiance" at 26.

[103] *Ibid.*

[104] *Ibid.*, at 28. It should be noted that Hart did not seem unaware of or unsympathetic to this "disjunctive view". In discussing coercion, he says: "There is nothing self-contradictory in such theories that the threat of legal punishment is required to create or maintain the voluntary practice of morality. But these are theories requiring empirical facts, and there is very little evidence to support the idea that morality is best taught by fear of legal punishment. Much morality is certainly taught and sustained without it, and where morality is taught with it, there is the standing danger that fear of punishment may remain the sole motive for conformity." Hart, *Law, Liberty, and Morality*, p. 58, and more generally see pp. 57–58.

political (either as *de jure* legitimate, or as something worth tolerating notwithstanding its illegitimacy), the development of ideas in the following sections should help explain the concerns and arguments to be explored in Chapter 8, which are representative of some of the most salient perspectives in public health law and ethics.

7.3.4.2 Subjects of the State and the scope of the community In defence of his "disjunctive view", Dan-Cohen pre-emptively raises and dismisses various possible responses to his argument that the State can not, in "good faith",[105] simultaneously appeal to citizens' moral reason for obeying its commands and threaten sanctions for non-compliance. Amongst the contemplated objections is one that features only in footnoted text, but which requires more attention than Dan-Cohen allows it. He says:

> It might be thought that the state addresses its threats only to recalcitrant citizens, while speaking in purely normative [i.e. moral] terms to the law-abiding ones. But this would be a delusion. No matter how small the number of recalcitrant citizens because of whom coercion is employed, given the generality of the law everyone's behavior falls within the scope of the threats.[106]

The treatment of this objection is unsatisfactory at two levels. First, it is not clear why the generality of law should lead to the morally upright citizens' being or feeling subject to the threat that Dan-Cohen alludes to. Second, it is not clear that citizens who may usefully or rightfully be subject to threats are exhausted by the category 'recalcitrant'. (And if in addressing the second point we find that the addressees of a policy contain others than competent moral agents, this may bear further on our response to the first issue.)

First, let us consider whether everyone *is* threatened simply by virtue of a threat being expressed in general terms. Provided the threat is qualified, which in the case of State's commands it is (no law simply says, for example, "People will be deprived of their liberty"), it is not clear how this would straightforwardly be the case. It is instructive to consider an analogy with English law concerning the effect of words on apparent assaults, and the law concerning justified battery. English law holds that there is no assault, notwithstanding a defendant's threatening actions, if an apparent assailant expresses words that have the effect of nullifying the ostensible threat.[107] And concerning battery at

---

[105] Dan-Cohen uses the term: Dan-Cohen, "In defense of defiance", at 49.

[106] *Ibid.*, at 49, fn. 40.

[107] *Tuberville* v. *Savage* [1669] EWHC KB J25, 86 ER 684, (1669) 1 Mod Rep 3. The plaintiff in this case put his hand on his sword. Such an action may be an assault,

law, people may use reasonable force to defend themselves from others' wrongful attacks.[108] These examples are instructive, as in each case they highlight the effect of contingency, and the importance of focusing not only on the assailant but also the understanding of the one he would put in fear of aggression. Should a person consider himself addressed in the way Dan-Cohen suggests if the contingency on which a threat hangs is forestalled by the circumstances of the *status quo*? Imagine there is no 'law'; that we only take normative direction from morality, but nevertheless recognise that we must act in the world as we find it. Imagine further that you are in a room with Barry, a man who you have good reason to believe will retaliate against any physical assault with greater force than you can possibly defend yourself against. That Barry's retributive tendencies and greater strength provide reasons for not hitting him do not clearly undermine your claims to have behaved morally by not hitting him. Simply, hitting him may not have featured as an idea that you would humour. This being the case, what may be described as the threat of violence in your case is better not thought of as an *additive* reason. Rather it is real – i.e. it exists in principle – but is in fact superfluous to your concerns. Likewise, if a State says it will apply coercive sanctions to those who do not do as they should, it can coherently claim only to be addressing recalcitrant agents. There is a contingency in the threat. An enlightened audience can assess for itself whether the contingency applies or not. If it does not, rather than feel the threat undermines the fact that it anyway would have done right, it can just see it is an irrelevant (inapplicable) further point. The level of understanding this requires of a citizen is not demanding; certainly not too demanding to puzzle a citizen with the rational competence of a moral agent worthy of the name.

To summarise, consider a final example. A State may declare that all people who earn over £100,000 a year must pay an income tax rate of 50 per cent. In doing this, the State thereby makes a general declaration in the sense indicated by Dan-Cohen. Nevertheless, the declaration clearly does not apply to everyone. Nor does it raise any confusion, incoherence, or difficulties in simultaneous (and equally general) demands for different levels of taxation for different earners. In the same way, the State may say that some coercive measure will apply to everyone who fits some other factual description (e.g. those who exceed the prescribed speed limits on public roads) without problematically

which may be constituted by any action if it leads another to apprehend physical violence. In *Tuberville*, the plaintiff expressed the words "If it were not assize-time, I would not take such language from you", thereby nullifying the assault.

[108] Criminal Law Act 1967, s. 3.

being seen to address those who anyway would not speed. The contingency on which the threat hangs does not apply in their cases, and there is no reason to suppose that – as rational agents, which they are taken by definition to be – they can not understand this, and see the reason as superfluous rather than either additional or disjunctive.

There is a further, separate problem with Dan-Cohen's description of the objection he seeks to refute. The way he frames it suggests that the law addresses only rational, autonomous moral agents, albeit both good and bad ones. A pressing difficulty arises when we consider that such moral agents do not exhaust the category of legal persons.[109] The communities that we – people – live in do not just comprise agents of the type imagined in support of Wolff's thesis on State legitimacy, or Dan-Cohen's presentation of the problem of the addressees of coercive threats. The communities also contain persons who are completely non-autonomous, and persons who lack to greater or lesser extents the capacity to reason. When considering the nature of the people in the communities we live in, we need to account for those with diminished mental capacity, including those with complete inability to act as agents.[110] But such extremes must not distract us: even adults who generally are able to demonstrate and exercise high levels of mental capacity will often not be in the position to act as agents.[111] And agency seems to be a developmental concept; as people develop and mature, so seems to develop the strength of their agency. Children are a complex category philosophically (which probably explains in part why many political theorists, especially those advancing more libertarian positions, choose to engage very little with how children fit into their theories[112]). Adults in dreamless sleep are tricky too. So are adults who are rendered unconscious following an accident, who may in due course make a recovery. These different complexities do not make implausible the idea that a community can only include what theorists such as John Harris label "persons",[113] with the other human non-persons' being possible sources of moral concern whilst not being of the same status. Indeed, these tensions seem to map quite precisely onto the normative underpinnings to the conflicts between 'choice-' and 'interest-theories'

---

[109] Nor need this be considered incoherent, see e.g. William Lucy, "Persons in law", *Oxford Journal of Legal Studies* (2009) 29:4, 787–804, especially at 799–800.

[110] At the extremes, neonates and those with severe brain damage: see Part III.

[111] See further the discussion in Chapter 10.

[112] E.g. Nozick's essential lip service in Part III of *Anarchy, State, and Utopia*. Note the engagement with the question of children in A. John Simmons, "Consent theory for libertarians", *Social Philosophy and Policy* (2005) 22:1, 330–356, at 344–345.

[113] Harris, *The Value of Life*.

of rights.[114] In each case, it is argued respectively that 'rights' exist to offer protection either to the decisions agents make – in essence, privileging their autonomy – or to protect aspects of their welfare. The two theories seem on their face to be incompatible, and to extend their concerns (potentially) to different extremes; the former only being applicable to the sorts of beings that can exercise choice, the latter extending possibly to anything that might be said to have welfare concerns.[115] Christopher Morris notes the way these debates are reflected in arguments about political legitimacy.[116] This insight is important. Without recognising the sorts of persons we consider to be in our community, we can not meaningfully establish what their 'rights' might obtain in, or understand where the boundaries of normative concern (moral or political) might lie.

It is not my purpose here to try to resolve these debates. I think they do permit of resolution, but in this part of the book my aim is to present and consider distinct attempts at addressing them, rather than to advance a single model. We have seen above that various theorists express considerable concern about the category 'human' as one that dictates specific normative concerns.[117] We might also note that those who do limit their concerns to humans, rarely do so in an unqualified fashion. To be a rights-holder, for example, it tends to be the case that an agent must be living (giving rise to heated debates about the best understandings of when life begins and ends, or should be considered to do so for normative purposes[118]). As a matter of fact, it is clear that human legal persons tend to be those who are considered as members

---

[114] On the distinctions, see Leonard Wayne Sumner, *The Moral Foundation of Rights* (Oxford: Clarendon Press, 1987); Matthew Kramer, Nigel Simmonds, and Hillel Steiner, *A Debate Over Rights* (Oxford University Press, 1998).

[115] I will go on in Part III to defend an interest theory account. It should be noted that on such an account, the importance of choice is not lost or undermined; rather, it obtains in finding in any given circumstance who is in the rightful position to define the content of welfare.

[116] Christopher Morris, "Natural rights and political legitimacy", *Social Philosophy and Policy* (2005) 22:1, 314–329.

[117] See e.g. Singer, *Animal Liberation*; Harris, "Taking the 'human' out of Human Rights".

[118] See e.g. K. Grandstand Gervais, *Redefining Death* (Yale University Press, 1986); David Lamb, *Death, Brain Death and Ethics* (London: Croom Helm, 1985); Calixto Machado and D. Alan Shewmon (eds.), *Brain Death and Disorders of Consciousness* (New York: Kluwer Academic, 2004); Jeff McMahan, *The Ethics of Killing – Problems at the Margins of Life* (Oxford University Press, 2002); Robert Veatch, *Death, Dying, and the Biological Revolution – Our Last Quest for Responsibility* (Yale University Press, 1976); Stuart Youngner, Robert Arnold, Renie Schapiro (eds.), *The Definition of Death: Contemporary Controversies* (Baltimore: John Hopkins University Press, 1999).

of communities. Whether this should be the case is in principle a separate question, though, like Geuss in his analyses of politics, we may not be as concerned as some analysts are about perfectly separating 'is' and 'ought' questions in understanding the practical boundaries of community.[119] That is not to say the fact/value distinctions are unimportant, but rather that where we engage with political communities, we will often engage with concepts of persons that (naturally enough) do not match perfectly the abstractions that form communities (political or moral) in the theories, for example, of Nozick and Wolff,[120] the rational negotiators in Rawlsian theory,[121] the psychological being implicit in Mill's conception of the human person,[122] or the rational chooser who features in much economic theory.[123] As long as children and other incompletely rational agents feature in political society, we have good reason to believe that it is wrong to limit the addressees of law to the good and bad moral agents that Dan-Cohen takes (albeit implicitly) to exhaust the subjects (and rightful beneficiaries?) of political society.

This is so important because it affects the very nature of normatively defensible claims that can be made, both about establishing the nature and scope of rights, duties, and so on, and about the role and nature of law as it addresses its subjects. The nature of rights holders within this community alters the determination of both the potential bases of rights (e.g. they can not just be about choice), and the way that rights may and should be exercised. The community is necessarily larger than one that would comprise only rational moral agents (even imperfect ones like the concession-laden conception of a person found in Harrisian philosophy[124]). Comprising people who can not exercise

---

[119] Geuss, *Philosophy and Real Politics*, p. 17.

[120] As James Griffin puts it in his analysis of human rights, in reference to theories based on the Kantian abstraction of an autonomous person: "Our aim must be the more modest one of understanding not the autonomy of a spare, abstract self, but the autonomy of *Homo sapiens.*" See Griffin, *On Human Rights*, p. 35.

[121] See Geuss' discussion of Rawls, including the passage quoted above in section 7.2.2. Geuss seems more willing to attribute (human) universality to Nozick's claims, whilst I read Nozick as being much more limiting, and raising real problems with regard to children as rights-holders: see Geuss, *Philosophy and Real Politics*, p. 64.

[122] In Hart's words: "Underlying Mill's extreme fear of paternalism there perhaps is a conception of what a normal human being is like which now seems not to correspond to the facts. Mill, in fact, endows him with too much of the psychology of a middle-aged man whose desires are relatively fixed, not liable to be artificially stimulated by external influences; who knows what he wants and what gives him satisfaction or happiness; and who pursues these things when he can." See Hart, *Law, Liberty, and Morality*, p. 33.

[123] Note the contrast described between *homo sapiens* and *homo economicus* in Thaler and Sunstein, *Nudge*, Part I.

[124] Cf Harris, *The Value of Life*.

their own rights, duties, and so on, the political community also alters the nature of claims that may be made against the autonomous individuals. For example, it implies practical duties to look after others as their needs and interests require. We have a different range of normative subjects than that provided in theories of moral rationality. The subjects and scope of the political community are muddied by human reality, even as rational moral arguments push the boundaries of concern one way or another. Just as this provides reason to embrace a separate normative realm – the political – it also suggests that we should possibly question our 'start point' in political philosophy. It is to this that I now turn.

7.3.4.3 The start point in politics   Much political theory starts with the idea of a 'state of nature'. Within this hypothesis, there is no political society, nothing held in common, no government, no legal system. Reference to the 'state of nature' is not best thought of as an anthropological or historical claim about pre-political society. Rather, it is a useful thought experiment, affording the potential for insights into the nature of moral rights that may be said to inhere in us individually, the benefits and harms of subjecting ourselves to some sovereign power, and the effects of so doing on our (putative) moral rights. The experiment is so potent that in some analyses, as we have seen, theorists find it hard to come far into the political realm because of the side-constraints that they find already exist in the state of nature. As this is taken as the original position, any moves away from it into politics may be said necessarily to require justification, because *a priori* moral laws logically precede the institution of politics and any man-made laws that come with it (whether the State is instigated formally, for example following a revolution, or develops as some manner of social evolution). For those who take this start point, there is little to be said to the side-constraints themselves. In this case, our task is fairly straightforward. We then have to ask, even if a State lacks legitimacy, whether its legitimacy is more important, for example, than concerns about justice or other things we might consider good. A. John Simmons finds political legitimacy only where citizens voluntarily submit to authority, and thus does not recognise the legitimacy of *any* existing States. This does not, however, preclude his acceptance of alternative "favorable evaluations" by which to test a political society:

A liberal egalitarian theory of justice and a consent theory of political legitimacy can be consistently conjoined if one accepts the distinction between what I have called "justification" and "legitimacy" – which I take to be two kinds of favorable evaluations of political institutions within quite different dimensions of evaluation. General good qualities and virtues of a political society – such as benevolence or justice – are what is appealed to in *justifying* that society's existence, in showing why such a society is *a good thing*. But the society's *legitimacy* is a function of its specific interactions with particular subjects and consists (in part) in its having a particular set of rights over a subject.[125]

Accordingly, "States can be evaluated independently in either dimension, sometimes producing mixed evaluations (as when we refer to 'benevolent dictatorships')".[126] This distinction is important. It shows, in line with the discussion above about normative and descriptive anarchists/statists, how we may coherently look to normative measures beyond deontological constraints abstracted from moral philosophy, in our evaluation of politics. Thus, if we part from Wolff's commitment to 'autonomy rights' as side-constraints, we can understand the apparent exasperation in McPherson's analysis of political obligation:

[W]hy should I obey government is an absurd question. We have not understood what it *means* to be a member of political society if we suppose that political obligation is something we might not have had and that therefore needs to be *justified*.[127]

For McPherson morality and politics are not part and parcel of the same thing. To be sure, it is possible to create a cogent moral critique of a political measure. Indeed such a critique may lead to a revision of the policy. But we need not, on this count, test political legitimacy in the same way that (for example because of prior metaphysical commitments concerning agency) we assess the scope and basis of moral claims. The extent to which politics *demands* practical action is not, and need not be, coextensive with the demands of morality. Whilst morality speaks to everything, but has no external enforcement mechanism, politics speaks only to matters of public concern – however these are established – and can employ external mechanisms, as considered in Chapter 4.

Even if we recognise this divide between morality and politics, however, we may still reject the cogency of the 'state of nature' as *really* being the start point the derivation from which requires justification. The actual and logical priority of the 'moral community' it implies may be said to offer too much strength to arguments concerning the political realm. There are two distinct arguments that I will use here as illustrations. Each suggests that the political society we find in the world

125 Simmons, "Consent theory for libertarians", at 354.
126 *Ibid.*   127 McPherson, *Political Obligation*, p. 64.

presents a normative reality that itself demands respect, in a distinct way to normative theories developed with an idealised, historically isolated, abstracted individual agent as its start point. First, let us consider George Klosko's questioning the strength of the role that voluntarism and consent have played in liberal theory. Klosko takes issue with the "isolated individual" of the political liberal tradition. In similar manner to that which I urge in Chapter 2, Klosko makes no strong metaphysical or ontological claims about what the community *is*, conceiving of it simply as "individuals jointly providing and receiving important benefits".[128] These benefits exist in the world in which moral agents develop, and are the basis on which Klosko builds his thesis. His focus falls particularly on non-excludable public goods, which – problematically for contract theory – cannot be procured individually, and instead require cooperation between people and governmental coordination. These nevertheless are basic to the protection of human welfare. Klosko therefore argues that they demand protection in accordance with Hart's principle of fairness.[129] Klosko provides three conditions that must be met for such benefits justifiably to impose burdens on citizens, regardless of their not having consented:

These conditions are met when the public goods supplied (1) are worth the costs required for their provision, (2) are indispensable for satisfactory lives, and (3) have benefits and burdens that are fairly distributed.[130]

The indispensable goods that Klosko takes as straightforward examples include defence, law and order, public health measures (which we may take to mean measures in accordance with the 'old public health' discussed above[131]), and protection from a hostile environment.[132] Thus if, for example, it is accepted that clean water is indispensable, an argument can be derived to the effect that people should have no choice but to contribute to the system necessary to provide it.[133] Klosko sums up his position as follows:

The fact that we *constantly* receive enormous benefits from the cooperative efforts of our fellows generates moral requirements for us to share their burdens. State of nature analysis is misleading because it implies that the baseline

---

[128] Klosko, "The natural basis of political obligation", at 95.
[129] See H.L.A. Hart, "Are there any natural rights?", *Philosophical Review* (1955) 64:2, 175–191.
[130] Klosko, "The natural basis of political obligation", at 97.
[131] Chapter 3, section 3.2.2.
[132] Klosko, "The natural basis of political obligation", at 99.
[133] *Ibid.*, see especially at 104. And note that Klosko does allow for the need that the empirical argument be made to support the State's case that it is needed to assure the coordination required for the provision of clean water.

position for questions of political obligation is that of an absence of obligations. On this account, if individuals do not consent or otherwise commit themselves to political bodies, then they do not have obligations. However, the fact that individuals are members of societies, conceived of as joint producers and consumers of essential benefits, entails a different starting point.[134]

Thus Klosko gives one reply to the normative anarchist. We do not, in truth, begin in a state of nature. Rather, we start in a political community that provides various goods that we could not do without. To deny obligation on the back of these benefits, the very least that most be shown (this is an empirical, not an ideological challenge) is that any particular goods can be better provided without governmental coordination. This must be a matter of case-by-case assessment. Whether or not a reader is convinced by, or sympathetic with, Klosko's argument, it provides a good example of an account that speaks to why politics is a defensible and satisfactory normative system, and to why we do well to frame our practical normative evaluations within a political frame.

A second account that repays brief consideration is Christopher Wellman's argument in favour of a positive "benefit principle", which he shows leads to reasons that demand political obligation.[135] Although Wellman does not believe that his presentation of "samaritanism" provides the complete source of State legitimacy, he argues that it nevertheless suggests the way to a theory that accounts not just for the benefits of the State, but also for its legitimacy. The empirical case in favour of the State, Wellman suggests, is easily made:

It does not require a full Hobbesian account of human nature to recognize that an environment with no political state would be an insecure place in which peace would be unavailable and moral rights would be disrespected. Put plainly, there will always be people unwilling to honor the moral rights of others if there were no legal repercussions of violating them. Moral rights will be respected and peace will be ensured only if police effectively protect individuals and recognized judges impartially adjudicate conflicts according to established rules.[136]

---

[134] *Ibid.*, at 113–114.
[135] Wellman, "Liberalism, samaritanism, and political legitimacy", at 211–237. We should note that Wellman in this paper forcefully distinguishes the focus of his analysis – political legitimacy – and the question of political obligation, which he takes to be separate (or only associated given further argument that often remains unstated). In the current analysis, I have not been at pains to separate the question of distinguishing the State's achieving a moral right to coerce, and the further work required (if it is) to establish that it also has a right to be obeyed. For reasons presented by Wellman (see 212), it may be considered important to do so, though I do not see that the analysis in this chapter is diminished for not addressing this question explicitly.
[136] *Ibid.*, at 216–217.

Some may contest this (consider e.g. Wolff's allusions to the post-political Utopia of anarchist America[137]), and certainly it is not a claim that *any* State is better than a state of nature. However, the empirical case in favour of the liberal State on this count seems compelling.[138] Given the truth of that claim, Wellman derives a situation in which even would-be dissenters have no right to fall outside of the political community.

> The reason *I* have no moral right to be free from political coercion (to secede) is because, even if *I* would rather forego the benefits of political society, *I* have a moral duty to others which allows my state to coerce me in order to secure political stability for *my fellow citizens*.[139]

In finally selling "samaritanism", Wellman urges that:

> This model is conceptually sturdy because its only contestable empirical premise is that political states are necessary to avoid the extreme perils of a lawless environment, and it is normatively inexpensive since its only controversial moral premise is its presumption of positive rights.[140]

The two theses we have considered here demonstrate alternative start points in political theory, and suggest that we may start with a positive account of politics that itself is at least prima facie a morally defensible normative theory without reference to the distinct evaluations approach that Simmons presents. And whilst Klosko's and Wellman's positions are, in some senses, both quite modest (i.e. neither describes the foundation of a strong welfare State), they present in clear terms considerations that may be salient in assessments of political community, and the normative issues to which these give rise.

Thus we see various arguments in favour of politics. Either we accept it as deriving from an alternative "favourable evaluation" to morality, or we question the nature of moral impositions on social norms and individual freedoms. Whichever theory is provided, it will need to mark some divergence from abstracted moral reasoning if it is to be practically applicable, and then practically applied. Chapter 8 will consider some such arguments in the specific context of public health law and

---

[137] Wolff, *In Defense of Anarchism*, p. 80.
[138] It is clear enough that I shall not try to prove it. As my account (see Part III) would be described as one of a 'descriptive statist', I am bound to accept the empirical upshot of different positions, and would take the one that does best, rather than be tied to any ideological commitments either for or against the State. I am not equipped here to make the formal knock-down case that people necessarily fare better in a State than in anarchism, but it seems close enough to self-evident that I am happy to leave it until I see convincing arguments to the contrary.
[139] Wellman, "Liberalism, samaritanism, and political legitimacy", at 219.
[140] *Ibid.*, at 237.

ethics. Prior to that, it is necessary briefly to speak to the issues of paternalism and the 'population perspective'.

7.3.4.4 A note on paternalism: politics, policy, and collateral paternalism

It seems necessary to consider paternalism under its own heading only because it is so commonly treated as a controversial theory, or even just a dirty word, in so much of the literature in bioethics and political philosophy. Particularly within bioethics, this has become rather tiresome. Consider the words of Angus Dawson and Marcel Verweij, writing in response to the Nuffield Council's report on public health ethics:

> A key part of their [i.e. the Nuffield Council's] modified liberal view is the attempt to distinguish the stewardship model from what they call 'paternalism'. They claim that the 'difference between paternalism and our stewardship model is that the latter is less likely to support highly coercive universal measures' (2007: 26). There are a number of problems with this. First, paternalism is a concept, not a normative position. Usually, and certainly in Gerald Dworkin's (2005) definition [which the Nuffield Council adopts], the term paternalism is used to describe specific types of action, performed for specific reasons. It is not a model, theory or view in any sense parallel to the stewardship model. Second, whilst, paternalistic actions may involve coercion, it seems a category mistake to claim [as the Council does] that paternalism *supports* coercion, and therefore very odd to claim that it implies acceptance of 'highly coercive' measures. Paternalism is a particular feature of acts motivated by beneficence: in essence it is wanting to do good for another person. The proposed intervention may be coercive (or it may not). There is certainly no reason why such acts are by definition 'highly coercive'.[141]

Dawson and Verweij are right here, and I will in this short section add to their claim with a general point about the controversy surrounding paternalism when we are conducting analysis in the context of politics.[142]

So-called "hard paternalism" – i.e. a decision made by a third party on behalf of a rational, moral agent, preventing his deciding for himself – is often treated as presumptively problematic in a way that is not true for "soft paternalism" – i.e. benevolent decisions made by a third party on behalf of a morally important but rationally defective being.[143] Whilst in a given instance we will find that many human persons are autonomous

---

[141] Dawson and Verweij, "The steward of the Millian State", at 194.

[142] See also Lawrence O. Gostin and Kieran G. Gostin, "A broader liberty: JS Mill, paternalism, and the public's health", *Public Health* (2009) 123:3, 214–221.

[143] See Joel Feinberg, "Legal paternalism", *Canadian Journal of Philosophy* (1971) 1:1, 105–124; Gerald Dworkin, "Paternalism", in Dan E. Beauchamp and Bonnie Steinbock (eds.), *New Ethics for the Public's Health* (Oxford and New York: Oxford University Press, 1999 [originally published in *The Monist* (1972) 56, 64–84]).

in the relevant sense that seems to give rise to problems with paternalism, we are clearly (empirically) not the ideal rational persons of
Kantian metaphysical abstraction. Douglas Husak notes as much in his
exploration of paternalism and its relationship with autonomy: "Ideal
persons, possessed of 'holy wills,' need no external laws."[144] Bearing in
mind that we are not these, and thus that we allow for external law to
make up for our deficiencies as agents, Husak speculates that:

> The shortcoming or deficiency that explains the failure of an agent to take
> proper care of himself, and thus makes him an appropriate subject of paternal-
> istic treatment, may be indistinguishable from the shortcoming or deficiency
> that explains the inclination of an agent to harm others and thus makes him an
> appropriate subject for non-paternalistic coercive legislation.[145]

In other words, if we accept external law for other reasons (e.g. to prevent people causing harm to others because they can not always be
trusted not to do so), we may well find that we legitimate paternalistic
policies in the process.

Furthermore, however we conceive it, the very notion of the State
may be best conceived as inherently paternalistic. This seems problematic if we take it that paternalism of necessity implies *active* intervention. But once we give a State normative grounding, we in principle
accept that it must provide the reason both for its interventions *and*
its non-interventions, all combined to conduce to whatever good we
deem the State necessary to protect. As such, paternalism is present
constantly, in all political systems. Where people are left free, this is
for their own good. Where they are not, this is for their good too.[146]
Regardless of this view, however, there is anyway a wider point that suggests that hard paternalism is a practical inevitability in a political society. Where policy is made for a community of people, there is bound to
be some imperfection in application, whatever the area of policy. In the
current context, we need to account for what I label 'collateral paternalism'. This applies where a "soft-paternalist" policy has some practical
overreach, resulting in instances also of "hard paternalism". We may

---

[144] Douglas Husak, "Paternalism and autonomy", *Philosophy and Public Affairs* (1981)
10:1, 27–46, at 42.
[145] *Ibid.*
[146] See further John Coggon, "What help is a steward? Stewardship, political theory, and
public health law and ethics", *Northern Ireland Legal Quarterly* (forthcoming 2012).
Contrast Wellman's appraisal of his own analysis in regard to paternalism: "[M]y
insistence that 'that person' receive the goods of political stability might have seemed
paternalistic and out of place. But we now see that allotting benefits to all citizens is
essential for political legitimacy not because of paternalism, but because these benefits are necessary to ensure that the burden of citizenship is not unreasonably costly."
See Wellman, "Liberalism, samaritanism, and political legitimacy", at 236.

compare this with the idea of collateral harm caused by policy, such as that involved in vaccination policies. At times, the general nature of a measure will mean that it reaches more than its intended or ideal beneficiaries.

Of particular concern in *medical* law and ethics, is the autonomy-limiting that may occur when legal tests are developed to assess a patient's decision-making capacity. These are a natural source of critical comment, and explain in part why paternalism is treated as so problematic. However, when making such assessments, it is important to do so in a political context, with a sound understanding of the inherent and often justified bluntness of policy. Although a liberal State works within a system of relatively high agnosticism concerning the content of 'the good' and thus of people's welfare, it nevertheless requires a concrete core, where presumptions (on whatever they are founded) tell us what is better or worse for us. These policies, for example, uncontroversially permit unconscious people to be rescued from road traffic accidents. Although when conscious they would have every right to refuse treatment the State can safely presume that treatment is good for the person. More controversial, but practically inevitable, are cases where a person is conscious, able to reason, but nevertheless his rational autonomy falls into doubt, and thus he is denied decision-making power. In such an instance, the State has to prevent harm to vulnerable people who lack decision-making capacity, whilst not denying the right of choice to those who are due this.[147] Ideally, these concerns would be reconciled perfectly; in practice, things will go wrong in each direction.[148] In instances where a policy has the effect, in good faith, of taking decision-making from an autonomous individual because he fails the legal test for mental capacity, we have an instance of collateral paternalism. Many manifestations of collateral paternalism will in fact be justifiable as an overall cost of a given policy. Assessments in public health ethics, and beyond, can not demonstrate the normative failure of a policy simply by pointing to an incident of its failing to work perfectly. An 'all things considered' policy assessment is needed. Only an advocate of normative anarchism, such as Wolff, can maintain otherwise.

---

[147] Cf Sheila McLean, "Live and let die", *British Medical Journal* (2009) 339:b4112, 837.

[148] See John Coggon, "Varied and principled understandings of autonomy in English law: justifiable inconsistency or blinkered moralism?", *Health Care Analysis* (2007) 15:3, 235–255; Michael Dunn, Isabel Clare, and Anthony Holland, "To empower or to protect? Constructing the 'vulnerable adult' in English law and public policy", *Legal Studies* (2008) 28:2, 234–253; John Coggon and José Miola, "Autonomy, liberty and medical decision-making", *Cambridge Law Journal* (forthcoming 2011).

7.3.4.5 Final reflections: beyond anarchism and into the realms of public and private   Politics imposes limits to liberty, even where political systems are designed to maximise the overall liberty that everyone can enjoy. Within political liberal systems, the liberty that is afforded and protected through law is represented by the private realm. Whilst this private sphere permits plural accounts of the good, and the freedom for citizens to live according to their own conceptions thereof, we must recognise two levels of value-certainty that must obtain in a political system. Each of these is necessary, given the demands of achieving the conditions of harmonious coexistence, and the fact that many members of society are too far from being meaningfully autonomous moral agents. At core, the State will have conceptions of the good that will stand regardless of any individual's acceptance. In terms of Millian liberalism, for example, we may consider this as providing the content of the 'harm principle'. The State must form policy around such a base conception, even if so doing is not agreed to by everyone (and thus, we may explore, for example, democratic or liberal mechanisms that can be best employed to find this core content). Outside of this core of hard certainty is a more transcendent certainty. This can form the basis, for example, of policy 'nudges'. The conception of good or harm is not sufficiently compelling to warrant enforced agreement. Yet it is sufficiently strong that policy can be framed to steer towards it, and it can provide presumptions about the good in cases where someone's agency is in doubt and 'soft paternalism' is called for.[149]

We have seen that philosophical anarchism means not recognising political authority, and thus that nothing can be made a public concern. We have seen too, however, that lack of moral legitimacy may not mean automatically that political framings are normatively indefensible. Finally, we have seen that arguments may be framed to suggest that political authority is itself morally sound, and something to which citizens should submit. So, whether we feel we can find a moral grounding for the State, or other normative reasons to act in accordance with its policies, we are able to make assessments about demands, imperatives, nudges, and so on, instituted on the basis that health concerns are a matter of shared concern. Philosophical anarchists may still join the analysis, asking something like "what makes health *de facto* public?" or "why would we make voluntary agreements to share concerns about health?". For those engaging in health as a subject of political concern, we see that the politics must come first. We can analyse models in public health ethics fully only by reference to the wider political model they

---

[149] Cf Sunstein and Thaler, "Libertarian paternalism is not an oxymoron".

are entailed in, or imply themselves to be in. Thus in Chapter 8 I will distinguish various accounts, and discuss how they may be understood against this political background. In the final section of this chapter, I will briefly discuss one final point of reference in public health ethics: the population perspective.

7.4   Conclusions: public health, politics, and the 'population perspective'

In Part I, we considered Geoffrey Rose's 'population perspective', descriptive of a methodological approach that allows analysis and understanding of causation in health through the study of populations, rather than just by ascertaining what can be learned from focusing on individual cases.[150] This scientific method has gained currency in the literature relating to public health law and ethics, more modestly for the insights it offers in support of practical decisions, and more boldly as the basis of a *normative* (as opposed to just a scientific) outlook. In the first sense, the population perspective helps analysts to understand the empirical world and the things that bear on it. In this way, descriptive anarchists and statists are at one in valuing an evidence base to inform their assessments of potential policy. In the second, stronger sense, the normative analyst looks at a population, and at means to target populations, and consider policies tailored to individuals *qua* group members, rather than individuals *qua* individuals. Theorists, including Angus Dawson and Marcel Verweij,[151] Daniel Goldberg,[152] and Wendy Parmet,[153] draw normative political models explicitly in line with the population perspective. In these normative guises, there is clearly interesting and detailed analysis. However, there is a more generalisable point that needs to be made here, which applies to any serious normative analysis of public health. As the relevant questions will be political, we necessarily take a population approach. This is something that is developed in the remainder of the book, but its simultaneous banality and profundity bears mention here, as sometimes it seems that the

---

[150] Geoffrey Rose, "Sick individuals and sick populations", *International Journal of Epidemiology* (1985) 14, 32–38. See Chapter 2, section 2.4, and Chapter 3, section 3.2.4.

[151] Marcel Verweij and Angus Dawson, "The meaning of 'public' in 'public health'", in Angus Dawson and Marcel Verweij (eds.), *Ethics, Prevention, and Public Health* (Oxford University Press, 2007).

[152] Daniel Goldberg, "In support of a broad model of public health: disparities, social epidemiology and public health causation", *Public Health Ethics* (2009) 2:1, 70–83.

[153] Parmet, *Populations, Public Health, and the Law*.

'population approach' is novel and controversial, and therefore needs to be defended.

When we are dealing with political communities, our approach must be directed at populations; we are addressing the regulation of populations by definition.[154] Policy-makers do not tailor each norm perfectly to each individual. Policy will, in the ideal, be as efficient, effective, and defensible as possible in terms of its effect on each individual, but there will be occasions where its bluntness means that there will be undue winners and losers. That there is under- or overstretch does not automatically prove that there is a problem. More profoundly, though, it reminds us of what it means to engage in political analysis: we necessarily 'de-atomise' individuals in the first place when we create a political community, whatever its basis and scope. As such, a population perspective is inevitable. Or to look at it another way, a normative theory that fails to allow for a population perspective will fail as a theory applicable in public health analysis, but also in analysis of public issues more generally. This point applies as strongly to the most minimal State libertarianism as it does to the most stringent forms of communitarianism. The disputes about how populations are best served, by minimal intervention and sharing of concerns or by greater State interference and wider sharing of responsibilities, are the interesting and important arguments in public health law and ethics. It is wrong-headed to imagine that any given political approach only 'allows' us to make individualistic appraisals.

Thus, the 'population perspective' should neither be looked at with suspicion, nor as something novel. Within political philosophy, we are interested in addressing the State and individuals found together in a shared *political* community. Incompatible or simplistic philosophising about autonomy, especially as we find it in many arguments in bioethics, can simply be put to one side. Certainly it should not make theorists in public health law and ethics apologetic about the need to look at protecting more than individuals' autonomy. Every aspect of every citizen's health is not everyone's business, and not therefore a public concern. Broad-sweeping claims, if they are taken as singular answers to tough normative questions, are therefore of little illumination. There is little merit (for our purposes) in engaging with claims such as: I own my body; health is purely private; interference with autonomous decisions can never be justified. They all ignore the nuance and complexity of shared sovereignty in a political society.

---

[154] Cf Hart, *The Concept of Law*, pp. 20–25.

It is a fact with important normative implications that as part of the social environment – a public – people are part of the environment in which other people live. If freedom is conferred, or its limitation may be justified, any freedom to be unhealthy impinges on the conditions in which people can be healthy. To the extent that health is public, *we* are part of the conditions in which people can be healthy. What remains to be decided is what the State should do in developing its policies. Should it be a very small State, or a larger, more ideologically communitarian one? This chapter has highlighted that the answer to this question will come from one of two directions. First, drawing from ideal theory, we might ask what rights, duties, and so on exist, and then establish what their practical institution requires. Alternatively, drawing from the best ends that can be achieved (and not excluding regard to some limitations), we look to the best outcome and establish what system is most conducive to achieving this. Whichever of these approaches we take, by uncovering the political system, we lead ourselves to answers that allow us to analyse public health issues. It is to this function that the next chapter turns.

8   Making health public

8.1   Introduction

Following the conceptual and analytic framing of the first half of this book, I seek now to explore the political framing of different arguments about how, why, and when health may be public. The particular works I discuss are familiar and influential, and can be mapped well onto the political spectrum from libertarianism to strong collectivism or contractarianism, described usefully as a heuristic device in the Nuffield Council on Bioethics' report on public health ethics.[1] The works I consider therefore provide a good representation of relevant arguments, and demonstrate how the work in the previous chapter relates to, and must come prior to, discussions in public health law and ethics. I will continue to argue that the meaningful normativity in the case of these arguments is political. As such, the common theme to normative analyses is the bindingly communitarian supposition entailed in politics of all brands. Equally, the most relevant analysis is that which is actually applicable to the world, and the most useful is that which is applicable given the practical normativity that can be achieved through liberal political structures (either existing, or ones that can realistically be established). None of this is about shirking moral responsibility or denying moral concern. Rather, it is about making two concessions in the face of real world concerns and idealistic abstracted responses to them. The first relates to moral epistemic uncertainty, and the (at least practical) truth of moral pluralism. Even if there were *a* single true moral system – encapsulated, for example, in a comprehensive theory of justice – we still in practice find what is best described as 'reasonable disagreement' about what it obtains in. And beyond differences of interpretation of single evaluative frames (such as justice), there are

---

[1] Nuffield Council on Bioethics, *Public Health – Ethical Issues* (London: Nuffield, 2007), pp. 13–14.

a great many "rationally incomparable"[2] value systems: I take it that these can functionally coexist and direct people's lives, provided there is an alternative source of normativity to morality (i.e. political normativity). And this leads to the second concession. If we are to live harmoniously we must sometimes sacrifice at least some ideal or valued positions. Political normativity does not demand that a 'right' answer be given to every practical problem, less still mechanisms to ensure that the 'right' decision be effectuated by everyone in every instance. But harmony can demand that "radical choices"[3] be made between values, to the exclusion – and practical denial – of other values. This must be done to give substantial content to, and allow protection of, the common good, however that is understood: it is necessary, for example, in order to give content to a 'harm principle', to assure a sufficiency of welfare amongst members of a population, or give content to and ensure that human rights are respected. Some theories will prioritise liberty, or their advocates emphasise the value of liberty. But to reinforce my own emphasis, in a political theory *the common good is the real default against which normative claims are to be tested*. A presumption in favour of liberty is really just a presumption only to regulate where and as the common good demands; an edict against random, unnecessary, or unjustifiable policy-making. Thus we need to establish what the public good demands, and in this chapter I discuss various ways this question has been addressed, focusing on works which are in – or at least brought into – public health law and ethics.

The way the arguments are divided is in some senses arbitrary, but is systematic and leads, I hope, to clear understanding. Each 'cluster' of positions is separated under one of three headings: narrow political models; models in the middle ground; and models representing a 'health theocracy'. The presentation of the arguments does not reflect an ordinal ranking of their strength or quality. Whilst I find some more and some less convincing, conclusive, or useful, each provides important insights to our analysis. It is important and interesting to contrast the persuasiveness of arguments by reference to their prior normative constraints, and where they are advocated because they offer the best practical means of achieving specific ends (i.e. how they relate to the discussion of normative *versus* descriptive statism discussed in the previous chapter). It is important too to remember that 'health' itself is not used throughout the different theories with a singular meaning. Where clarification seems necessary, and it is possible to do so, I describe what

---

[2] See John Gray, *Isaiah Berlin* (Princeton University Press, 1996), ch. 1.
[3] *Ibid.*, see ch. 2.

health means in each argument considered. In Part III, where I provide my own views on the best approach to political liberalism and its implications for analysis of public health issues, I will draw from insights found in the works considered in this chapter. As already noted, some of the divides between the approaches here are somewhat artificial, just as is the case when 'liberals' and 'communitarians' are distinguished as shorthand in the political literature more widely. The shorthand is useful, but can obscure the communitarian commitments of those who only support a small State, or the concerns for liberty of those who are more collectivist. One significant upshot of ignoring such apparent divides is the capacity it affords to draw salient ideas, when these can be coherently adopted, from apparently opposing theorists' perspectives. Thus, whilst I separate the arguments in what follows, and go some way to stress the contrasts between different positions, this must not be taken to suggest that all aspects of each theory are mutually incompatible or contradictory.

8.2   Narrow models and public health

8.2.1   Libertarianism and community in the small State

The first 'cluster' of arguments that I want to consider position themselves within libertarian political models, broadly understood. To stress the point of contrast drawn in the last chapter, these are *not* anarchist positions. They cross the controversial threshold into politics and demand a concession to the complex process of justifying or legitimating submission to the State, and the creation of a public; a politically bounded group with shared interests that foreclose some incompatible actions based on contradictory interests. Thus, although libertarian models are not communitarian in the sense of presenting a strong, 'big State' (and often are associated with deep suspicion of the State), they are nonetheless born of a robust sense of political community, and must be recognised as doing so.[4] This point bears stressing, as libertarians

[4] H. Tristram Engelhardt, some of whose arguments I consider in the next section, argues that community and society are separate concepts, which ought not to be conflated. Engelhardt's division here seems to be aimed at strong communitarian theories that see political society and moral community as obtaining in the same thing: H. Tristram Engelhardt, "Health care reform: a study in moral malfeasance", *Journal of Medicine and Philosophy* (1994) 19:5, 501–516, at 509–510. It should be clear that the sense in which I am using community does not entail a commitment to such a view (i.e. a conflation of moral and political community), but rather emphasises the controversial normative commitment of political theorists of any approach, including a libertarian one.

are often seen as presenting the 'liberty friendly' face of politics, leaving the more 'intrusively' communitarian theorists alone with the job of justifying their positions. At a minimum, and as noted previously, the claim that a libertarian always or best maximises liberty is not straightforwardly true: many forms of libertarianism seem to prioritise *property* rather than liberty.[5] Both where this is and is not the case, libertarianism tends to entail the following: scepticism about the efficiency of the State in securing goods; scepticism about its right to claim sovereignty on many matters beyond the security of minimum 'rights' (classically to life, liberty, and property) and thus about the rightfulness of the involuntary sharing of a wide range of concerns; an outright denial of the justifiability of 'hard paternalism';[6] and an outright or implicit denial of the justifiability of many State-administered 'soft-paternalist' measures (because the plight of a vulnerable, non-rational person is not everyone else's concern). Political libertarianism in its most robust form is derived from a commitment to a strong conception of morality; for example, Lockean accounts, such as A. John Simmons' or Robert Nozick's limit the scope of State legitimacy *because* of the compelling demands of morality.[7] Other forms of libertarianism, by contrast, such as some based on interpretations of the 'Millian paradigm', are compatible with strong claims about moral pluralism and value-agnosticism. Although I do not – and could not – here exhaust accounts of libertarianism, I will relate the arguments I consider to the descriptivist/normativist divide outlined above: descriptive libertarians are those who argue for a small State on the empirical basis that this leads to the best outcome (however that is calculated), rather than because of a commitment to some prior side-constraints; normative libertarians, by contrast, urge that the State's right to rule is limited in principle, and should be limited in practice accordingly. Given that these two approaches use different manners of 'favourable evaluation',[8] it is possible that a person can argue in favour of a libertarian position on both grounds simultaneously, or acknowledge competing arguments that at once make him endorse libertarianism *and* some other political position. Within

---

[5] See Samuel Freeman, "Why libertarianism is not a liberal view", *Philosophy and Public Affairs* (2001) 30:2, 105–151, and Chapter 7, section 7.3.1.

[6] As discussed above, "hard paternalism" refers to paternalist decisions made on behalf of autonomous agents. See Chapter 7, section 7.3.4.4, and Gerald Dworkin, *The Theory and Practice of Autonomy* (Cambridge University Press, 1988), p. 124.

[7] *Cf* A. John Simmons, *On the Edge of Anarchy: Locke, Consent, and the Limits of Society* (Princeton University Press, 1993); Robert Nozick, *Anarchy, State, and Utopia* (Oxford: Blackwell, 1974).

[8] See A. John Simmons, "Consent theory for libertarians", *Social Philosophy and Policy* (2005) 22:1, 330–356, at 354; and Chapter 7, section 7.3.4.3.

the context of State health policy, I will focus in this section on four libertarian theorists whose arguments relating to public health issues are well noted: Richard Epstein, Ivan Illich, Petr Skrabanek, and H. Tristram Engelhardt.

8.2.2   Public health and libertarianism

Richard Epstein is clear that libertarianism is not to be conflated with anarchism:

> [N]o careful defender of laissez-faire has ever confused property and liberty with anarchy; all have indeed recognized the case for some state regulation under the police power. Even though the classical writers on the subject, such as Ernst Freund, were reluctant to offer any precise or comprehensive definition of the term, the received wisdom *confined* its application to laws and regulations that advanced the *public* safety, health, and morals as well as the catchall general welfare category.[9]

The way Epstein presents his case in favour of the 'old public health', which we considered above,[10] can be seen to fall into the descriptive frame, and is posited as an economic case in favour of minimal regulation:

> [T]he proper approach recognizes that there are always two kinds of error: the danger of stopping activities that turn out to be harmless, or allowing activities to go forward that turn out to be deadly.[11]

Throughout, his arguments rest on (often speculative) empirical claims about the greater harm caused by a more invasive State system designed to improve public health.[12] Public health measures such as enforced taxation to ensure clean water and sewerage, which only a "madman" or "knave" would oppose, do not, he takes it, require argument (we might note the utility of having a comprehensive class of tacitly self-defining protagonists such as "madmen" and "knaves", whose positions are of necessity refutable!). The "conflict" requiring argument, Epstein suggests, presents itself with more controversial measures, such as quarantine, vaccination, and the destruction of property.[13] In other words, there is a baseline of justified State action, on which everyone who is not

---

[9] Richard Epstein, "In defense of the 'old' public health", *Brooklyn Law Review* (2004) 69:4, 1421–1470, at 1428–1429 (emphasis in original).

[10] Chapter 3, section 3.2.2.

[11] Epstein, "In defense of the 'old' public health", at 1458.

[12] For example, *ibid.*, at 1464, Epstein appeals to the strength of his "own deep suspicion" that the "new public health is likely to reduce overall life expectancy".

[13] *Ibid.*, at 1444–1445.

mad can agree (disagreement itself debars a protagonist's being taken seriously, and thus precludes him from the debate). Beyond this bare minimum, arguments are needed, and the strength of an argument is evidenced by reference to its overall effect (in the current analysis on health). Epstein is sure of his case, taking it that his analysis as applied to public health is but one example of the empirical superiority of 'classical liberalism' over 'modern welfarism'. Private economic actors are better able to secure the good; and thus a community of agents who in the main take responsibility for, and care of, themselves will be better off than a population of agents who cede more responsibility to each other, and allow it more generally to be mediated through the State. At times the truth of such claims seems to rely on an apparently logical certainty given some uncontestable premise; at times it is evidenced by reference to practical upshots. Notwithstanding Epstein's conviction in these arguments, as they are justified by reference to the real world, as opposed to *a priori* side-constraints (e.g. as we find in a Nozickian small State), it is worth noting that some scepticism is due to his analysis. The dubious reliability of his factual claims is emphasised by Lawrence Gostin and Gregg Bloche, who suggest that Epstein's descriptive libertarianism is in reality just a means of disguising a less easily sold normative libertarianism.[14] If for the sake of argument we say that the jury is still out, increasing empirical research has focused on these questions, and if the evidence against Epstein's case is not compelling, it should at least give readers sympathetic to his views reason to reflect on their cogency. There is very good reason to believe that health*care* is more efficiently provided in systems that are less laissez-faire, and that better health obtains in societies that are more egalitarian, and much more closely regulated than Epstein would allow.[15] It should be stressed,

---

[14] Lawrence O. Gostin and M. Gregg Bloche, "The politics of public health: a response to Epstein", *Perspectives in Biology and Medicine* (2003) 46:3, S160–S175.

[15] Cf Michael Marmot, Geoffrey Rose, Martin Shipley, and P.J.S. Hamilton, "Employment grade and coronary heart disease in British civil servants", *Journal of Epidemiology and Community Health* (1978) 32, 244–249; Norman Daniels, Bruce Kennedy, and Ichiro Kawachi, "Why justice is good for our health: The social determinants of health inequalities", *Daedalus* (1999) 128:4, 215–251; Richard Eckersley, Jane Dickson, and Bob Douglas, *The Social Origins of Health and Well-being* (Cambridge University Press, 2001); Lawrence O. Gostin and Madison Powers, "What does social justice require for the public's health? Public health ethics and policy imperatives", *Health Affairs* (2006) 25:4, 1053–1060; Michael Marmot, *Status Syndrome: How Your Social Standing Directly Affects Your Health and Life Expectancy* (London: Bloomsbury, 2004); Jonathan Wolff, "Disadvantage, risk and the social determinants of health", *Public Health Ethics* (2009) 2:1, 214–223; Clare Bambra, Marcia Gibson, Amanda Sowden, Kath Wright, Margaret Whitehead, and Mark Petticrew, "Tackling the wider social determinants of health and health inequalities:

though, that even if Epstein's case is not convincingly made by simple reference to health outcomes, this may not be damning overall for the libertarianism he defends. His conception of health is narrow, relating to absence of disease or maladies that are pathogenic or "directly linked to particular ... substances".[16] We have already seen how his theories in this regard lead him to limit the definition of 'public health' to narrowly circumscribed governmental competences.[17] Doubtless Epstein recognises the disease implications of, for example, obesity; simply, he does not think they are most effectively (and thus best) addressed through regulatory intervention. Even if he is wrong in this claim, his empirical libertarianism is overall only destroyed if health is our baseline. If we have concerns other than health as he understands it, we may yet find his libertarianism compelling *all* things considered. (Then again, we may not.)

Epstein's approach, which within the context of public health law and ethics is linked to a narrow conception of health, may be contrasted with the libertarian perspective presented by Ivan Illich.[18] Illich is arguably the most noted critic of orchestrated, professionalised attempts that will – or will be said to – serve health. His celebrated work *Medical Nemesis* presents a principled and an empirical case against late-twentieth century, Western healthcare. The thesis essentially claims that professionalism has led to doctors' (and the State's) adverse possession of the concept of health, and with it their misappropriation of the power to decide how people's health should be served. Pointing to the iatrogenic harm that ensues, Illich provides a powerful critique, which still holds strong resonance in debates today.[19] Yet interestingly, he creates his own conceptual problems when he deals with health as a concept.[20]

evidence from systematic reviews", *Journal of Epidemiology and Community Health* (2010) 64, 284–291; Bob Roehr, "US gets least for healthcare spending; Netherlands the most", *British Medical Journal* (2010) 340:c3406, 14–15.

[16] Richard Epstein, "Let the shoemaker stick to his last: a defense of the 'old' public health", *Perspectives in Biology and Medicine* (2003) 46:3, S138–S159, at S141.

[17] See Chapter 3, section 3.2.2.

[18] Ivan Illich, *Limits to Medicine – Medical Nemesis: The Expropriation of Health* (London: Marion Boyars, 1995 [1976]).

[19] See eg Nicholas A. Christakis, "Indirectly doing harm", *British Medical Journal* (2009) 339, 782. Christakis applies what he labels "classic iatrogenesis" to public health considerations, raising the issue of groups that are simultaneously benefited and harmed by a public health policy, and going on to question the justifiability of "social iatrogenesis" where one group is harmed by a public health policy that benefits a different group.

[20] Possibly this is due to the wrong sort of understanding by analysts such as me; or at least an understanding that Illich had not foreseen when writing the book. See the preface to the 1995 edition of the book: Illich, *Limits to Medicine*. Nevertheless, what follows in the text seems to be valid comment.

Illich argues that it is wrong for health to be made public: with sickness a "public affair", he suggests, "it is no longer the concern of those who are ill".[21] Rather, he thinks health is best defined by the individual, not constrained and given practical authority through a scientific, medical epistemology. There is something a little paradoxical, however, about this approach. He simultaneously seeks to allow individuals to define their own health, and provides a robust definition himself. This ties health to a strong conception of autonomy, with the assured claim that we are best off when responsible for ourselves (and provided we are not harming others' rights). Whether or not Illich's claim is sound, health itself and its maintenance come to imply and be logically entailed by a theory of political libertarianism. In Illich's words:

"Health," after all, is simply an everyday word that is used to designate the intensity with which individuals cope with their internal states and their environmental conditions. In *Homo sapiens*, "healthy" is an adjective that qualifies ethical and political actions. In part at least, the health of a population depends on the way in which political actions condition the milieu and create circumstances that favour self-reliance, autonomy, and dignity for all, particularly the weaker. In consequence, health levels can only decline when survival comes to depend beyond a certain point on the heteronomous (other-directed) regulation of the organism's homeostasis. Beyond a critical level of intensity, institutional health care – no matter if it takes the form of cure, prevention, or environmental engineering – is equivalent to systematic health denial.[22]

Whilst Illich may make sound arguments about the 'use' of concepts such as health and disease by the State and the medical profession, it is surely arguable that he too, by claiming a necessary and strongly normative definition of health, misappropriates the term to reinforce his own conception of the good of people and the best manner of social order. This is somewhat ironic in an argument that criticises others for taking their definitions too far away from what 'health' might reasonably denote. And it serves well to demonstrate the potency of health as a term in arguments that claim through it some sort of political authority, even if those arguments recommend *less* rather than more State interference. We have a claim about what best serves people's good – small government and professions as servants rather than holders of power – and these are themselves bolstered by use of the term "health".[23]

---

[21] *Ibid.*, p. 155. As the point is made, Illich refers to a change in views on health at the time of the French Revolution, but it is intended to speak of something with long-standing effect.

[22] *Ibid.*, p. 7.

[23] Although the focus is on health and health services, Illich presents it as one amongst a more general range of problems with society governed by dominant industry.

In the context of health policy, Petr Skrabanek also marries both normative and descriptive libertarian approaches in an argument that explicitly owes much to Illich's concerns about unduly privileged professionalism (discussed further below), and fears of authoritarianism and totalitarianism.[24] Skrabanek is critical of policies' ostensible legitimisation in accordance with the World Health Organization's definition of health as "a state of complete physical, mental and social well-being and not merely the absence of disease or infirmity".[25] He describes "coercive healthism" as the political phenomenon whereby apparently objective, scientific, and technical fact is used through cynical altruism as a means to increase governmental power. Public health policies move beyond "legitimate preventive medicine, such as immunisation, pasteurisation, or sewage treatment, to the social, philosophical, and spiritual domains".[26] Medicalisation and prescribed social *mores* enable treatment to be forced on unwilling patients, whose rationality is more easily questioned when linked to health; an apparently objective concept. The medical profession's capacity to define normal, and stigmatise abnormal, is used to legitimate the limiting of people's behaviour in the name of health promotion.[27] This "coercive altruism" is a form of authoritarianism, and conformity as a result of a State's prescriptive system reflects a "creeping totalitarianism".[28] According to Skrabanek, this political phenomenon is fed by both the left and the right in Western liberal States:

[T]he Left starts from the premise that man is perfectible, as Rousseau believed, and by changing the unhealthy environment, created by an unfettered capitalism, man can be made healthy and happy, even though at times some degree of coercion might become necessary ... By linking poverty with disease (which is not unreasonable on its own), Marxists promise that in a classless society the health of the poor will improve. This has not been the experience of the working class in communist countries ...

The Right, on the other hand, is more concerned about the 'nation' than about the individual. To maintain the nation in a high state of readiness to defend the supremacy of the race, people should be responsible for their own health ... Patients 'should be made to pay', particularly when most diseases are now said to be 'caused' by unhealthy lifestyles ...

Any prescriptive system to make man free, or healthy, ends by enslaving him, or by taking health away from him.[29]

---

[24] Petr Skrabanek, *The Death of Humane Medicine and the Rise of Coercive Healthism* (Bury St Edmunds: St Edmundsbury Press, 1994).

[25] See the declaration in the WHO's constitution, available at http://apps.who.int/gb/bd/PDF/bd47/EN/constitution-en.pdf.

[26] Skrabanek, *The Death of Humane Medicine*, p. 47.

[27] *Ibid.*, p. 140.   [28] *Ibid.*, pp. 156–157.   [29] *Ibid.*, pp. 155–156.

As this last sentence suggests, Skrabanek too works from a robust conception of health. Yet for Skrabanek, it does not seem amenable to definition. He shares Illich's prizing of autonomy and liberty, but in contrast with Illich, he does not commit himself to making health another way of saying these things. Rather:

Health, like love, beauty or happiness, is a metaphysical concept, which eludes all attempts at objectivisation. Healthy people do not think of health, unless they are hypochondriacs, which, strictly speaking, is not a sign of health ... It is the absence of health that gives rise to dreaming about health, just as the real meaning of freedom is only experienced in prison.[30]

And just as Skrabanek finds individual pursuit of health to be unhealthy, so he argues that health as a political ideology, pursued by the State, is "a symptom of political sickness".[31]

It is useful finally to consider the approach of H. Tristram Engelhardt. Engelhardt acknowledges more forcefully than Epstein the rich and normatively potent effect of value judgements within the definition of health. Health on Engelhardt's count is not simply reducible to the absence of a scientific judgement of disease. Nevertheless, he does argue that what counts as good health will be relatively generalisable amongst people, notwithstanding the values inherent in teleological claims that will be made in any given assessment that something harms health.[32] In his words:

Our ideologies and expectations concerning the world move us to select certain states as illnesses because of our judgment as to what is dysfunctional or a deformity and to select certain cause sequences, etiological patterns, as being of interest to us because they are bound to groups of phenomena we identify as illnesses. Although there is a stark reality, it has significance for us only through our own value judgments, in particular through our social values.[33]

In 1994, Engelhardt published an argument that focuses specifically on US healthcare policy under the Clinton administration, but which has wider principled application relevant to our analysis of the role of politics in public health issues.[34] In this argument, he voices a radical scepticism of any "common content-full understanding of morality, justice, and fairness",[35] seeking to refute the plausibility of such theories as the

---

[30] *Ibid.*, p. 15.   [31] *Ibid.*
[32] See H. Tristram Engelhardt, "Is there a philosophy of medicine?", *Proceedings of the Biennial Meeting of the Philosophy of Science Association* (1976) 2, 94–108; H Tristram Engelhardt, "Ideology and etiology", *Journal of Medicine and Philosophy* (1976) 1:3, 256–268.
[33] Engelhardt, "Ideology and etiology", at 267.
[34] Engelhardt, "Health care reform: a study in moral malfeasance".
[35] *Ibid.*, at 506.

basis of practical political normativity. However one seeks to apply a moral theory, he argues – be it through a utilitarian judgement, by reference to game theory, the balancing of goods, the rational formation of contracts by hypothesised disinterested actors, or something else – the approach will question-beggingly demand an attachment to prior (and thus inherently controversial) values. In this sense, the critique seems to be as strongly sceptical of Epstein and Illich as it is of any bigger-State models. Indeed, as Søren Holm has argued, it seems to be *self-defeatingly* sceptical, as even a minimal model of political normativity is governed by a partisan and exclusive "rationality".[36]

Nevertheless, Engelhardt advances a contractarian theory of political legitimacy that seems to share its moral foundations, for example, with Simmons' libertarianism. Yet unlike Simmons, Engelhardt also denies the alternative practical good of political theories of justice that accord with an alternative normative theory:

> It is because of these difficulties that appeals to the governed for moral authority, not appeals to God, rational argument, or consensus, provide the most plausible justification for governmental moral authority. Consent must be actual or plausibly integral to resolving issues by agreement without the presumption of a common moral vision.[37]

This strong democratic commitment, which practically can not permit much by way of consensus, commits Engelhardt to defending only a minimal State (though one may wonder how the strong demands of valid contract-making does not lead in fact to the total anarchism advocated by Robert Paul Wolff[38]); like John Gray,[39] he does this in concession to the (at least practical) fact of moral pluralism. Engelhardt denies that his project is libertarian.[40] In some senses this seems reasonable: rather than entrench his political views in a moral perspective *based on* self-ownership, as many libertarian theories do, he simply seeks to protect *modus vivendi*. Nevertheless, the practical upshot is clearly that desirability and legitimacy can be said to obtain only in a libertarian regime.[41] This is all the coexistence of different moralities requires. As Engelhardt explains in a subsequent paper:

---

[36] Søren Holm, "Secular morality and its limits", *Medicine, Health Care and Philosophy* (1998) 1:1, 75–77, at 76.

[37] Engelhardt, "Health care reform: a study in moral malfeasance", at 508.

[38] Robert Paul Wolff, *In Defense of Anarchism* (with a new preface) (Berkeley: University of California Press, 1998).

[39] John Gray, *Two Faces of Liberalism* (Cambridge: Polity Press, 2000).

[40] Engelhardt, "Health care reform: a study in moral malfeasance", at 510–512.

[41] As Holm puts it, "the substantive conclusions which Engelhardt draws from his views about secular morality as a morality of mutual agreement, are indistinguishable from

None of these practices requires an agreement requiring a common, content-full understanding of the good and the right. It is enough that individuals by themselves or in different communities approach each other from their own wellsprings of concerns and interests, however diverse, so as to collaborate in a web of agreements, however sparse.[42]

Echoing Holm's critique, it is not quite clear how contractarianism can with any certainty be said to offer justified common morality, or how real Engelhardt's apparently more robust (as opposed to imputed or implicit) contractarianism is in practice. In other words, it remains unclear quite how Engelhardt establishes legitimate political authority. It is likewise possible, however, to see how his libertarianism (as I would continue to label it) may be persuasive to a 'descriptive libertarian' who was attracted to the liberal 'toleration' and the licence for contradictory moralities to be sustained in society through the political formulation of a large private sphere. Surely on some counts so narrow a libertarianism is not all that could be demanded by, or compatible with, sustaining plural moralities, but Engelhardt's view is a forceful one that may be attractive to a whole range of analysts.[43]

8.2.3   Health libertarians and scepticism about expertise

One further issue that we should consider here is a feature that is not exclusive to libertarian critiques, but is often associated with them: the question of scepticism of expert opinion. Where more collectivist State theories may recommend measures that are designed to enhance

---

the standard libertarian conclusions. His basic premises are ... non-libertarian, whereas his conclusions are libertarian". Holm, "Secular morality and its limits", at 75.

[42] H. Tristram Engelhardt, "Keynote address: bioethics at the end of the millennium: fashioning health-care policy in the absence of a moral consensus", Stephen Wear, James Bono, Gerald Logue, and Adrianne McEvoy (eds.), *Ethical Issues in Health Care on the Frontiers of the Twenty-First Century* (New York/Boston/Dordrecht/London/Moscow: Kluwer Academic Publishers, 2002), p. 10.

[43] See similarly Matti Häyry's treatment of competing 'rationalities' and his separation of moral and political (legal) normativity, and the scope for legal *neutrality*, as a means of overcoming the problem of equally plausible moral positions: Matti Häyry, *Rationality and the Genetic Challenge – Making People Better?* (Cambridge University Press, 2010), especially ch. 4. Note that in some senses Häyry's project in this regard seems a little confused, as the means he uses to establish neutrality looks markedly similar to a moral approach based on contractarianism that he claims to reject: John Coggon, "Confrontations in 'genethics': rationalities, challenges and methodological responses", *Cambridge Quarterly of Healthcare Ethics* (2011) 20:1, 46–55; see also Ronald M. Green, "Confronting rationality", *Cambridge Quarterly of Healthcare Ethics* (2011) 20:2, 216–227.

people's welfare, and demand taxation to underwrite such measures, there seems to be a need for a limiting imperative to make reasonably certain that only *good* welfare-protection be offered. To illustrate, consider Allen Buchanan's (non-libertarian) treatment of human rights. He takes it that these are legitimate tools for protecting people's interests. Part of the means to ascertain their proper employment is to ensure that specialist bodies gather and assess factual claims that support or undermine policy.[44] As we have already seen, libertarian theorists following Epstein would not necessarily doubt the value of this expertise; rather, they would imagine that the best results given the expertise would be achieved if individuals were left to make ensuing private arrangements themselves. We have also seen that in contrast Illich and Skrabanek have advanced critiques that are suspicious of a technocratic medicalisation that they perceived in late-twentieth century liberal societies, in approaches that are endorsed, developed, or expanded upon and carried through to the present day.[45] Although *Medical Nemesis* focused on the medical profession, and thus may be seen as less relevant in a (putatively) more 'patient-empowered' era, Illich was concerned about professionalism more generally having malign effects on society.[46] As he argues in *Disabling Professions*, "the new dominant professions claim control over human needs, *tout court*".[47] The wide problem of professional authority is found in three things:

[T]he sapiential authority to advise, instruct and direct; the moral authority that makes its acceptance not just useful but obligatory; and charismatic authority that allows professionals to appeal to some supreme interest of his client that not only outranks conscience but sometimes even the *raison d'état*.[48]

[44] Allen Buchanan, "Human rights and the legitimacy of the international order", *Legal Theory* (2008) 14:1, 39–70, especially at 61–64.

[45] See, for example, the following, very distinct, analyses: Michael Fitzpatrick, *The Tyranny of Health – Doctors and the Regulation of Lifestyle* (London and New York: Routledge, 2001); Stale Fredriksen, "Tragedy, utopia and medical progress", *Journal of Medical Ethics* (2006) 32:8, 450–453; Fred Paccaud, "Implausible diseases and public health", *European Journal of Public Health* (2007) 17:5, 410; Nicola Glover-Thomas and John Fanning, "Medicalisation: the role of e-pharmacies in iatrogenic harm", *Medical Law Review* (2010) 18:1, 28–55.

[46] In *Medical Nemesis* itself, Illich explains how "Iatrogenesis will be controlled only if it is understood as but one aspect of the destructive dominance of industry over society, as but one instance of that paradoxical counterproductivity which is now surfacing in all major industrial societies". Illich, *Limits to Medicine*, p. 211, and Part IV. See also Ivan Illich, "Disabling professions", in Ivan Illich, Irving Kenneth Zola, John McKnight, Jonathan Caplan, and Harley Shaiken, *Disabling Professions* (New York and London: Marion Boyars, 1977).

[47] Illich, "Disabling professions," *ibid.*, p. 16.   [48] *Ibid.*, pp. 17–18.

By becoming "experts of the public good",[49] the liberal professions become dominant, and their claims (both epistemic and normative) are thus to be treated with considerable suspicion and scepticism.

To return to health, this may be particularly problematic in regard to health defined as 'social well-being', although the concern applies to narrower definitions too. If we are to formulate positive public health policy, we must confront the problem of deciding who we trust to define health (or 'well-being') satisfactorily. Consider Skrabanek's reflection on Illich's work:

> [The medical profession] may not stop at 'advising', but move on to monopolis-ing the power to prescribe and codify. They not only define what is bad, but they also dictate what is good. Illich made a clear distinction between medi-cine as a liberal profession (in which medical knowledge and skills are used to alleviate the suffering of fellow men) and medicine as a dominant profession, dictating what constitutes a health need for people in general and turning the whole world into a hospital ward.[50]

It is not necessary to buy fully into these theories to accept that they invoke a serious problem that ought to be heeded, at least if there is good reason to believe in plural theories of the good, to doubt the soundness of the understanding of the good employed by experts, and to be wary of the *bona fide* motivation of all in positions of power. Given the wide variety of definitions of health that exist, at the least some scepticism recommends itself of policy justifications that are purportedly based on health benefits.

8.2.4   *Concluding comments on libertarianism and small State models*

Arguments about public health that urge a normativity limited to a political libertarian perspective may draw from any of various grounds. Although the four theorists considered in this section are all advocates of political libertarianism, and each frames his arguments by refer-ence to health, their reasoning varies, as does their treatment of the concept of health itself. The above analysis is intended to be illustra-tive rather than comprehensive. Complemented by the discussions of anarchism in the previous chapter, it is sufficient to allow us to make and carry forward the following points. An analyst may advocate a small State model for any of various reasons. For example: he might

---

[49] *Ibid.*, p. 20.
[50] Skrabanek, *The Death of Humane Medicine*, p. 19. See also Skrabanek, pp. 146–150, on "The doctor as agent of the state"; Thomas Szasz, *The Theology of Medicine – The Political-Philosophical Foundations of Medical Ethics* (Oxford University Press, 1979), ch. 1.

advocate political libertarianism because of prior moral constraints, as in Nozickian libertarianism;[51] he might find that efficiency recommends private means of securing the bulk of overlapping (but therefore not politically shared) goods, as in the case of Epstein;[52] he may be a moral pluralist and defend a small State as it protects against the crushing of *modus vivendi*, as in the cases of Skrabanek and Engelhardt;[53] he might be sceptical about the normative status of expertise, and the fear of creeping technocratic regulation based upon it, as in the cases of Illich and Skrabanek.[54] Furthermore, even as exemplified by the small number of arguments we have considered here, it is important to recognise how health assumes distinct understandings in different theories that are presented in public health law and ethics. Even those of us who are not convinced by the sorts of concerns raised in this section would be sensible to take seriously the elements of some of the expressions of scepticism. Finally, it should be noted that attachment to political libertarianism need not denote a negative, or even narrow, view of the value or strength of community, or the good of community. Simply, it presents limits to great elements of communal cohesion's being the business of the State. Where, for example, these concerns manifest themselves not on the basis of epistemic uncertainty about the (actual or probable) content of people's interests, a libertarian position may suggest policy initiatives that go short of coercion, as notably advocated by Richard Thaler and Cass Sunstein.[55] We should bear in mind, then, the discussion of policy and regulatory approaches in Chapter 4, but also the claims in Chapter 7 about the need to justify the rationale underpinning policy (or failure to make positive policy), even where this is not coercive. There is a clear tension, which warrants consideration, between the less sceptical approach to the good taken by Epstein, and the much more pluralist Skrabanek. Whatever political theory we might adopt, it is of considerable importance to address the epistemic problems this suggests exist.

---

[51] Nozick, *Anarchy, State, and Utopia*.

[52] Epstein, "Let the shoemaker stick to his last: a defense of the 'old' public health"; Epstein, "In defense of the 'old' public health".

[53] Skrabanek, *The Death of Humane Medicine*, especially pp. 185–190; Engelhardt, "Health care reform: a study in moral malfeasance"; Engelhardt, "Keynote address: bioethics at the end of the millennium".

[54] Skrabanek, *The Death of Humane Medicine*; Illich, *Limits to Medicine*; Illich, "Disabling professions".

[55] Cass Sunstein and Richard Thaler, "Libertarian paternalism is not an oxymoron", *The University of Chicago Law Review* (2003) 70:4, 1159–1202; Richard Thaler and Cass Sunstein, *Nudge: Improving Decisions About Health, Wealth, and Happiness* (London: Penguin Books, 2009).

8.3   Public health and the 'middle ground'

8.3.1   Moving into the middle ground

Most approaches found in public health law and ethics would roughly be categorised as falling in the 'middle ground'. In the space available here, it is only possible to give short accounts of different perspectives, if I am to provide a sufficiently broad representation. Although this risks an inevitable 'thinness' and simplification, what follows demonstrates the range and manner of analyses that seek to balance concerns for health (variously conceived) with other concerns such as sustaining liberty, sharing responsibility, and practically assuring sufficient concern for vulnerable individuals who are part of political society. It is common for the libertarian approaches to derive political norms from conceptions of people as rational, autonomous, persons. These works' treatment of people who do not come close to matching this – for example, young children, the temporarily or permanently mentally incapacitated – is often rather sparse, simplistic, or question-begging. Rather than ignore the variety that is inherent in the political community, it is important to account for and respond to it: for example, we need to ask what sorts of rights (and so on) do young children have; how are these established; and what does this imply in terms of practical obligations (and so on) for other members of the community? Where libertarian accounts inadequately respond to such questions we do well to look to more realistic appraisals of political communities, and (potentially) reconsider guiding norms in the light of that.

To assist the analysis, I separate the approaches considered in this section under four broad subheadings. The means of 'clustering' the theories is primarily for clear presentation. It must not be taken as denoting deep-seated commonalties between the theories placed under the same heading, or complete distinctions between theories under different headings. A different analyst may have taken the same theories and grouped them alternatively. This is not problematic, provided the following draws out well the pressing normative concerns. Although the theories are not exhaustive of approaches in the middle ground in public health law and ethics, they give a good overview of many salient concerns that must be accounted for in an assessment of the political question "what makes health public?". I will consider 'principle-based' approaches; theories associated with questions of social justice; those that claim a 'communitarian' focus;[56] and human rights arguments.

---

[56] Note that despite using 'communitarian' as a distinct label here I use the term generally to denote theories that accept and work with a robust concept of political community,

8.3.2   Ethical principles

Readers familiar with the medical ethics literature will be aware of the dominance of 'the four principles' in that field, particularly as it applies to professional ethics.[57] Given their vogue, it is unsurprising that when there is apparently something new to be explored in 'public health ethics', commentators investigate the utility and applicability of 'the four principles' approach,[58] or its underlying rationale, in order to develop general principles that may transcend moral divides. They thereby enunciate important values or considerations of general application, to assist analysis. Here I consider three such approaches, all published shortly after the turn of the century. In each case, the main 'target audience' seems to be public health professionals, rather, for example, than 'ethicists'. As such, the papers (at least ostensibly) do not present political theories. Indeed, they may be seen as attempts to get past distinct or competing political theories. Nevertheless, to be normatively valid within a legitimate liberal political system (which each would surely claim to be) there must at least be tacit background claims that amount to, or imply, some substantial manner of political normativity. These works may best be considered, then, as aids to people who need to be *reminded* of the relevant considerations entailed in a wider political model to which (in principle) they are already committed. As they are so influential they demand explicit attention here. However, it is crucial to voice an important *caveat* to analysts who come to public health issues from critical positions in legal, moral, or political philosophy. Principles can be helpful, and the three papers considered here are all clear, well-considered, and robust. Nevertheless, analysts need to read them as consequential to a prior political theory, and locate their normative stipulations there. Neither 'public health', nor any given 'principle of public health ethics' is the start point. Should it become so, much analysis in 'public health ethics' will become as normatively impoverished and practically useless (if not harmful!) as is the case with so much other work in bioethics.

---

and have used this to help establish that theorists of quite distinct political hues share a commitment to the idea of a *shared* and thereby constraining community.

[57] Tom Beauchamp and James Childress, *Principles of Biomedical Ethics* (6th edn) (Oxford University Press, 2008). The 'four principles' are autonomy, non-maleficence, beneficence, and justice.

[58] See Stephen Holland, *Public Health Ethics* (Cambridge: Polity, 2007), pp. 26–28, and on adapted or alternative 'principles-based' approaches, see pp. 28–32.

With that *caveat* in mind, let us first consider a paper by Nancy Kass.[59] Kass considers the development of an ethical approach that would prevent the wrongful use of power that would ostensibly be justified in the name of public health. In her words:

The need for a code of ethics for public health, then, might be viewed as a code of restraint, a code to preserve fairly and appropriately the negative rights of citizens to noninterference.[60]

At the same time, Kass argues, the code must account for the positive political rights (and thus obligations) relevant to public health issues, that are properly addressed in a framework such as the one she outlines. She thus contextualises her perspective on professional ethics within a morally pluralistic, political liberalism. Her framework may therefore be seen as the logical upshot of such liberalism, which analytically can be traced back to derive an understanding of at least approximately how the political theory is framed. Kass advocates a six-step approach to public health ethics analysis. First, check the goals of any proposed programme, to ensure they relate to the reduction of morbidity or mortality. Second, be sure about the effectiveness of a programme, by reference to good data and understanding, for example, of uptake. Especially where liberty will be infringed, Kass suggests that the "burden of proof" is with the government to demonstrate the programme will succeed (noting too that success in terms of health improvements alone does not signal acceptability). Third, she argues that it is important to consider the likely burden of a programme, saying:

Although a variety of burdens or harms might exist in public health programs, the majority will fall into 3 broad categories: risks to privacy and confidentiality, especially in data collection activities; risks to liberty and self-determination, given the power accorded public health to enact almost any measure necessary to contain disease; and risks to justice, if public health practitioners propose targeting public health interventions only to certain groups.[61]

Fourth, Kass says that ways of minimising burdens should be explored, by considering alternative interventions and choosing the least burdensome option. Fifth, there is an appeal to fairness (which seems in Kass' usage to be synonymous with justice), and a suggestion that public health programmes ought to be employed as a means of addressing existing social injustices. Finally, it is argued that the benefits and

---

[59] Nancy Kass, "An ethics framework for public health", *American Journal of Public Health* (2001) 91:11, 1776–1782.
[60] *Ibid.*, at 1777.   [61] *Ibid.*, at 1779.

burdens of a proposed programme must be fairly balanced. Here Kass notes the inevitability of disagreement, resultant of competing value systems, and urges that resolution be found in open systems of democratic procedural justice (which is not to be conflated with the tyranny of the majority):

[I]t is important to acknowledge that there will always be some number of persons who do not want their water fluoridated, do not want their children immunized, do not want to wear seat belts, and do not want speed limits on public roads. That there is dissent is insufficient justification for blocking a public health program; indeed, dissent is inevitable in all proposals. Dissent must be considered, however, and it deserves special attention if it is raised exclusively by a particular identified subgroup such as an ethnic minority, a particular age group, or residents of a particular neighborhood.[62]

Kass allows for both moral and political pluralism, suggesting that measures deemed acceptable in one State may not be acceptable in another. Even as this bears on questions of what is burdensome, and what is excessively burdensome, a presumption against coercion seems to prevail. That policies will differ can indicate that fair process has been followed against a background of legitimate pluralism, rather than that one or more of the policies is necessarily wrong.

In her conclusion, Kass notes explicitly that public policy is not based only on health concerns. In fact, the development of her six stages account well for this, and whilst they speak to officials charged with the implementation of policy, they speak well also to the political system in which they are to operate. Kass clearly envisages a morally pluralistic, liberal democracy, and ties her ethical claims not to a monistic account of morality, but rather to a political normativity that accommodates distinct moralities, albeit with some solid 'ground rules', relating to liberty as a default, coercion as a last resort, (at least something like, if not straightforward) Rawlsian justice as a prevalent consideration,[63] and deliberative democratic process as a means of resolving otherwise intractable moral disputes.

The second paper that I want to consider here is by James Childress and colleagues.[64] Again the approach seems primarily to be addressed to practitioners in public health, and thus does not claim to form a political theory in and of itself. Furthermore, the authors describe it as relating to "moral considerations" at a level of generality that "does not entail

---

[62] *Ibid.*, at 1781.

[63] John Rawls, *A Theory of Justice – Revised edition* (Oxford University Press, 1999).

[64] James Childress, Ruth Faden, Ruth Gaare, *et al.*, "Public health ethics: mapping the terrain", *Journal of law, Medicine and Ethics* (2002) 30:2, 169–177.

a commitment to any particular theory or method".[65] Nevertheless, to sustain a coherence it also seems to be traceable back to a commitment to a theory of political liberalism, or one of a number of political theories: without their explicitly providing this normative start point, we see the upshot of political liberalism, albeit not its foundation. As such, any political theories that conduce to a similar result may be under description here. As with Kass' single-authored argument, there is some further detail about the political system that supports the directions. The authors list the following nine considerations, claiming that the list is not exhaustive:

- producing benefits;
- avoiding, preventing, and removing harms;
- producing the maximal balance of benefits over harms and other costs (often called utility);
- distributing benefits and burdens fairly (distributive justice) and ensuring public participation, including the participation of affected parties (procedural justice);
- respecting autonomous choices and actions, including liberty of action;
- protecting privacy and confidentiality;
- keeping promises and commitments;
- disclosing information as well as speaking honestly and truthfully (often grouped under transparency); and
- building and maintaining trust.[66]

The authors do not suggest that there is any presumptive ordering or weighting that can properly be given to the different moral considerations; "absolute" priority is given to none. That no algorithm or universally applicable means of resolution is presented is reflective of the moral and value pluralism against which their proposal is set. In order to assist resolution when there is conflict between a moral consideration's supporting a public health "goal" and the demands of the other moral considerations, five "justificatory conditions" are appealed to. Problem solving is assisted by considerations of effectiveness, proportionality, necessity, least infringement, and public justification.[67] The authors' reference to public justification is cast "in terms that fit the overall social contract in a liberal, pluralistic democracy".[68] Although the wider elaboration in their paper is of doubtless utility to people facing problems in public health ethics, it seems clear that everything can actually be reduced back to this *political* system of normativity, and resolution on all counts is found in accordance with the norms that

---

[65] *Ibid.*, at 170.   [66] *Ibid.*, at 170–171.
[67] *Ibid.*, at 172.   [68] *Ibid.*

implies. More specifically, they endorse Norman Daniels' "account-ability for reasonableness" method as the right means of overcoming moral disagreement in politics.[69] They summarise Daniels' approach as including:

[T]ransparency and publicity about the reasons for a decision; appeals to rationales and evidence that fair-minded parties would agree are relevant; and procedures for appealing and revising decisions in light of challenges by various stakeholders.[70]

Throughout, the argument ostensibly focuses on moral considerations, but it is clear that the prevalent normativity is political. The context in which public health activity 'happens' is social, and the society is morally pluralistic and governed politically.

The final paper we will consider here is by Ross Upshur.[71] Upshur argues that the four principles approach is "robust" and "useful" in medical ethics. He therefore seeks a similar tool for those interested in public health issues, but suggests that the distinct issues raised – notably the questions associated with moral pluralism in a political community – require an alternative list. As, again, we have an argument focused on the *justification* of public health activity, we are given a theory whose background is in politics, and whose normativity derives directly from that applied to the State. Upshur's four principles of public health ethics are: the harm principle; least restrictive or coercive means; the reciprocity principle; and the transparency principle. It is clear that, whilst Upshur claims the principles are derived from "the nascent literature in public health ethics", these are really articulations, again, of a theory of democratic political liberalism. The harm principle is a simple iteration of the oft-cited passage from John Stuart Mill's essay *On Liberty*.[72] The principle of least restriction is self-explanatory. The reciprocity principle denotes a duty on "society" to help people discharge their duties, compensating those who are burdened. And the

---

[69] The authors cite Norman Daniels, "Accountability for reasonableness", *British Medical Journal* (2000) 321, 1300–1301. See also Norman Daniels and James Sabin, "Limits to health care: fair procedures, democratic deliberation, and the legitimacy problem for insurers", *Philosophy and Public Affairs* (1997) 26:4, 303–350.

[70] Childress, Faden, Gaare, *et al.*, "Public health ethics: mapping the terrain", 173–174.

[71] Ross Upshur, "Principles for the justification of public health intervention", *Canadian Journal of Public Health* (2002) 93:2, 101–103.

[72] As quoted by Upshur: "The only purpose for which power can be rightfully exercised over any member of a civilized community, against his will, is to prevent harm to others. His own good, either physical or moral, is not a sufficient warrant." *Ibid.*, at 102.

transparency principle is again a nod to deliberative democracy, this time attributed to Habermas.[73]

In conclusion to his paper, Upshur says "[e]thics in public health requires systematic attention".[74] It is clear that he has not been alone in so thinking, and the last decade has seen an explosion in literature on public health ethics. Yet it is also apparent – and exemplified in the three papers considered here – that what tends to happen, and what usefully happens, is not the development of some sub-discipline in ethics – such as medical ethics – but rather a series of exercises in political philosophy. As such, rather than forming a new discipline, we see attempts to provide a particular focus to modes of inquiry that are as old as philosophy itself. And unlike medicine or health care, which themselves provide at some level a narrowing focus, the study of normative issues in public health can not be undertaken in a vacuum. Theorists may refer to 'moral principles', but where they allow for 'reasonable disagreement', and look for means of resolution, this suggests the necessity of an alternative normative system: politics. Beneath the approaches considered in this section is a need to establish a sense of the common good and to recognise what counts as a public concern (and thus an indication for a limit to the private realm). To be useful analytically, the political theory itself must be articulated, and in the following sections, I consider a few examples of how this has been done.

8.3.3   *Justice, equality, capability, and opportunity*

Claims about justice are central to many endeavours in public health law and ethics. There are now several monographs detailing distinct theories of justice that focus specifically on the bearing of justice on health, and the practical normative implications of the relationships between health and society.[75] It is highly likely that their number will increase substantially over the next decade. Each theory has political implications, and makes a rich addition to debates both in public health law and ethics,

---

[73] Jürgen Habermas, *The Theory of Communicative Action. Vol 1. Reason and the Rationalization of Society* (translated by T. McCarthy) (Boston: Beacon Press, 1984).

[74] Upshur, "Principles for the justification of public health intervention", at p. 103.

[75] See Madison Powers and Ruth Faden, *Social Justice: The Moral Foundations of Public Health and Health Policy* (Oxford University Press, 2006); Norman Daniels, *Just Health: Meeting Health Needs Fairly* (Cambridge University Press, 2008); Shlomi Segall, *Health, Luck, and Justice* (Princeton and Oxford: Princeton University Press, 2010); Jennifer Prah Ruger, *Health and Social Justice* (New York: Oxford University Press, 2010).

and to wider inquiries in political philosophy. There are things that the different theories share, but also wide basic divergences, and countless subtle distinctions in nuance and development. For present purposes, I propose to consider two works that focus directly on public health: the theory of social justice articulated by Madison Powers and Ruth Faden, and Norman Daniels' development of John Rawls' *Theory of Justice*. I will also consider Jonathan Wolff and Avner de-Shalit's *Disadvantage*. This last text is not placed, by its authors anyway,[76] within 'public health ethics'. However, as with the other two theories, 'health' is treated as one important category in a wider scheme, emphasising its importance in analysis of a just or equal society.

Powers and Faden's theory of social justice is rightly considered a leading work in this area.[77] The subtitle of their book – "the moral foundations of public health and health policy" – may suggest a narrow focus, simply on health. However, whilst their principal focus in terms of policy outputs is on health-related issues, they develop an argument that the normative questions raised in this regard can not be considered without attention being given to *all* things relevant to the underpinnings of political normativity. Where many works in bioethics are based in some abstracted moral position, such as a universe of just two people (e.g. a doctor and patient isolated from everyone else and only concerned by the clinical issue at hand), Powers and Faden's crucial insight is that the relevant foundations can not be found there. As they say in the book's preface:

> We contend that it is impossible to make progress in our understanding of the demands of justice *within* medical care without looking *outside* of medical care to public health and to the other determinants of inequalities in health and indeed without situating an analysis of justice and health policy in the wider social and political context.[78]

Their account thereby "denies that there are separate spheres of justice, within health policy or within social policy more generally".[79]

Powers and Faden's theory of justice places itself firmly in the real world, seeking means of establishing "which inequalities matter most", and gaining an understanding of how to address them. They approach this by developing an essentialist account of human well-being,[80]

---

[76] Though Wolff does apply the theory directly to questions portrayed explicitly as ones in public health ethics, for example, in Jonathan Wolff, "Disadvantage, risk and the social determinants of health", *Public Health Ethics* (2009) 2:1, 214–223.

[77] Powers and Faden, *Social Justice*.   [78] *Ibid.*, p. x (emphasis in original).

[79] *Ibid.*, p. xi. See also *ibid.*, ch. 4.

[80] More specifically, they describe it as a "moderate essentialist" account: "While a threshold level of well-being across each dimension of well-being may not be present

around which an understanding of the good of people can be established, and thus a theory explaining what are just norms in a human society. Well-being, they argue, comprises six "plural, irreducible dimensions, each of which represents something of independent moral significance".[81] Their account draws only from these issues of universal importance. In so doing, it allows that there are further matters of significance peculiar to different people, but their contention is that the six are crucial to everyone, and are the basis of finding answers to questions of social justice. The political imperatives demanded by justice are to secure a sufficiency, insofar as is possible, of the six dimensions of well-being: health; personal security; reasoning; respect; attachment; and self-determination.[82] For Powers and Faden, it is essential that the six components be recognised as qualitatively distinct. Therefore, their approach to the concept of health entails a rejection of the WHO's definition, which suggests that 'health' comprises all of human well-being; physical, mental, and social. The WHO's understanding, they say, "conflates virtually all elements of human development under a single rubric and thereby makes almost any deficit of well-being into a health deficit".[83]

In fact, it is not entirely clear at what level this criticism should be taken to bite. After all, there at least appears to be scope for differentiation within the WHO's definition, and Powers and Faden themselves ultimately relate their concerns about the human good under a single rubric. The overall rubric may best not be labelled 'health' – perhaps because it is misleading, beyond the competence of the WHO, or

---

(or even possible) for everyone, our list of essential dimensions of well-being is offered as an account of those things *characteristically* present within a decent life, whatever a person's particular life plans and personal commitments." *Ibid.*, p. 15. For elaboration, see *ibid.* pp. 29–30.

[81] *Ibid.*, p. 15.

[82] Beyond health, I can not here explore in depth the meanings of each of these. Briefly, they may be taken as follows. Personal security is used to denote the sorts of personal invasion that denote, for example, some manner of *abuse* (threatened or actual), as opposed to simple bodily violations that may cause harm, but not unacceptably (e.g. as in the case of a consensual surgical intervention). Reasoning relates to reflective capacities necessary for existence as practical, morally cognisant beings. Respect refers to equal treatment of people (others and oneself) "as independent sources of moral worth and dignity" and "appropriate objects of sympathetic identification" (*ibid.*, p. 22). Attachment relates to the bonds and sense of association with the community, as well as closer, more intimate relationships. Self-determination, which they describe as "the linchpin of liberal political theory" (*ibid.*, p. 26), does not entail a completely atomising theory that sanctifies personal choice, but reflects the way in which "our lives [should] be shaped at least in part by our choices, informed by our values and interests" (*ibid.*, p. 28). Overall, see *ibid.*, ch. 2.

[83] *Ibid.*, p. 17.

renders the term 'health' redundant or useless – but it is surely no less tenable or coherent an approach, at least in the abstract, than describing the bases of human good under the term 'well-being'. Nevertheless, Powers and Faden seek to differentiate health under its own, more narrow heading, so that particular, exclusive matters of moral significance can be assessed in due isolation from the other five distinct aspects of well-being. They therefore work with an:

[O]rdinary-language understanding of physical and mental health that is intended to capture the dimension of human flourishing that is frequently expressed through the biological or organic functioning of the body.[84]

Their definition is not, however, reducible to species-typical functioning or biological criteria. It entails concerns:

[O]f public health and clinical medicine, including premature mortality and preventable morbidity, malnutrition, pain, loss of mobility, mental health, the biological basis of behavior, reproduction (and its control), and sexual functioning.[85]

Thus their conception of health looks beyond issues that are limited to "the vectors of disease, injury, or illness",[86] and their basis for assessment of health policy finds imperatives associated with other aspects of well-being, rather than just health considered in a vacuum.

Whilst their approach relates to ideal concepts within the six dimensions, they do not rest it upon any metaphysical claims about the human good. Furthermore, the imperatives that they draw, though aspirant to the ideals of social justice, are practically grounded and give "practical guidance on questions of which inequalities matter most when just background conditions are *not* in place".[87] They do not, therefore, work within the hypothetical bounds of a society of just institutions and atomised rational actors, but rather develop a relational account that applies to a society of people who are mixed in terms of power, vulnerability, advantage, dependence, and interdependence. In contrast with other comparable theories, the theory advanced by Powers and Faden shares most with Amartya Sen's and Martha Nussbaum's 'capabilities approaches'.[88] Nevertheless, they distance themselves from simple capabilities, and urge that the *achievement* of well-being is of central concern, not least because in regard, for example, to vulnerable groups, or children, who could not be in a position to exercise agency, it is

---

[84] *Ibid.*   [85] *Ibid.*   [86] *Ibid.*, p. 18.   [87] *Ibid.*, p. 30.

[88] See *ibid.*, pp. 37–41, and cf Amartya Sen, *Development as Freedom* (Oxford University Press, 1999), especially ch. 3; Martha Nussbaum, "Capabilities as fundamental entitlements: Sen and social justice", *Feminist Economics* (2003) 9:2–3, 33–59.

the attainment of well-being that matters. In careful elaboration of an egalitarian outlook that concerns itself primarily with people's having a sufficiency of well-being, Powers and Faden summarise their position as follows:

[T]he point of a nonideal theory of justice, expressed positively, is to achieve a level of sufficiency for each of the dimensions of well-being. Those inequalities that are most urgent to address, for a theory that aims ultimately at a sufficiency of dimensions of well-being, are ones that are a consequence of systematically related overlapping social determinants affecting multiple dimensions of well-being. Justice, therefore, requires both obligations to remedy existing systematic patterns of disadvantage that profoundly and pervasively undermine the prospects for well-being, as well as prospective obligations to design social institutions and structures in order to prevent such patterns of disadvantage from arising.[89]

These factors can only be assessed by reference to the real world, with a view to the way systematic disadvantages materialise, and with due concern given to the determination of matters across a "whole life view". In particular, they insist on proper account being given to development from childhood, when many concerns are not properly conceived by reference to limits to choices.[90] And in contrast with the apparent straightforward acceptance in the arguments of Kass, Childress *et al.*, and Upshur, Powers and Faden recognise a much more limited scope for useful or even justified engagement with deliberative democratic mechanisms, such as "accountability for reasonableness". Instead, Powers and Faden suggest that the hard choices are to be made by government, and the more pressing constraints on its freedom to make 'radical choices' between potential policy positions are imposed by the demands of justice.[91] Thus, their approach requires a sound and defensible normative theory, but also sound knowledge of the world to which it applies. Only then can we understand systematic disadvantage, which disadvantages are worst, and achieve means of addressing the problems we find.

It is interesting to note, therefore, that Powers and Faden could just as well have entitled their book *Disadvantage*, as Jonathan Wolff and Avner de-Shalit chose to do.[92] Wolff and de-Shalit deny that theirs is a theory of justice,[93] yet their approach shares a great deal with Powers

---

[89] Powers and Faden, *Social Justice*, pp. 71–72.
[90] *Ibid.*, ch. 3, especially pp. 73–79.   [91] *Ibid.*, ch. 7.
[92] Jonathan Wolff and Avner de-Shalit, *Disadvantage* (Oxford and New York: Oxford University Press, 2007).
[93] They say in note 1 to chapter 1: "In general we will avoid using the terminology of 'justice' and 'injustice'. In our view society has an obligation to address many forms

and Faden's. They too assume a 'non-ideal' approach, and attach great value to empirical work: so much so that their account of normatively important disadvantage is substantiated, in part, through an empirical methodology.[94] Their concern is again a study of inequality, with a view to addressing systematic, socially determined disadvantaging of groups. In particular, they are concerned about the 'clustering' of disadvantage within specific social groups. Like Powers and Faden, they draw particularly from the 'capabilities approach', once more in a revised form. In their case, they replace the idea of 'capability' with that of 'genuine opportunity',[95] which they argue is a less vague measure to assess the security of the functionings that are crucial to well-being. It is interesting to compare and contrast their arguments with Powers and Faden's, as their insights complement well those discussed immediately above.

Wolff and de-Shalit argue in favour of a pluralist account, urging that aspects crucial to human flourishing are not reducible to a single measure (and thus a deficit in individual aspects of well-being is not readily recompensable through, for example, financial alternatives). They choose directly to expand and develop Martha Nussbaum's list of essential human functionings. It is Nussbaum's contention that without substantive detail, discussion of capabilities and what justice requires to permit human flourishing will come to nothing. This is why she develops a specific list, which bears citing in full here:

The list itself is open-ended and has undergone modification over time; no doubt it will undergo further modification in the light of criticism. But here is the current version.

The Central Human Capabilities

1. **Life**. Being able to live to the end of a human life of normal length; not dying prematurely, or before one's life is so reduced as to be not worth living.
2. **Bodily Health**. Being able to have good health, including reproductive health; to be adequately nourished; to have adequate shelter.

---

of disadvantage, whether or not they are injustices, strictly speaking. Hence to concentrate only on injustice would be to risk imposing an unhelpful restriction on our subject matter." *Ibid.*, p. 194.

[94] This methodology entailed the conducting of interviews with members of the public to evaluate, understand, and add to a theory of the 'functionings' necessary to sustain human well-being, and to understand when inequalities in disadvantage give particular rise to concerns: on the methodology see *ibid.*, Appendix 1.

[95] See especially *ibid.*, ch. 4.

3. **Bodily Integrity**. Being able to move freely from place to place; to be secure against violent assault, including sexual assault and domestic violence; having opportunities for sexual satisfaction and for choice in matters of reproduction.

4. **Senses, Imagination, and Thought**. Being able to use the senses, to imagine, think, and reason – and to do these things in a 'truly human' way, a way informed and cultivated by an adequate education, including, but by no means limited to, literacy and basic mathematical and scientific training. Being able to use imagination and thought in connection with experiencing and producing works and events of one's own choice, religious, literary, musical, and so forth. Being able to use one's mind in ways protected by guarantees of freedom of expression with respect to both political and artistic speech, and freedom of religious exercise. Being able to have pleasurable experiences and to avoid non-beneficial pain.

5. **Emotions**. Being able to have attachments to things and people outside ourselves; to love those who love and care for us, to grieve at their absence; in general, to love, to grieve, to experience longing, gratitude, and justified anger. Not having one's emotional development blighted by fear and anxiety. (Supporting this capability means supporting forms of human association that can be shown to be crucial in their development.)

6. **Practical Reason**. Being able to form a conception of the good and to engage in critical reflection about the planning of one's life. (This entails protection for the liberty of conscience and religious observance.)

7. **Affiliation**.
   A. Being able to live with and toward others, to recognize and show concern for other human beings, to engage in various forms of social interaction; to be able to imagine the situation of another. (Protecting this capability means protecting institutions that constitute and nourish such forms of affiliation, and also protecting the freedom of assembly and political speech.)
   B. Having the social bases of self-respect and nonhumiliation; being able to be treated as a dignified being whose worth is equal to that of others. This entails provisions of nondiscrimination on the basis of race, sex, sexual orientation, ethnicity, caste, religion, national origin.

8. **Other Species**. Being able to live with concern for and in relation to animals, plants, and the world of nature.

9. **Play**. Being able to laugh, to play, to enjoy recreational activities.

10. **Control Over One's Environment**.

    A. Political. Being able to participate effectively in political choices that govern one's life; having the right of political participation, protections of free speech and association.
    B. Material. Being able to hold property (both land and movable goods), and having property rights on an equal basis with others; having the right to seek employment on an equal basis with others; having the

freedom from unwarranted search and seizure. In work, being able to work as a human being, exercising practical reason, and entering into meaningful relationships of mutual recognition with other workers.[96]

Wolff and de-Shalit add to this list:

1. **Doing good to others**. Being able to care for others as part of expressing your humanity. Being able to show gratitude.
2. **Living in a law-abiding fashion**. The possibility of being able to live within the law; not to be forced to break the law, cheat, or to deceive other people or institutions.
3. **Understanding the law**. Having a general comprehension of the law, its demands, and the opportunities it offers to individuals. Not standing perplexed facing the legal system.[97]

Following their interviews, they also add a further category, bringing the total to fourteen:

[T]he functioning of being able to communicate, including being able to speak the local language, or being verbally independent.[98]

Like Nussbaum, Wolff and de-Shalit are clear that their list is a provisional one.[99] They are also clear that they take their list to illustrate "components of well-being" rather than "a philosophical analysis of 'the human good'".[100]

With this list, or a further refined version thereof, Wolff and de-Shalit consider it possible to make a cogent and persuasive critique of social policy (including public health policy[101]), and for policy-makers to recognise and prioritise areas that demand political attention. This is to be done by aiming to eradicate the worst systematic disadvantage; instances where the more problematic inequalities are found in achievement or security of well-being. Their model is useful because,

---

[96] Nussbaum, "Capabilities as fundamental entitlements", at 41–42.

[97] Wolff and de-Shalit, *Disadvantage*, ch. 2. The additional categories are listed at pp. 50–51. Note, for methodological reasons, as Wolff and de-Shalit's research is heavily reliant on interviews discussing this understanding of well-being and disadvantage, they also include what they label a "dummy libertarian category", which they use "both to see if it provoked a different kind of reaction and to see if people, especially the disadvantaged, were particularly attracted to it". This category was called: "Complete independence. Being able to do exactly as you wish without relying on the help of others." Following the interviews, they found only a small minority in support of this category, and inasmuch as it received qualified acceptance, they felt it was adequately captured in categories 6 and 10; practical reason and control over the environment (see pp. 57–58).

[98] *Ibid.*, pp. 60–61.   [99] *Ibid.*, p. 61.

[100] *Ibid.*

[101] Wolff, "Disadvantage, risk and the social determinants of health".

whilst being based on a strong philosophical footing, it allows analysts to recognise what should be considered a public problem,[102] requiring remedial political action. Although they do not consider any of the functionings to be 'lexically prior', their study leads to a claim, which they consider to be strong whilst accepting that it may be modified given further, wider research, that six of the functionings are most important: life; bodily health; bodily integrity; affiliation; control over one's environment; and sense, imagination, and thought.[103] Where the government finds groups particularly susceptible to clusterings of absences of these functionings, it has a discernible reason to believe there is a particularly problematic disadvantaging that demands political attention. Wolff and de-Shalit use this narrowing to forestall objections that their pluralist outlook entails insurmountable 'indexing problems' for practical decision-making. They contend that such problems can be overcome, and a non-arbitrary or question-begging means of prioritisation established.[104]

The idea of disadvantages being most insidious when clusterings of disadvantage are found is informative and important. One other aspect of Wolff and de-Shalit's argument should be mentioned here. This relates to the security of an agent's existing functionings, and the important consideration that should be given to risk.[105] Perhaps to a reader with a background in epidemiology or policy, this is a plain point. But it carries considerable force, and offers a further point of interesting comparison with the explication given by Powers and Faden. Wolff and de-Shalit say:

[W]e do not recommend that *achieved* functionings should be the sole measure of well-being ... In their zeal to emphasize freedom to achieve functionings, capability theorists have failed to bring out a somewhat different issue of great importance: the freedom to *sustain* functionings.[106]

People's involuntary exposure to risks, or their being forced to take risks, represent a further dimension to disadvantage that must be accounted

---

[102] Note, Wolff and de-Shalit do not cast the issue in this way, remaining agnostic as to "whether there is a legitimate distinction to be drawn between the public and private": *Disadvantage*, p. 175. The formulation here is a continuance of my own usage throughout this book's analysis.

[103] *Ibid.*, ch. 5. It is interesting to contrast this with Powers and Faden's (complete) list of six aspects of well-being: health; personal security; reasoning; respect; attachment; and self-determination.

[104] Wolff and de-Shalit also give detailed consideration of the problem of measuring functionings. This is not something I address here, but note the discussion of internal *versus* external evaluations in Chapter 11, section 11.2.2, below.

[105] See especially Wolff and de-Shalit, *Disadvantage*, ch. 3.

[106] *Ibid.*, p. 65 (first emphasis added).

for when considering social ethics and policy. A lack of security of functioning is important to well-being, and should be accounted for as well as its current achievement. And where clustering of all or many of the six (arguably) most important functions is in evidence, there is an instance of problematic disadvantage, which requires redress.[107] In particular, they urge that governments find and tackle "corrosive disadvantages" (i.e. ones that lead to others) and find and encourage "fertile functionings" (i.e. ones that lead to others). The best sort of State is one where everyone enjoys well-being, and it is not possible to tell who is the most disadvantaged. And necessarily, health in such a State will be of a generally good level, whilst being well balanced against other important functions that contribute to people's overall well-being.

In contrast with the theories of Powers and Faden, and Wolff and de-Shalit, we should consider finally Norman Daniels' influential revision of John Rawls' theory of justice[108] in his book *Just Health*.[109] This forms an important and contrasting justice-based account of how, when, and why health should be made a public issue. Daniels' theory differs from the other two considered in this section both for being formulated as a 'social contract' model, and in being based in 'ideal theory'. Nevertheless, his concern too is to establish which health inequalities are normatively problematic, and how properly to address health needs when they can not all be met. As Daniels puts it:

> When is an inequality in health status between different socioeconomic groups unjust? More generally, when is an inequality in health status between different demographic groups unjust? An account of just health should help us determine which health inequalities are unjust and which are acceptable. Recognizing these distinctions will help us to remedy injustice and establish just institutions.[110]

Daniels' project in this work marks a shift from his earlier thesis in *Just Health Care*,[111] addressing a wider focus of concern, notably providing

---

[107] Wolff and de-Shalit do not conclusively argue that clustering occurs, but do provide a prima facie case at least, and suggest cogent means of testing the theory: see *ibid.*, ch. 7.

[108] Rawls, *A Theory of Justice*.

[109] Daniels, *Just Health*. Note that with specific regard to Sen and Nussbaum, Daniels claims that following his (Daniels') modification of Rawlsian justice the contrast between his theory of justice and the capabilities approach is "more apparent than real" (see p. 64ff.), and Norman Daniels, "Equality of what: welfare, resources, or capabilities?", *Philosophy and Phenomenological Research* (1990) 50, Supplement, 273–296. Note that in *their* respective projects of refinement, both Powers and Faden, and Wolff and de-Shalit create further points of contrast and comparison.

[110] Daniels, *Just Health*, p. 79.

[111] Norman Daniels, *Just Health Care* (Cambridge University Press, 1985). Daniels reflects on the developments and fundamental changes to his thinking on questions

a "broader evaluation of all the determinants of health, not just health care or traditional public health".[112]

As with the other book-length works considered in this chapter, it is not possible to condense Daniels' treatise without losing much of its nuance. Even so, it is useful for illustrative purposes to consider how he frames his argument, as many working in public health ethics, and those in policy, are influenced by this approach. According to Rawls' theory of justice, our understanding of what constitute just social institutions, and how we should shape our political structures in society, is derived by reference to principles that would be agreed upon by rational, disinterested contractors, agreeing terms behind a veil of ignorance. A combination of rationality, self-interest, and the ignorance of where each 'contractor' will end up in actual society, it is argued, will lead to the most fair institutions, where liberty *and* equality of opportunity will be prized and given due protection. By putting ourselves in the contractors' position, the argument suggests, we can come to a view of what justice requires. Daniels famously departs from Rawls by allowing and demanding that the contractors consider questions of disease and disability to feature in deliberations (an intended omission on Rawls' part). It has long been Daniels' contention that equality in health is fundamental to satisfactory equality of opportunity, and therefore a matter that ought to be considered when establishing what the demands of justice are.

Daniels begins his inquiry in *Just Health* with what he labels "the Fundamental Question": "As a matter of justice, what do we owe each other to promote and protect health in a population and to assist people when they are ill or disabled?"[113] To answer this question, Daniels advances three levels of argument. First, he seeks to establish that health itself is of special moral importance.[114] As already indicated, he does this by arguing that it is a necessary condition if people are to be able to achieve equality of opportunity. Without health, or with diminished health, the opportunities open to us are fewer. In assessing social justice, it is therefore crucial he argues, *pace* Rawls, to know about and be prepared to address social determinants of ill health. An interesting point to note, given his claim of its moral importance, is that Daniels takes health itself to be an only "modestly" normative concept.[115] It is conceivable that a teleological

of health and social justice since engaging in this seminal work in the introduction to *Just Health*.

[112] Daniels, *Just Health*, p. 4.   [113] *Ibid.*, p. 11.   [114] *Ibid.*, ch. 2.

[115] As noted above Daniels adopts Christopher Boorse's 'naturalist' conception of health: Christopher Boorse, "On the distinction between disease and illness", *Philosophy and Public Affairs* (1975) 5:1, 49–68; "Health as a theoretical concept", *Philosophy of*

concept of health can be advanced that contains no intrinsic *moral* criteria,[116] and *purely* scientific and purely normative concepts can also be established. But Daniels mounts a forceful defence that health as species-typical functioning, whilst not a moral concept, is something of sufficient moral importance that it demands special attention throughout a public if the demands of justice are to be met.[117] By appealing to species-typicality, Daniels considers it possible to give objective content to claims about 'needs' as well as founding a definition of health that does not, for example, conflate health with happiness. It sets an objective baseline, from which a list of health needs can be drawn:

1. Adequate nutrition
2. Sanitary, safe, unpolluted living and working conditions
3. Exercise, rest, and such important lifestyle features as avoiding substance abuse and practicing safe sex
4. Preventive, curative, rehabilitative, and compensatory personal medical services (and devices)
5. Nonmedical personal and social support services
6. An appropriate distribution of other social determinants of health[118]

Daniels' second task is to establish a means of assessing which health inequalities are unjust.[119] In order to assess this as a question of social justice, it is necessary to look to differences between *groups* within a society, to see whether there are systematic inequalities. Without overstating claims about causation (as opposed to correlation) between sex, socio-economic, racial, ethnic status and health status, Daniels joins others in recognising the strength of theses pertaining to the social determinants of health. And as he says, "[t]o the extent that these social determinants are socially controllable, we clearly face questions of distributive justice".[120] Though his theorising is distinct, in similar vein to

---

Science (1977) 44:4, 542–573; "A rebuttal on health", in James Humber and Robert Almeder (eds.), *What is Disease?* (Totowa, NJ: Humana Press, 1997). Unlike Boorse, however, Daniels concedes "a modest form of normativism" in the concept of health: see Daniels, *Just Health*, p. 42.

[116] See Mahesh Ananth, *In Defense of an Evolutionary Concept of Health* (Aldershot: Ashgate, 2008).

[117] By taking a 'naturalist conception', Daniels acknowledges that there is still need for a normative judgement – i.e. to decide which pathologies demand practical attention – but he argues that conceiving things this way is attractive because of "*where* it locates normative judgments about health, not that it avoids them altogether". See Daniels, *Just Health*, p. 38, and see his discussion on pp. 36–42.

[118] *Ibid.*, pp. 42–43.   [119] *Ibid.*, ch. 3.

[120] *Ibid.*, p. 81.

Wolff and de-Shalit, Daniels notes how social determinants of health "cluster", and thus how applying principles of justice as fairness will lead to a remediation of unjust health inequalities. His claim is powerful: "*In effect, social justice in general is good for population health and its fair distribution.*"[121] This claim is evidenced in Daniels' work by reference to what is known about social determinants of health and the nature of principles and institutions derived in accordance with his account of Rawlsian justice.

Daniels' third "focal question" asks how health needs can be met justly when there are too few resources to meet them all.[122] At this stage of deliberation, he suggests that the principles of justice as fairness "are too general and too indeterminate to resolve many reasonable disputes about how to allocate resources fairly to meet health needs, and we lack a consensus on more fine-grained principles".[123] (Note, it is taken that 'we' do not lack a consensus on the more general principles.) By accepting the scope and import of reasonable disagreement, Daniels must find a legitimate means of overcoming practical differences. He finds market accountability, majority rule, or cost-value methodologies unsatisfactory. Instead, as described above in discussion of principle-based approaches, he draws on his work with James Sabin on accountability for reasonableness, which in summary holds that:

[T]he reasons or rationales for important limit-setting decisions should be publicly available. In addition, these reasons must be ones that fair-minded people can agree are relevant for appropriate patient care under resource constraints[.][124]

By appealing to a practical, public mechanism, Daniels moves from a straightforwardly principled theory to norms of *procedural* justice (though there is more contention than Daniels allows in the idea of "fair-minded people", who are still something of an abstraction[125]).

Taken together, Daniels claims the answers to the focal questions create an integrated approach that allows us to work out who owes what to whom; in the terms of this book, to establish when health is made public. Like the other two approaches considered in this section, Daniels' work demonstrates a concerted effort to ensure the practical utility of

---

[121] *Ibid.*, p. 82 (emphasis in original).
[122] *Ibid.*, ch. 4.   [123] *Ibid.*, p. 103.   [124] *Ibid.*, p. 117.
[125] Andreas Hasman and Søren Holm, "Accountability for reasonableness: opening the black box of process", *Health Care Analysis* (2005) 13:4, 261–273.

his theory.[126] It is also very clear that the works are in political theory, and the authors are all concerned with addressing the political norms that govern society. It would be insufficient simply to provide a moral theory and list what good agents would do given it. Rather, they present a clear understanding that the relevant normativity for arguments about making health public is political, and must account for the sorts of limitations (principled and practical) that apply given this. In the next section we will consider works that in some respects can be closely associated with these, but which I think are most usefully presented in a different light.

8.3.4 'Communitarianism'

Another strong and growing theme in public health ethics relates to more 'overtly communitarian' theories, especially ones associated with civic virtue and republicanism. To force the point about political normativity generally, I have described all who accept (liberal) political government, from libertarians through to extreme collectivists, as communitarian, noting that many libertarians will not likely accept the label. I have acknowledged also that *within* political philosophy, 'communitarians' are often seen as a discrete camp, generally contrasted with 'liberals'. In this section, I focus on more specific understandings of communitarian, wherein the focused purpose of politics is to 'promote' community, rather than the interests, rights, good, etc. of individuals who form a community. In the context of public health law and ethics, there is a range of communitarian arguments now prevalent, and theories of civic republicanism look set to make a considerable upsurge over the next few years. Here I wish to consider works of two prominent theorists in the field: Dan Beauchamp and Bruce Jennings.

The development of a benign, inclusive, and powerful sense of community has been central to Dan Beauchamp's analysis over more than thirty years.[127] Beauchamp often presents his view as one of "social justice", and is clear that this creates positive obligations on the back of a shared responsibility for minimising death and preventable disability and disease.[128] In contrast with the theories presented in the previous section, however, Beauchamp draws from a robust conception of the ethics

---

[126] In Daniels' case, this is drawn out in Parts II and III of the book, which have not been considered in any detail in my overview of his approach.

[127] See the reflective discussion in Dan Beauchamp, *Health Care Reform and the Battle for the Body Politic* (Philadelphia: Temple University Press, 1996), especially ch. 1.

[128] Dan Beauchamp, "Public health: alien ethic in a strange land?", *American Journal of Public Health* (1975) 65:12, 1338–1339; "Public health as social justice", *Inquiry*

'of' public health itself (one imagines he takes public health to mean either a professional approach or a social mission conception[129]), and looks to the way the community *qua* community is served, rather than the social norms derived for the benefit of a community *qua* a group of individuals (though he does make a detailed assessment of the nature of justice through a carefully modified Rawlsian perspective[130]). Nowhere does Beauchamp give absolute primacy to health goals. His understanding of health seems to be associated, at least approximately, with a 'biomedical understanding', and he clearly recognises that alternative goods exist. He treats community and civic republicanism as follows:

Community in public health does not imply intimate association but rather connotes the possessing of something in common, like an interest or a purpose, an idea closer to the Roman notion of *communitas*. Indeed, the Latin maxim, *Salus populi suprema lex est* ("the health of the people is the supreme law") has been a frequently cited justification of the power to regulate property and liberty on behalf of the common good ...

The maxim rests on a central principle of republican governments: the elected official is chosen in significant part to advance the interests of the community as a whole, i.e., of the public. Of course, legislators also address the interests of the well-organized, yet the challenge of representation must be to rise above organized interests where required and to advance "the permanent and aggregate interests of the community" (to use James Madison's language from *Federalist* 10).[131]

And it is by reference to community that Beauchamp would seek to answer the question "what makes health public?", or as he puts it, "what is 'public' about public health[?]".[132] In his response to the question, he works within the political liberal paradigms discussed in Chapter 2, acknowledging a "private sphere" as well as a "collective" (public) sphere.[133] Conceptually, the public sphere is where the matters of shared concern are found: as discussed above, this means that we need

---

(1976) 13:1, 1–14; "Public health and individual liberty", *Annual Review of Public Health* (1980) 1:1, 121–136.

[129] For example, in Dan Beauchamp, "What is public about public health?", *Health Affairs* (1983) 2:4, 76–87, Beauchamp suggests that public health "is an ill-defined label for a disparate number of activities", but is "fundamentally about community and about shared values of life, health, and security". In Beauchamp's works it is interesting to note how many of the different 'faces' of public health, explored in Chapter 3 of the current book, present themselves.

[130] See Beauchamp, "Public health and individual liberty".

[131] Dan Beauchamp, "Injury, community and the republic", *Law, Medicine and Health Care* (1989) 17:1, 42–49, at 43.

[132] Beauchamp, "What is public about public health?", at 78.

[133] He also mentions the market sphere, but that need not concern us here. See *ibid.*, at 78–79.

means of establishing how and why concerns are shared. Beauchamp seeks to establish this by a mixture of economic and idealistic claims, suggesting that sharing responsibility for various goods is more efficient and effective, and also that it reinforces common ties and community commitment. Meanwhile, the private sphere constrains the legitimate bounds of public health activities. In regard to US constitutional theory, Beauchamp discerns a:

[V]iew of political association [that] blends social contract and republican thought with Judeo-Christian notions of covenant. It ascribes to the individual private interests and rights that political association is designed to protect; it also defines the individual as part of a political community that, despite diversity and pluralism, is more than the sum of private interests. As a member of that community, the citizen is subject to laws and regulations designed to advance the interests of all – the common good.[134]

Thus, Beauchamp recognises – and urges – that health should not be considered either purely private or purely public:

By insisting that individual responsibility coexist with collective rules to protect the common good, we can save tens of thousands of lives and limit disease.[135]

In contrast with Beauchamp's approach, which has a powerful, more-than-the-sum-of-its-parts conception of community, we can consider Bruce Jennings' civic republicanism. We saw in Chapter 2 Jennings' insistence on theorists not reifying 'the public'. Even so, his is a strongly – in the US context in which he writes, perhaps even radically – communitarian theory, which he applies to debates in public health law and ethics.[136] Jennings addresses the question of 'what makes health public' by combining a morality born of political notions of civic virtue and republicanism, and a careful understanding of the empirical world that draws from how things and people are, rather than how more idealised, abstracted versions of them would be.[137] Thus it is his view that:

---

134 *Ibid.*, at 80.
135 *Ibid.*, at 83. See also Dan Beauchamp, "Community: the neglected tradition of public health", *Hastings Center Report* (1985) 15:6, 28–36; Jean Forster, "A communitarian ethical model for public health interventions: an alternative to individual behavior change strategies", *Journal of Public Health* (1982) 3:2, 150–163.
136 During my writing of this work, Bruce Jennings has been kind enough to share with me the October 2009 draft of his forthcoming book, *Civic Health: Political Theory in Public Health and Health Policy*, which is a comprehensive analysis of his theory of civic republicanism, and its application to questions relating to public health.
137 See especially Willard Gaylin and Bruce Jennings, *The Perversion of Autonomy: Coercion and Constraints in a Liberal Society* (2nd edn) (Washington DC: Georgetown University Press, 2003).

[C]ontemporary epidemiology is taking us from statistical correlation to the design and redesign of personal relationships, institutional capacities, moral connections, and in the broadest sense of the term political space itself. The new epidemiology has less to do with the causal nexus than it does with a kind of moral ecology[.][138]

The basis of this observation has driven Jennings towards the de-atom-ising "civic bioethics" that he would apply to questions of what makes health public in all of the senses considered above: "what it means to have a public space, to be public selves, and to share a common or pub-lic good".[139] Jennings stresses how important the questions are to all analysis in bioethics: without a social ontology and a political under-standing, we simply can not address specific questions in bioethics, or relate them to the wider normative system that we espouse. And the individualistic liberal paradigms that predominate, built on ahistoric universalism, argues Jennings, are often ill-equipped to respond well to the social reality that we face.[140] Through individualism, difference between persons is emphasised, and the political system that results is guided primarily to 'negative rights'; freedoms from interference. The civic system, by contrast, explores the good ends of human life, the shared or common goods, and builds institutions and norms directed towards ensuring their achievement, through a sufficiency also of 'posi-tive rights'; claims against others (thus sharing the Aristotelian trap-pings of the analyses drawing from Sen and Nussbaum, considered in the previous section). In a way echoed in my previous chapter, Jennings asks why we would enter politics in the first place:

What is the basic human problem for which the invention of political space ... holds the solution? For liberalism, it is overcoming obstacles to cooperation; for civic theory, it is overcoming obstacles to community.[141]

---

[138] Bruce Jennings, "From the urban to the civic: the moral possibilities of the city", *Journal of Urban Health* (2001) 78:1, 88–103, at 90.

[139] *Ibid.*

[140] *Ibid.*, at 91–92. Specifically, Jennings describes the predominant paradigms as com-ing from "the tradition of Western philosophical liberalism and moral individual-ism in its contractarian, neo-Kantian, utilitarian, and libertarian guises" (at 92). It should be noted that in drawing his distinctions, Jennings consciously overlooks the more subtle nuances of contemporary philosophical inquiry, and dichotomises on the basis of the "grounded liberalism" as found in popular discourse (in the United States). His dichotomy serves a heuristic purpose, and is thus fine and works well, but when we engage – as we do in this book – with the more careful accounts, we see that Jennings is more usefully considered as part of a debate where overlaps can be found, rather than one side of two necessarily oppositional camps.

[141] *Ibid.*, at 100.

The communitarianism that Jennings supports does not commit him to a totalitarian agenda, or to a conception of autocratic State government that some libertarian theorists fear. Whilst supporting the notion of shared goods, Jennings is an advocate of a pluralist liberalism, born of the tradition of John Stuart Mill as explicated and advanced by Isaiah Berlin.[142] Berlin famously describes two concepts of liberty: a "negative liberty" that entails protection from interference; and a "positive liberty", which is entailed in the mental capacity for self-government. Positive liberty, combined with an understanding of the plurality of goods, is argued to warrant a protection of negative liberty so that each person can make his life his own, free from tyranny or the constraints of a monist ethic that would claim a single, universal good, tied to a unitary rationality (as espoused, for example, in Kantian philosophy).[143] Whilst Jennings endorses this approach, he considers it incomplete. He therefore complements Berlin's pair with a third concept of liberty: *relational liberty*. To characterise it in the typical framing, negative liberty is 'freedom from'; positive liberty is 'freedom to'; and relational liberty is 'freedom through'.[144] More specifically, Jennings describes it as "mutual care or *freedom through transactions and relationships with others*"[145] (which we might note is redolent *inter alia* of political theory within aspects of associated feminist literature[146]). He goes on to say:

[Freedom through] is a warrant to live one's own life in one's own way that results from embedding that way of life in a tradition, a civic life of shared purpose, and rooting that life in membership in broader community. Just as there are certain kinds of practice or activity that by their very nature cannot be done alone, so there is a kind of freedom that subsists not in separation from others but through connection with them. Not in protections but in pacts of association; not in locked doors but in open ones; not in fences but in circles; not in rights but in relationships.[147]

Absent the due evaluation of community, and its role in sustaining everyone's good, a political account is simply too impoverished to convey all that it should, and to explain, for example, the basis of positive health obligations. The understanding that Jennings advocates

[142] See John Stuart Mill, *On Liberty*, Edward Alexander (ed.) (Broadview, 1999); Isaiah Berlin, "Two concepts of liberty", in Isaiah Berlin, *Four Essays on Liberty* (Oxford University Press, 1969).

[143] See Gray, *Two Faces of Liberalism*.

[144] Bruce Jennings, "Public health and liberty: beyond the Millian paradigm", *Public Health Ethics* (2009) 2:2, 123–134; Bruce Jennings, *Civic Health* (forthcoming).

[145] Jennings, "Public health and liberty: beyond the Millian paradigm", at 130.

[146] See e.g. Françoise Baylis, Nuala Kenny, and Susan Sherwin, "A relational account of public health ethics", *Public Health Ethics* (2008) 1:3, 196–209.

[147] Jennings, "Public health and liberty: beyond the Millian paradigm", at 130.

is presented as a middle way in the disputes that define much contemporary political philosophy and its application to public health issues:

We are all torn between our private wills and our civic wills, between our interests as isolated individuals or consumers and our moral interests and commitments as members of a community of shared purpose broader than ourselves. This is the symbiosis of the public and the private. In my view, it should not be eliminated, but lived with and worked through. There will always be free riders. And there will also be fanatics of civic virtue. Most of us will be caught in the middle, neither wishing to live in a society of privatization and selfishness nor in a society of total commitment.[148]

Thus Jennings' work is focused not just on defending people from government, but also on ensuring that the community give them the support they need. Concerning health, he seems to endorse both a species-typical understanding,[149] and something more abstract: "When public health talks about health it means a state of biological, psychological, and social functioning of a human organism/person in a social context."[150] This is a very wide-spanning understanding, which may be seen to bring Jennings close to the WHO in his understanding both of health, and the 'jurisdiction' of public health workers and agencies.

There are clear overlaps between the approaches to public health ethics of both Beauchamp and Jennings and Powers and Faden and Wolff and de-Shalit. Nevertheless, the value of community seems to be distinctly emphasised in Jennings' and Beauchamp's works, and may be taken as representative of an alternative manner of argumentation to be developed in public health law and ethics.

8.3.5   Human rights

Finally within the middle ground I want to give brief attention to arguments presented in terms of human rights. For some analysts, human rights provide *the* answer to all of the problems – analytic and practical – that are faced in otherwise imperfect societies. George Annas,

---

[148] *Ibid.*, at 132.
[149] See e.g. Bruce Jennings, "Public health and civic republicanism", in Angus Dawson and Marcel Verweij (eds.), *Ethics, Prevention, and Public Health* (Oxford University Press, 2007), where he seems to endorse Norman Daniels' preferred understanding.
[150] *Ibid.*

for example, argues that the Universal Declaration of Human Rights (UDHR):

[I]tself sets forth the ethics of public health, since its goal is to provide the conditions under which people can flourish. This is also the goal of public health. The unification of public health and human rights efforts throughout the world could be a powerful force to improve the lives of every person.[151]

Human rights might be seen primarily as international instruments, useful particularly for securing basic needs in 'developing' rather than 'developed' States. But they have legal application and political effect in policy development in 'developed nations' too. As well as evoking profound (if sometimes opaque or contested) moral values, they are powerful practical tools, which can be used to advance radical programmes in support of global welfare, and to assess discrepancies between health situations in different countries.[152] Annas argues that human rights are the forgotten foundation of bioethics, and that public health, bioethics, and health law exist in symbiosis. Furthermore, this he takes to be to the good. Human rights are universal, progressive, and conduce to the basic needs of people, and thus give content to the necessary obligations.[153]

There can be little doubt about the effectiveness of human rights' application in public health issues, or their utility in defining the scope of entitlements both to conditions conducive to greater health (however this is understood) and to the limits of such claims.[154] Even commentators who explicitly doubt the philosophical coherence of human rights endorse them as tools that should be used in practice.[155] To be clear, though, there are quite a few pinches of salt that need to be taken when basing arguments on human rights. First, the claims of universalism are not terribly enlightening. They apply to 'everyone', but do not give

---

[151] George Annas, "Human rights and health – The Universal Declaration of Human Rights at 50", *New England Journal of Medicine* (1998) 339:24, 1778–1781, at 1780.

[152] See Jonathan Mann, "Medicine and public health, ethics and human rights", *Hastings Center Report* (1997) 27:3, 6–13; Solomon Benatar, "Global disparities in health and human rights: a critical commentary", *American Journal of Public Health* (1998) 88:2, 295–300; Gunilla Backman, Paul Hunt, Rajat Khosla, *et al.*, "Health systems and the right to health: an assessment of 194 countries", *The Lancet* (2008) 372, 2046–2085.

[153] George Annas, "American bioethics and human rights: the end of all our exploring", *Journal of Law, Medicine and Ethics* (2004) 32, 658–663.

[154] John Coggon, "Public health, responsibility and English law: are there such things as no smoke without ire or needless clean needles?", *Medical Law Review* (2009) 17:1, 127–139, especially at 133–139.

[155] See e.g. Daniels, *Just Health*, ch. 12; Amartya Sen, *The Idea of Justice* (London: Penguin, 2009), ch. 17.

a perfect picture of who 'everyone' is. Within the UDHR there seem to be at least three different conceptions of "human": primarily it seems to be a born, living human being; at times it is a person of "full age";[156] and at times it is a rational, moral agent (or a 'legal fiction' to the effect that all are this).[157] This suggests something of a conceptual fudge, which leads in theoretical debates – in essence – to the appropriation of the term 'human rights' by theorists who are seeking to advance a thesis that does not limit itself to the biological category 'human', and instead speaks to a philosophical basis for normative protection. This is fine, though it raises questions about how these are human rights theories; i.e. it does not make clear why they should be considered theories of human rights as opposed just to ones of rights. James Griffin, for example, writes a treatise on human rights that essentially is a defence of 'personhood theory' – in which moral status attaches to specific mental capacities of reason and evaluation – and thus is universal, but not universal to all subjects of legal protections in liberal democracies, excluding, for example, neonates and young children.[158] Or Deryck Beyleveld and Roger Brownsword transpose their rights-based account of morality onto the language of human rights. Although their theory also applies only to rational agents, their efforts to embrace a concession to empirical scepticism allows them to broaden their conception of a human rights-holder to the unconscious, the dead, and to species and things that are not biological humans.[159] The literature on human rights theory is vast. The point I use these two theories to exemplify is that at a theoretical level there is considerable disagreement about what human rights are, and the sense that some theorists will claim the label without too much concern for whether there was a coherent concept to begin with. In other words, they take it first that human rights exist,

---

[156] See e.g. Art. 16, on the right to marry and found a family; and consider the scope of the "universal" right to take part in government and to vote in Art. 21; the right to work in Art. 23; and the right to paid holiday in Art. 24.

[157] See e.g. Art. 1, which states: "All human beings are born free and equal in dignity and rights. They are endowed with reason and conscience and should act towards one another in a spirit of brotherhood."

[158] Griffin, *On Human Rights*.

[159] Deryck Beyleveld and Roger Brownsword, *Human Dignity in Bioethics and Biolaw* (Oxford University Press, 2001). Søren Holm and I have argued that these authors fail to create a practically useful theory to satisfy the epistemic limitations to assessments of agency: see Søren Holm and John Coggon, "A cautionary note against 'precautionary reasoning' in action guiding morality", *Ratio Juris* (2009) 22:2, 295–309. Deryck Beyleveld and Shaun Pattinson have responded to our argument, though seem still to fail to account for the sceptic's objections that form the basis of their theory's extension: see Deryck Beyleveld and Shaun Pattinson, "Defending moral precaution as a solution to the problem of other minds: a reply to Holm and Coggon", *Ratio Juris* (2010) 23:2, 258–273.

and only secondarily inquire into them, and in so doing happen to find that human rights 'mean' what their prior analytic convictions already told them was right. In this regard 'human rights' seem to present an ironic and not terribly informative clash of legal positivism and natural rights.

None of this is to speak against human rights as practical instruments, or to suggest a greater coherence in other conceptions (not least the concept of law itself!). Rather, it is an echo of Gostin's call for a more tempered approach to claims about human rights. As he argues:

> [T]here is considerable imprecision in the way that modern scholars and practitioners use the language of human rights. Consider the different, but overlapping meanings of human rights. Some use human rights language to mean a set of entitlements under international law, others use human rights to mean a set of ethical standards that stress the paramount importance of individual interests, and still others use human rights for its aspirational, or rhetorical, qualities. A scholar is bound to be concerned when the terminology of human rights is invoked without clarifying the sense in which it is intended.[160]

The point that Gostin is making is that legal professionals and scholars engaged in human rights law are speaking within a separate normative frame to 'ethicists' employing the language of human rights, with no real view to international law norms. There may be a common language, but there is not a common theory. Especially given the moralistic tone to human rights instruments, it is often not clear whether an argument based on human rights is rooted in a moral claim or a legal one.[161] Fundamentally, then, it is wrong-headed to treat human rights as 'self-evident truths'. Rather, it is necessary to articulate the theory on which they are founded, which means at the level of legal, moral, or political theory that they of themselves do less work than would reasonably be hoped. As with other theories presented here, the basis, scope, and reasoning needs to be provided. And once this is done, appeal is not so much found *in* human rights, as human rights are the final articulation of the theory.

At the level of practical application, there are just a couple of points worth stating explicitly concerning human rights' import. Jurisprudentially, human rights are rights held against States, and are typically conceived and contrasted as two categories, some denoting 'negative' obligations and some denoting 'positive' obligations. Negative rights are rights to be left free to act in certain ways – e.g. to practise a

---

[160] Lawrence O. Gostin, "Public health, ethics, and human rights: a tribute to the late Jonathan Mann", *Journal of Law, Medicine and Ethics* (2001) 29:2, 121–130, at 126.
[161] *Ibid.*, at 128.

religion, to have children – whilst positive rights are claims to certain things – e.g. here we may think of a claim to provision of healthcare. As Annas notes, the positive/negative divide is a little misleading, as the supposedly negative obligations demand positive action of governments.[162] Likewise, in order to assure the rights, positive obligations must be imposed back down on citizens. In other words, citizens' own human rights entail obligations that they essentially hold against themselves. Onora O'Neill has made the point well in an argument that provides a critical warning of the likely upshot of a proliferation in the number and nature of 'fundamental' rights. She clearly expresses the burdens imposed by human rights – such as a right to health – by reference to the *second-order obligations* that they logically involve:

> The deepest problem may be that the obligation assigned to states by some of the most significant Declarations and Covenants are *not* the corollaries of the human rights that the documents proclaim. The Covenants do not assign states straightforward obligations to respect liberty rights (after all, liberty rights have to be respected by all, not only by states), but rather second-order obligations to *secure* respect for them. Equally, they do not assign states obligations to meet rights to goods and services, but rather second-order obligations to *ensure* that they are met.[163]

This is not a damning point: in accordance with whatever political theory a State is governed this applies. However, it bears stressing in relation to human rights as it highlights that they do not only confer goods on citizens as recipients, but impose burdens on these rights-holders too. Human rights on any theory, and certainly in practice, are qualified not only by limitations expressly linked to each of them taken individually (e.g. in derogation clauses). They all also qualify each other. Thus a sound development of a theory of human rights applicable to public health issues can not ignore other 'competing' matters that must be touched by the theory. Human rights arguments may be used explicitly to argue that a State has overreached its health-related obligations to the abnegation of other, more important goods in a given instance, which are also protected by human rights. Although some analysts (and others) take it that human rights are foundational, they are a philosophically weak basis for political models in the middle ground. Nevertheless, they are practical concepts of undoubted strength, and a useful legal mechanism.

---

[162] Annas, "American bioethics and human rights", at 660.
[163] Onora O'Neill, "The dark side of human rights", *International Affairs* (2005) 81:2, 427–439, at 433.

8.3.6   Concluding comments on middle ground models

Section 8.3 has considered some of the most prevalent theories and positions that arise in arguments concerning public health law and ethics. I have continued to demonstrate the political nature of the normative argumentation. As we saw in section 8.3.2, even positions that claim to speak to ethics *qua* morality fall back into a liberal political framing. And it is right that they should do so. In the following three sections, I have drawn out three rough categorisations. There is a good deal of overlap. This raises problems for neat classifications, but is useful for analysis. It allows us to recognise matters within ostensibly distinct theories that overlap, and can reinforce or add to arguments. In particular, we might note the contrasts that exist between 'ideal' and 'non-ideal' theories. It is also interesting to speculate about the extent to which one can discuss a coherent concept of political liberalism without being specific; or whether and to what extent one can meaningfully speak approximately, and thereby address various different political theories, endorsing all at once even as they would contradict each other. Finally, although the models with most appeal will likely be those in the middle ground, it is important to look to the underpinnings, and not just the conclusions, when making an assessment of the models themselves. And it is crucial to look to an all-things-considered analysis, rather than seek to segregate the health-related issues and make an assessment of the whole model by reference simply to these. The less 'mystique' there is surrounding a political theory, the easier it will be to assess and accept, modify, or reject.

8.4   Modelling towards a 'health theocracy'

8.4.1   'Healthism': benign or threatening?

In academic and public debates, the concerns of analysts such as Skrabanek, considered in section 8.2, can raise apparent problems for the theorists who occupy what I have cast as the middle ground. For example, as we have seen, Bruce Jennings is amongst the theorists who advocate a civic republicanism that explicates a political normativity to govern society generally, and guide its public health policies specifically. However, given the nature of caricatures that often appear in debates between 'individualists' and 'communitarians', Jennings raises the idea of the 'health theocracy' that analysts such as Skrabanek urge so strongly against. As Jennings puts it:

Will a more communitarian public health, one that does base its public ethical justification on a conception of community and the human good, lead towards a kind of health theocracy in which the main tenet of faith is: *Mens sana in corpore sano*? That, I take it, is a conclusion that liberal individualists always fear and that indeed no civic, progressive communitarian should want.[164]

Jennings recognises the fear of totalitarianism, but suggests that it is as anathema to his own political position as it is to the more libertarian critiques. The idea of a 'health theocracy' is, however, a powerful and instructive one that warrants a level of serious engagement. Although few analysts seem to defend such a position, it is interesting to reflect how and why it might be a good or bad thing. In evaluation, there are two approaches that we might usefully draw from here. The first is found most strikingly in parts of the WHO's literature, such as that concerning the human right to health. Here it does seem that health, broadly understood as a utopian aspiration to *complete* physical, mental, and social well-being, is taken as *the* end at which political society ought to be directed (and tacitly that physical, mental, and social well-being are compatible and harmonious conceptions). The second is in theories that present themselves as giving narrow articulations of what 'health' should be taken to mean, when in fact they are complete political theories.

8.4.2   Health totalitarianism[165]

The WHO's famous definition of health is often embraced, but is also much maligned. It states that: "Health is a state of complete physical, mental and social well-being and not merely the absence of disease or infirmity."[166] As discussed in Chapter 1, the definition encapsulates a commitment to two distinct conceptions, which are generally labelled positive and negative definitions of health. In its negative form, health

---

[164] Bruce Jennings, "Community in public health ethics", in Richard Ashcroft, Angus Dawson, Heather Draper, and John McMillan (eds.), *Principles of Health Care Ethics* (2nd edn) (Chichester: Wiley, 2007), p. 545. Health/religion metaphors are widespread in the literature: from texts considered above, see e.g. Skrabanek, *The Death of Humane Medicine*, p. 166; Engelhardt, "Health care reform: a study in moral malfeasance", at 509. And classically see Thomas Szasz, *The Theology of Medicine – The Political-Philosophical Foundations of Medical Ethics* (Oxford University Press, 1979).

[165] The following discussion draws from papers I presented at the "Human Right to Health Conference", 14–15 May 2009, in the Centre for Philosophy, Justice and Health, University College, London and the O'Neill Institute for National and Global Health Law, School of Law, Georgetown University on 26 May 2010. I am grateful to participants at both for stimulating discussion and useful feedback.

[166] See the declaration in the WHO's constitution, available at http://apps.who.int/gb/bd/PDF/bd47/EN/constitution-en.pdf.

assumes the 'biomedical definition': the absence of disease, illness, and the like. By assuming also a potent, positive form, the WHO claims a broad manner of concern and expertise, assuring enormous scope to the 'territory' under its 'jurisdiction'. Through noted twentieth-century critiques, some of which we considered above, this positive definition has been seen as a source of the misappropriation of moral freedom and the widening, tyrannical domain of experts. Skrabanek, for example, mocks the WHO definition, suggesting that complete well-being would be the "sort of feeling ordinary people may achieve fleetingly during orgasm, or when high on drugs", and goes on to say that "[e]ven Christians, in their boundless optimism, have been more realistic in deferring the promise of complete happiness to the afterlife".[167]

As part of its work to push towards the universal achievement of its understanding of health, the WHO has sought to make a political instrument of "the human right to health". It describes the right to health as a "progressively realisable" right to the "highest attainable standard of health", imposing on governments obligations not only to provide healthcare, but to ensure that the entire social infrastructure supports the best possible health for everyone.[168] The "right to health" has critics such as Onora O'Neill, who insist that it is conceptually flawed. She argues, for example, that:

There are ... occasional demands for a supposed (but literally speaking incoherent) 'right to health', a fantasy that overlooks the fact that no human action can secure health for all, so that there can be no human obligation to do so, and hence no right to health.[169]

Making a similar point later in the same work, when reflecting on a discussion at a WHO meeting, she says:

At most, I suggested, we might argue for a right to health care of a certain level, with coherent corresponding obligations to provide that health care. My critic insisted that health is so important to human beings – which it is – that we should never in any circumstances cast doubt on the supposed right to health! Evidently he – and many others – did not view rights and obligations as requirements, but rather as ideals or aspirations. In my view this well-intentioned reinterpretation fatally weakens the entire point and purpose of talking either about rights or about obligations, because it does not construe them as

---

[167] Skrabanek, *The Death of Humane Medicine*, pp. 42–43.
[168] WHO and Office of the UN High Commission for Human Rights, *Fact Sheet 31 on the Right to Health* (2008), available at www.ohchr.org/Documents/Publications/Factsheet31.pdf.
[169] Onora O'Neill, *Autonomy and Trust in Bioethics* (Cambridge University Press, 2002), p. 10.

requiring action: a disaster that will corrode and weaken all subsequent claims about rights and obligations.[170]

We can see two broad issues within O'Neill's criticisms. The first concerns the conceptual coherence of the right to health; it is argued that a right to health would demand a correlative duty that could not be met. The second, seeking to address this, suggests that what is really under issue is a narrower, more pragmatic concern for remedial measures when personal health has been harmed; i.e. a right to healthcare.

I am unconvinced by both arguments. The first I take at best to be rather an unsympathetic reading of legal rights generally. Of course the right is qualified; almost every right is qualified. The question is whether, and to what extent, the qualification needs to be presented in the very articulation of the right. Relatively few rights, beyond a very small number presenting absolute, unqualified protections against State *actions* – e.g. against torture – come without qualification. O'Neill's criticism speaks against succinct description, and suggests that the whole of law ought to be framed in accordance with a straightforward maxim such as "be just" or "be reasonable". The enunciation of anything more specific risks the same fate as the right to health; my right to life will be derided as merely aspirational because death is inevitable; my right to property denied because of duties such as taxation; and so on. To say that the "right" is only an "aspiration" says too much; it entails a much wider claim – one that O'Neill would surely deny – that law and morality too are mere aspirations, or that their breach or negation by human action in some way coherently curtails or limits them. That, clearly I think, gets matters the wrong way around. And having denied that the right to health is simply an aspiration, I would also contend that there is no reason to suppose that what it does cover need only relate to healthcare. It is possible that broad-sweeping rights – such as the right to life, to health, to privacy, to found a family – coherently denote complex mixes of claim rights and freedoms, and corresponding obligations on States, often filtered back to the citizenry through legal or policy norms. There is no reason to limit such obligations to the competence of one government department, such as the Department of Health.[171]

The WHO itself seems to respond to the manner of objection made by O'Neill when it addresses "common misconceptions about the

---

[170] *Ibid.*, p. 79.
[171] See also Daniels, *Just Health*, pp. 144–147.

right to health" and emphatically writes in bold print: "**The right to health is NOT the same as the *right to be healthy*.**"[172] Equally, the WHO denies that it fails to impose obligations, or that financial limitations disoblige States. Nevertheless, it can be fairly accused of being misleading in its description of the right, which suggests that it imposes positive obligations only on the State. For citizens it describes the right in purely beneficial terms, holding that it is inclusive, contains freedoms and entitlements, demands against discrimination, and guarantees quality.[173] The obligations it is said to impose are of three sorts:

Respect: This means simply not to interfere with the enjoyment of the right to health.
Protect: This means ensuring that third parties (non-state actors) do not infringe upon the enjoyment of the right to health.
Fulfil: This means taking positive steps to realize the right to health.[174]

Not only is the right progressively realisable, it has no stated end point. True, it has what may be labelled a contemporaneous sufficiency clause, to avoid asking the impossible of States, but over time the right seems to demand more and more, and satisfaction will not be achieved, one imagines, except perhaps when the concept of health that the WHO subscribes to is everyone's. Given this, the right to health seems to assume a supreme role of its own, rather than featuring as one amongst various other rights. Theorists from many camps will be wary of this explicit progression to a 'health theocracy', even if they at once also value the great work that can be done with such a forceful rhetorical and political tool.

8.4.3   Health as politics

There is an apparently converse manner in which we might find health theocracies in the literature. In this sense, health is not described explicitly as the total of human well-being and the sole end of the State. Rather, it is presented as if it were just an *aspect* of concern, when in reality it is so wide, and so powerfully normative, that it ends up presenting a veiled political theory. Let us take as an example David Seedhouse's "enabling" concept of health:

---

[172] WHO and Office of the UN High Commission for Human Rights, *Fact Sheet 31*, p. 5.
[173] *Ibid.*, pp. 3–4.
[174] WHO/OHCHR, *The Right to Health – Joint Fact Sheet* (2007), available at www.who.int/mediacentre/factsheets/fs323_en.pdf, p. 2. For more detail, see *ibid.*, pp. 25–28.

A person's (optimum) state of health is equivalent to the state of the set of conditions which fulfil or enable a person to work to fulfil his or her realistic chosen and biological potentials. Some of these conditions are of the highest importance for all people. Others are variable dependent upon individual abilities and circumstances.[175]

Seedhouse reflects on the similarity between the governance imperatives surrounding his concept of health and the political liberalism of John Stuart Mill in *On Liberty*. Seedhouse argues that his account "is not simply co-opted from Mill, nor is [the 'harm principle'] merely a taken-for-granted social assumption, rather it stems from the foundations theory of health itself".[176] Seedhouse is claiming that his theory of health's leading *de facto* to a political framework similar to Millian liberty is coincidental. However, it is not clear that the arguments that favour what he describes as health are not also those that favour a State system that accords with Mill's liberty. In other words, the upshot of his model of health is a much wider political theory, rather than something particularly to do with anything meaningfully narrowed by the term 'health' (or the work of healthcare professionals, whom Seedhouse seems primarily to be addressing). Strikingly, then, Seedhouse's claim about health and the imperatives it demands can not be divorced from strong moral claims about what is good for everyone, strong political claims about the function of the State as a provider and protector of people's interests, and a staked position on what people ought to care about. Of significance here, in its detail the commitment to enabling people to realise their chosen potentials is remarkably redolent of Amartya Sen's "capabilities approach".[177] When considering debates in public health law and ethics, Sen's approach is intellectually more honest than Seedhouse's. If a theory of health (or of public health) is actually a strong claim about the good of humans, and this is used to obscure rather than shed light on a wider political theory that it logically implies, there is a problem. Noting the proximity between the ultimate positions implied by Sen and Seedhouse, it should be clear why Sen's approach is preferable. Sen's position more openly relates to securing human flourishing, whilst Seedhouse's seems only to speak for part of it: i.e. that relating to health, which is treated as something discrete, or

---

[175] David Seedhouse, *Health: The Foundations of Achievement* (2nd edn) (Chichester: John Wiley & Sons, 2005), p. 84.

[176] *Ibid.*, p. 107.

[177] See Sen, *Development as Freedom*, ch. 3. The point I make here has been previously noted in a review of another of Seedhouse's books: see Joann Sy and Anthony Kessel, "[Review of] *Health Promotion: Philosophy, Prejudice and Practice – 2nd edition*", *Journal of the Royal Society of Medicine* (2005) 98, 132–133.

separable from other goods. Seedhouse is well aware of, and has argued for, the necessity of political philosophy to assume a critical role in these sorts of arguments,[178] but his approach to understanding health and what its protection requires gets everything confusingly mixed, and leaves unstated more that must be accepted for the practical effects of his definition to be realised.[179] As analysts become aware of the normative import of meanings of health, and bind this to normative matters that they consider important, the ostensible *health* aspect becomes of decreasing importance, or anyway distinct from the normative basis of some wider, all-encompassing, political model that is in fact at the core of their concern. When this is the case, it is better to be open about it, and not constrain or blind ourselves (or others) by pretending our focus is on health, if more accurately it is on, for example, autonomy, welfare, or capabilities.[180]

8.4.4 *Conclusions on health theocracies*

Works of quite distinct character in public health law and ethics cite the maxim *salus populi est suprema lex*, and draw distinct inferences of what it might entail, and with what qualifications.[181] Where health is treated as the overall good to which a State directs itself, however, some caution is to be recommended. First, it is important to establish precisely what health is taken to mean, and explore whether it sufficiently exhausts the categories of things of normative importance. Where it does, we might echo Powers and Faden's concern about the WHO definition and wonder if it leaves anything distinctive in the term 'health', or whether it becomes something of a redundant expression. Second, 'health' is a term that is by definition good. Yet as this chapter has re-emphasised, it may be taken to mean many different things. There is a danger of pre-analytic loading of normativity.

---

[178] See e.g. David Seedhouse, "Why bioethicists have nothing useful to say about health care rationing", *Journal of Medical Ethics* (1995) 21, 288–291.

[179] See also the criticisms in Donald Hill, "A response to David Seedhouse's 'Commitment to health: a shared ethical bond between professions'", *Journal of Interprofessional Care* (2002) 16:3, 261–264, especially at 264.

[180] Compare also Holland's discussion of Seedhouse: Holland, *Public Health Ethics*, pp. 95–96.

[181] Contrast, for example, Onora O'Neill, "Informed consent and public health", *Philosophical Transactions of the Royal Society B* (2004) 359, 1133–1136; Epstein, "Let the shoemaker stick to his last: a defense of the 'old' public health"; Wendy Parmet, *Populations, Public Health, and the Law* (Washington DC: Georgetown University Press, 2009); Lawrence O. Gostin and Lesley Stone, "Health of the people: the highest law?", in Dawson and Verweij (eds.), *Ethics, Prevention, and Public Health*.

Taken to extremes, we have seen, this can result in an apparently modest concept of health implying a wide, or even complete, political theory. Where, as in the case of Daniels, a correlation between levels of justice and a concept of health can be shown and explained that is one thing. But where an apparently benign conception is used to smuggle or disguise a whole political theory, that is quite another. It may imply a lot more than its arguments will carry, or prioritise certain goods at the cost of others.

8.5   Conclusions: distinctions with and without differences

The different theories and arguments presented in this chapter demonstrate key points on the spectrum of political positions that are foundational to distinct arguments about public health law and ethics. There are five general observations that bear stressing in this conclusion. First, we have seen how the theories are well expressed in political framings, and I take this point to be completely generalisable. Even those positions that are cast in moral terms are well revised politically, and some of the most prominent 'ethical' models relating to public health issues have a fundamental political liberalism explicitly or implicitly in the background. Second, a political framing need not present a rejection of some ideal-type theory. In this chapter we have come across a mix of ideal and non-ideal theories, as well as ideal theories that make concession to real world limitations (e.g. through the mechanism of 'progressive realisation'). Third, we have found more than once that different authors have been concerned about achieving the same end (e.g. assuring the highest levels of a particular conception of health), or are motivated to protect the same good (e.g. assuring a maximum of freedom to flourish or pursue one's preferred ends), and disagree politically because of tensions in beliefs about the effect of political intervention. Fourth, we have seen the great importance of clarifying what 'health' means in a given argument, as different authors present it under different lights, which means at times they are only ostensibly speaking to the same issue. Finally, I would stress again that when we enter the political realm, we may think we sustain a presumption that liberty is to be respected unless there is good reason to interfere. In fact, this is not the case. Rather, we presume that regulation is not made – and thus liberty not interfered with – unless there is good reason. Only in an unreflective sense do we have the liberal default. Really, our presumption is that we be faithful to the overarching conception of the good or right that gives shape to our political system in the first place. And thus our default presumption is that the good or right be done. We always presume that regulation *may be* permissible in any case. The argument must be made. But non-regulation can call for justification just as much as regulation can. With the shared commitment that provides a political normativity comes a pressing basis of interference with negative liberty.

9   Conclusion to Part II

The conceptual groundwork on public health law and ethics in Part I demonstrated the plural meanings of public health itself, and also raised the political connotations of an inquiry into the public nature of questions including ones relating to health. Part II has confirmed an earlier unproven thesis, that normative analysis of public health requires an assessment in the light of viable political norms, and thus a complete political framework to guide compelling conclusions. In other words, it is impossible to have a study 'just' of public health law and ethics: health is important, but public health raises political questions, and these can not be answered with just a partial view. It is therefore necessary to be clear what the political requires both for analytic study, and as a practical source of normativity.

For this reason, I have sought to establish why we would be interested in politics as opposed to morality: after all, a critique in 'ethics' seems to aspire to moral norms, and many critiques in health law are rooted explicitly in moral philosophy. Having established what political inquiry entails, in particular by emphasising its focus on issues relevant to and in light of the State, I have discussed anarchism. This is particularly instructive given debates that abound in moral and political philosophy about the difficulty of finding terms of legitimacy for the State. The nature of argumentation this inspires (regardless of whether it accords with my own presentation) is particularly instructive as it forces analysts to establish how and why they would make matters the subject of political – and thus public – concern. Some may remain anarchists. Others will present arguments in favour of a political model, and in so doing they will develop their background account that will allow meaningful conclusions in public health law and ethics.

In the light of this methodology, I have presented some accounts that feature prominently in the public health law and ethics literature, and have tried to make clear the political nature of the argumentation. In some cases the authors do this themselves. In others they do not. Where there is disagreement this is sometimes a question of principle,

for example due to particular normative side-constraints. Sometimes
it is due to disagreements about empirical questions (e.g. whether the
State provides the necessary or most efficient means to reallocate certain goods). I have noted the differences and the similarities between
approaches, emphasising where arguments are harmonious or capable
of mutual reinforcement. Because 'the political' speaks positively to
fewer things than 'the moral' – i.e. because, as discussed in Chapter 2,
some things are 'none of the law's business' – analysts must not only
show that something is a problem, but also that it is one that is rightly
addressed through political measures. In so doing, they are framing
arguments about instances where health is or should be made public
(or not). In line with others, I have noted the utility of the 'population
approach' that is associated with scientific analyses in public health.
However, I have guarded against claims that this presents a novelty;
indeed, presenting it as innovative needlessly fuels conservative critiques of law. Rather, the population approach that is rightly adopted by
analysts engaged in politics and law might equally be termed the 'policy
approach'. This is necessarily not perfectly nuanced in every situation,
or designed to account ideally to every person's needs and characteristics. However, as shown in Chapter 4, it need not represent too blunt a
mechanism either. A policy or population approach demands that the
right account be given to effective, practical, practicable and generally defensible normative mechanisms. It necessarily allows individual
problems – both 'collateral harms' and 'collateral paternalism' – but any
alternative approach would be flawed for its naivety or indifference.

Parts I and II have presented and elaborated on the central thesis
of this book, and I hope it is clear that public health law and ethics
require studies in politics. In Part III my purpose is to present and
defend a particular understanding of liberalism that I would use in my
own assessments of public health measures.

Part III

Tackling responsibility: liberal citizens as subjects and sovereigns
Introduction to Part III

In Part III I present and defend an approach to developing and understanding the scope of political liberalism. My aims here, as in the rest of the book, carry two prominent themes: first to demonstrate a 'methodological approach'; second to offer my own views on what I take to be the best applicable approach to normative analysis. This means that even where my conclusions are not accepted, I hope to raise provocative and useful ideas for alternative, contradictory theories. This 'building' of a theory is the work of Chapter 10, which exposes the nature of *us* as concepts in politics and under the law, and the consequent normative implications. Chapter 11 then takes this theory, and through discussion of its bearing on various substantive questions presents it in relation to public health law and ethics. Necessarily, given all that has come in the previous sections, it is not a theory 'of' public health law and ethics. Rather, it is a political theory that can be applied *to* public health issues. Equally, and again of necessity, it can be applied to all other manner of questions facing a political society. Such a theory is demanded prior to study in public health law and ethics. An interesting observation, then, is that this book began with the specific, and through its deconstruction and analysis has worked out to the general. It should by now be clear why this is the case, and why final positions on questions in public health law and ethics – Should the wearing of seatbelts be enforced at law?; Should smoking be banned in public places?; Should the drug ecstasy be decriminalised? – require the manner of inquiry outlined here as a start point. To gain meaningful answers to questions of what makes health public, we need to look to political framing, not, for example, to norms that seem to emanate from the various 'faces' of public health presented in Chapter 3.

10 Liberal citizens: defining non-individuated individuals

10.1 Introduction

In this chapter I describe and defend an approach to political liberalism. It will be clear following Part II that this, like any approach, will not appeal or be acceptable to everyone, given conflicting analytic and conceptual constraints that bind other analysts engaged in alternative theories. For reasons that I will explain, the population the approach speaks to includes all born, living human beings within the jurisdiction of a liberal State. Therefore, my account includes members that some theorists would *ex*clude (e.g. due to a commitment to a 'rationalised personhood account'[1]) and denies a *special* normative protection to potential members that some theorists would *in*clude (e.g. due to a commitment to 'preference utilitarianism'[2]). I emphasise the word "special" because nothing in what follows precludes alternative bases and mechanisms for affording legal protections to non-humans or unborn humans. Simply, the account creates a system that affords 'legal personhood' – and thus legal rights, duties, etc. – to all born, living humans. Furthermore, I should stress that while the liberalism I describe speaks universally (albeit necessarily to a contestable classification of 'everyone'), its normativity applies practically within a bounded jurisdiction; it could not be applied everywhere in the world as we find it, and should be conceived as relating to a geographically defined political State. It is important 'to be upfront' about each of these controversial points, because they go to the heart of some of the most contested ethical problems that we will face when presenting conclusions on policy problems. Moreover, I initially present the points succinctly and explicitly, as I want to be clear that I know that they may lead to accusations of

---

[1] Cf Michael Tooley, "Abortion and infanticide", *Philosophy and Public Affairs* (1972) 2:1, 37–65; James Griffin, *On Human Rights* (Oxford University Press, 2008); John Harris, "Taking the 'human' out of Human Rights", *Cambridge Quarterly of Healthcare Ethics* (2011) 20:1, 9–20.

[2] See Peter Singer, *Animal Liberation* (2nd edn) (London: Pimlico, 1995).

parochialism or a localised *status quo* bias. Although the localism may be true, it is not a *biased* perspective, and I do not intend that the upshot of the analysis be understood as unduly conservative, morally blind, or morally imperialistic. Rather, I aim to explore a sustainable and defensible understanding of political normativity that is applicable in the context of contemporary State liberalism, and which can be engaged in a positive progression within such a system. I would emphasise that this analytic focus is of considerable importance in the current political climate, it does not preclude wider considerations of transnational obligations, and many of the issues discussed above and below have application outside of the approximate political structure that I take as the necessary backdrop to analysis.[3] Equally, whilst I am driven by some ideal-type concerns, I consider it crucial to develop the analysis in a manner that makes it realistically applicable to contemporary societies, and consider mine a 'non-ideal' theory. (If a label is needed, it approximates what might be described as soft-perfectionism.) The following analysis draws from, and is influenced by, many of the theorists whose works we have considered in the preceding chapters. While I do not claim to have stumbled upon a new political theory, in the context of the debates I am addressing I do hope that the following work is elucidating, useful, and provocative. Where it does not convince all readers, I aim at least to bring to the fore the pressing issues that demand attention in theorising about public health law and ethics. I develop my position in this chapter through four stages of argument, which allow me to articulate the basis, shape, and scope of the political liberalism that I would have underpin policy.

10.2   Abstraction away and the normative implications of mental capacity

One of the most notable discrepancies in the accounts considered in Part II was the divide between theorists whose starting place is an abstract account of morality, and theorists who start with a concern for the world as they find it. I presented approaches to political analysis under three different lights: ideal accounts that attach to a singular conception of morality; ideal accounts that accommodate a plurality of moralities, and thus seek to articulate a separate normative system; and non-ideal accounts that seek to learn about politics as a non-ideal phenomenon centred on questions of real world power relations.[4] I argued

---

[3] Cf Stephen Holland, *Public Health Ethics* (Cambridge: Polity, 2007), pp. x–xii.
[4] See Chapter 7, especially sections 7.2.1 and 7.2.2.

that it is possible and informative to draw coherently from aspects of each in the formation of critiques in public health law and ethics, and in the development of a morally informed account of politics. In Chapter 8 we saw that some of the authors whose specific works were considered choose to theorise in such a non-idealistic framing. Although it would be wrong to claim that any of their concerns or approaches are mirrored precisely in my own, I will seek in this section to establish that approaches such as those found in the works of Powers and Faden,[5] Gaylin and Jennings,[6] and Wolff and de-Shalit[7] are close to what we should aim at. However, for my own part, the political picture is closest to a development of the liberalism John Gray explores and advocates in his books *Isaiah Berlin* and *Two Faces of Liberalism*.[8] Some of the concerns he expresses are reflected in others of the works I have just cited. To explain the rationale for going beyond a unitary moral account as representative of politics, it is useful to begin with the words of Jonathan Wolff, whose commitment to robust political philosophy is wedded to a careful assurance that the theory can have application in practice. Considering the role of the political philosopher in debates on drugs policy, he contrasts two methods. The first says that:

[I]t is one thing to set up laws for an ideal society of the imagination, but the task in hand is to deal with the world we have. Inevitably, then, for policy reasons what needs to be discussed is not ideal law and regulation, but changes to the existing law.[9]

The alternative, by contrast, seeks to work in abstraction from any empirical grounding, and looks only to 'philosophical arguments' to provide an answer for what policy should do.[10]

Having contrasted the two methods, Wolff contends:

It would be absurd to argue that there is no place for speculation about ideals – of course this is necessary, otherwise there would be nothing to inspire or direct change. However, speculation about ideals is the start, not the finish, and if philosophers want to have an influence on the direction policy takes, then

---

[5] Madison Powers and Ruth Faden, *Social Justice: the Moral Foundations of Public Health and Health Policy* (Oxford University Press, 2006).

[6] Willard Gaylin and Bruce Jennings, *The Perversion of Autonomy: Coercion and Constraints in a Liberal Society* (2nd edn) (Washington DC: Georgetown University Press, 2003).

[7] Jonathan Wolff and Avner de-Shalit, *Disadvantage* (Oxford University Press, 2007).

[8] John Gray, *Isaiah Berlin* (Princeton University Press, 1996); John Gray, *Two Faces of Liberalism* (Cambridge: Polity Press, 2000).

[9] Jonathan Wolff, "Harm and hypocrisy – Have we got it wrong on drugs?", *Public Policy Research* (2007) 14:2, 126–135, at 133.

[10] *Ibid*.

there is no alternative to accepting that the status quo does have a privileged position in the debate.[11]

Part of the 'realism' that Wolff appeals to is about the messy nature of principle underpinning policy. In a democratic society, policies are born of political wrangling, opportunity, and compromise. To suppose that any single principle underpins each and every policy is naive.[12] As we have seen in consideration of his methodological outlook, and in slight contrast with Wolff's statement here, Raymond Geuss would go further in political analysis and place investigation of the empirical world first.[13] The order does not matter, I suggest, but we clearly do not do well to express normative conclusions on developed ideals without also exploring ourselves and the world conceptually; we can not usefully develop norms pertaining to people in abstraction from an understanding of what people are. I therefore explain in the following passages the problem with analysis that does not heed warnings such as that voiced by Wolff, and seek to address it as I develop my own principled account. The problem is abstraction away in the development of analytic concepts. It can prove a useful technique in argumentation, but can be damaging when it comes to practical application.

10.2.1   Abstraction away

The term 'abstraction away' denotes a technique in argumentation that 'purifies' thought by eradicating supposedly irrelevant, mundane, or trivial conceptual features to allow clearer analysis. It may be done for various reasons: for example, to allow argument to remain succinct; to lay aside matters that (it is taken) all are agreed on; or to allow the description of an ideal State or system. As already noted, some theorists treat this as the quintessence of their methodology, and would not qualify it according to 'real world' limitations. At a meeting I attended on public health ethics, a philosopher was told his theory could not work in practice. He indifferently shrugged off the criticism: "I'm interested in the normative, not the empirical." Such a level of theorising is of interest, and indirectly perhaps of use, but it does not lead to analysis that particularly bears on, let alone serves to help understand and improve,

---

[11] *Ibid.*

[12] See also Søren Holm, "'Parity of reasoning' arguments in bioethics – some methodological considerations", in Matti Häyry and Tuija Takala (eds.), *Scratching the Surface of Bioethics* (Amsterdam: Rodopi, 2003).

[13] Raymond Geuss, *Philosophy and Real Politics* (Princeton and Oxford: Princeton University Press, 2008), p. 59.

the society we create and live in.[14] There seem to me to be two prominent forms of abstraction away to consider. The first relates to the conceptual construction of 'persons', the second to that of the environment (social and physical).[15]

10.2.1.1 Abstracted persons   Abstraction away in regard to persons often occurs when theorists wish to distil from their analysis those parts of us or our being that are morally or functionally unimportant or irrelevant. There is no doubting the value or importance of this exercise. What we see is abstraction from persons in a grounded sense – generally understood as meaning adult, human people with their attendant foibles and failings – to persons in an abstract sense – generally understood as something featuring various capacities relating to self-awareness. This abstraction is made, essentially, so that the matters of importance can be analysed without the distraction of normatively uninteresting diversions. The benefit of so doing is presented, for example, in the refining theorising found in Kant's analysis of autonomy, the theory of morality that he presents given autonomy,[16] and subsequent theorising by others on its basis.[17] And insofar as a reader may be persuaded by such theory, that is all to the good. But it is important not to be carried too far by conclusions based on such analysis. If we assume *people* to be, for example, 'Kantian persons', we risk creating *false paradigms*, and around these will tend to construct further false paradigms that support practically dubious premises and eventually a completely inapplicable framework for our analysis. We will have a model that is well suited to abstract moral analysis of theoretical beings, but it will not speak to *us*. There is no use or sense in designing a society for autonomous 'Kantian persons' (not least as for them – if they exist – society will not be designed, it will just be, and any external law will be useless; and for us it is useless because we are not they). In the words of James Griffin:

Our aim must be the more modest one of understanding not the autonomy of a spare, abstract self, but the autonomy of *Homo sapiens*.[18]

[14] See Thomas McPherson, *Political Obligation* (London: Routledge and Kegan Paul, 1967), ch. 4.

[15] Note how these are parallel with the ideas about assessing the public/private distinction in section 2.3.

[16] Immanuel Kant, *Groundwork of the Metaphysics of Morals*, ed. Mary Gregor (Cambridge University Press, 1998).

[17] E.g. Robert Paul Wolff's analysis of political philosophy, considered above: Robert Paul Wolff, *In Defense of Anarchism* (with a new preface) (Berkeley: University of California Press, 1998).

[18] Griffin, *On Human Rights*, p. 35.

Speaking to the subjects of our analysis as if they are hyper-rational, logically atomised (though also logically fully absorbed in one another by virtue of 'the moral law'!) beings is to speak to beings out of this world. This criticism is clear, and well made in many quarters. As well as analysts such as Griffin, we find it, for example, in feminist critiques of dominant liberal models,[19] and in the communitarian critiques of theorists such as Bruce Jennings.[20] It is crucial that as our theories develop, they remain suited to the people they speak to. Where we face practical constraints, it is better to accept this than to fictionalise our way around them.[21] We need to develop a theory of social normativity that entails concepts that are true to us. This is an endeavour, as discussed in previous chapters, that will lead to varied results in part because of radical disagreements about the scope of the term 'us'. In what follows, I will seek to present a liberalism whose subjects are born, living humans, and will aim to respond to accusations of arbitrary over- or under-inclusion.

10.2.1.2 Abstracted environments   As is the case with persons, concerns arise in relation to the environment, situation, or universe, against which analysis takes place. Environments here should be understood as both physical and social spaces. As can be the case when an excess of artificial conditions skews the real world utility of data found in medical trials,[22] if normative theorising operates in too distant abstraction, we gain little for practical application because our conclusions can only coherently function in an artificial world too different from our own. Within bioethics, this is perhaps most obvious when analysis is conducted as if the universe contains just two agents – a doctor and a patient – and does not extend beyond the physician's surgery. Theories such as 'relational' accounts have proliferated as a counter-flow to this manner of analysis, and speak well to its deficiencies. (It should be

---

[19] Catriona MacKenzie, Natalie Stoljar (eds.), *Relational Autonomy: Feminist Perspectives on Autonomy, Agency, and the Social Self* (Oxford University Press, 2000).

[20] Bruce Jennings, "Autonomy and difference: The travails of liberalism in bioethics", in Raymond Davies and Janardan Subedi (eds.), *Bioethics and Society: Constructing the Ethical Enterprise* (New York: Prentice Hall, 1998); Gaylin and Jennings, *The Perversion of Autonomy*.

[21] Parallel to the moral abstractions described here, it is worth noting the equivalent problem in economic theory, which of course also has considerable bearing on arguments in public health law and ethics, and are well addressed by Richard Thaler and Cass Sunstein's distinction between *homo sapiens* and '*homo economicus*': Richard Thaler and Cass Sunstein, *Nudge: Improving Decisions About Health, Wealth, and Happiness* (London: Penguin Books, 2009).

[22] Marie Fox and Michael Thomson, "HIV/AIDS and male circumcision in public health discourse and practice" (forthcoming).

noted, too, that the law operates outside of such analytic constraints, though whether it always does so well in any given jurisdiction is a separate question.) The important point for present purposes, however, is that drawing practical conclusions from unrealistic theories of the content of the environment is problematic as soon as it leads to our designing a normative framework that is only suited to government within some alien place, reflective only of an incomplete picture of the important aspects of the society we live in.[23] Where the physical environment bears importantly on questions that at least raise the possibility that State governance is attractive, these must be factored into the reasoning. In public health analysis, this entails an openness to understanding environmental questions relating to pollution, access to clean water, the best means of dealing with waste, and so on, and people's practical capacity to act. It also will be well informed by understandings of people and how they behave. Thinking back to Chapter 4, and the reference to "really responsive regulation",[24] it is crucial to understand humans' actions if we are to know what governmental responses are necessary, and which will be manageable and effective.

Equally, the social environment is important. In this chapter, I am developing an account that does not define 'everyone' with philosophical purity. It does not rest on a strong essentialist account of ideas such as the good, well-being, or flourishing of *all* human beings. Indeed, the plausibility of claims of universal truths about all human organisms are something of which to be sceptical. The putative interests of a human embryo – for example in continued life or in not being subjected to medical tests – are qualitatively distinct to those of a developed human being. I choose not to rely on dubious or speculative theological or metaphysical claims about the essence of humanity as if the biological species naturally carries with it a robust and broad bunch of general goods or rights that can be said actually to apply to all, at all stages of existence. I do, though, consider it important to account for various facts about the social environment as it is constructed by people. In Chapter 2, I followed Bruce Jennings and adopted Benedict Anderson's 'imagined communities' thesis in seeking to understand what 'the public' *qua* a political community is.[25] I will reflect further on that here, to develop an understanding of the social environment.

---

[23] Margaret Brazier, "Do no harm – do patients have responsibilities too?", *Cambridge Law Journal* (2006) 65:2, 397–422.

[24] Robert Baldwin and Julia Black, "Really responsive regulation", *Modern Law Review* (2008) 71:1, 59–94.

[25] Bruce Jennings, "Public health and civic republicanism: toward an alternative framework for public health ethics," in Angus Dawson and Marcel Verweij (eds.), *Ethics,*

I have agreed that a sustainable public requires the 'shared imagination' of its constituents; a shared belief in the *fact* of, and in broad terms the nature of, their association. This 'imagining' comes from two directions: people's self-reflections (e.g. my believing myself to be British) and people's reflections on others (e.g. my neighbours believing me to British).[26] In some cases, each of these is sufficient to endow someone with an identity, in some cases both are necessary before an identity is formed. This will depend in part on the specific nature of identity within any given group, and in part on the nature of the group itself: to become a member of a club may require internal and external recognition; to be classified as a criminal may only require external recognition; to be a Christian may only require internal recognition. In regard to the social environment, it is important to note therefore that there is no need to have universal consensus about group membership for a group functionally to exist. Taken at the level of a political association (which is the extent of my concern in this book), we do not need, for example, all Canadians to believe that they are Canadian, or even to believe that all legal Canadian nationals are Canadian. Rather, we need a sufficiency for this to become a 'practical truth'.

The interesting thing to note here is the potential for some form of 'imaginative creep' through external identification, that leads to the development of a practical truth that bears directly on the facts about the world that we seek to subject to normative inquiry and control. Where a sufficiency of people believes that all of x people form part of the public, they will eventually do so as a matter of fact. Thus, for example, whilst some philosophical theories would deny the inclusion of newborn infants in the political community, and those infants are unable to imagine themselves within the community, the fact of brute belief in their inclusion can (and currently does) nevertheless render it a practical – and thence a political – truth. In this sense, part of the real world situating of a normative account or response must accommodate this truth, even in cases where it would seek too to modify or move beyond it. To be clear, this is not an argument that because sufficient people believe x we must take it that x is right. Rather, it is the

Prevention, and Public Health (Oxford University Press, 2007); Benedict Anderson, *Imagined Communities – Reflections on the Origin and Spread of Nationalism – Revised edition*, (London: Verso, 1991).

[26] Richard Jenkins, "Rethinking ethnicity: identity, categorization and power", *Ethnic and Racial Studies* (1994) 17:2, 157–223; Rogers Brubaker, "Ethnicity without groups", *European Journal of Sociology* (2002) 43:2, 163–189.

claim that this makes it *practically* true. And any account that seeks to move things progressively must be able to respond to the practical truth about human communities as they practically exist in the social world that people create and have foisted upon them, as much as it does in the physical world they find themselves in. A priority, of course, must be eradicating harmfully formed groups (e.g. *exclusion* on grounds of race is indefensible in a way that *inclusion* (if we take it to be wrongheaded) on grounds of simply being a born member of the biological species human is not). As such, part of my cautioning against abstraction from the environment demands that attention be paid to the social world that we actually live in. To change it, should we so choose, we must understand it, and speak to it in terms that can actually bear on policy-making.

One final note in this regard relates to the use of the term 'health' itself in social settings, an issue I shall consider in relation to my own theory in the next chapter. As seen in Chapter 1, Amartya Sen highlights the importance of the potential for discrepancy in internal and external perspectives on health.[27] This contrasts self-perception with the observation of some outside expert. The distinction is useful, and assumes great relevance when we consider the substantial content of concepts such as health, welfare, and well-being, and question *who* should be the effective arbiter of such matters in terms of policy. Noted accounts of social perceptions of what is healthy suggest that health itself may be usurped, grounded in an 'externalist' perspective, and used to control or castigate individuals, groups, or behaviours.[28] Equally, there are notable instances of ill-health that are not felt or recognised by their subjects, but which are seen legitimately to demand external interference.[29] Just as there may be some 'imaginative creep' that includes people in publics they are unable to conceive or are doggedly opposed to entering, so 'imaginative creep' might have more particularised upshots in policy and practice, leading to general beliefs about what and who is healthy or unhealthy.

---

[27] Amartya Sen, "Health achievement and equity: external and internal perspectives", in Sudhir Anand, Fabienne Peter, and Amartya Sen (eds.), *Public Health, Ethics, and Equity*, (Oxford University Press, 2004).

[28] Perhaps most notably Ivan Illich, *Limits to Medicine – Medical Nemesis: The Expropriation of Health* (London: Marion Boyars, 1995[1976]). See also Jonathan M. Metzl and Anna Kirkland (eds.), *Against Health – How Health Became the New Morality* (New York and London: New York University Press, 2010).

[29] For a stark example, see e.g. H Tristram Engelhardt, "The disease of masturbation: values and the concept of disease", *Bulletin of the History of Medicine* (1974) 48:2, 234–248. See also Metzl and Kirkland, *Against Health*.

10.2.2   *A practical upshot: contrasting mental and legal capacity*

The foregoing arguments render it important to make an observation about the practical freedom of human agents in liberal political systems. Working with a community of 'non-perfect agents' gives us reason to develop a political realm, and makes it defensible to do so. People do not have access to perfect knowledge, yet need to get on, and thus an external order is required to address 'coordination problems'. And people are morally imperfect (i.e. sometimes act amorally and immorally), and at least as a practical truth are committed to distinct understandings of morality. Thus an external order is also required to address and prevent (some) wrongful and/or harmful behaviour, and to overcome distinct interpretations of the demands of morality. People's agency is what allows them to be treated as responsible beings. And their flaws in agency are what permits them to be treated not as the sole governors of their lives.

In legal terms, a person is responsible when he has capacity to be so.[30] The ways capacity may be ascribed are various; it is common to distinguish three means.[31] First, capacity given a status (e.g. being over 18 years old); second, capacity given mental competence (e.g. a medical patient who passes a 'functional test' demonstrating the ability to understand, reason, and come to a decision); or third, capacity given the 'right' decision-making (e.g. holding a person free to make decisions provided he makes the right ones, as judged against some external standard). Whether there is a presumption that a person has decision-making capacity or that he lacks it, at law it is rightly just a presumption. And whilst the anarchism of Robert Paul Wolff may derive from the paradigm example of a 'mentally competent adult', as soon as we step into a political system – even a strongly libertarian one – we will see that the presumption of capacity in any given case may be doubted.[32] And, as mentioned in the discussion of 'collateral paternalism', when policy is made, it will necessarily not be applied perfectly in practice: at times, a person will wrongly be treated as if he has capacity; and at times a person will wrongly be treated as if he lacks capacity. Equally, there will

---

[30] There is in practice, of course, considerable ambiguity and equivocation in such a statement: see Barry Lyons, "Dying to be responsible: adolescence, autonomy and responsibility", *Legal Studies* (2010) 30:2, 257–278.

[31] See e.g. Margaret Brazier and Emma Cave, *Medicine, Patients and the Law* (4th edn) (London: Penguin, 2007), pp. 125–126.

[32] This is, again to draw from McMahon's phraseology, reflective of our "peculiarly human" nature and the need to accommodate this in an appropriate political normativity: Christopher McMahon, "Autonomy and authority", *Philosophy and Public Affairs* (1987) 16:4, 303–328, at 325.

be compelling reasons, at times, to prohibit or anyway regulate various activities, bringing a limit to people's freedom to act. Recognition of this allows us to see that there is no necessary paradox in an individual being found mentally competent to make a decision, but not having legal capacity to act upon it.[33] Assisted suicide under English law is a case in point. Without worrying here whether the policy is defensible, we can see a position where assisting a suicide is prohibited on the grounds that vulnerable groups will be harmed by anything but a blanket policy criminalising assisted suicide. In this situation, we can without contradiction find that a person has the mental capacity to ask for assisted suicide, find that he has a willing assister, and still deny the person the freedom he wants. Mental capacity to make a decision does not of itself denote a rightful legal capacity to act;[34] further argument is needed to account for policy concerns (i.e. it is necessary to test the empirical claims about the threats to those who are vulnerable, and not limit assessment to individual cases that would certainly be acceptable when considered in isolation).[35]

The point of all this is that in a political system it is insufficient to speak of specific acts or actors without considering the wider framework, and accounting for the wide range of legal persons. Much work in medical ethics is impoverished to the point of uselessness as a result of failures to recognise this. The general norms that underpin law and policy, when they are justified, make it permissible to limit freedoms, even in cases of people who, like Wolff's authority-denying Kantian anarchist, think the rule should not speak to them. In a specific analysis of what is right, or should or should not be the case, it is insufficient simply to point to the fact that someone has 'mental capacity' and then claim that he functions as a moral agent and thus deserves detachment from general constraints founded by political society. If, for example, we are to assess proposed or existing drugs policy, we can not do so well by reference just to the people who will not be harmed, or by reference

---

[33] See further John Coggon and Jose Miola, "Autonomy, liberty, and medical decision-making", *Cambridge Law Journal* (forthcoming 2011).

[34] Cf Philip Bielby, "The conflation of competence and capacity in English medical law: a philosophical critique", *Medicine, Health Care and Philosophy* (2005) 8:3, 357–369.

[35] See the European Court of Human Rights' decision in the case of Dianne Pretty: *Pretty* v. *UK* (2002) 35 EHRR 1. See also the discussion in John Coggon, "Assisted-dying and the context of debate: 'medical law' *versus* 'end-of-life law'", *Medical Law Review* (2010) 18:4, 541–563; Richard Huxtable, "Whatever you want? Beyond the patient in medical law", *Health Care Analysis* (2008) 16:3, 288–301; Claire McIvor, "Bursting the autonomy bubble: a defence of the Court of Appeal decision in *R (On the Application of Oliver Leslie Burke)* v. *GMC*", in Stephen W. Smith and Ronan Deazley (eds.), *The Legal, Medical and Cultural Regulation of the Body: Transformation and Transgression* (Farnham: Ashgate, 2009).

to an ideal construct of the person and the law as it should apply to him. Similarly, if we are to assess road traffic laws, we need to account for the range of people who will use public roads, not design regulation around the capacities of the ideal-typical driver. As we have seen, in drafting defensible policy, we may come to a judgement that suggests the legal permissibility of some wrong-doing; which does nothing to advocate political or legal interference. Likewise, we may come to a moral judgement that taken alone a proposed conduct is fine, but no workable policy could allow a general freedom to do it without devastating wider effect. As our focus is in the political realm, we need to understand the political community, and develop workable norms within that. And it is these that establish judgements in analyses in public health law and ethics.

10.3   'Law's persons' and universalism

10.3.1   Conceiving persons and the coexistence of different conceptions

As a singular class, human beings do not fit neatly into some conceptual categories.[36] Their plural and conflicting natures and interests make it hard to classify them, and easy to pick at any specific definition that may be advanced by reference either to someone who presumptively should be 'in' but who does not fit the bill, or someone who should be 'out' yet inexplicably is not. As I have stressed above, the normativity to address this question is political, and the voice of the political is the legal. To explore the scope of political community, this section therefore borrows from a title of a work by Ngaire Naffine, whose central question is "Who are law's persons?".[37] As Naffine notes, whilst her analysis is "essentially conceptual":

[I]t is of considerable practical and political importance. Perhaps the greatest political act of law is the making of a legal person (simply put, he who can act in law) and, in the same move, the making of legal non-persons (those who cannot act in law and who are generally thought of as property).[38]

Naffine's approach is useful in separating the answer to her question into three possible categories. First she argues that 'legal persons' may simply be whoever 'the law' says they are, thus *ex ante* with "no necessary

---

[36] Harris, "Taking the 'human' out of Human Rights".
[37] Ngaire Naffine, "Who are law's persons? From Cheshire cats to responsible subjects", *Modern Law Review* (2003) 66:3, 346–367.
[38] *Ibid.*, at 347.

moral or empirical content".[39] The second "is necessarily linked with biological and also metaphysical definitions of humanity",[40] and will generally denote a born, living human. In contrast with the first concept, this is not purely legal, as it includes moral and biological considerations, and is evidenced in accounts of law where 'human being' and 'legal person' are considered naturally synonymous. This inevitably means that:

What counts as a legal biological human is therefore not just subject to medical (which of course are also cultural) determinations about the beginnings and ends of a human being. What it means to be a biological human is also influenced by cultural ideas of what it is to be a whole and proper metaphysical person.[41]

In this sense, which Naffine argues is heavily informed by dominant liberal paradigms, persons are conceived as "whole, integrated and individuated beings".[42] The third concept of a person is "the rational and therefore responsible human legal agent or subject: the classic contractor".[43] On this understanding, rational agency denotes the status of moral agent, which in turn permits the conception of a legal person. This person is thus "essentially a mental rather than a biological being".[44]

Naffine suggests that as one moves from the first to the third conception, the classification becomes increasingly exclusive; the first, potentially endowing anyone (and anything) with personhood, the second, (in some senses arbitrarily) limiting personhood to humans, and the third, limiting it to beings able to exercise agency. Naffine argues that claims in justice may mean that the first concept should be more widely embraced to ensure that we have "the basis of a law for everyone".[45] There is something a little hollow in this aspiration, as she clearly does not (I trust) mean to make every *thing* a legal person, and thus still needs to perform some limiting exercise (engaging with what she would seem to label "metaphysical" reasoning). Nevertheless, what is most usefully taken from Naffine's analysis is that these three conceptions in fact coexist at law, and if law's persons include the conceptual variety of beings that it does, and drives to cover different concerns, there will have to be some manner of unclarity or incoherence. To put it another way, as a legal and political conception, the biological class 'human' does not form a unitary category. Looking from the perspective of the 'rational personhood theorist', we have already noted that people are

---

[39] *Ibid.*, at 351.   [40] *Ibid.*, at 357.   [41] *Ibid.*, at 359–360.
[42] *Ibid.*, at 360.   [43] *Ibid.*, at 362.   [44] *Ibid.*, at 364.
[45] *Ibid.*, at 367.

variously imperfect. And as a matter of fact, even those who are 'whole-sale incompetent' (e.g. the permanently comatose, neonates, those with severe mental disability) are still a part of society, and thus legal rights-holders. The inclusion of all of these people reflects a common concern for, and importance in, their interests. Furthermore, even people who would tend to have decision-making capacity are flawed from the rational personhood perspective. Thus everyone in a political system is a subject as well as a sovereign. The universalism of law is expressed in who it protects, which must be decided in accordance with some prior means of analysis (i.e. we do not come to the table knowing who 'everyone' is). Its universalism, at least within the political realm, does not denote a unitary nature to all legal subjects, or a unitary concept of morality to govern them. And the fact of the political realm conjoins everyone. Whilst they are individual subjects, they are not fully individuated. This all bears directly on how we should conceive legal rights.

10.3.2   Legal rights

A point raised in Chapter 7, which resurfaces here, is that the obvious conceptual tension amongst different accounts of 'legal persons' is reflected in the debates between will- and interest-theories of rights. Briefly, will-theories hold that rights are protections of choices made by agents, thus applying only to beings that are autonomous and able to exercise their rights on their own behalves. Interest-theories, by contrast, hold that rights protect particular interests, and focus not so much on who exercises the right as on the interest the right protects.[46] Within the political scheme under discussion here, legal rights are best thought of not as foundational, prior concepts on which a theory is based (as may happen in some ideal-type deontological theories of law[47]). Rather, 'rights language' permits us to speak the practical upshots, often in shorthand terms, of the political system that we are working within.[48] 'Rights' and associated concepts are used as a technical expedient, describing the nature and practical demands of relationships between

---

[46] See Leonard Wayne Sumner, *The Moral Foundation of Rights* (Oxford: Clarendon Press, 1987); Matthew Kramer, Nigel Simmonds, and Hillel Steiner, *A Debate Over Rights* (Oxford University Press, 1998); Matthew Kramer, "On the nature of legal rights", *Cambridge Law Journal* (2000) 59:3, 473–508; Leif Wenar, "The nature of rights", *Philosophy and Public Affairs* (2005) 33:3, 223–252; Matthew Kramer and Hillel Steiner, "Theories of rights: is there a third way?", *Oxford Journal of Legal Studies* (2007) 27:2, 281–310.

[47] E.g. Deryck Beyleveld and Roger Brownsword, *Law as a Moral Judgment* (London: Sweet and Maxwell, 1986).

[48] Cf John Gray, *Two Faces of Liberalism* (Cambridge: Polity Press, 2000), pp. 84–85.

persons with regard to each other, and between persons and the State.[49] Thus, I do not 'just have' a right not to be hit, reflecting in others a duty not to hit me. It must be possible to appeal to a prior principle (for the purposes of this book's analysis, one that is inherent in political liberalism) that holds that it is generally wrong for people to hit each other, and from which we can derive the articulation of a right not to be hit. Equally, we must recognise that when we describe such a right, we must not generalise it too far; it will almost always, for example, be something that can be qualified, or waived, or overridden.

Put this way, it becomes apparent that it is not a being's moral perfection that makes rights-talk necessary, but everyone's 'imperfections'. In a community of persons described within the autonomous Kantian abstraction, no one would need to articulate his rights, as they would just be 'respected' as a matter of course. Rather than frame legal rights in terms of abstract academic inquiry into questions of what a rational person would do or will, we frame rights to protect legal persons in the manner and to the extent that such protection is warranted and if necessary underpinned by the interference of the State. Given that 'law's persons' are rationally varied, and can not all or always exercise their own rights, a complete theory of legal rights must accommodate matters that can not be deduced by reference just to a hypothetical, abstract, autonomous, individuated person. People are not simply rights-holders to the extent that they can exercise choice, or under conditions where they have the capacity to do so. They remain rights-holders in a dreamless sleep, when incarcerated, when drunk, and so on.

Given this, the best way to conceptualise legal rights is through an interest theory.[50] It is possible for this to apply equally well to those with and those without mental capacity or the power to exercise a right, and need not imply that choice is unimportant.[51] This is not the trite observation that 'it can be in someone's interests to make a choice'. Rather, it is the more substantive claim that often each individual is best placed to ascertain what his interests obtain in.[52] It is about accommodating a political and legal freedom reflective of value-pluralism and epistemic humility, whilst also holding as a practical truth that rights

[49] This is most usefully done within the Hohfeldian framing of rights: Wesley Newcomb Hohfeld, *Fundamental Legal Conceptions as Applied in Judicial Reasoning*, David Campbell and Philip Thomas (eds.) (Aldershot: Ashgate Dartmouth, 2001).

[50] See Kramer, "On the nature of legal rights".

[51] *Ibid.*

[52] Noting which is not to deny the potential for *this* view to become a more generalised (and also trite) refrain reflective of an empirical untruth: see Cass Sunstein and Richard Thaler, "Libertarian paternalism is not an oxymoron", *University of Chicago Law Review* (2003) 70:4, 1159–1202; Thaler and Sunstein, *Nudge*.

protect interests with substantive content, and that that content may be limited where necessary in order to sustain the political society and a sound legal order.[53] Thus let us start by considering a mentally competent adult, who can choose between drinking whisky and not drinking whisky as of right (i.e. he has a double-liberty whose protection poses a duty on the State or others not to interfere with his choice). His choice is between two mutually exclusive options, he is the beneficiary of the right, and it is his power to exercise the right. We do not need to consider this right as being protected in accordance with a choice theory because of a belief that as they are contradictory choices, they can not each be said potentially to serve his interests. Rather, we can say that *he* is best positioned to assess his own interests, and thus himself to give the content to the interest that this right serves as a mechanism in protecting. Within this conceptualisation, we are able to accommodate value-pluralism, so that within the political society different people can live in accordance with their own moralities. It is likewise possible for this pluralistic outlook to be employed for people who lack decision-making capacity. Although they may not be in a position to exercise rights for themselves, whoever may be charged with this power can inform his understanding of the person's interests by reference to the values that person holds or held, as evidenced explicitly or implicitly.[54] The most complex category here is people who have never had any, or only very limited, psychological existence as it is not possible even approximately to infer the holding of one way of life over another. In such instances, values will have to be imputed with a level of artificiality.[55] It is still possible, but is more complex.[56]

In summary, legal rights are well conceived as protections of interests. At core, there will be certain 'individual interests' that are put beyond the pale (classically, for example, we might say that someone's interest in killing his parents to inherit their estate is not a legitimate

---

[53] Contrast the more robust 'perfectionism' of Joseph Raz, who is deeply critical of the manner of scepticism I advocate here: Joseph Raz, "Liberalism, scepticism, and democracy", in Joseph Raz, *Ethics in the Public Domain* (Oxford: Clarendon, 1994).

[54] In English law, for example, such an approach is legally required: see Mental Capacity Act, s. 4; *Re A (Medical Treatment: Male Sterilisation)* [2000] 1 FCR 193; *In Re S (Adult Patient: Sterilisation)* [2001] Fam 15; *Ahsan* v. *University Hospitals Leicester NHS Trust* [2007] PIQR P19.

[55] See *Re Y (Mental Patient: Bone Marrow Donation)* [1997] Fam 110.

[56] See further John Coggon, "Best interests, public interest, and the power of the medical profession", *Health Care Analysis* (2008) 16:3, 219–232; John Coggon, "Doing what's best: organ donation and intensive care", in Christopher Danbury, Christopher Newdick, Carl Waldmann, and Andrew Lawson (eds.), *Law and Ethics in Intensive Care* (Oxford University Press, 2010); Andreas Dimopoulos, *Issues in Human Rights Protection of Intellectually Disabled Persons* (Farnham: Ashgate, 2010).

grounding of a right to do so in a liberal political system). Nevertheless, by not giving more than presumptive content to the great majority of interests that might be served and protected through the mechanism of legal rights, we allow a rich pluralism that reflects the practical reality of varied moral perspectives and values, and protects their coexistence within a pluralist, political liberalism. This pluralism extends to all citizens, not just those in a situation to exercise choice, and presents a position that allows us well to conceive, as we must do, legal persons as subjects as well as sovereigns.

10.3.3 Legal persons as subjects and sovereigns

Having shunned anarchism, it is right now to reiterate and reaffirm the importance of taking a 'policy perspective', and the upshot of political normativity for the government of people. Within a liberal political system, we are all subjects as well as sovereigns. The political community is a part of us, and we are a part of it. The principle underpinning this, though not the breadth of its practical implications, is as true for small State libertarians as it is for big State communitarians. And it demands that any given manner of regulation be tested not just by reference to an individual case, but appraised in the full context of the political society in which it applies. The best way to think about this is through the lens of effective government (again with no need to preconceive a particular brand of political philosophy, though in half of what follows I will clearly preclude some), and under the shadow of two frames of epistemic blindness. First, contrary to some political views, there is a recognition of some moral uncertainty, which operates to allow conditions of moral pluralism, and no *ex ante* presumption that morality implies a monistic and exclusive normative system. Rather than political normativity being a means to drive people towards and in accordance with a specific morality, it transcends or ignores many moral questions and allows for harmonious coexistence given distinct moral values. Second, and this applies to any political system that would work in practice, is acceptance that we can not know to a certainty whether or to what extent any given citizen has mental capacity (or the capacity to act as a moral agent in his own right). Thus, in a community comprising only agents who are imperfect, and imperfect to various degrees and in various ways, *presumptions* must be made about when people define their own interests, and what defaults to appeal to when it is decided that they can not define their own interests. And as ever, in the background are considerations that may recommend blanket policies, for example where prevention of harm to vulnerable or incompetent people can only be achieved in such manner.[57] This is a price that, in principle, must be paid by everyone for living in a varied society. In practice, tension arises because of disputes over who *should* have sovereignty in a given situation. This is not about choice *in se*, or even necessarily about *mental* capacity. It is about the distribution of sovereignty: i.e. who says what is in my interests in this situation; me, the State, my doctor, my mentor, my parents, my spouse, my children, or someone else? And when must decisions be made collaboratively? In what follows, I shall seek to argue that the best way to mediate these practical questions, given the conceptual nature and variety of members of human communities, is through a *modus vivendi* liberalism, derived in its articulation from John Gray.

10.4   The shape of liberalism

We have seen, in particular in Chapter 8, some of the very different ways in which analysts articulate their preferred political systems, and the distinct concerns and reasons that push them in different directions. Throughout Part II, and in the preceding sections of this chapter, I have presented points of consideration in the development of a political theory, against which it must be defended. In the remainder of the chapter I will present what I take the best defensible political liberalism to be. This is the framework that I (and others, should they so choose) can apply both to general and specific questions concerning public health law and ethics.

So, where does the above analysis leave us? If we take it that people are not 'rationally perfect', does it mean that we ought to reject familiar ideas associated with liberalism – for example that 'individual autonomy' is worthy of considerable protection; that people should be responsible for their lives; that liberty is not to be interfered with unless there is some well argued warrant – because they are based on spurious paradigms? The answer is no. But we need to modify our system to account for the conceptual differences that reality presents us with. Even with a community that contains some 'incompetent' people, and no 'fully competent' people, there will be an enormous amount of freedom that is best left with individuals for the oft-cited reasons that make political liberalism defensible. Simply, a revised, or more carefully articulated, liberal framework requires us to reconceptualise matters that have become 'received wisdom' in much analysis, and re-conceive our paradigms accordingly.

---

[57] As per the above discussion of *Pretty* v. *UK* (2002) 35 EHRR 1.

10.4.1   Locating the individual and society

In arguments concerning political norms, and those relating to public health imperatives, it is common to find the apparent problem – sometimes cast as a 'dilemma' even – of the individual *versus* society, or a conflict between the rights of individuals and the rights of the community. In many cases, the reasoning behind the articulation of this supposed conflict renders it a bogus notion. And for the purposes of the theory I am elaborating, it is important to lay this to rest, by reference to ideas of 'the good' within politics. First of all, in accordance with the arguments of Chapter 2, I do not accept that 'the public' should be reified. Physical harms or threats to 'the public' or 'society' are actually threats to people. In other words, we may find conflicts between individuals *within* a society, but we can not find a conflict between any individual *and* the political community. 'Society' does not exist in the strong sense implied by some in this regard. If a person is denied a level of physical liberty that is generally held, for example because he carries a harmful, contagious disease, this restriction is not because he may harm some reified abstract called 'the public' of which he is not a part. It is because he is part of that public and he may harm other people within it. His interests in going out are pitted unsuccessfully against others' interests in not being harmed. A good political system will allow for the mediation of this conflict, and allow us to see which interests are legitimate (i.e. shared by all) and which are self-interest and not sufficient to justify State (or State-sanctioned) interference. By forming a public, people are well considered as joint custodians (with and through the State) of their bodies. Government is split, and there may be a conflict over who ought to govern in a particular situation: for example, over whose appraisal of my interests prevails if I think my interests would not be served by wearing a seatbelt and the government thinks that they would be.

At the conceptual level, whilst we may talk of the mediation exercise as being one about 'balancing rights', this is not what happens. On some theories, pluralities mean that dilemmas exist, wherein one is bound to make a decision, and of all the options none permits an outcome with no rights-violation. In cases where there are plural moralities, such as in the world John Gray describes, it may seem analytic (as he takes it to be) that rights and liberties can not be harmonised. He argues, for example, that:

Unless we know the interests they protect, rights lack content. When we know these interests, we find that rights, even a single right, may make incompatible demands. Then we have no alternative to choosing between them.[58]

This view is sustainable on the bases that an account of the good is necessary to give content to liberties and rights, there are plural accounts of the good, and the good can take priority over the right. Gray thus discounts the perspectives of theorists as distinct as Mill, Rawls, and Nozick in accordance with his concern for the truth of *modus vivendi*, and the inevitable contentiousness of staking a claim that has the practical effect of denying a person the freedom to live according to his own conception of morality. So for example where Gray denies the plausibility of Mill's 'harm principle' as a means of limiting practical freedom, he says:

Even where there is agreement on the facts of the matter, people with different views of human well-being will disagree on whether harm has been done. Or, if they agree that harm has been done, they will differ on its severity.[59]

Millian liberalism, like other forms of liberalism, "does not enable us to avoid making moral judgements. It requires them".[60]

It seems clear that Gray is right; we can seek to limit freedom by reference to models of 'rational consensus', or appeal to principles such as well-being or welfare. But to make these effective, we must endow them with positive content that carries its own values, and thus speaks negatively to the values of those who disagree:

It does not matter whether liberal values are conceived in terms of the promotion of autonomy, the priority of negative liberty, the demands of equality, the protection of human rights or – though this is the most useful rule of thumb that liberal philosophy has produced – the prevention of harm to others. In every case, liberal values prescribe rival freedoms. By so doing, they engender dilemmas for which liberal principles have no answer.

If we think of liberalism as a prescription for an ideal regime, it is undone by conflicts of value that liberal principles are powerless to resolve. It is better to step back from Kant to Hobbes, and think of the liberal project as a pursuit of *modus vivendi* among conflicting values.[61]

Gray is right to suggest that the acknowledgment of plural values does not permit of a principle from within liberalism to judge how good liberalism is or what it should permit. He is right too that such pluralism suggests that legitimacy can not be tested conclusively, and that several distinct systems can exist, none of which is more legitimate than the next, and that one system can change qualitatively over time without

---

[58] Gray, *Two Faces of Liberalism*, p. 84.   [59] *Ibid.*, p. 87.
[60] *Ibid.*   [61] *Ibid.*, p. 104.

gaining or losing legitimacy. So, I agree both that between regimes we may find justifiable distinctions, and that 'rights' are no starting point for a political theory. However, where Gray denies the plausibility of an "overall theory of rights",[62] he is speaking across time and globally in a world of many different States. He and I part company if by doing this it is taken that he is denying that *legal* rights in the sense I have described above exist within a single given State at a given time. Indeed, he recognises that some manner of compromise, detached from any single moral theory, must be taken to ensure that harmonious living can continue, and that commonly held and recognised institutions are needed to resolve conflicts between citizens. Within a given jurisdiction, it seems clear that rights *do not*, at least at the level of principle, conflict at all. And more strongly, in practice when they are tested, principle demands that they be treated as harmoniously reconcilable in accordance with a positive – albeit morally contestable – system of values. Understood in this way, we see that effective *legal* rights do exist, and do not conflict. When these are articulated as short hand descriptions of conclusions – which is what they are – we may find prima facie conflicts, but their necessary tacit qualifications allow for this to be remedied. As for liberties, where a person has a freedom to act, he may choose one way of life that precludes his choosing others, but this has no practical effect for another person's liberties. Thus, talking about special liberties – for example, 'freedom of religion', 'scientific freedom,' and 'freedom of speech' – as if they actually denote separate spheres is wrong-headed. Particular values will underpin how we estimate a particular use of freedom, but liberty can not conflict with itself, and employing adjectives to suggest that there are different 'sorts' of liberty only confuses things. It is important to note too that the scope of liberty need not denote an area of 'anything goes'; rather, it exhausts the list of options wherein people live according to their evaluation of interests rather than in the constraints of some legally imposed conception.

Thus, we may say that it is a basic analytic truth that any right within a political system is qualified by all other rights. And it is a practical truth that there is little to be gained, as a general rule, in stipulating all qualifications to a right, even if this is possible. Rather, we need to draw the qualifications out only when we face the ostensible (but necessarily illusory) conflict. So it may be helpful to presume there is such a thing as 'a right to healthcare' as a basic proposition within a political system that places positive value on its citizens' welfare. When working out precisely what it entails, however, we look at other rights

---

[62] *Ibid.*, p. 113.

and obligations that lead to effective claims on the things that might be entailed in a bald right to healthcare.[63] By confusing claims that can be made in timeless universality, and claims that can be made within a single jurisdiction at a point in time, Gray wrongly gives insufficient attention to the fact that we can quite usefully, plausibly, and credibly – within a scheme of *modus vivendi* – distinguish a hard core of commensurable legal rights and associated duties, and a wider, freer, harmonious space comprising liberties and no-rights. For the political system to have practical bite, through the legal institutions it requires, this is a necessary upshot, and need not obtain in a specific and exclusive morality. Indeed, the point of accepting politics is to describe a normative system that, for practical purposes, transcends the problems of having competing moralities. The common good that this requires is necessarily contentious, but acknowledging that does not get us nearer or further from the problem of having to do so. And seeing this conceptualisation allows us to be clear that there is little in claims that individuals sacrifice their rights to 'the rights of the community'.[64]

10.4.2   Giving solid content in a system of pluralism and uncertainty

The task that the foregoing assessment leaves us is a troublesome one, and necessarily will alienate my views from some readers' own perspectives. Even on my own terms, I have left little solid ground on which to base arguments about the good that founds laws and regulations.[65] I seek to defend a theory of liberalism that promotes some welfare, for example by providing a level of care and attention to vulnerable people and those who are incapacitated in various senses. I also want it to allow, insofar as is practicable, for people to live according to their own value systems, in recognition of moral pluralism at the very least as a practical truth, and one that can not be surpassed by reference to any particular theory being demonstrably superior on independent terms.

---

[63] See also the discussion of O'Neill on the right to health: Onora O'Neill, "The dark side of human rights", *International Affairs* (2005) 81:2, 427–439, Chapter 8, section 8.4.2.

[64] Gray seems to commit the converse of the problem Sen describes of Bentham, where Sen describes Bentham as treating it as analytic that rights are positive legal constructs and thus not amenable to assessment by reference to purported moral rights, whilst also having his own non-legal means of assessing laws (utilitarianism): see Amartya Sen, *The Idea of Justice* (London: Penguin, 2009), ch. 17. Gray's denial of the foundational nature of *moral* rights does not speak, though he seems to take it otherwise, to the practical nature of *legal* rights.

[65] See e.g. Raz, "Liberalism, scepticism, and democracy"; William M. Curtis, "Liberals and pluralists: Charles Taylor *vs* John Gray", *Contemporary Political Theory* (2007) 6:1, 86–107.

In so doing, I have denied myself the independent grounds on which to make any of the relevant valuations. Equally, I deny the plausibility of contractarian theses that either work at a level of abstraction that means we articulate the values people *should* accept, or demand the tolerability of anarchism based on the fact that everyone has not *in fact* accepted a political system. Even the more sophisticated democratic theories that have proliferated, such as Norman Daniels and James Sabin's "account-ability for reasonableness" thesis,[66] fail for the abstracted citizen to which they appeal when dictating the limits of political acceptability or in circumscription of what is 'reasonable'.[67] I am working from a non-ideal account of politics, which, in the words of Andrew Vincent "embodies … *both* the fact of conflict and plural uncertainty *and* its possible mediation".[68] In essence, I resolve to take it as a fact that in a 'state of nature', and in many political situations, power relations form a fundamental aspect of social structuring (whether it occurs 'organically' or through design). Thus I heed (though not to the extent of accepting all his conclusions) the warnings articulated by Geuss.[69] Furthermore, I take it as a fact that whilst people disagree about the specific content of the good in many situations, and the question of there being a singular moral foundation to the State, it is not contentious to be a 'descriptive statist', and urge that people are actually better off (even given their plural understandings of what 'better off' means) within some State systems than in anarchy or some other State systems. If these claims are accepted, we can conceive of a political system that is founded as a prudential and partial understanding held between people, which exists for their good. To label it a "contract" would be too strong. To claim its basis is moral would be an overstatement. However, amongst competing conceptions of the good, it is possible to gain an approximate account of the manner and scope of an operable and defensible liberal system, if we allow too that democratic limitations take practical effect in the local governance; in other words, like Gray, we allow for variation from State to State, so norms can be local and localised. Equally, we can allow for side-constraints against wrongheaded or harmful demands of

---

[66] Norman Daniels and James Sabin, "Limits to health care: fair procedures, democratic deliberation, and the legitimacy problem for insurers", *Philosophy and Public Affairs* (1997) 26:4, 303–350.

[67] Andreas Hasman and Søren Holm, "Accountability for reasonableness: opening the black box of process", *Health Care Analysis* (2005) 13:4, 261–273.

[68] Andrew Vincent, *The Politics of Human Rights* (Oxford University Press, 2010), p. 160 (emphasis in original).

[69] Geuss, *Philosophy and Real Politics*; and see Chapter 7.

the majority through legal and political mechanisms that are developed within the State.

I thus offer a robust but contingent concept of the State. Its foundations are contestable, but this hardly distinguishes it from other conceptions that may actually relate to the world we live in. It is a distinct understanding, however, and for some it will be too weak, or too devoid of a specific form of content (e.g. they might argue that it gives insufficient account for a particular democratic mechanism; insufficient regard for a moral foundation in some theory of moral rights). The prudential partial understanding model is the logical upshot of the systematised epistemic limitations that play on a society of humans, alongside the varied conceptual natures of persons as they actually are. Accordingly, it seems that the easiest measure of acceptability of legal measures in such a society can be found in a revised formulation of the 'harm principle', with emphasis on imperfections of agents, and on risk. In essence, we move from:

[T]he only purpose for which power can be rightfully exercised over any member of a civilized community, against his will, is to prevent harm to others.[70]

To:

The only purpose for which power can be rightfully exercised over any likely competent member of a civilized community against his will, is to prevent unacceptably likely harm to others, or to secure the benefits due to others.

Gray is right that benefit and harm prove to be unfixed concepts. But we have seen that we require an inner core of certainty, in which there is no pluralism. And beyond that – within the sphere of liberty – we *can* have various accounts of harm and benefit, properly protected through law. I thus suggest the above revision, in order to assist our understanding of good governance. There are a few layers to unpack. First, the meaning of competent needs to account both for mental competence (i.e. we trust the wisdom of those who are rightly judged wise) and legal capacity (i.e. we do not permit activities that sound policy demands be prohibited across the board). The inherently paternalist undertone to this, and the need to rule on competence (even if we *presume* people are competent, it is still a judgement that allows the presumption to hold), are necessary in a shared society, of themselves, to protect others as well as individuals for their own good. It is crucial, then, to recognise that at any time a person is judged a sovereign, it is because it is *probably*

---

[70] This is the 'harm principle' as classically presented by Mill: see John Stuart Mill, *On Liberty*, Edward Alexander (ed.) (Peterborough, Ontario: Broadview, 1999), p. 52.

right that that be so. Equally, it is not that he *surely* knows his interests best; rather, he *probably* does. One aspect of probability and harm that requires explicit attention is the equivocal way in which something may be described as a likely harm. Given the pluralism we are working within, and the epistemic uncertainty that we must accept, it may be that by "likely harm" we mean that something can not be described to the point of certainty as harmful, either because a harm will not necessarily follow in a specific case (e.g. as in the claim "smoking causes lung cancer") or because in the individual case a perhaps prima facie harm does not in the end constitute a harm for some reason (e.g. as in the case of an invasive bodily intervention that a person reasonably considers an enhancement, where others might reasonably consider it harmful). There is also the real disadvantage in exposure just to risk,[71] regardless of whether the harm finally materialises (e.g. again claims about smoking). So, there is complexity of something's probably rather than certainly occurring, and the complexity of its manifestation probably rather than certainly being harmful. There is also uncertainty about an individual's competence to judge this, and a need where the individual is not placed to do so to set a default and act in accordance with it. Finally there is the conferring of benefits onto others. Obligations here are founded through shared membership of a political community, and the needs that some members have.[72] In this sense, we might for example find taxation used to secure some basic standard of healthcare or environmental protections. Controversies will arise in the degree to which assuring positive benefits narrows the scope for legitimate liberty and pluralism, and to the extent that the State is not considered an efficient means of redistributing goods. However, at the level of principle this should be no more (or less) difficult to justify than the harm to others justification for limiting liberty. As we saw in the arguments above, although it is attractive (and sometimes expedient) to distinguish 'negative' and 'positive' liberties, both require positive obligations to be imposed on citizens if they are to be sustained.[73] I would suggest too that in practice many issues could equally reasonably be described as justified either for reasons relating to not causing harm, or for reasons

---

[71] As carefully discussed by Wolff and de-Shalit: Jonathan Wolff and Avner de-Shalit, *Disadvantage* (Oxford and New York: Oxford University Press, 2007). See also Jonathan Wolff, "Health risks and the people who bear them", available at http://sas-space.sas.ac.uk/dspace/bitstream/10065/677/1/J_Wolff_Health.pdf.

[72] This may be seen as an extension of the principle explored in George Klosko, "The natural basis of political obligation", *Social Philosophy and Policy* (2001) 18:1, 93–114.

[73] See section 8.3.5.

of creating benefit (see e.g. the example of compulsory seatbelt wearing in the next paragraph).

In the next chapter I will discuss the approach to analysis using this understanding of political liberalism in public health law and ethics, but will briefly here exemplify the implications by reference to a common example from debates about public health: the enforced wearing of seatbelts. This raises questions about paternalism and coercion,[74] and draws out the policy angle that must be taken by governments in the development of law and regulation. My above position can lead to the following stages of reasoning and counter-reasoning about the legally obligatory wearing of seatbelts:

1. Tom does not want to wear a seatbelt.
2. Because, Tom argues, an ideal conception of Tom ought to be free to decide not to do so, he ought to be granted the freedom to choose, and left free not to wear the seatbelt.
3. In response, it is argued that Tom is not an ideal conception of Tom, and the State thus can make an argument that *its* wisdom ought to prevail rather than his.
4. Furthermore, even in a situation of moral pluralism and value agnosticism, it is necessary to devise a strong account of harm and benefit, on the back of which law can be made.
5. Added to this, even where what is decided to be a harm is less than certainly going to eventuate, the State can still make an offence of running the risk.
6. Compulsory wearing of seatbelts is argued to be justified in the interests of the individual, even if he disapproves, because the risk is of a great and (reasonably described) objective harm, and the burden imposed on the individual (even the unwilling Tom) is small.
7. Thus, the law imposes a right that Tom can not waive (in Hohfeldian terms, a right coupled with only a single liberty, and a duty), because seatbelt-wearing is deemed to be in his interests.
8. This is justified, because it probably is in his interests, and if he thinks that it is not, he is probably wrong.
9. And finally, the argument is bolstered by a kind of harm/benefit-to-others argument: it is reasonable to presume that it is in most people's interests to wear seatbelts. If Tom does happen to be sophisticated enough to establish that it is not in his interests to do so, he should nevertheless submit to it as a general policy where this is necessary

---

[74] Note that it is, at least in the first instance, an example of 'rational coercion': Grant Lamond, "The coerciveness of law", *Oxford Journal of Legal Studies* (2000) 20:1, 39–62.

for the policy to work in those cases where the non-conformists lack the requisite capacity (i.e. if it is shown to be a justified instance of collateral paternalism).

10. I.e. Tom owes a political duty to himself and all others to obey the policy, as its blanket nature is needed to ensure that those who do not have capacity do not wrongly fail to wear their seatbelts (a manifestation of collateral paternalism).[75]

In specific cases, the arguments will have to be made in a manner that is acceptable to – and accepted by – a sufficient number of the polity they speak to. Given the contingency of policy-making, many policies will vary from State to State, both in general and in the detail. More multicultural societies will perhaps find it more difficult to conceive wide-reaching and compelling conceptions of harm and benefit. Equally, extant background conditions will qualify the level and nature of coordination needed by the State (for example, in a system where a sufficient number of people voluntarily submit to vaccination programmes, compulsion will not be necessary; where they do not, there may be an argument for the State's compelling people legally[76]). The 'agnostic liberalism' here, as I have emphasised throughout, does not in logic require a homogeneity to every legal system even in 'Western democracies'. It does, however, offer the rationale for accepting a political normativity, and the nature of reasoning that should be engaged in the development of policy, including policy that will predictably compel even rational, autonomous adults. The contingency of this liberalism means that the specific arguments must be made against and in light of local background conditions. But without strong metaphysical claims about the 'nature' of humans or human flourishing, a political concern for people's welfare, including both negative claims about their avoiding harm and positive claims about their being able to achieve benefit, can give the framework for building useful and defensible political institutions and policies. And such politics can work coherently even where there are plural, coexisting conceptions of harm and the good.

10.5   Conclusion

Often claims about universalism are too easily made. For example, to praise human rights for their virtue of applying to 'everyone' overlooks

---

[75] This argument ignores the other harm-to-others arguments that are advanced on this sort of question; such as the cost of healthcare should Tom come to grief; the harm to his family; etc.

[76] Cf Stephen John, "Expert testimony and epistemological free-riding: the MMR controversy", *The Philosophical Quarterly* (2011) 61:244, 496–517.

the real problem not of everyone having rights, but of understanding *who* everyone is. Furthermore, in the real world, practical questions of governance mean that in most cases we must limit questions to distinct jurisdictions. This non-idealism is what our theorising *must* apply to (if anything), so it ought not to be seen as a weakness that we should 'start from here'. In the above, I have started with a notion of the public that comprises people including those who can not be self-reliant. Bringing everyone together, this has practical implications both for the nature of rights, and their scope and the means by which they are exercised. Sometimes they will be exercised by the beneficiaries on their own behalves; sometimes they will be exercised regardless of the will of the beneficiary. As members of the political community, we are in part responsible for each other's being able to benefit within the society, and to avoid harms therein. In order to give voice to the normative mechanisms that express how this may be done, we can use the language of legal rights, liberties, and so on. In this way, the political framework can be used to articulate, explore, and describe complex relationships between, for example, freedoms and obligations. Chapter 11 will consider it and the light it sheds on inquiry into questions that arise in relation to public health issues.

11 Health made public: rights, responsibilities, and shared concerns

11.1 Introduction

In this chapter I present some of the implications of the political liberalism described in Chapter 10 for analysis in public health law and ethics. This book has demonstrated the need to commit to a political model or framework for any meaningful normative discussion to take place in relation to public health. Thus, even readers who are opposed to the political position that I take should be able to see and accept the wider analytic and 'methodological' point about political engagement with public health issues. The political context that I defend includes in its community people with and without their own decision-making capacity, and narrows the legitimate freedom people have to act on some of the decisions they would make. This applies not only where their actions themselves may cause harm to others, but also where a general and perhaps generally latent freedom that would allow them to perform harmful acts would lead to unacceptable harm amongst members of the wider population. In this sense, not only are people part of the environment, but their legal rights, freedoms, and so forth are too. Such a point is well demonstrated by a claim made by the British Medical Association's (BMA) Board of Science in its report "Under the influence – The damaging effects of alcohol marketing on young people".[1] Alcohol regulation is one of the BMA's four public health priorities.[2] Core to the argument in the report is that excessive alcohol consumption is a public health problem, and that young people (by which it means people under 25) face particular problems. However, the Board of Science rejects the idea that simply targeting young people will provide a satisfactory response. Rather, it argues, regulations to protect

[1] British Medical Association Board of Science, *Under the Influence – The damaging effect of alcohol marketing on young people* (London: BMA, 2009).
[2] On its website, the BMA says it "maintains a proactive interest in the following key public health areas: Reducing alcohol-related harm; doctors taking action on climate change; tackling the obesity crisis; working towards a tobacco-free society": www.bma.org.uk/health_promotion_ethics/index.jsp.

this group must be targeted across the board. The report describes the regulatory system in the UK as providing a "pro-alcohol environment", where advertising, popular culture, marketing, fiscal arrangements, and widespread availability are amongst the malign factors that conspire in sustaining an unacceptable public health problem. Elsewhere I have suggested that the BMA's position is interesting:

> Not least as each person's part in the "pro-alcohol environment" means even directly harmless, or only self-harming behaviour, may be a matter of public interest: my freedoms to extol the joys of drinking, to buy alcohol at any time of the day, to consume intoxicating drinks that taste non-alcoholic, to see entertainment that is subsidised by the industry, to drink cheaply, and to find dense collections of bars, pubs, and clubs are all harmful, even if I do not exercise them. In other words, the apparently benign presence of latent or responsibly exercised freedoms amongst some citizens is deemed to be sufficiently troublesome that they must be curbed for the greater good.[3]

What we see here then is the importance of the 'context' provided by general rights, which clearly can be mapped onto the concept of public discussed in Chapter 2.[4] Likewise, we see an argument advanced by the BMA in favour of a specific manifestation of 'collateral paternalism' in the context of public health policy. More generally, much of the recent upsurge of interest in the fields of public health law and ethics is evidenced in works that address the sorts of observations underpinning the BMA report, and develop or criticise the sorts of arguments that it raises. There are disputes about the understandings of, rationales for, and means of allocating responsibilities when we understand the community to comprise people who can not always take responsibility for themselves. And beneath these disputes is the problem of there being something inherently contestable in claims about what constitutes harm and benefit, and by implication in terms such as 'health'.

Within a liberal political community there are shared concerns, some of which manifest themselves as legal duties, as well as a great deal of liberty left (in varying degrees) to citizens to live their own lives in the manner they choose, given what they are able to do: we have norms developed to protect important 'private realms', reflective of the importance of personal decision-making, and private space. Part of the role of the State is to safeguard and respect liberty. National defence and policing are the most obvious means by which the State has a positive obligation

---

[3] John Coggon, "The British Medical Association, young people's alcohol consumption, and public health: everyone's problem", *Journal of Bioethical Inquiry* (2010) 7:1, 5–7, at 7.

[4] See section 2.3, especially the concept of public/private drawn from the decision in *Pretty* v. *UK* (2002) 35 EHRR 1.

to protect citizens' rights to be left alone (which in turn places positive obligations on citizens, for example, to pay taxes to sustain the governmental protections, in some cases to participate in national service, and so on). In parallel, the State assumes responsibility for assuring public goods that require a coordinated, communal effort, such as ensuring a supply of potable water and working sewage systems (again in turn placing positive obligations on citizens to pay taxes necessary to sustain these or assure adequate oversight of private bodies that do so). And part of the role of the liberal State I have described is to 'enable' or 'empower' citizens, most obviously perhaps through the provision of education and some level of social welfare.

The basis for demanding positive assistance, and thus enforceable and unwaivable duties, varies between theories. Some, for example, argue that it is necessary insofar as would be demanded in a system agreed by rational drafters of a social contract, concerned to design political institutions in a way that assures a fair opportunity to all citizens.[5] Others suggest that there is a minimum duty on States to ensure conditions in which humans can flourish.[6] In some sort of echo of these latter theories, my own commitment is to a manner of liberalism that recognises plural benefits and harms that may bear on people's lives, and sees the State as a means of ensuring that people can live sufficiently good lives. This entails enforced taxation, and sometimes 'hard paternalism' (as a proportionate collateral effect of necessary blanket policy to protect citizens who require 'soft paternalist' measures). The basis of this liberalism is not founded on 'basic rights', but rather an appeal to overall consequences, within a system of plural goods. It thus maps onto a development of Millian liberalism, drawing in part from qualifications made in subsequent works, in particular those of Isaiah Berlin, and later John Gray. Within a community, political duties conjoin us, and law and regulation can be advanced to ensure these duties are met where necessary. In this sense, the ultimate basis of the assessment works back to some sort of 'harm and benefit principle' that is defensible by reference to the goods it leads to.

As areas of principled concern, 'real politics' and political need vary over time and between States, meaning the 'negative' and 'positive'

---

[5] John Rawls, *A Theory of Justice – Revised edition* (Oxford University Press, 1999); Norman Daniels, *Just Health: Meeting Health Needs Fairly* (Cambridge University Press, 2008).

[6] Madison Powers and Ruth Faden, *Social Justice: The Moral Foundations of Public Health and Health Policy* (Oxford University Press, 2006); Jonathan Wolff and Avner de-Shalit, *Disadvantage* (Oxford and New York: Oxford University Press, 2007); Bruce Jennings, *Civic Health: Political Theory in Public Health and Health Policy* (forthcoming).

roles will complement one another in different ways depending on the situation as it presents itself, and lead to particularised practical demands in the sharing of concerns. Likewise, the very natures of those who are part of the community has a bearing. If we take it that all born, living humans are within the fold, needs abound that can not be addressed just by leaving people alone to look after themselves; obligations necessarily arise that in some cases can not be (immediately, anyway) reciprocated (e.g. obligations to young children). Although certain duties can be exercised on behalf of 'incompetent' individuals (e.g. the payment of tax), and many duties are exercised 'passively' (e.g. duties not to commit battery), there are many people who require positive assistance, which a liberal society will mediate or oversee through the State.[7] This does not negate the distinction that, for example, Nozick or Engelhardt would, in their different ways, draw between 'community' as some naturally (and in an over-simplistic manner voluntarily) forming apolitical association, and the community as 'the public'. However, the value of not 'enforcing' duties, whilst keeping an eye on the good, is eminently plausible in political terms if we acknowledge the wide and nuanced regulatory sphere, rather than conceive of 'the law' as something that will only coerce, prohibit, or permit.[8] People's voluntary activity may limit the need to *exercise* political power to ensure that duties are met: where people generally do what is required or desirable, 'light touch' regulation can be quite defensible, even if this means there will be some 'free riders' or some missed beneficiaries. Importantly, the test of acceptability of non- or limited interference here is made by reference to the outcome, not some moral imperative that dictates a 'trumping' value in voluntariness.[9] And to be clear, this argument does not deny that political association costs. It obviously does narrow some of the freedoms of 'autonomous adults' who become obliged to share in the responsibility of other members of the public. (We should note, though, that this narrowing may lead to a net increase in practical freedom as a result.)

With regard to questions in public health, what does this mean? Potentially a great deal, if we recall how broad an interpretation of the

---

[7] John Coggon, "Intellectual Disability, Autonomy, and Legal Rights," *European Journal of Health Law* (2011) 18:4, 447–459.

[8] See Chapter 4.

[9] See Anthony Ogus, "Regulation revisited", *Public Law* (2009) 332–346. Cf Stephen John's view that it is "telling" that a regulator should seek to coerce where voluntary conduct fails to produce the desired outcome: Stephen John, "Expert testimony and epistemological free-riding: the MMR controversy", *The Philosophical Quarterly* (2011), 61:244, 496–517.

field can be, essentially allowing that it can relate to the study of anything that possibly bears on health.[10] This chapter explores some of the more common overarching issues from the perspective provided by the political liberalism developed in Chapter 10. I will begin by addressing the problems with understanding concepts such as 'health' and 'harm'. I will then reflect on the practical upshots for policy-makers and analysts alike, in a mode that will allow further critical appraisal and application in works beyond this book. The answer to normative questions concerning proposed and existing public health policy will always be found by establishing what makes health public, which is in turn found by establishing what health is and what makes anything public; establishing how and in what ways health exists within and bears on the political sphere.

11.2   Health, welfare, harm, and benefit

I noted in Chapter 1 that theorists vary greatly in what they take health to denote. To reinforce the point, and to demonstrate some of its implications, in Chapter 8 I tried to draw out what different theorists themselves think it best implies, bringing to the fore some of the stark distinctions, and the consequent problem that we may end up talking across each other even when we seem to be debating similar questions. In some arguments, health was one amongst various necessary aspects of human flourishing;[11] in others, it was a basic good necessary for the achievement of basic entitlements in justice;[12] in others still it seemed to be a complete normative theory of human well-being, or even a thinly veiled political theory;[13] and we also found an intentional failure to commit to a clear understanding, with claims that it is too abstract or personal a concept to permit of useful definition.[14] Where it is defined, we find negative and positive definitions, and ones that take on more or fewer normative criteria.[15] In this section I will argue for what I

---

[10] See Part I, especially Chapters 3 and 5.

[11] E.g. Powers and Faden, *Social Justice*; Wolff and de-Shalit, *Disadvantage*; Jennings, *Civic Health*.

[12] E.g. Daniels, *Just Health*.

[13] E.g. Ivan Illich, *Limits to Medicine – Medical Nemesis: The Expropriation of Health* (London: Marion Boyars, 1995 [1976]); David Seedhouse, *Health: The Foundations of Achievement* (2nd edn) (Chichester: John Wiley & Sons, 2005).

[14] Petr Skrabanek, *The Death of Humane Medicine and the Rise of Coercive Healthism* (St Edmundsbury Press: Bury St Edmunds, 1994).

[15] A little crudely, it might be suggested that the 'extremes' run from Boorse's naturalist conception to the World Health Organization's all-encompassing well-being conceptions: Christopher Boorse, "Health as a theoretical concept", *Philosophy of Science*

consider to be the best way to understand health. I will maintain that it is necessarily a normative concept, but one that I would only separate categorically for practical rather than principled reasons (in contrast, for example, with theorists such as Powers and Faden, and Wolff and de-Shalit, who consider health in its own right for normative reasons[16]). As far as political argument is concerned, I consider it best to treat health as forming an aspect of a wider category of welfare, which must then be related to politically relevant concepts of benefit and harm.[17]

11.2.1   From health to welfare

Richard Hare is right in his observation that:

[O]ne is perhaps being over-ambitious if one thinks that one will be able to capture our understanding of words like 'health' and 'disease' in cut-and-dried definitions. Wittgenstein has made us familiar with the idea that a word may have a spread of meanings; there are a whole lot of conditions for its use, and perhaps none of them is necessary or sufficient.[18]

In recognition of this, I do not propose to settle questions of what health means, less still to establish that 'we' have all been talking about the same thing when we draw together distinct discussions that claim to be about (public) health.[19] Nevertheless, I do aim to place my position within the debates on what health means, and think there is considerable practical utility in so doing.

As discussed above, two of the key dichotomies that arise in debates about health are over the questions of whether it is a positive or negative concept, and whether it is a 'normativist' or 'naturalist' concept. A positive definition of health holds that it obtains in some state of being. Most famously, the World Health Organization (WHO) definition of health as states of well-being fits this definition. A negative definition, by contrast, defines health by reference to the absence of some state, such as one of disease. It is possible coherently to adopt positive and negative approaches simultaneously (as the WHO does). The

---

(1977) 44:4, 542–573; Constitution of the World Health Organization, available at http://apps.who.int/gb/bd/PDF/bd47/EN/constitution-en.pdf.

[16] Powers and Faden, *Social Justice*; Wolff and de-Shalit, *Disadvantage*.

[17] *Cf* Margaret Brazier and John Harris, "Public health and private lives", *Medical Law Review* (1996) 4:2, 171–192.

[18] Richard Hare, "Health", *Journal of Medical Ethics* (1986) 12, 174–181, at 178. See also Bjørn Hofmann, "The concept of disease – vague, complex, or just indefinable?", *Medicine, Health Care and Philosophy* (2009).

[19] See the discussions in Chapters 1 and 3. Especially in view of Chapter 3, it is hard to maintain that people could be found to have spoken about one thing when discussing 'public health'.

normative/naturalist split, however, describes two mutually exclusive positions. A normative understanding finds that health is necessarily a good thing, and thus has background criteria about what is good for people. A naturalist conception treats health as a scientific question, often to stand in contradistinction with a scientific understanding of disease. Theorists who appeal to a naturalist understanding will tend to triumph its lack of normativity, noting that they make no pre-analytic claims about the goodness of being healthy, or the badness of being diseased.[20] Perhaps particularly where scientific understandings take a teleological approach to analysing how the human organism 'works', however, there will often seem to be a *correlation* between good health and a desirable end state, from which theorists may try to draw strong political conclusions.[21]

Nevertheless, I voiced above considerable scepticism of claims that theorists are able *usefully* to treat health as a non-normative, or even a minimally normative, concept. Although this seems an attractive means of denying or avoiding further analytic groundwork, if we – or policy-makers – are to be rationally motivated to advance health, it needs to be established first that it is a good thing. For this reason, I position myself in the normative camp in debates on the meaning of health. I do not deny that a science of health could be developed, where inquiry focuses, for example, on the statistical incidence of observable traits. I do, however, deny the utility of this to analysts in public health law and ethics, and to policy-makers. Furthermore, I look to positive and negative health concepts. In part, this is due to an underlying failure to recognise the positive/negative distinction as being quite as sharp as some consider to be the case. Once we see health as a value-laden term, we do so too with disease, or whatever property's absence conduces to health. As such, health logically assumes a positive conception in the sense that, with health necessarily good, it is something we have a *prima facie* reason positively to pursue, and with disease necessarily bad, it is something we have a *prima facie* reason positively to avoid.[22] By conceiving things like this, however, we must move away from something

---

[20] See the comparisons of a scientific concept of health with other concepts found in life sciences: Christopher Boorse, "On the distinction between disease and illness", *Philosophy and Public Affairs* (1975) 5:1, 49–68, at 55–56.

[21] *Ibid.*, at 60. And for the most noted example of this leading to potent political claims, see Daniels, *Just Health*.

[22] As such, I am less concerned than some analysts about distinguishing 'treatments' and 'enhancements', or seeing a normative divide between the two. I find persuasive the arguments advanced in John Harris, *Enhancing Evolution – The Ethical Case for Making Better People*, (Princeton and Oxford: Princeton University Press, 2007), ch. 3, see especially pp. 44–58. Cf Allen Buchanan, Dan W. Brock, Norman Daniels, and

that is simply 'told to us by science', and thus medical models of disease become inadequate alone to tell us what health is, even if we accept that health does not exhaust all of what is good for us. So where does this take health?

Juha Räikkä suggests that the important argument may be taking place in a different sphere than many protagonists imagine: normativists and naturalists disagree on the substance of health, but are largely one in the belief that they are debating a medical concept. In contrast, he contends "the concept of disease used in discussing social questions is not the medical concept of disease, but what might be called the *social concept of disease*".[23] As we have seen, the medical (or scientific) concept can not without being normative suggest that we should aim to enhance health or lessen disease. Yet in general usage these are seen to be good things to do. Räikkä suggests three prevalent reasons why disease (and by implication health) is thought to be normative:

First, people observe that health is on the whole *desirable*, while disease is on the whole undesirable. Second, they note that what counts as disease seems to *depend on the culture* where the condition occurs. And third, they point out that diseases and pathological conditions are considered *abnormal*.[24]

But in Räikkä's argument, it seems that the key reason for deciding that something is a disease is the "special services, care and assistance"[25] that are *due* to the unhealthy. For those interested in social theory, this sense of disease will be most important because it poses the practical question: "Is it justified or obligatory to treat people with this condition differently from others?"[26] Adopting this social sense, we move two steps further. First, it is not just diseased people who may be treated differently, but also conditions and things that likely bear on them.[27] Second, just as we may be interested in the special treatment of disease, so we may also be interested in the special treatment of health; in other words, we do not just seek to create an absence of disease, but hold to a stronger, positive sense of health.

Daniel Wikler, *From Chance to Choice – Genetics and Justice* (Cambridge University Press, 2000), ch. 4.

[23] Juha Räikkä, "The social concept of disease", *Theoretical Medicine* (1996) 17:4, 353–361, at 355, emphasis in original.

[24] *Ibid.*, at 354, emphasis in original, footnote omitted.

[25] *Ibid.*, at 360.   [26] *Ibid.*

[27] Richard Hare notes the value of the "non-committal word 'condition'" in arguments on health-related concepts: 'condition' does not commit one to ascribing a particular aetiology to a condition, and it does not commit one to holding that something is pathological or necessarily a *bad* condition: Hare, "Health", at 175.

From this, a concept is beginning to develop that might be mean-ingfully employed in political analysis of public health issues. I have argued that a value-free concept is of no practical use, and is of little use or interest to normative theorists, be their immediate concern moral, legal, or political. Räikkä's social concept appears to apply to the sort of health conception that is likely to occupy us in public health law and ethics because it relates precisely to conditions and states that we have (or think we have) good reason to control in a particular manner. It allows us to sidestep the *traditional* normative *versus* naturalist debate. However, there are some further concerns that must be addressed. By following Räikkä, we are assuming a social-constructionist model of health as described, for example, some years earlier by Peter Sedgwick.[28] There is a danger, when assigning to health a meaning that is consistent with a social understanding, that the medical sphere holds considerable relevance after all. Sedgwick describes the way the medical (or scien-tific) concept gains some sort of privileged status even within 'social' definitions:

Practice and concept continue their mutual modification over the ages. In a society where the treatment of the sick is still conducted through religious rit-ual, the notion of illness will not be entirely distinct from the notion of sin-fulness or pollution. Correspondingly, with the growth of progressively more technical and more autonomous specialisms of therapy, the concepts of disease and illness themselves become more technical, and thereby more alienated from their implicit normative background. Thus we reach the position of the present day where any characterization of an "illness" which is not amenable to a diagnosis drawn from physiology or to a therapy based on chemical, elec-trical, or surgical technique becomes suspect as not constituting, perhaps, an illness at all.[29]

This idea of expertise in health has more import than a straightfor-ward model providing the social construction, for example, of deviancy can allow. The gloss provided by a health professional's rationale for dubbing a matter 'health-related' should not be underestimated. Thus, we can not quite so straightforwardly avoid biomedical conceptions, even if the reason for this failure is of dubious rational quality. As long as policies claim to have some evidence base, or appeal to a scientific rationale, health is a narrower concept than *all* conditions that we can and would have good reason to address. (Or what constitutes a 'health professional' becomes someone with a much wider-reaching span of

---

[28] Peter Sedgwick, "Illness: mental and otherwise", *The Hastings Center Studies* (1973) 1:3, 19–40.
[29] *Ibid.*, at 35.

expertise.[30]) Whilst it is clear that simply because people *do* think in a certain way it does not follow that they *should do* so, it is important to account for the concern articulated here as it will bear on the apparent rationale of much policy that is advanced, and also a great deal of argument in academic and policy literature.[31] We need not be beholden to the continuing 'claims' of, or appeals to, science or medicine, but must be aware of them. As health seems to be something susceptible to expertise and professional assessment, but also something that relates precisely to 'what is good for us', we need to treat carefully policy arguments based on health benefits or harms (this point is discussed further in section 11.2.2, below).

So now we come to the important question for policy analysis concerning public health: if health is best understood as a normative concept, how can it fit into and relate to a complete theory of political normativity? We have two options: we make health a complete normative theory itself; or we develop some 'meta-theory' either to mediate between it and other normative concepts, or to fit them all together coherently. In Chapter 8 I discussed reasons to be wary of the former approach, placing it under the heading of a 'health theocracy'.[32] In regard to the latter, it is useful to note a point made by Lennart Nordenfelt, who emphasises that discourse on health does not take place solely within a medical context, or even a purely scientific context. Given this, he argues that there is a concept of health that forms part of the "philosophy of welfare" rather than the "philosophy of medicine", and which is worth exploring thus.[33] Health in this context relates to something wider than the concern of doctors and patients, but is not the whole of welfare. Giving substance to this definition of health *does*, in practice, involve the views of the medical establishment.[34] As discussed just above, even if we take health to be a social concept, there is a role played by those with medical expertise. This pragmatic approach draws Nordenfelt to the following conclusion (note that I have added the word "health" to his references to disease and illness, in a manner that I trust is acceptable):

---

[30] See Chapter 3, section 3.2.4.
[31] This is one of the strengths of adopting Powers and Faden's "ordinary-language understanding": see Chapter 8, section 8.3.3, and Powers and Faden, *Social Justice*.
[32] See Chapter 8, section 8.4.1, and Bruce Jennings, "Community in public health ethics", in Richard Ashcroft, Angus Dawson, Heather Draper, and John McMillan (eds.), *Principles of Health Care Ethics* (2nd edn) (Chichester: Wiley, 2007).
[33] Lennart Nordenfelt, "On the relevance and importance of the notion of disease", *Theoretical Medicine and Bioethics* (1993) 14:1, 15–26.
[34] *Ibid.*, at 19.

The concepts of [health,] disease and illness figure in a number of moral and legal contexts. In some of these contexts they play *as a matter of fact* a decisive role for important decision-making. In response to this we ought to ask the following two questions. Is the role played by these concepts clear and coherent? Can we rationally defend it? And in order to answer these questions we must know the meaning of the notions of [health,] disease and illness in these contexts.[35]

One upshot of this, in the light of earlier analysis, is that we should be wary where 'health' is said to underpin a critique or proposed measure. Only by having our eyes open to what is in fact being discussed can we equip ourselves to measure its validity.

But we see too that Nordenfelt hints at another problem: if health is part of welfare but not its whole, how does it distinguish itself from the other parts, and how do we profit from the distinction? This depends in part on what we mean by welfare, and if health is part of welfare it seems that there is no rational reason to concern ourselves especially with health. Most usefully, health may be said to relate to a specific subcategory of welfare, though by no means one that – even presumptively – should receive special priority. It is, in this regard, a potentially useful concept, but one that is neither perfect nor always illuminating. In fact, the risk it raises of privileging itself – being considered 'special' when it is not – may, in some instances make it a damaging or misleading concept, or one whose apparent importance obscures that of more fundamental values.[36] In the next section I discuss the wider concept of welfare, the role of expertise in understanding it, and its relationship to harm and benefit in social policy.

Just prior to that, it should be stressed that if we consider health as a part of welfare, we can see how there might be expertise in it that is not applicable to all of welfare; some aspects of welfare may not permit of scientific examination or understanding.[37] That is to say, 'health experts' can exist, and they can be presumed to look at what is good for us. But as health is not all of welfare, their conclusions still leave us having to rank the importance of health protection, promotion, etc. in

---

[35] *Ibid.*, at 24, emphasis in original.

[36] Cf. James Wilson, "Not so special after all? Daniels and the social determinants of health", *Journal of Medical Ethics* (2009) 35:1, 3–6; Stephen John, "Why 'health' is not a central category for public health policy", *Journal of Applied Philosophy* (2009) 26:2, 129–143.

[37] Without needing to become either too abstract, or make any strong ontological claims, we can look to issues that are 'matters of taste' or just incomprehensible (e.g. enjoyment of *The X Factor*).

any situation.[38] It is useful to note the following observation, made by Daniel Callahan:

> The acceptable range of uses of the term "health" should, at the minimum, capture the normative element in the concept as traditionally understood while, at the maximum, incorporate the insight (stemming from criticisms of the WHO definition) that the term "health" is abused if it becomes synonymous with virtue, social tranquillity, and ultimate happiness.[39]

The alternative position is to assume that health is all of the good. In doing this, we at once dilute health expertise and make it broader. We do best to think of health as relating to aspects of what is good for us physically and mentally, and to an extent subject to scientific understanding. Nevertheless, to use health to describe all of welfare is to render the term practically redundant, and may wrongly suggest that all of the human good can be diagnosed in a politically sterile, value-free environment. Furthermore, health and welfare both permit of equally reasonable but contradictory understandings, even within the scheme just described. I will now turn to this issue, and highlight its implications.

11.2.2 *From welfare to benefit and harm*

I have said that health is a part of welfare without giving in this chapter a substantive account of welfare. This omission is principally due to the pluralist outlook I endorsed in Chapter 10. It is not my view that welfare permits of a singular formula that can be applied universally. Nor do I see it as usefully reduced to combinations of (supposedly) universally applicable 'functionings'. Rather, it parallels the conception of interests described by John Gray, founded on competing but equally valid perspectives of the good.[40] The pluralism described in Gray's defence of *modus vivendi*, and in his wider discussion of Isaiah Berlin's liberalism, is what I have argued political normativity ought to be designed to protect. In saying this, it is not possible to give a singular account of what is in everyone's interests. Gray seems to skirt over the depth of this issue

---

[38] See Brazier and Harris, who think we should treat the risk of disease as in principle no different to other risks to safety: "Public health and private lives", at 191 and 177–178.

[39] Daniel Callahan, "The WHO definition of health", *The Hastings Center Studies* (1973) 1:3, 77–87, at 84.

[40] This is to be distinguished with the multi-dimensional accounts of well-being described by Powers and Faden and Wolff and de-Shalit, though its practical significance is clearly very similar. I do not, however, see the value in seeking to deduce and list universal components of human flourishing.

by making problematic claims about a small amount of matters that *are* of universal benefit and harm.[41] A difficulty we have encountered a few times in this book when considering differences between some forms of moral and political argument is that of establishing who is part of the community in the first place. I would reiterate here that claims of universalism are only attractive if they include everyone who should be 'in'. And this is a matter on which there is radical disagreement. When it comes to claims about (albeit limited) universal interests, this creates problems when counter-examples suggest exclusion or undermine the universality. For example, arguments about the common interests of a human embryo, an eight-month-old foetus, an eight-month-old child, an eight-year-old, an eighteen year old, a 48 year old, and an 88 year old will either rely on fiction, or rest on appeal to controversial metaphysical claims or tenuous assertions about intrinsic normative nature.[42] The biological category 'human' (even if it is taken to relate only to those who are born and alive) does not present a collection of conceptually singular beings.[43] But if, as I suggested in Chapter 10 is important, we address our concerns to human societies – e.g. we care for and about babies and the mentally incapacitated regardless of whether they are 'moral persons' – then even modest appeal to meaningfully universal benefits and harms will founder.

We can, however, make a pragmatic concession to this manner of principled criticism, and still establish general truths about harm and benefit that apply to people. To do so is more useful than allowing ourselves to become crippled by theoretical objections or our inevitable epistemic limitations and distinct reasons for ascribing membership to the community. So notwithstanding these complications, the pluralist understanding of (human) legal persons, and human welfare, to which this discussion gives rise can be afforded practical protection in a functioning political system. However, we also saw in the previous chapter that there is a deficiency in a practical political theory that permits pluralism but has no core of objective value certainty on which to base policy presumptions, or even at times to define the limits of normatively

---

[41] John Gray, *Two Faces of Liberalism* (Cambridge: Polity Press, 2000), especially pp. 8–9, 66–68, and ch. 4.

[42] Amongst the more widely accepted (though I would not argue convincing) such theories, see e.g. John Finnis, *Natural Law and Natural Rights* (Oxford University Press, 1980); Leon Kass, *Life, Liberty and the Defense of Dignity: The Challenge for Bioethics* (San Francisco, CA: Encounter Books, 2002); Jürgen Habermas, *The Future of Human Nature* (Cambridge: Polity Press, 2003).

[43] See e.g. John Harris, *The Value of Life* (London: Routledge, 1985); John Harris, "Taking the 'human' out of Human Rights", *Cambridge Quarterly of Healthcare Ethics* (2011) 20:1, 9–20.

permissible conduct.[44] Where positive welfare claims are being made – e.g. where a person is exercising a right to healthcare against the State – definition of the content of the claims can not just be left with the individual.[45] At times, putative healthcare rights in English law are derided because, although there seems to be the basis of a corresponding duty in the Secretary of State for Health to provide healthcare,[46] people are not entitled to all treatments that they demand.[47] Rights-based analytic criticisms lose their sting, however, if it is seen that the right to healthcare is one whose positive content is not to be defined purely by the individual, and that rather there is something transactional in its exercise.[48] In the case of a mentally competent adult patient, he has the right to refuse any intervention whatsoever (that would be given purely for his own good); the wisdom and sovereignty on the content of his interests are entirely his in this negative sense.[49] However, where he seeks to claim something (a treatment, medication, etc.) from the State, his agreement *and* that of an expert are legally required; the law demands a consensus between them on what serves his interests.[50] This can still permit for pluralism; several therapeutic options may be available, and choices may even be narrowed beyond what would generally be clinically acceptable because of a patient's particular values.[51] But this consensus is crucial to the law's understanding of positively exercisable welfare rights.

---

[44] Joseph Raz, "Liberalism, scepticism, and democracy", in Joseph Raz, *Ethics in the Public Domain* (Oxford: Clarendon, 1994).

[45] *Cf* Mark Sheehan, "It's unethical for GPs to be commissioners", *British Medical Journal* (2011) 342:d1430, 601.

[46] National Health Service Act 2006, s. 1.

[47] *R (On the Application of Oliver Leslie Burke)* v. *The General Medical Council* [2005] EWCA Civ 1003.

[48] General Medical Council, *Consent: Patients and Doctors Making Decisions Together* (London: GMC, 2008).

[49] One worrying qualification to this long held and widely understood statement of principle stems from the recent jurisprudence relating to 'vulnerable adults', where the High Court has declared its inherent jurisdiction to make welfare decisions on behalf of adults who do not fail the law's test for capacity, as now enshrined in s. 3 of the Mental Capacity Act 2005. There is not space here to critique this area of development, but see: Michael Dunn, Isabel Clare, and Anthony Holland, "To empower or to protect? Constructing the 'vulnerable adult' in English law and public policy", *Legal Studies* (2008) 28:2, 234–253; and *Re G (An Adult) (Mental Capacity: Court's Jurisdiction)* [2004] EWHC 222 (Fam); *Re SK (An Adult) (Forced Marriage: Appropriate Relief)* [2005] 2 FLR 230; *Re SA (Vulnerable Adult with Capacity: Marriage)* [2006] 1 FLR 867; *A Local Authority* v. *DL & Ors* [2010] EWHC 2675 (Fam).

[50] *Burke* v. *GMC*.

[51] See further John Coggon, "Assisted-dying and the context of debate: 'medical law' *versus* 'end of life law'", *Medical Law Review* (2010) 18:4, 541–563, section IV; Mark Sullivan, "The new subjective medicine: taking the patient's point of view on health care and health", *Social Sciences and Medicine* (2003) 56, 1595–1604.

This position is defensible. At least within a system of finite resources that relies on the compulsory taxation of others, it would be most difficult to sustain an argument to the contrary; i.e. it is hard to imagine quite how one would justify a general compulsion to pay taxes that are then used to satisfy everyone's desires with no sort of check or brake on acceptable spending. The precise role of expertise may prove controversial, but it is an essential part of the political process.[52] Nevertheless, it has implications, alluded to in the previous chapter, for the scope of people's positive freedom as guaranteed by the State. It should be noted, though, that it also has implications for the scope of negative freedoms available, for example as the judgements affect regulation of what food products may be available on the market, or what limits may be imposed on people's freedom to release substances into the natural environment. Where it is accepted that people benefit sufficiently from some regulation (i.e. where *caveat emptor* does not suffice as a means of justifying non-regulation of the market), restrictions will be imposed on freedom, justified by reference to an understanding of what is (most probably) good for people, or necessary to create the conditions that allow them (most probably) to achieve what is good for them.[53] In regard to health, and welfare more widely, we see a crucial tension in substantiating 'the good'. This is captured by reference to the coexistence of internalist and externalist understandings of health, discussed by Amartya Sen:

[T]here is a conceptual contrast between the 'internal' view of health, as seen by the person in question, and 'external' views that others may take of the person's state of health. The contrast goes well beyond incidental differences between two assessments, and can reflect different ideas as to what can be understood as 'good health' of a person.[54]

As Sen notes, this has implications for the validity of data on health in a population, with consequent effects on policy that is formulated. He defends both perspectives: the internal perspective alone can account for matters that necessarily require a subject's view, such as whether

---

[52] Compare the reasoning in Allen Buchanan, "Human rights and the legitimacy of the international order", *Legal Theory* (2008) 14:1, 39–70.

[53] See for example the quite generally applicable arguments in Cass Sunstein and Richard Thaler, "Libertarian paternalism is not an oxymoron", *University of Chicago Law Review* (2003) 70:4, 1159–1202 (who notably finish their argument by saying that their reasoning can even support instances of 'hard paternalism': see 1201).

[54] See Amartya Sen, "Health achievement and equity: external and internal perspectives", in Sudhir Anand, Fabienne Peter, and Amartya Sen (eds.), *Public Health, Ethics, and Equity*, (Oxford University Press, 2004), p. 263. See also Sullivan, "The new subjective medicine".

there *is* pain, or how symptoms are actually felt; the external perspective, by contrast, profits from its detachment and wider view of the matter. Sen suggests that the two should complement each other. For as he puts it:

> The internal view of the patient is not only *informed* by knowledge to which others do not have access, but it is also *limited* by the social experience of the person in interpreting what is happening and why. A person reared in a community with a great many diseases may tend to take certain symptoms as 'normal' when they are clinically preventable. Also, a person with little access to medical care and little education on medical matters can take certain bodily conditions as inescapable even when they are thoroughly amenable to effective medical treatment.[55]

It is hard to see how Sen's reasoning here is disputable. If we focus purely on what people report or feel, we abandon them to a limited outlook. And if we focus purely on external observations we miss important facts because of a detached (and thus distinctly limited) outlook that can not perceive all that is relevant. A combination is required for a sufficiently full picture.

It should be clear how this approach to health can be transposed directly onto the framing described above, and cast more generally in terms of wider welfare. It should also be clear how it highlights the most salient tension for a political system of good governance, with the State being required to mediate between competing conceptions of people's interests in order satisfactorily to serve their interests. Although this does not suggest that the State straightforwardly has a mandate to step in to improve people's welfare as the government or judges perceive this concept and against people's will, it does suggest that people benefit from alternative perspectives on their welfare, and may be harmed by not having access to alternative understandings. It also opens up the possibility of arguments that favour paternalist policies, in the name of some form of 'harm principle' and a parallel 'benefit principle'. However, it demands cautious acceptance before we take it that measures scientifically proven to serve an understanding of welfare ought to be introduced.

We might here think of drawing examples from one of the biggest public health campaigns of recent times; the increasing legal and regulatory restrictions in relation to the smoking of tobacco. In England, the most notable development in this regard has been the Health Act 2006, which provides various limitations, including a general ban on smoking in workplaces and enclosed or substantially enclosed public spaces.

---

[55] Sen, "Health achievement and equity", pp. 265–266, emphasis in original.

Although the general ban attracts criticism,[56] it has been welcomed as part of a new trend in regulation.[57] Of some importance is the fact that, at least ostensibly, the legislation is justified according to harm-to-others reasoning. People are still allowed to smoke, for example, in open spaces, and in their homes. Furthermore, regulations drafted in accordance with the Act provide for exemptions from the general ban, including in care homes, hospices, and prisons.[58] Part of the justification for this is the idea that people resident in such places are due some sort of recognition of privacy rights. However, as discussed in Chapter 2, the regulations only allowed a comparable exemption for patients resident in psychiatric units for a year following the introduction of the smoking ban.[59] Of interest to scholars in public health law and ethics is not just the legitimacy and coherence of the ban, but also of the exemptions. In particular, the Rampton smokers' legal challenge (in judicial review) to the termination of the exemption for mental health units makes for fascinating analysis.[60] To recap, patients at Rampton Hospital, a secure psychiatric unit, argued that their right to respect for private and family life, enshrined in Article 8 of the European Convention on Human Rights (ECHR), was breached by the ban. As they could not go outside, and were not allowed to smoke inside, smoking was completely foreclosed to them as an option.

Their case was unsuccessful both in the High Court and in the Court of Appeal (albeit with one dissenting judgment). The judicial reasoning provides scope for analysis on various grounds, but of immediate relevance is the question of the applicants' smoking being subject to a decision that was out of their hands. The State's access to this decision was made through suggested limits to their 'spatial privacy', i.e. the law would protect their sovereignty less highly in their place of residence; and to their 'decisional privacy', i.e. smoking could not be a matter of sufficient personal importance that a decision to do it should receive the law's protection. No one disputes the negative health effects of smoking tobacco. But when the government denies a specific group of people the freedom to smoke, it is making that aspect of that group's lives public. For psychiatric patients in secure mental health units, in contrast for

---

[56] See e.g. www.amendthesmokingban.com.
[57] Howard K. Koh, Luk X. Joossens, and Gregory N. Connolly, "Making smoking history worldwide", *New England Journal of Medicine* (2007) 356:15, 1496–1498.
[58] Smoke-Free (Exemptions and Vehicles) Regulations 2007, reg. 5.
[59] *Ibid.*, reg. 10.
[60] *R (G and B)* v. *Nottinghamshire Healthcare NHS Trust; R (N)* v. *Secretary of State for Health* [2008] EWHC 1096 (Admin); *R (N)* v. *Secretary of State for Health; R (E)* v. *Nottinghamshire Healthcare NHS Trust* [2009] EWCA Civ 795.

example with prisoners, any internal or subjective view on the value of smoking is given no practical weight, and an external or 'objective' view is imposed from without. Particularly noteworthy is the Court of Appeal's acceptance (albeit in *obiter dictum*) of the applicability of the "protection of health" justification for interfering with an individual's right to respect for private and family life, enshrined in the derogation clause in Article 8(2) ECHR. The Court held that:

[A]rticle 8(2) refers to the protection of health, not the health of others. In these circumstances we accept the submission that it is a potentially legitimate aim to restrain a person's article 8 rights for the protection of [his own] health. It was necessary and proportionate for the health of both the patients, which of course includes the appellants, and others.[61]

The Rampton smokers' case provides a good example of arguments for why and how health can be made public, and the role of individuals' reasons and reasoning in relation to that of State actors.[62] I have not here made a critical analysis of the issues it raises (which would be quite a lengthy undertaking). Rather, I use it to exemplify the way analyses in public health law and ethics require us to frame such questions, and the epistemic and political tensions that are inherent in health policy.

As long as a political framework protects plural conceptions of the good, there needs to be account for this, and policies such as that just described should be analysed with the pluralism in mind.[63] It is implausible that everyone should be permitted simply to live according to their own, internal perspectives. Equally, there are good reasons to believe that people are well served by being exposed to alternative conceptions, such as those based on scientific observations about how their welfare *could* be; i.e. that they may be wrong about what serves their interests. Recall in this regard the nature of a policy-maker's perspective means it must account both for the fact that a person may be wrong (i.e. there is a substantive judgement of his appraisal of his interests), or the fact that any given person may not be in a position to appraise his interests (i.e. there is a judgement of his capacity to make the assessment).[64] This means that there are even good reasons to believe that he is well served

---

[61] *R (N) v. Secretary of State for Health; R (E) v. Nottinghamshire Healthcare NHS Trust* [2009] EWCA Civ 795, para. 71.

[62] John Coggon, "Public health, responsibility and English law: are there such things as no smoke without ire or needless clean needles?", *Medical Law Review* (2009) 17:1, 127–139; John Coggon, "No right to smoke in high security psychiatric hospitals", *Journal of Bioethical Inquiry* (2009) 6:4, 405–408.

[63] Dennis Raphael, "The question of evidence in health promotion", *Health Promotion International* (2000) 15:4, 355–367.

[64] See Chapter 10.

by living in an environment (social and spatial) wherein he is *de facto* forced to live in accordance with various externally defined conceptions of the good; i.e. whatever he thinks, the State may regulate for example to ensure clean water, limits on emissions of what are deemed to be hazardous pollutants, prohibit the sale of foodstuffs that do not comply with standardised norms. There is in essence a question here of assuring that more trivial matters on which the State might otherwise be agnostic be subject to regulation, in order to allow people a broader freedom to achieve their own conceptions of the good. This may be described as amounting to a 'soft perfectionism', wherein practically real but epistemically modest claims about the human good are protected through the manifestation of a State, with consequent institutions, laws, and policies.

This leaves an important role for expertise within politics. As we have seen,[65] expertise attracts suspicion, particularly from more libertarian critics who see it either as intrinsically bogus (e.g. where the things the experts would speak to are beyond 'rational proof') or intrinsically dangerous politically (e.g. because it gives States a mandate to institute a coercive and totalitarian agenda with an undue sheen of scientific legitimacy). Such critics provide useful cause to think, but the level of scepticism (even cynicism) that they recommend is unduly strong.[66] It is unduly strong because resignation to it means ignoring the welfare of members of the community who need a less detached State to ensure they are properly 'empowered'. Nevertheless, we do well to combine what the libertarian critics hint to with a sober reflection on the implications of pluralism, and Sen's reflections on the subjective *versus* the externally observed assessments of health. With pluralism in welfare, we have to treat with caution evaluations of interests that form the basis of (both coercive and non-coercive) policy. A strong external conception – whether established through scientific consensus, a prevalent political 'common sense', or some other means – brings a risk of a more monist or anyway preclusive understanding of health, and thus welfare, than a robust pluralist account would comfortably allow. The concern this gives rise to is important, and is perhaps why Skrabanek is so keen to claim that health does not permit of definition, and is rather a 'metaphysical' concept like love.[67] The potential for political oppression based on claims about certainty concerning the human good underpins

---

[65] Chapter 8, section 8.2.
[66] See e.g. Skrabanek, *The Death of Humane Medicine*, and the discussion of his work in Chapter 8.
[67] *Ibid.*, p. 15.

one strand of twentieth-century liberalism and liberal critique (notably that advanced by Isaiah Berlin and later by John Gray[68]). The current trend of twenty-first century scientific enlightenment[69] should assist our understanding, be used to eradicate demonstrably false beliefs, and inform policy-makers and analysts in their efforts to design good policy. But it does entail a danger of 'monistic creep' or, with less concern for philosophical truth, a danger just of authoritarianism in the name of the State's duty to protect its citizens when they fail to recognise what is good for them.

The goal of policy-makers in regard to health, welfare, and other issues, should be to draw from evidence-bases and expert opinion in developing regulation.[70] Regulation is required to minimise unacceptable harms, and to ensure necessary benefits. Judging the content of the terms "unacceptable harms" and "necessary benefits" is necessarily a political task. It requires that regard be given to reasons that freedoms – including harmful ones – ought to be preserved, as well as reasons for limiting them. The tyranny of 'health and safety' has become a popular political caricature (in the same vein as 'political correctness gone mad').[71] But some responsibility for welfare *is* the responsibility of government. This sometimes requires 'trickle-back obligations' on citizens, for example through the imposition of taxes, or their being subject to other general duties or restrictions on liberty for the good of them and others (resulting at times in instances of 'collateral paternalism'). This, and the assessments both in favour and against regulation, requires paternalistic judgement. That is not of itself problematic: it would be perverse if the State did not exist to serve its people's interests.

11.3   Politics, public health, and the sharing of responsibility

The key outcome for analysts in public health law and ethics is to understand the proper allocation of practical responsibility for health

---

[68] Isaiah Berlin, *Four Essays on Liberty* (Oxford University Press, 1969); John Gray, *Isaiah Berlin* (Princeton University Press, 1996); John Gray, *Two Faces of Liberalism* (Cambridge: Polity Press, 2000).

[69] See e.g. Peter Atkins, *On Being: A Scientist's Exploration of the Great Questions of Existence* (Oxford University Press, 2011).

[70] Buchanan, "Human rights and the legitimacy of the international order", especially at 61–64.

[71] See HM Government, *Common Sense, Common Safety – A report by Lord Young of Graffham to the Prime Minister following a Whitehall-wide review of the operation of health and safety laws and the growth of the compensation culture* (London: Cabinet Office, 2010).

in different instances. I have detailed my own, and other analysts', perspectives on how to find measures of assessment to make this analysis, and using practical examples have demonstrated some of the 'points of entry' for analysts seeking to make an applied critique of a public health measure. The courts and policy-makers can also easily be viewed as routinely dealing with these questions. Judges are asked to assess where responsibility should lie given existing legal frameworks. This can mean they hear challenges against the State for failing to meet its health responsibilities, or for claiming responsibility where it has no right to do so.[72] Legal principles are used in many ways to establish an environment more conducive to good health, through litigation, legislation, policy-making, and accepted practice.[73] By way of example, consider matters as diverse as occupational health law, environmental regulation, criminal and civil law controls on (potentially) harmful conduct, taxation policy on (potentially) harmful products, and road safety legislation, which all may reasonably be described as 'serving public health'. It is easy to see how we could add and add to the list, which is why one may reasonably express some doubt about the boundedness of public health law and ethics as areas of study or practice. But it also becomes clear what a useful mechanism the law can be both in advancing the public's health, and in limiting interferences where they are not due.[74] I will not consider in detail here the ways that practical measures may be invoked in debates on public health. However, the foregoing work and the means it affords to assess measures should make clear the way to evaluate the desirability of different practical questions that fall under the heading of public health.[75] A defensible background political theory

---

[72] Compare, for example, *Shelley* v. *UK* (2008) 46 EHRR SE16, where the claimant sought (unsuccessfully) to argue that the government had greater responsibility for his health than it was accepting, with the Rampton smokers' case, discussed above, where the applicants sought (unsuccessfully) to argue that the government had assumed too great a responsibility for their health. See also Coggon, "Public health, responsibility, and English law".

[73] And arguments are developed to *use* the law as a tool to advance public health; see e.g. Jonathan Mann, "Medicine and public health, ethics and human rights", *Hastings Center Report* (1997) 27:3, 6–13; Robyn Martin, "The limits of law in the protection of public health and the role of public health ethics", *Public Health* (2006) 120, 71–80; Roger S. Magnusson, "Mapping the scope and opportunities for public health law in liberal democracies", *Journal of Law, Medicine and Ethics* (2007) 35:4, 571–587; Lawrence O. Gostin, *Public Health Law: Power, Duty, Restraint* (2nd edn), (Berkeley: University of California Press, 2008); Keith Syrett and Oliver Quick, "Pedagogical promise and problems: Teaching public health law", *Public Health* (2009) 123, 222–231; Wendy Parmet, *Populations, Public Health, and the Law* (Washington DC: Georgetown University Press, 2009).

[74] Gostin, *Public Health Law*.

[75] Given the breadth of the project this implies, it is hard to imagine that a book length work could comprehensively speak to public health law's dominion.

is needed for *evaluation* to take place, and the evaluation can be made only insofar as that theory permits. We need to work in accordance with a robust understanding of fact, but also in accordance with a defensible approach to values. We must therefore contrast arguments that evaluate in accordance with some non-political – or even 'scientific' – measure, and ones that claim to provide a politically directive conclusion. To illustrate, consider how we might read a paper in the *British Medical Journal* that examines the (vogue in current UK government) idea of 'nudges' as the basis of health policy.[76] The paper's aim is to assess whether or not nudges 'work'. It is important to recognise, however, how the term 'work' permits an equivocation between an evaluation made by a public health scientist, and an evaluation made by an analyst in public health law and ethics. The authors' arguments are an example of the former, and the points they raise are significant: the effectiveness of a policy-approach that only uses nudges is to be doubted, but further directed research is needed to assess questions of its efficacy.[77] As their argument develops, they say that:

> While nudging relates more closely to whole population approaches to disease prevention, indirect harm might arise if an emphasis on nudging resulted in neglect of population level interventions that were potentially more effective.[78]

Their position is of clear use and interest to analysts in public health law and ethics, especially given the dominance of the ideals embodied in 'nudge'. Nevertheless, that nudges do not produce maximal health outcomes should not be taken as, or considered indicative of, a moral, legal, or political conclusion. The knowledge the paper provides will usefully inform further argument, but any separate political arguments must be made clear. If, for example, someone is a libertarian, he can (in principle) quite coherently accept that nudges' efficacy is slight whilst also maintaining that they are the only legitimate policy option. In contrast, according to the critical model I have advocated, some coercive paternalist interventions could be acceptable. But the important point here is to note that I can not refute a more libertarian model by bald reference to nudges' relative ineffectiveness. I need the reference point of a

---

Foremost amongst work in this direction, however, must be Gostin's *Public Health Law, ibid.*

[76] Theresa M. Marteau, David Ogilvie, Martin Roland, Marc Suhrcke, Michael P. Kelly, "Judging nudging: can nudging improve population health?", *British Medical Journal* (2011) 342:d228, 263–265. The 'nudge' thesis is, of course, attributed to Richard Thaler and Cass Sunstein, *Nudge: Improving Decisions About Health, Wealth, and Happiness* (London: Penguin Books, 2009).

[77] Marteau *et al.*, "Judging nudging", at 264.   [78] *Ibid.*

considered and defensible political theory, and persuasive arguments in favour of it. These may be bolstered by reference to better policy (recall the discussion of 'descriptive statism'), but the reasoning must be made rather than presumed to be tacit.

In the final short sections of this chapter, I will consider these 'methodological' issues in a way that applies broadly to analyses undertaken in public health law and ethics. As has been evident, these are often characterised as explorations of ideas concerning responsibility for health. As such, it is useful to start this final set of points by making reference to the normativity in concepts of health, and with an emphasis on ensuring awareness of the environmental context (physical and social) under discussion. Analysis can then be made using the overall political framework that is advocated, leading to an understanding of how we should think about proposed and actual policies, practices, and institutions; about when, how, why, and to what extent health is public.

11.3.1   Moral determinants in health

Before considering arguments concerning the social determinants of health, which assume central importance in debates on how political responsibility should be allocated, it is necessary to consider moral determinants *in* health. 'Health' as deployed in policy and in debates in public health law and ethics is a normative concept. When it is offered as a reason for action or policy the underpinning presumption is that health is a good thing. In this sense, there is presumed to be a robust (even compelling) conception of the good, which is preclusive of other accounts and concerns. It is possible to make too much of this: often it is apparent what is meant, and we do not always need to worry about achieving complete conceptual clarity or consensus. However, it is possible too to overlook the danger where the concept is not made clear, particularly as things can often harm health in one respect, yet enhance it in another. With a monist account of health, "health-health trade-offs" will often have to be made, where policies aimed at serving health in one way will harm it in another.[79] And if we allow for plural accounts of health – either because we, for example, worry about health separately as it relates to physical, mental, and social matters,[80] or because we accommodate arguments working from competing understandings

---

[79] See Cass Sunstein, "Health-health tradeoffs", *University of Chicago Law Review* (1996) 63:4, 1533–1571, and note Sunstein's practical examples presented at 1535–1536.
[80] As per the World Health Organization's definition.

of health[81] – then a health benefit in one regard may be a health dis-benefit in another; for example, limiting certain recreational activities on the grounds that they are physically harmful may simultaneously cause considerable psychological harm. Finally, looking at the here and now in contrast with an individual across his lifespan, or individuals as members of a population, or looking across generations of populations (a 'public's lifespan') can give rise to distinct manners of argument for prioritising health.[82] For example, smoking a cigarette is of minimally negligible (if any) harm to health, yet is well described as harmful to health if considered as part of a manner of behaviour with a cumulative effect whose later manifestation can be said to bear on the individual who currently exists, or who is one amongst a number a significant pro-portion of whom will be harmed. To be clear, the majority of the cases are simultaneously more prosaic and more complex. Is it, for example, harmful to my health not to have a pension policy? It would not injure my health now, and there are many uncertainties in the meantime (per-haps most salient among them whether I or the pension policy will still exist when the time would come to draw it!). This, like so many other things, can be cast as a health problem, and as a matter that obtains within a polity it can equally be cast as (at least ostensibly) a public health problem.

The principal point to note here is that just because something can reasonably be said to serve health, it does not mean that it automatically presents a knock-down argument in favour of the policy it would seem to recommend. It is analytic that 'health' is good. Yet that the term is by definition good neither means that every concept presented under its name should be taken as such, nor that it should prevail over other things that are good. There are moral (and other normative) determin-ants to a protagonist's given definition of health, and imperatives that bite, or whose reward is presented, at different stages. This inherent normativity will drive the concept, and must be accounted for. As we have seen, at times policy may be framed to force people to do things, or refrain from doing things, for their own good. In a liberal political system this can be justified, but we do well to heed arguments that warn against 'moral imperialism'.

---

[81] As per Sen, "Health achievement and equity: external and internal perspectives".

[82] Cf Geoffrey Rose, "Sick individuals and sick populations", *International Journal of Epidemiology* (1985) 14, 32–38; Raymond Geuss, *Public Goods, Private Goods* (Princeton and Oxford: Princeton University Press, 2003), ch. 3, especially pp. 36–39; Norman Daniels, "A lifespan approach to health care", in Helga Kuhse and Peter Singer, *Bioethics: an Anthology* (2nd edn) (Oxford: Blackwell, 2006).

11.3.2   Social determinants of health

Social determinants of health theses have come into their own, not just in the academic literature[83] but in the political and public consciousness too.[84] There are several layers here that require brief discussion. First, there are those who deny social determinants altogether.[85] Their position should be mentioned, though it seems not to be even thinly credible, given the compelling evidence that stands to the contrary. Nevertheless, one often senses when reading their attempted refutations that there is a principled (or even just paradigmatic) source to their contention,[86] and this bears directly on the normative question of who should take responsibility for health matters. This difficulty may be said to stem from hypothesising in accordance with an abstraction such as Richard Thaler and Cass Sunstein's *homo economicus*.[87] If people are rational, self-interested actors then naturally we can not hold that their social environments dictate the choices they make, and the network of decisions that surround their development (first by their parents, and then by themselves) are voluntary in a pure sense of the term, uncontaminated by background psycho-social criteria that appear

[83] M. Marmot, G. Rose, M. Shipley, and P. Hamilton, "Employment grade and coronary heart disease in British civil servants", *Journal of Epidemiology and Community Health* (1978) 32, 244–249; Norman Daniels, Bruce Kennedy, and Ichiro Kawachi, "Why justice is good for our health: The social determinants of health inequalities", *Daedalus* (1999) 128:4, 215–251; Richard Eckersley, Jane Dickson, and Bob Douglas, *The Social Origins of Health and Well-being* (Cambridge University Press, 2001); Lawrence Gostin and Madison Powers, "What does social justice require for the public's health? Public health ethics and policy imperatives", *Health Affairs* (2006) 25:4, 1053–1060; Michael Marmot, *Status Syndrome: How Your Social Standing Directly Affects Your Health and Life Expectancy* (London: Bloomsbury, 2004); Jonathan Wolff, "Disadvantage, risk and the social determinants of health", *Public Health Ethics* (2009) 2:1, 214–223; C. Bambra, M. Gibson, A. Sowden, K. Wright, M. Whitehead, and M. Petticrew, "Tackling the wider social determinants of health and health inequalities: evidence from systematic reviews", *Journal of Epidemiology and Community Health* (2010) 64, 284–291.

[84] Nuffield Council on Bioethics, *Public Health – Ethical Issues*, (London: Nuffield, 2007); Commission on Social Determinants of Health, *Closing the Gap in a Generation: Health Equity Through Action on the Social Determinants of Health* (Geneva: World Health Organization, 2008); Andrew Lansley MP, "Secretary of State for Health's speech to the UK Faculty of Public Health Conference – 'A new approach to public health'" (7 December, 2010), available at www.dh.gov.uk/en/MediaCentre/Speeches/DH_117280.

[85] See Richard Epstein, "In defense of the 'old' public health", *Brooklyn Law Review* (2004) 69:4, 1421–1470.

[86] Lawrence Gostin and M. Gregg Bloche, "The politics of public health: a response to Epstein", *Perspectives in Biology and Medicine* (2003) 46:3, S160–S175.

[87] Thaler and Sunstein, *Nudge*, Part I.

to be in evidence in more realistic critiques.[88] More fundamentally, it might be argued that if we want to engage with people as responsible moral actors, amenable to concepts such as praise, blame, and desert, we must shirk determinist claims that would otherwise undermine our endeavours.

In response to this position, there are salient theoretical and empirical counter-arguments. First is the anti-absolutist claim: there is no principled reason why a theory of agency need demand the premise that a person be in *complete* control of his will. Theories can permit weak-wills, or non-dualistic concepts of persons that allow for their forming and acting on both rational and irrational ideas.[89] In theory, we can without contradiction or incoherence allow for some determinism and rational fragility without dispossessing ourselves altogether of a potent concept of agency. Second, working within the empirical world at the level to which we are able to observe it, it *is* apparent that the social determinants thesis is true. Complex questions are raised about where free choice is engaged, but where trends are discernable, it seems perverse to deny them simply because we would rather that they were not the case; because we have developed moral paradigms that we wish we could match. Quite where and how lines between voluntary and involuntary action should be drawn is a complex and controversial matter. However, it is clear that political mechanisms can be developed to modify people's behaviour, and these need not be based exclusively by reference to just desert (which does not preclude their basis being in justice). In parallel with discussions of justifications for punishment, policies may develop to create deterrents and incentives concerning conduct that bears on welfare.

Whilst further research is of doubtless benefit, arguments affirming the determinative effects of the social environment should not in

---

[88] Amongst others discussed and referred to in this book, see especially Thaler and Sunstein, *ibid.*; Willard Gaylin and Bruce Jennings, *The Perversion of Autonomy: Coercion and Constraints in a Liberal Society* (2nd edn) (Washington DC: Georgetown University Press, 2003); Powers and Faden, *Social Justice*; Wolff and de-Shalit, *Disadvantage*.

[89] We may take as an example Ronald Dworkin's conception of the "competent person" who reaches the threshold for being treated as autonomous by possessing the "general ability ... to act out of genuine preference or character or conviction or a sense of self": Ronald Dworkin, *Life's Dominion: an Argument about Abortion and Euthanasia* (London: Harper Collins, 1993), p. 225. On an account such as this, 'perfect' agency is not required for a person to be worthy of respect. See also, e.g., the concepts of the person discussed in Harris, *The Value of Life*; James Griffin, *On Human Rights* (Oxford University Press, 2008); or indeed the concepts of the person discussed in Chapter 10.

themselves be considered contentious.[90] Contention comes, however, with the *political* arguments about how we should respond to the situation. Moving beyond denials of social determinants, we face the question of establishing *which* social determinants should be subject to political amendment: which social determinants are *public* matters? This is a central question in public health law and ethics, and we saw in Chapter 8 how different of the key authors in the field would respond to such questions. An anarchist can agree that others' behaviour affects how he will behave without having to concede that a political system ought therefore to exist to change this. If we revisit the libertarianism of Skrabanek, we can recall that he derides messages that urge health promotion, and finds repugnant the idea that the State should control behaviour in the name of health.[91] His position holds that whilst there is something insidious in officious 'healthism' (which may justify imposing limits to freedom of expression?), there is something abhorrent in the forced political assuming and sharing of health responsibilities. The human environment is crucial to the context of analysis, but that something happens in that environment does not make it automatically the business or responsibility of the State. Thus, the social determinants theses provide crucial empirical information, and feed well the practical targets of theses concerned with unfair disadvantage, or the distribution of welfare. However, they require political input before we know how and to what extent they are public concerns.

11.3.3 Political determinants and health

Important to the analysis in Part II of this book was the need to account for issues of 'real politics'. As well as questions of normatively defensible political systems, we need to allow for the question of actual power in human society.[92] This bears not only on issues of malevolent rulers and actors, but conditions within benevolent or apparently benign regimes too. The point is especially significant where we develop political support for a society that espouses moral pluralism, and shun models where a singular and exclusive moral account is developed and its practical conclusions forced onto citizens. The considerations are pervasive, but raise the greatest practical concern where we face a strong and questionable ideology, and create difficulties particularly in relation to

---

[90] Bambra *et al.*, "Tackling the wider social determinants of health and health inequalities".
[91] Skrabanek, *The Death of Humane Medicine*.
[92] Raymond Geuss, *Philosophy and Real Politics* (Princeton and Oxford: Princeton University Press, 2008).

people who are vulnerable. Good governance demands concern for sufficient autonomy and liberty whilst also assuring adequate regard to welfare. Whilst these can be cast as 'competing antagonists', a good political theory guarantees due regard to both.[93] So when approaching a potential public health policy, the pertinent questions that require consideration are captured under the following headings:

1. What is the substance and meaning of welfare needs in a given instance, how controversial is this, and how are the costs (e.g. in liberty, money, opportunity) and benefits (e.g. in welfare, opportunity, security) to be understood?
2. In the light of the potential costs and benefits, what manner of regulation is called for? Possibly a 'hard' legal measure; legal incentives or disincentives; private and 'civil society' mechanisms beneath regulatory oversight; no regulation at all.
3. Are there particular problems or groups that demand specific attention? Possibly e.g. those who are particularly vulnerable or systematically disadvantaged.
4. In any given case, who should be empowered to exercise 'health rights' (individuals on their own behalves, in collaboration with others, or others on behalf of individuals), when must these rights be exercised, and when is there a discretion concerning their exercise?
5. What political constraints are there on the advancement of health in a given case?
6. What governmental freedoms exist to ensure the advancement of health in a given case? I.e. beyond setting rules or providing incentives, how free is the government to police these matters?

These questions are broadly applicable, and can – and should – be addressed to the whole range of specific matters of interest to public health law and ethics scholars, from traffic regulation to vaccination policy, from food regulation to town-planning. I intentionally pose them in terms that imply the possibility of a calculus, though I do not take this to imply that I am of the view that a single, monistic model can be employed in the resolution of policy problems. Rather, this framing should be taken as a means of accessing the salient governance issues, whatever the political model to be applied to a given problem. As we have seen in Chapter 8, how the assessment will actually be made, allowing e.g. for indexing problems, alternative values, side-constraints, will

---

[93] Cf Michael Dunn and Charles Foster, "Autonomy and welfare as *amici curiae*", *Medical Law Review* (2010) 18:1, 86–95.

vary between analysts, who must each also be prepared to defend their preferred background theory.

Within the framework described in Chapter 10, there is no avoiding the political contentions that will arise, but it does permit a reasoned model. It does not recommend a complete failure of moral scrutiny, or rely on legal abstracts such as 'the reasonable man'. This manner of politics can permit distinct understandings of the fundamentals, whilst upholding robust values through legal protections.[94] The policy-perspective also demands wider considerations than 'just deserts'. This is double-edged. On one hand, it would recommend against State-indifference to people who bring ill-health on themselves. On the other, it requires support from the citizenry for each others' health (and welfare more widely). Liberty can be seen as important enough that we 'forgive' people's failure to care always for their welfare. Yet welfare is important enough that we limit people's freedom (e.g. through imposition of taxation) to assure its sufficient protection. It is these political judgments that answer the important questions in public health.

11.4   Conclusions: tackling responsibility

The analysis and reflections in this chapter have demonstrated how scholars should approach problems in public health law and ethics. The model of liberalism that I have described is something I would seek to apply to practical problems concerning public health, but provides the basis for analysis of *all* manner of political concerns. This is not coincidental. *Only* a model capable of this wider task is suitable for serious application to the narrower questions. The theory I advocate will face objections. Nevertheless, such a form of 'agnostic liberalism' is, I think, a crucial component of a liberal State that is committed to respecting moral pluralism.[95] There are good reasons to defend such a State. Where these give rise to theoretical difficulties – e.g. in establishing robust and compelling concepts of benefit and harm – it is better to face these than to deny them, or bury them beneath ethereal references to 'the reasonable', 'the rational', or 'the wills' of some hypothesised abstract. The practical examples we have considered in this chapter – matters such as the regulation of alcohol and tobacco – raise complex issues, and these can not be resolved without due care to the politico-legal housing that does or should contain them. Analysts in public health law and ethics

---

[94] Cf Cass Sunstein, *Legal Reasoning and Political Conflict* (Oxford University Press, 1998).
[95] I take the term 'agnostic liberalism' from Gray, *Isaiah Berlin*.

will often be tasked to resolve such difficult questions, but sound analyses can not be made in a vacuum; a defensible background theory must be present, and proper account should be made for the knock-on implications of any norms or imperatives that are invoked in response to a problem.

In the relevant literatures, we find arguments about responsibility for health taking place on two planes; there are concerns about moral responsibilities, and there are concerns about political (and legal) responsibilities. In regard to the former, we find arguments saying what people should do, and why they should be praised or condemned morally. In regard to the latter, by contrast, we find arguments about what people can legitimately be forced, or at least given incentives, to do by the State. Commonly, these distinctions are explicitly made.[96] It is in the latter instances that theorists are asking *what makes health public?* This book has demonstrated why *that* is *the* important question, and the nature of the theoretical ground that needs to be covered if it is to be answered.

---

[96] Cf Gerald Dworkin, "Taking risks, assessing responsibility", *The Hastings Center Report* (1981) 11:5, 26–31; Daniel Wikler, "Who should be blamed for being sick?", *Health Education and Behavior* (1987) 14:1, 11–25; Meredith Minkler, "Personal responsibility for health? A review of the arguments and the evidence at century's end", *Health Education and Behavior* (1999) 26:1, 121–140; Alexander W. Cappelen and Ole Frithjof Norheim, "Responsibility in health care: a liberal egalitarian approach", *Journal of Medical Ethics* (2005) 31:8, 476–480; Bruce N. Waller, "Responsibility and health," *Cambridge Quarterly of Healthcare Ethics* (2005) 14:2, 177–188; Harald Schmidt, "Patients' charters and health responsibilities", *British Medical Journal* (2007) 335, 1187–1189; Ofra Golan, "The right to treatment for self-inflicted conditions", *Journal of Medical Ethics* (2010) 36:11, 683–686.

12   Conclusion

A sweeping claim that 'health is a public matter' is as unhelpful as its counter; that 'health is a private matter'. Health, and welfare more widely, touch on many issues – physical, behavioural, environmental – some of which can be argued to fall into the public sphere, others of which can not. There are many points of controversy, and it is not always clear which answers are definitively right. The role for analysts in public health law and ethics, and for policy-makers concerned about health issues, is to establish which things are public, to what extent, in what regard, and how and why this is so. We have seen repeated a point that can be missed when political paradigms present a 'presumption of liberty', suggesting that State inaction is ostensibly benign: States are accountable for their omissions as well as their acts. On one hand this means that States can not shirk responsibility for their failures. On the other, it means that every social determinant of health is under the State's view, yet each is not ultimately the business of the State. It is for this reason that political analysis is essential: it is this that establishes which matters are of political concern, and the legitimate sources of political obligation.

Beyond the political arguments, any number of moral arguments may be made to individuals, advocating distinct practices in the name of health. There may be strongly felt moral imperatives about what people should do with, to, and for their minds and bodies. But where health is public, we go beyond moral argumentation, and seek to establish the role of the State in assuring or encouraging compliance with health-related imperatives, and the means it would use to do so. In one instance, compulsion may be recommended in response to a problem, in another no governmental action may be required whatsoever. In most cases, the regulatory structures will 'nudge' and persuade, rather than coercively direct.

This manner of inquiry is what public health law and ethics are about: working out what is in the political realm, and how effectively to see that the political imperatives are properly met (or assessing the claims of others about these questions). Some analysts are keen to learn, for example, whether we would be morally justified in denying someone treatment to remedy a self-inflicted harm. Concerning public health issues, however, the question is not ultimately about moral justifiability or deserts in regard to individual cases considered in a vacuum. The question is whether something can be politically justified. This does not mean asking whether it could be 'sold' politically, though that will be important information. It means assessing it as a policy; accounting for practical limitations in understanding (e.g. of causation), allowing for human frailty, considering the general effect of the policy itself, and appraising the potential costs in welfare and liberty. Sound assessment requires the evaluation to be made in accordance with a defensible political theory. It is that that tells us what would make health public in a given instance, and much more besides.

Bibliography

Acheson, Donald, *Public Health in England* (Cmnd. 298) (London: HMSO, 1988)

Allen, Neil, "A human right to smoke?", *New Law Journal* (2008) 158 (7326), 886–887

Ananth, Mahesh, *In Defense of an Evolutionary Concept of Health* (Aldershot: Ashgate, 2008)

Anderson, Benedict, *Imagined Communities – Reflections on the Origin and Spread of Nationalism – Revised edition* (London: Verso, 1991)

Annas, George, "American bioethics and human rights: the end of all our exploring", *Journal of Law, Medicine and Ethics* (2004) 32, 658–663

"Human rights and health – The Universal Declaration of Human Rights at 50", *New England Journal of Medicine* (1998) 339:24, 1778–1781

Atkins, Peter, *On Being: A Scientist's Exploration of the Great Questions of Existence* (Oxford University Press, 2011)

Ayres, Ian and Braithwaite, John, *Responsive Regulation: Transcending the Deregulation Debate* (Oxford University Press, 1992)

Backman, Gunilla, Hunt, Paul, Khosla, Rajat, Jaramillo-Strouss, Camila, Fikre, Belachew Mekuria, Rumble, Caroline, Pevalin, David, Acurio Páez, David, Pineda, Mónica Armijos, Frisancho, Ariel, Tarco, Duniska, Motlagh, Mitra, Farcasanu, Dana, Vladescu, Cristian, "Health systems and the right to health: an assessment of 194 countries", *The Lancet* (2008) 372, 2046–2085

Baldwin, Robert and Black, Julia, "Really responsive regulation", *Modern Law Review* (2008) 71:1, 59–94

Baldwin, Tom, Brownsword, Roger, and Schmidt, Harald, "Stewardship, paternalism and public health: further thoughts", *Public Health Ethics* (2009) 2:1, 113–116

Bambra, Clare, Fox, Debbie, and Scott-Samuel, Alex, "Towards a politics of health", *Health Promotion International* (2005) 20:2, 187–193

Bambra, Clare, Gibson, Marcia, Sowden, Amanda, Wright, Kath, Whitehead, Margaret, and Petticrew, Mark, "Tackling the wider social determinants of health and health inequalities: evidence from systematic reviews", *Journal of Epidemiology and Community Health* (2010) 64, 284–291

Bayer, Ronald and Fairchild, Amy, "The genesis of public health ethics", *Bioethics* (2004) 18:6, 473–492

Bayer, Ronald, Gostin, Lawrence O., Jennings, Bruce, Steinbock, Bonnie (eds.), *Public Health Ethics: Theory, Policy, and Practice* (Oxford University Press, 2007)

Baylis, Françoise, Kenny, Nuala, Sherwin, Susan, "A relational account of public health ethics", *Public Health Ethics* (2008) 1:3, 196–209

Beauchamp, Dan, "Community: the neglected tradition of public health", *Hastings Center Report* (1985) 15:6, 28–36

   Health Care Reform and the Battle for the Body Politic (Philadelphia, PA: Temple University Press, 1996)

   "Injury, community and the republic", *Law, Medicine and Health Care* (1989) 17:1, 42–49

   "Public health: alien ethic in a strange land?", *American Journal of Public Health* (1975) 65:12 1338–1339

   "Public health and individual liberty", *Annual Review of Public Health* (1980) 1:1, 121–136

   "Public health as social justice", *Inquiry* (1976) 13:1, 1–14

   "What is public about public health?", *Health Affairs* (1983) 2:4, 76–87

Beauchamp, Dan and Steinbock, Bonnie (eds.), *New Ethics for the Public's Health* (New York: Oxford University Press, 1999)

Beauchamp, Tom and Childress, James, *Principles of Biomedical Ethics* (6th edn) (Oxford University Press, 2008)

Benatar, Solomon, "Global disparities in health and human rights: a critical commentary", *American Journal of Public Health* (1998) 88:2, 295–300

Berlin, Isaiah, *Four Essays on Liberty* (Oxford University Press, 1969)

Beyleveld, Deryck and Brownsword, Roger, *Human Dignity in Bioethics and Biolaw* (Oxford University Press, 2001)

   Law as a Moral Judgment (London: Sweet and Maxwell, 1986)

Beyleveld, Deryck and Pattinson, Shaun, "Defending moral precaution as a solution to the problem of other minds: a reply to Holm and Coggon", *Ratio Juris* (2010) 23:2, 258–273

Bielby, Philip, "The conflation of competence and capacity in English medical law: a philosophical critique", *Medicine, Health Care and Philosophy* (2005) 8:3, 357–369

Bonell, Chris, McKee, Martin, Fletcher, Adam, Wilkinson, Paul, and Haines, Andy, "One nudge forward, two steps back", *British Medical Journal* (2011) 342:d401, 241–242

Boorse, Christopher, "A rebuttal on health", in James Humber and Robert Almeder (eds.), *What is Disease?* (Totowa, NJ: Humana Press, 1997)

   "Health as a theoretical concept", *Philosophy of Science* (1977) 44:4, 542–573

   "On the distinction between disease and illness", *Philosophy and Public Affairs* (1975) 5:1, 49–68

Brassington, Iain, *Public Health and Globalisation – Why an NHS is Morally Indefensible* (Exeter: Imprint Academic, 2007)

Brazier, Margaret, "Do no harm – do patients have responsibilities too?", *Cambridge Law Journal* (2006) 65:2, 397–422

Brazier, Margaret and Cave, Emma, *Medicine, Patients and the Law* (4th edn) (London: Penguin, 2007)

Brazier, Margaret and Harris, John, "Public health and private lives", *Medical Law Review* (1996) 4:2, 171–192

Brink, David, "Mill's deliberative utilitarianism", *Philosophy and Public Affairs* (1992) 21:1, 67–103

British Medical Association Board of Science, *Under the Influence – The damaging effect of alcohol marketing on young people* (London: BMA, 2009)

Brownsword, Roger, "So what does the world need now? Reflections on regulating technologies", in Roger Brownsword and Karen Yeung (eds.), *Regulating Technologies: Legal Futures, Regulatory Frames and Technological Fixes* (Portland, OR: Hart Publishing, 2008)

Brubaker, Rogers, "Ethnicity without groups", *European Journal of Sociology* (2002) 43:2, 163–189

Buchanan, Allen, "Human rights and the legitimacy of the international order", *Legal Theory* (2008) 14:1, 39–70

Buchanan, Allen, Brock, Dan W., Daniels, Norman, and Wikler, Daniel, *From Chance to Choice – Genetics and Justice* (Cambridge University Press, 2000)

Callahan, Daniel, "The WHO definition of health", *The Hastings Center Studies* (1973) 1:3, 77–87

Cane, Peter, *Atiyah's Accidents, Compensation and the Law* (6th edn) (Cambridge University Press, 2004)

Cappelen, Alexander W. and Norheim, Ole Frithjof, "Responsibility in health care: a liberal egalitarian approach", *Journal of Medical Ethics* (2005) 31:8, 476–480

Casciani, Dominic "Profile: Professor David Nutt", *BBC Online News* (30 October 2009), available at http://news.bbc.co.uk/1/hi/uk/8334948.stm

Chadwick, Ruth, "Defining bioethics", *Bioethics* (2007) 21:2, ii

Charlesworth, Lorie, *Welfare's Forgotten Past* (Abingdon: Routledge, 2009)

Childress, James, Faden, Ruth, Gaare, Ruth, Gostin, Lawrence O., Kahn, Jeffrey, Bonnie, Richard, Kass, Nancy, Mastroianni, Anna, Moreno, Jonathan, and Nieburg, Phillip, "Public health ethics: mapping the terrain", *Journal of Law, Medicine and Ethics* (2002) 30:2, 169–177

Christakis, Nicholas A., "Indirectly doing harm", *British Medical Journal* (2009) 339, 782

Cochrane, Alasdair, "Animal rights and animal experiments: an interest-based approach", *Res Publica* (2007) 13:3, 293–318

Coggon, John, "Assisted-dying and the context of debate: 'medical law' *versus* 'end-of-life law'", *Medical Law Review* (2010) 18:4, 541–563

"Best interests, public interest, and the power of the medical profession", *Health Care Analysis* (2008) 16:3, 219–232

"Confrontations in 'genethics': rationalities, challenges and methodological responses", *Cambridge Quarterly of Healthcare Ethics* (2011) 20:1, 46–55

"Does *public health* have a personality (and if so, does it matter if you don't like it)?", *Cambridge Quarterly of Healthcare Ethics* (2010) 19:2, 235–248

"Doing what's best: organ donation and intensive care", in C. Danbury, C. Newdick, C. Waldmann, and A. Lawson (eds.), *Law and Ethics in Intensive Care* (Oxford University Press, 2010)

"Harmful rights-doing? The perceived problem of liberal paradigms and public health", *Journal of Medical Ethics* (2008) 34:11, 798–801

"Intellectual disability, autonomy, and legal rights", *European Journal of Health Law* (2011) 18:4, 447–459

"No right to smoke in high security psychiatric hospitals", *Journal of Bioethical Inquiry* (2009) 6:4, 405–408

"Public health, responsibility and English law: are there such things as no smoke without ire or needless clean needles?", *Medical Law Review* (2009) 17:1, 127–139

"The British Medical Association, young people's alcohol consumption, and public health: everyone's problem", *Journal of Bioethical Inquiry* (2010) 7:1, 5–7

"Varied and principled understandings of autonomy in English law: justifiable inconsistency or blinkered moralism?", *Health Care Analysis* (2007) 15:3, 235–255

"What help is a steward? Stewardship, political theory, and public health law and ethics", *Northern Ireland Legal Quartely* (forthcoming 2012)

Coggon, John and Miola, José, "Autonomy, liberty and medical decision-making", *Cambridge Law Journal* (forthcoming 2011)

Commission on Social Determinants of Health, *Closing the Gap in a Generation: Health Equity Through Action on the Social Determinants of Health* (Geneva: World Health Organization, 2008)

Copp, David "The idea of a legitimate State", *Philosophy and Public Affairs* (1999) 28:1, 3–45

Cox White, Becky and Zimbelman, Joel, "Abandoning informed consent: an idea whose time has not yet come", *Journal of Medicine and Philosophy* (1998) 23:5, 477–499

Cribb, Alan, *Health and the Good Society-Setting Healthcare Ethics in Social Context* (Oxford University Press, 2005)

"Translational ethics? The theory-practice gap in medical ethics", *Journal of Medical Ethics* (2010) 36:4, 207–210

Curtis, William M., "Liberals and pluralists: Charles Taylor *vs* John Gray", *Contemporary Political Theory* (2007) 6:1, 86–107

Dan-Cohen, Meir, "In defense of defiance", *Philosophy and Public Affairs* (1994) 23:1, 24–51

Daniels, Norman, "Accountability for reasonableness", *British Medical Journal* (2000) 321, 1300–1301

"A lifespan approach to health care", in Helga Kuhse and Peter Singer, *Bioethics: an Anthology* (2nd edn) (Oxford: Blackwell, 2006)

"Equality of what: welfare, resources, or capabilities?", *Philosophy and Phenomenological Research* (1990) 50, Supplement, 273–296

Just Health Care (Cambridge University Press, 1985)

Just Health: Meeting Health Needs Fairly (Cambridge University Press, 2008)

"Just health: replies and further thoughts", *Journal of Medical Ethics* (2009) 35:1, 36–41

Daniels, Norman and Sabin, James, "Limits to health care: fair procedures, democratic deliberation, and the legitimacy problem for insurers", *Philosophy and Public Affairs* (1997) 26:4, 303–350

Daniels, Norman, Kennedy, Bruce and Kawachi, Ichiro, "Why justice is good for our health: The social determinants of health inequalities", *Daedalus* (1999) 128:4, 215–251

Davies, Peter "Is this the end of the road for the PFI?", *British Medical Journal* (2010) 341, 176–177

Dawson, Angus, "Political philosophy and public health ethics", *Public Health Ethics* (2009) 2:2, 121–122

"The future of bioethics: three dogmas and a cup of hemlock", *Bioethics* (2010) 24:5, 218–225

Dawson, Angus and Verweij, Marcel, "Public health ethics: a manifesto", *Public Health Ethics* (2008) 1:1, 1–2

"The steward of the Millian State", *Public Health Ethics* (2008) 1:3, 193–195

Department of Health, *The NHS Constitution for England* (London, 2010), available at www.dh.gov.uk/en/Publicationsandstatistics/Publications/PublicationsPolicyAndGuidance/DH_113613

Dimopoulos, Andreas, *Issues in Human Rights Protection of Intellectually Disabled Persons* (Farnham: Ashgate, 2010)

Dunn, Michael and Foster, Charles, "Autonomy and welfare as *amici curiae*", *Medical Law Review* (2010) 18:1, 86–95

Dunn, Michael, Clare, Isabel and Holland, Anthony, "To empower or to protect? Constructing the 'vulnerable adult' in English law and public policy", *Legal Studies* (2008) 28:2, 234–253

Durkheim, Emile, *The Division of Labour in Society* (trans. George Simpson) (New York: Macmillan, 1933 [1893])

Dworkin, Gerald, "Paternalism", in Dan E. Beauchamp and Bonnie Steinbock (eds.), *New Ethics for the Public's Health* (Oxford and New York: Oxford University Press, 1999 [originally published in *The Monist* (1972) **56**, 64–84])

"Taking risks, assessing responsibility", *The Hastings Center Report* (1981) 11:5, 26–31

The Theory and Practice of Autonomy (Cambridge University Press, 1988)

Dworkin, Ronald, "Liberalism", in Stuart Hampshire (ed.), *Public and Private Morality* (Cambridge University Press, 1978)

Life's Dominion: an Argument about Abortion and Euthanasia (London: Harper Collins, 1993)

Eckersley, Richard, Dickson, Jane and Douglas, Bob, *The Social Origins of Health and Well-being* (Cambridge University Press, 2001)

Edwards, Geoff, "Clarifying the status of policy", *Australian Journal of Public Administration* (2000) 59(2), 109–114

Elliott, Mark, "'Public' and 'private': defining the scope of the Human Rights Act", *Cambridge Law Journal* (2007) 66:3, 485–487

Engelhardt Jr, H. Tristram, "Health care reform: a study in moral malfeasance", *Journal of Medicine and Philosophy* (1994) 19:5, 501–516

"Is there a philosophy of medicine?", *Proceedings of the Biennial Meeting of the Philosophy of Science Association* (1976) 2, 94–108

"Ideology and etiology", *Journal of Medicine and Philosophy* (1976) 1:3, 256–268

"Keynote address: bioethics at the end of the millennium: fashioning health-care policy in the absence of a moral consensus", Stephen Wear, James Bono, Gerald Logue, and Adrianne McEvoy (eds.), *Ethical Issues in Health Care on the Frontiers of the Twenty-First Century* (New York/Boston/Dordrecht/London/Moscow: Kluwer Academic Publishers, 2002)

"The disease of masturbation: values and the concept of disease", *Bulletin of the History of Medicine* (1974) 48:2, 234–248

Epstein, Richard, "In defense of the 'old' public health", *Brooklyn Law Review* (2004) 69:4, 1421–1470

"Let the shoemaker stick to his last: a defense of the 'old' public health", *Perspectives in Biology and Medicine* (2003) 46:3, S138–S159

Etzioni, Amitai, "Public health law: A communitarian perspective", *Health Affairs* (2002) 21:6, 102

Evans, H. Martyn, "Do patients have duties?", *Journal of Medical Ethics* (2007) 33:12, 689–694

Feinberg, Joel, "Legal paternalism", *Canadian Journal of Philosophy* (1971) 1:1, 105–124

Finnis, John, *Natural Law and Natural Rights* (Oxford University Press, 1980)

Fitzpatrick, Michael, *The Tyranny of Health – Doctors and the Regulation of Lifestyle* (London and New York: Routledge, 2001)

Forster, Jean, "A communitarian ethical model for public health interventions: an alternative to individual behavior change strategies", *Journal of Public Health* (1982) 3:2, 150–163

Fox, Marie and Thomson, Michael "HIV/AIDS and male circumcision in public health discourse and practice" (forthcoming)

Frankfurt, Harry G., "Freedom of the will and the concept of the person", *Journal of Philosophy* (1971) 68:1, 5–20

Fredriksen, Stale, "Tragedy, utopia and medical progress", *Journal of Medical Ethics* (2006) 32:8, 450–453

Freeman, Michael, *The Ethics of Public Health,* vols I and II (Aldershot: Ashgate, 2010)

Freeman, Samuel, "Why libertarianism is not a liberal view", *Philosophy and Public Affairs* (2001) 30:2, 105–151

Gaffney, Declan, Pollock, Allyson, Price, David, Shaoul, Jean, "The politics of the private finance initiative and the new NHS", *British Medical Journal* (1999) 319, 249–253

Gaylin, Willard and Jennings, Bruce, *The Perversion of Autonomy: Coercion and Constraints in a Liberal Society* (2nd edn) (Washington DC: Georgetown University Press, 2003)

General Medical Council, *Consent: Patients and Doctors Making Decisions Together* (London: GMC, 2008)

Geuss, Raymond, *Philosophy and Real Politics* (Princeton and Oxford: Princeton University Press, 2008)

Public Goods, Private Goods (Princeton and Oxford: Princeton University Press, 2003)

Glover-Thomas, Nicola and Fanning, John, "Medicalisation: the role of e-pharmacies in iatrogenic harm," *Medical Law Review* (2010) 18:1, 28–55

Golan, Ofra, "The right to treatment for self-inflicted conditions", *Journal of Medical Ethics* (2010) 36:11, 683–686

Goldberg, Daniel, "In support of a broad model of public health: disparities, social epidemiology and public health causation", *Public Health Ethics* (2009) 2:1, 70–83

Gostin, Lawrence O., "From a civil libertarian to a sanitarian", *Journal of Law and Society* (2007) 34:4, 594–616

"National and global health law: a scholarly examination of the most pressing health hazards", *Georgetown Law Journal* (2008) 96:2, 317–329

"Public health, ethics, and human rights: a tribute to the late Jonathan Mann", *Journal of Law, Medicine and Ethics* (2001) 29, 121–130

Public Health Law and Ethics: A Reader (Berkeley, CA: University of California Press, 2002)

Public Health Law and Ethics – A Reader (2nd edn) (Berkeley, CA: University of California Press, 2010)

Public Health Law: Power, Duty, Restraint (Berkeley, CA: University of California Press, 2000)

Public Health Law: Power, Duty, Restraint (2nd edn) (Berkeley, CA: University of California Press, 2008)

Gostin, Lawrence O. and Gostin, Kieran G., "A broader liberty: JS Mill, paternalism, and the public's health", *Public Health* (2009) 123:3, 214–221

Gostin, Lawrence O. and Bloche, M. Gregg, "The politics of public health: a response to Epstein", *Perspectives in Biology and Medicine* (2003) 46:3, S160–S175

Gostin, Lawrence O. and Powers, Madison, "What does social justice require for the public's health? Public health ethics and policy imperatives", *Health Affairs* (2006) 25:4, 1053–1060

Gostin, Lawrence O. and Stone, Lesley, "Health of the people: the highest law?", in Angus Dawson and Marcel Verweij (eds.), *Ethics, Prevention, and Public Health* (Oxford University Press, 2007)

Gostin, Lawrence O. and Taylor, Allyn, "Global health law: a definition and grand challenges", *Public Health Ethics* (2008) 1:1, 53–63

Gostin, Lawrence O, Heywood, Mark, Ooms, Gorik, Grover, Anand, Røttingen, John Arne and Chenguang, Wang, "National and global responsibilities for health", *Bulletin of the World Health Organization* (2010) 88:10, 719–719A

Grandstand Gervais, K., *Redefining Death* (Yale University Press, 1986)

Gray, John, *Isaiah Berlin* (Princeton University Press, 1996)

Two Faces of Liberalism (Cambridge: Polity Press, 2000)

Green, Leslie, "Authority and convention", *The Philosophical Quarterly* (1985) 35:141, 329–346

Green, Ronald M., "Confronting rationality", *Cambridge Quarterly of Healthcare Ethics* (2011) 20:2, 216–227

Griffin, James, *On Human Rights* (Oxford University Press, 2008)

Griffiths, Rod, "Fluoride: a whiter than white reputation?", *British Medical Journal* (2007) 355, 723

Griffiths, Sian, Jewell, Tony, and Donnelly, Peter, "Public health in practice: the three domains of public health", *Public Health* (2005) 119, 907–913

Habermas, Jürgen, *The Future of Human Nature* (Cambridge: Polity Press, 2003)

    The Theory of Communicative Action. Vol 1. Reason and the Rationalization of Society (trans. by T. McCarthy) (Boston, MA: Beacon Press, 1984)

Hall, Mark, "The scope and limits of public health law", *Perspectives in Biology and Medicine* (2003) 46:3, S199-S209

Hare, Richard, "Health", *Journal of Medical Ethics* (1986) 12, 174–181

Harris, John, *Enhancing Evolution – The Ethical Case for Making Better People* (Princeton and Oxford: Princeton University Press, 2007)

    "Taking the 'human' out of Human Rights", *Cambridge Quarterly of Healthcare Ethics* (2011) 20:1, 9–20

    The Value of Life (London: Routledge and Kegan Paul, 1985)

Hart, H.L.A., "Are there any natural rights?", *Philosophical Review* (1955) 64:2, 175–191

    Law, Liberty, and Morality (Stanford University Press, 1963)

    The Concept of Law (2nd edn) (Oxford University Press, 1997)

Hasman, Andreas and Holm, Søren, "Accountability for reasonableness: opening the black box of process", *Health Care Analysis* (2005) 13:4, 261–273

Häyry, Matti, "Can arguments address concerns?", *Journal of Medical Ethics* (2005) 31:10, 598–600

    "Public health and human values", *Journal of Medical Ethics* (2006) 32:9, 519–521

    Rationality and the Genetic Challenge – Making People Better? (Cambridge University Press, 2010)

Herring, Jonathan, *Medical Law and Ethics* (Oxford University Press, 2006)

Hervey, Tamara K. and McHale, Jean V., "Law, health and the European Union", *Legal Studies* (2005) 25:2, 228–259

Hesslow, Germund, "Do we need a concept of disease?", *Theoretical Medicine* (1993) 14:1, 1–14

Hill, Donald, "A response to David Seedhouse's 'Commitment to health: a shared ethical bond between professions'", *Journal of Interprofessional Care* (2002) 16:3, 261–264

Hill, Mark and Sandberg, Russell, "Is nothing sacred? Clashing symbols in a secular world", *Public Law* (2007) 488–506

Hill, Michael and Hupe, Peter, *Implementing Public Policy: Governance in Theory and Practice* (2nd edn) (London: Sage, 2009)

HM Government, *Common Sense, Common Safety – A report by Lord Young of Graffham to the Prime Minister following a Whitehall-wide review of the operation of health and safety laws and the growth of the compensation culture* (London: Cabinet Office, 2010)

Hofmann, Bjørn, "The concept of disease – vague, complex, or just indefinable?", *Medicine, Health Care, and Philosophy* (2009)

Hogwood, Brian and Gunn, Lewis, *Policy Analysis for the Real World* (Oxford University Press, 1984)

Hohfeld, Wesley Newcomb, *Fundamental Legal Conceptions as Applied in Judicial Reasoning* (eds. David Campbell and Philip Thomas) (Aldershot: Ashgate Dartmouth, 2001)

Holland, Stephen, *Public Health Ethics* (Cambridge: Polity, 2007)

Holm, Søren, "If you have said A, you must also say B: Is this always true?", *Cambridge Quarterly of Healthcare Ethics* (2004) 13:2, 179–184

"'Parity of reasoning' arguments in bioethics – some methodological considerations", in Matti Häyry and Tuija Takala (eds.), *Scratching the Surface of Bioethics* (Amsterdam: Rodopi, 2003)

"Secular morality and its limits", *Medicine, Health Care and Philosophy* (1998) 1:1, 75–77

Holm, Søren and Coggon, John, "A cautionary note against 'precautionary reasoning' in action guiding morality", *Ratio Juris* (2009) 22:2, 295–309

Horwitz, Morton, "The history of the public/private distinction", *University of Pennsylvania Law Review* (1982) 130:6, 1423–1428

House of Commons Health Committee, *Alcohol: First Report of Session 2009–10 – Volume I*, HC 151-I (London: The Stationery Office, 2010), available at www.publications.parliament.uk/pa/cm200910/cmselect/cmhealth/151/151i.pdf

Hunter, Nan D., "'Public-private' health law: multiple directions in public health", *Journal of Health Care Law and Policy* (2007) 10, 89–119

Husak, Douglas, "Paternalism and autonomy", *Philosophy and Public Affairs* (1981) 10:1, 27–46

Huxtable, Richard, "Whatever you want? Beyond the patient in medical law", *Health Care Analysis* (2008) 16:3, 288–301

Illich, Ivan, "Disabling professions", in Ivan Illich, Irving Kenneth Zola, John McKnight, Jonathan Caplan, and Harley Shaiken, *Disabling Professions* (New York and London: Marion Boyars, 1977)

Limits to Medicine – Medical Nemesis: The Expropriation of Health (London: Marion Boyars, 1995 [1976])

Institute of Medicine, *The Future of Public Health* (Washington DC: National Academy Press, 1988)

Jenkins, Richard, "Rethinking ethnicity: identity, categorization and power", *Ethnic and Racial Studies* (1994) 17:2, 157–223

Jennings, Bruce, "Autonomy and difference: the travails of liberalism in bioethics", in Raymond Devries and Janardan Subedi (eds.), *Bioethics and Society: Constructing the Ethical Enterprise* (New York: Prentice Hall, 1998)

Civic Health: Political Theory in Public Health and Health Policy (forthcoming)

"Community in public health ethics", in Richard Ashcroft, Angus Dawson, Heather Draper, and John McMillan (eds.), *Principles of Health Care Ethics* (2nd edn) (Chichester: Wiley, 2007)

"Frameworks for ethics in public health", *Acta Bioethica* (2003) IX:2, 165–176

"From the urban to the civic: the moral possibilities of the city", *Journal of Urban Health* (2001) 78:1, 88–103

"Public health and civic republicanism", in Angus Dawson and Marcel Verweij (eds.), *Ethics, Prevention, and Public Health* (Oxford University Press, 2007)

"Public health and liberty: beyond the Millian paradigm", *Public Health Ethics* (2009) 2:2, 123–134

Jochelson, Karen, *Nanny or Steward? – The Role of Government in Public Health* (London: King's Fund, 2005)

John, Stephen, "Expert testimony and epistemological free-riding: the MMR controversy", *The Philosophical Quarterly* (2011) 61:244, 496–517

"Why 'health' is not a central category for public health policy", *Journal of Applied Philosophy* (2009) 26:2, 129–143

Kahn, Jeffrey P., "Why public health and politics don't mix", *American Journal of Bioethics* (2007) 7:11, 3–4

Kant, Immanuel, *Groundwork of the Metaphysics of Morals* (ed. Mary Gregor) (Cambridge University Press, 1998)

Kass, Leon, *Life, Liberty and the Defense of Dignity: The Challenge for Bioethics* (San Francisco, CA: Encounter Books, 2002)

Kass, Nancy, "An ethics framework for public health", *American Journal of Public Health* (2001) 91:11, 1776–1782

Kennedy, Duncan, "The stages of decline of the public/private distinction", *University of Pennsylvania Law Review* (1982) 130:6, 1349–1357

Kindig David and Stoddart, Greg, "What is population health?", *American Journal of Public Health* (2003) 93:3, 380–383.

Kingma, Elselijn, "What is it to be healthy?", *Analysis* (2007) 67:2, 128–133

Klosko, George, "The natural basis of political obligation", *Social Philosophy and Policy* (2001) 18:1, 93–114

Koh, Howard K., Joossens, Luk X., and Connolly, Gregory N., "Making smoking history worldwide", *New England Journal of Medicine* (2007) 356:15, 1496–1498

Kramer, Matthew, "On the nature of legal rights", *Cambridge Law Journal* (2000) 59:3, 473–508

Kramer, Matthew and Steiner, Hillel, "Theories of rights: is there a third way?", *Oxford Journal of Legal Studies* (2007) 27:2, 281–310

Kramer, Matthew, Simmonds, Nigel and Steiner, Hillel, *A Debate Over Rights* (Oxford University Press, 1998)

Lamb, David, *Death, Brain Death and Ethics* (London: Croom Helm, 1985)

Lamond, Grant, "The coerciveness of law", *Oxford Journal of Legal Studies* (2000) 20:1, 39–62

Landale, James, "Whitehall turf war saves cows' hides", *BBC Online News* (25/11/2009), available at http://news.bbc.co.uk/1/hi/uk_politics/8379759.stm

Lansley, Andrew, "Secretary of State for Health's speech to the UK Faculty of Public Health Conference – 'A new approach to public health'"

(7 December, 2010), available at www.dh.gov.uk/en/MediaCentre/
Speeches/DH_117280

Lowi, Theodore, "Law vs. public policy: a critical exploration", *Cornell Journal of Law and Public Policy* (2003) 12, 493–501

Lucy, William, "Persons in law", *Oxford Journal of Legal Studies* (2009) 29:4, 787–804

Lyons, Barry, "Dying to be responsible: adolescence, autonomy and responsibility", (2010) *Legal Studies* 30:2, 257–278

Machado, Calixto and Shewmon, D. Alan (eds.), *Brain Death and Disorders of Consciousness* (New York: Kluwer Academic, 2004)

MacKenzie, Catriona and Stoljar, Natalie (eds.), *Relational Autonomy: Feminist Perspectives on Autonomy, Agency, and the Social Self* (Oxford University Press, 2000)

Magnusson, Roger S., "Mapping the scope and opportunities for public health law in liberal democracies", *Journal of Law, Medicine and Ethics* (2007) 35:4, 571–587

Mann, Jonathan, "Medicine and public health, ethics and human rights", *Hastings Center Report* (1997) 27:3, 6–13

Mariner, Wendy K., "Public health and law: past and future visions", *Journal of Health Politics, Policy and Law* (2003) 28:2–3, 525–552

Marks, Linda, Cave, Sally, and Hunter, David J., "Public health governance: views of key stakeholders", *Public Health* (2010) 124, 55–59

Marmot, Michael, *Status Syndrome: How Your Social Standing Directly Affects Your Health and Life Expectancy* (London: Bloomsbury, 2004)

Marmot, Michael, Rose, Geoffrey, Shipley, Martin, and Hamilton, P.J.S., "employment grade and coronary heart disease in British civil servants", *Journal of Epidemiology and Community Health* (1978) 32, 244–249

Marteau, Theresa M., Ogilvie, David, Roland, Martin, Suhrcke, Marc, Kelly, Michael P., "Judging nudging: can nudging improve population health?", *British Medical Journal* (2011) 342:d228, 263–265

Martin, Robyn, "The limits of law in the protection of public health and the role of public health ethics", *Public Health* (2006) 120, 71–80

Martin, Robyn and Coker, Richard, "Conclusion: where next?", *Public Health* (2006) 120, 81–87

Mason, Elinor, "Consequentialism and the 'ought implies can' principle", *American Philosophical Quarterly* (2003) 40:4, 319–331

Mason, J.K. and Laurie, Graeme, *Mason & McCall Smith's Law and Medical Ethics* (8th edn) (Oxford University Press, 2010)

McCormick, James, "Death of Petr Skrabanek", *The Lancet* (1994) 344, 52–53

McHale, Jean, "Law, regulation and public health research: a case for fundamental reform?", *Current Legal Problems* (2010) 63, 475–510.

McHale, Jean and Fox, Marie, *Health Care Law – Text and Materials* (2nd edn) (London: Sweet and Maxwell, 2007)

McIvor, Claire, "Bursting the autonomy bubble: a defence of the Court of Appeal decision in *R (On the Application of Oliver Leslie Burke)* v. *GMC*", in Stephen W. Smith and Ronan Deazley (eds.), *The Legal, Medical and*

Cultural Regulation of the Body: Transformation and Transgression (Farnham: Ashgate, 2009)

McLean, Sheila, "Live and let die", *British Medical Journal* (2009) 339:b4112, 837

McMahan, Jeff, *The Ethics of Killing – Problems at the Margins of Life* (Oxford University Press, 2002)

McMahon, Christopher, "Autonomy and authority", *Philosophy and Public Affairs* (1987) 16:4, 303–328

McPherson, Thomas, *Political Obligation* (London: Routledge and Kegan Paul, 1967)

Metzl, Jonathan M. and Kirkland, Anna (eds.), *Against Health – How Health Became the New Morality* (New York and London: New York University Press, 2010)

Mill, John Stuart, *On Liberty*, Edward Alexander (ed.) (Peterborough, Ontario: Broadview, 1999 [1859])

Minkler, Meredith, "Personal responsibility for health? A review of the arguments and the evidence at century's end", *Health Education and Behavior* (1999) 26:1, 121–140

Mnookin, Robert, "The public/private dichotomy: political disagreement and academic repudiation", *University of Pennsylvania Law Review* (1982) 130:6, 1429–1440

Mohr, Richard, "AIDS, gays, and State coercion", *Bioethics* (1987) 1:1, 35–50

Montgomery, Jonathan, *Health Care Law* (2nd edn) (Oxford University Press, 2002)

Morris, Christopher, "Natural rights and political legitimacy", *Social Philosophy and Policy* (2005) 22:1, 314–329

Naffine, Ngaire, "Who are law's persons? From Cheshire cats to responsible subjects", *Modern Law Review* (2003) 66:3, 346–367

Nordenfelt, Lennart, "On the relevance and importance of the notion of disease", *Theoretical Medicine and Bioethics* (1993) 14:1, 15–26

Novak, William, "Private wealth and public health: a critique of Richard Epstein's defense of the 'old' public health", *Perspectives in Biology and Medicine* (2003) 46:3, S176–S198

Nozick, Robert, *Anarchy, State, and Utopia* (Oxford: Blackwell, 1974)

Nuffield Council on Bioethics, *Public Health – Ethical Issues* (London: Nuffield, 2007)

Nussbaum, Martha, "Capabilities as fundamental entitlements: Sen and social justice", *Feminist Economics* (2003) 9:2–3, 33–59

Ogus, Anthony, "Regulation revisited", *Public Law* (2009) 332–346

O'Neill, Onora, *Autonomy and Trust in Bioethics* (Cambridge University Press, 2002)

"Informed consent and public health", *Philosophical Transactions of the Royal Society B* (2004) 359, 1133–1136

"The dark side of human rights", *International Affairs* (2005) 81:2, 427–439

Paccaud, Fred, "Implausible diseases and public health," *European Journal of Public Health* (2007) 17:5, 410

Parmet, Wendy, *Populations, Public Health, and the Law* (Washington DC: Georgetown University Press, 2009)

Powers, Madison, "Bioethics as politics: the limits of moral expertise", *Kennedy Institute of Ethics Journal* (2005) 15:3, 305–322

Powers, Madison and Faden, Ruth, *Social Justice: The Moral Foundations of Public Health and Health Policy* (Oxford University Press, 2006)

Räikkä, Juha, "The social concept of disease", *Theoretical Medicine* (1996) 17:4, 353–361

Raphael, Dennis, "The question of evidence in health promotion", *Health Promotion International* (2000) 15:4, 355–367

Rawls, John, *A Theory of Justice – Revised edition* (Oxford University Press, 1999)

Raz, Joseph, "Liberalism, scepticism, and democracy," in Joseph Raz, *Ethics in the Public Domain* (Oxford: Clarendon, 1994)

The Morality of Freedom (Oxford University Press, 1988)

Reich, Michael, "Public-private partnerships for public health", *Nature Medicine* (2000) 6:6, 617–620

Roberts, Marc and Reich, Michael, "Ethical analysis in public health", *The Lancet* (2002) 359, 1055–1059

Roehr, Bob, "US gets least for healthcare spending; Netherlands the most", *British Medical Journal* (2010) 340:c3406, 14–15

Rose, Geoffrey, "Sick individuals and sick populations", *International Journal of Epidemiology* (1985) 14, 32–38

Rothstein, Mark, "Rethinking the meaning of public health", *Journal of Law, Medicine and Ethics* (2002) 30, 144–149

"The limits of public health: a response", *Public Health Ethics* (2009) 2:1, 84–88

Ruger, Jennifer Prah, *Health and Social Justice* (New York: Oxford University Press, 2010)

Ruger, Theodore W., "Health law's coherence anxiety", *Georgetown Law Journal* (2008) 96:2, 625–648

Sandberg, Russell and Doe, Norman, "Religious exemptions in discrimination law", *Cambridge Law Journal* (2007) 66:2, 302–312

Schmidt, Harald, "Patients' charters and health responsibilities", *British Medical Journal* (2007) 335, 1187–1189

Sedgwick, Peter, "Illness: mental and otherwise", *The Hastings Center Studies* (1973) 1:3, 19–40

Seedhouse, David, *Health: The Foundations of Achievement* (2nd edn) (Chichester: John Wiley & Sons, 2005)

"Why bioethicists have nothing useful to say about health care rationing", *Journal of Medical Ethics* (1995) 21, 288–291

Segall, Shlomi, *Health, Luck, and Justice* (Princeton and Oxford: Princeton University Press, 2010)

Sen, Amartya, *Development as Freedom* (Oxford University Press, 1999)

"Health achievement and equity: external and internal perspectives", in Sudhir Anand, Fabienne Peter, and Amartya Sen (eds.), *Public Health, Ethics, and Equity* (Oxford University Press, 2004)

The Idea of Justice (London: Penguin, 2009)

Sheehan, Mark, "It's unethical for GPs to be commissioners", *British Medical Journal* (2011) 342:d1430, 601

Simmons, A. John, "Consent theory for libertarians", *Social Philosophy and Policy* (2005) 22:1, 330–356

   On the Edge of Anarchy: Locke, Consent, and the Limits of Society (Princeton University Press, 1993)

   "The anarchist position: a reply to Klosko and Senor", *Philosophy and Public Affairs* (1987) 16:3, 269–279

Singer, Peter *Animal Liberation* (2nd edn) (London: Pimlico, 1995)

Skrabanek, Petr, *The Death of Humane Medicine and the Rise of Coercive Healthism* (Bury St Edmunds: St Edmundsbury Press, 1994)

Skrabanek, Petr and McCormick, James, *Follies and Fallacies in Medicine* (Glasgow: Tarragon Press, 1989)

Stephenson, Terence, "Ban smoking in cars with children", *BBC Online News* (17 June 2009), available at http://news.bbc.co.uk/1/hi/health/8079357.stm

Sterba, James, "The decline of Wolff's anarchism", *The Journal of Value Inquiry* (1977) 11:3, 213–217

Sullivan, Mark, "The new subjective medicine: taking the patient's point of view on health care and health", *Social Sciences and Medicine* (2003) 56, 1595–1604

Sumner, Leonard Wayne, *The Moral Foundation of Rights* (Oxford: Clarendon Press, 1987)

Sunstein, Cass, "Health-health tradeoffs", *University of Chicago Law Review* (1996) 63:4, 1533–1571

   Legal Reasoning and Political Conflict (Oxford University Press, 1998)

Sunstein, Cass and Thaler, Richard, "Libertarian paternalism is not an oxymoron", *University of Chicago Law Review* (2003) 70:4, 1159–1202

Sy, Joann and Kessel, Anthony, "[Review of] *Health Promotion: Philosophy, Prejudice and Practice – 2nd edition*", *Journal of the Royal Society of Medicine* (2005) 98, 132–133

Sypnowich, Christine, "The civility of law: between public and private", in Maurizio Passerin d'Entrèves and Ursula Vogel (eds.), *Public and Private – Legal, Political and Philosophical Perspectives* (London and New York: Routledge, 2000)

Syrett, Keith and Quick, Oliver, "Pedagogical promise and problems: teaching public health law", *Public Health* (2009) 123, 222–231

Szasz, Thomas, *The Theology of Medicine – The Political-Philosophical Foundations of Medical Ethics* (Oxford University Press, 1979)

Thaler, Richard and Sunstein, Cass, *Nudge: Improving Decisions About Health, Wealth, and Happiness* (London: Penguin Books, 2009)

Thomas, Kendall, "Beyond the privacy principle", *Columbia Law Review* (1992) 92, 1431–1516

Tooley, Michael, "Abortion and infanticide", *Philosophy and Public Affairs* (1972) 2:1, 37–65

Upshur, Ross, "Principles for the justification of public health intervention", *Canadian Journal of Public Health* (2002) 93:2, 101–103

Veatch, Robert, *Death, Dying, and the Biological Revolution – Our Last Quest for Responsibility* (Yale University Press, 1976)

Veitch, Kenneth, *The Jurisdiction of Medical Law* (Aldershot: Ashgate, 2007)

Verweij, Marcel and Dawson, Angus, "The meaning of 'public' in 'public health'", in Angus Dawson and Marcel Verweij (eds.), *Ethics, Prevention, and Public Health* (Oxford University Press, 2007)

Vincent, Andrew, *The Politics of Human Rights* (Oxford University Press, 2010)

Waller, Bruce N., "Responsibility and health", *Cambridge Quarterly of Healthcare Ethics* (2005) 14:2, 177–188

Weait, Matthew, "Knowledge, autonomy and consent: R. v Konzani", *Criminal Law Review* (2005) 763–772

Wellman, Christopher, "Liberalism, samaritanism, and political legitimacy", *Philosophy and Public Affairs* (1996) 25:3, 211–237

Wenar, Leif, "The nature of rights", *Philosophy and Public Affairs* (2005) 33:3, 223–252

WHO and Office of the UN High Commission for Human Rights, *Fact Sheet 31 on the Right to Health* (2008), available at www.ohchr.org/Documents/Publications/Factsheet31.pdf

  The Right to Health – Joint Fact Sheet (2007), available at www.who.int/mediacentre/factsheets/fs323_en.pdf

Wikler, Daniel, "Who should be blamed for being sick?", *Health Education and Behavior* (1987) 14:1, 11–25

Williams, Bernard, "From freedom to liberty: the construction of a political value", *Philosophy and Public Affairs* (2001) 30:1, 3–26

Williamson, Laura, "Scotland: leading the way for alcohol policy in the United Kingdom?", *Journal of Bioethical Inquiry* (2009) 6(3): 265–266

Wilson, James, "Not so special after all? Daniels and the social determinants of health", *Journal of Medical Ethics* (2009) 35:1, 3–6

Wilson, James and Dawson, Angus, "Giving liberty its due, but no more: Trans fats, liberty, and public health", *American Journal of Bioethics* (2010) 10:3, 34–36

Wise, Jacqui, "MPs criticise government for ignoring doctors' advice on alcohol", *British Medical Journal* (2010) 340:c136

Wolf, Susan, "Two levels of pluralism", *Ethics* (1992) 102:4, 785–798

Wolfe, Alan, "Public and private in theory and practice: some implications of an uncertain boundary", in Jeff Weintraub and Krishan Kumar (eds.), *Public and Private in Thought and Practice: Perspectives on a Grand Dichotomy* (Chicago and London: The University of Chicago Press, 1997)

Wolfenden Committee, *Report of the Committee on Homosexual Offences and Prostitution* (Cmnd. 247) (London: HMSO, 1957)

Wolff, Jonathan, "Disadvantage, risk and the social determinants of health", *Public Health Ethics* (2009) 2:1, 214–223

  "Harm and hypocrisy – have we got it wrong on drugs?", *Public Policy Research* (2007) 14:2, 126–135

  "Health risks and the people who bear them", available at http://sas-space.sas.ac.uk/dspace/bitstream/10065/677/1/J_Wolff_Health.pdf

Wolff, Jonathan and de-Shalit, Avner, *Disadvantage* (Oxford and New York: Oxford University Press, 2007)

Wolff, Robert Paul, *In Defense of Anarchism* (with a new preface) (Berkeley, CA: University of California Press, 1998)

Younger, Stuart, Arnold, Robert and Schapiro, Renie (eds.), *The Definition of Death: Contemporary Controversies* (Baltimore: John Hopkins University Press, 1999)

Zemans, Frances "Legal mobilization: the neglected role of the law in the political system", *The American Political Science Review* (1983) 77:3, 690–703

Index